WILLS, TRUSTS, AND ESTATES IN CONTEXT

ASPEN COURSEBOOK SERIES

WILLS, TRUSTS, AND ESTATES IN CONTEXT

SCOTT ANDREW SHEPARD

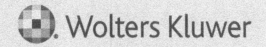

Published by Wolters Kluwer in New York.

Wolters Kluwer Legal & Regulatory U.S.serves customers worldwide with CCH, Aspen Publishers, and Kluwer Law International products. (www.WKLegaledu.com) No part of this publication may be reproduced or transmitted in any form or by any means, electronic or mechanical, including photocopy, recording, or utilized by any information storage or retrieval system, without written permission from the publisher. For information about permissions or to request permissions online, visit us at www.WKLegaledu.com, or a written request may be faxed to our permissions department at 212-771-0803.

To contact Customer Service, e-mail customer.service@wolterskluwer.com, call 1-800-234-1660, fax 1-800-901-9075, or mail correspondence to:

Wolters Kluwer
Attn: Order Department
PO Box 990
Frederick, MD 21705

Printed in the United States of America.

1 2 3 4 5 6 7 8 9 0

ISBN 978-1-4548-9118-5

Library of Congress Cataloging-in-Publication Data

Names: Shepard, Scott Andrew, author.
Title: Wills, trusts, and estates in context / Scott Andrew Shepard.
Description: New York : Wolters Kluwer, [2018] | Includes index.
Identifiers: LCCN 2018034385 | ISBN 9781454891185
Subjects: LCSH: Wills—United States. | Trusts and trustees—United States. |
    Probate law and practice—United States. | Estate planning—United States.
Classification: LCC KF755 .S54 2018 | DDC 346.7305/4—dc23
LC record available at https://lccn.loc.gov/2018034385

About Wolters Kluwer Legal & Regulatory U.S.

Wolters Kluwer Legal & Regulatory U.S. delivers expert content and solutions in the areas of law, corporate compliance, health compliance, reimbursement, and legal education. Its practical solutions help customers successfully navigate the demands of a changing environment to drive their daily activities, enhance decision quality and inspire confident outcomes.

Serving customers worldwide, its legal and regulatory portfolio includes products under the Aspen Publishers, CCH Incorporated, Kluwer Law International, ftwilliam.com and MediRegs names. They are regarded as exceptional and trusted resources for general legal and practice-specific knowledge, compliance and risk management, dynamic workflow solutions, and expert commentary.

To Shelby, Hailey, Colby, Paige and Tommy, who can now tell their friends that they've appeared in a real, published book . . . and don't need to mention that it's a textbook.

SUMMARY OF CONTENTS

CONTENTS

PART III
Law of Wills   105

PART IV
The Law of Trusts

ACKNOWLEDGMENTS

I'd like most particularly to thank the following people whose assistance and support absolutely made this project possible: My family, of course, and also Ellen Caplin, Emily Davis, Tawnda Dyer, Ryan Farrell, Jodie Needham and Erin Sheley. I also thank the students in a series of Trust & Estates classes at John Marshall and Willamette Law Schools, stretching back to the spring of 2013, who served as the first subjects—and first, insightful reviewers—of this text while it was abuilding. Thanks to the authors who allowed me to excerpt their research articles in this text. Finally, thanks to the help and faith of Rick Mixter, Dana Wilson, and the editorial and publication team at Wolters Kluwer, who took the chance and dedicated the time to seeing this text published.

WILLS, TRUSTS, AND ESTATES IN CONTEXT

PART I

OVERVIEW AND INTRODUCTION

A. OVERVIEW: AN OVERDUE CHANGE IN THE LAW-SCHOOL LANDSCAPE

This text introduces a new way of studying for both trusts and dece-dents' estates (T&E) law. Compared to standard casebooks in the area, it strips out many cases, which we have concluded provide a poor return on student attention and class discussion time, opting instead for a more straight-forward and efficient treatment of many subjects. By decreasing the time required to convey the fundamental doctrine of trusts and wills law, while increasing the clarity of exposition, this text adopts a pedagogy more modern than that that still prevails in many law school classrooms, but almost nowhere outside of legal education.

Section I of this text addresses the generalities of the T&E field. These include consideration of why the Anglo-American system of transfer-in-anticipation-of-death (or end-of-life) dispositions developed as it did, what practical and philosophical premises inform(ed) that development, and other potential but as-yet-declined alternatives. More generally, Section I explains both the rules that our system has devised for those who forfeit the opportunity to make their own end-of-life dispositions (i.e., the default rules, essentially the law of intes-tacy), and the rules that have come to obtain broadly (if not quite universally) to all attempted end-of-life dispositions, regardless of the form that they take and that serve to curb the property owners' otherwise fairly complete freedom in fashioning such dispositions (i.e., the mandatory rules).

Then we will turn to the law of wills. It is here that this text does the most solid work, because many of the Wills Act rules do not require deep dives into cases that are often complicated in ways tangential to point they are used to establish. It is here that we pick up the brunt of the time that can now be used in achieving the second virtue of the new course design, considered shortly.

Finally, we will turn to the law of trusts. Perhaps the most important distinction between the law of wills and that of trust is that the latter lacks many of the formal drafting rules that have traditionally rendered an error in will drafting so easy and, in this day of vigorous malpractice law, so potentially dangerous to attorneys practicing in this field.

The new structure frees up enough time to allow instructors to conduct a genuine (though still primarily classroom-bound) practice-regarding exercise, at least in classes of three or more credits. In classes that include this practical component, each student will be asked to take on a persona (or possibly more than one) for the purposes of conducting a practicum in the final quarter (approximately) of the semester. If your professor elects to use the practicum, then about midway through the semester additional information about this exercise should be forthcoming, including perhaps examples of previous practicum problems.

B. INTRODUCTION TO THE SUBJECT MATTER: THE ANGLO-AMERICAN SYSTEM OF DESCENT

In this text we will focus—with brief detours down occasional relevant by-ways—primarily on the laws that govern and instruments that facilitate the transfer by owners of their worldly possessions (usually, though not always, at the time of their deaths). The law of trusts, of wills, of intestate transfer, of an increasing multiplicity of supplementary options: These will inform our efforts.

Yet before these inquiries begin, there arise a pair of issues predicate to—back of and necessary to—the more specific considerations that await. First, note that the very notion of transfer of one's property upon death presumes the institution of private property and that dedicating an entire upper-division law-school class merely to this narrow aspect of the treatment of private property argues quite strongly for the vigor and the fundamental nature of the tradition of descent within the institution of private-property holding.

1. Limited Options

As a theoretical matter, though, this need not necessarily be the case. Various philosophers, sages, politicians, and some of less-dignified stripe have argued for centuries that "property is theft"[1] of some sort, from some other entity. That these authors (whether explicitly or implicitly) are discussing *private* property arises from this consideration: A system of property is merely a systematic answer to the question, "What shall be the relationship between people (with their endless wants), and things (which are, while often wildly substitutable and expandable in economically and intellectually vibrant societies, still inevitably scarce)?" And, in fact, there can only be three (or four, depending on how they're counted, as will become immediately apparent) possible answers to that question.

First, as already considered, private individuals can hold title to and authority over property.

Second, government—or, more specifically, those who run a particular government—can actually or in effect hold that title and authority.

Third, property can be communally owned. This third category is different than the second because under government ownership, the individuals or groups who wield political power control the distribution and use of resources. Under "pure" communal (or "commons") ownership, *no one* controls that distribution and use.[2] This third system presents a bit of a paradox, in that it is a perfectly efficient system in *exactly* those situations in which no property regime is required, i.e., in which there is no scarcity of a given resource. If, say, there are (as was true for much of history) too few people—possessed of too few productive

---

1. *"Property is theft!"* Pierre-Joseph Proudhon, *What Is Property? An Inquiry into the Principle of Right and of Government*, Ch. I (1840).

2. Many scholars have noted that informal rules can often develop about who amongst those entitled to access common property may do so at what times, for what purposes, and to what extent. To the very extent that these informal rules arise, however, they represent the informal development of property-type rights (e.g., "I get the commons from 10-11 a.m. and may exclude others at that time"), or government-type regulation (e.g., "We will watch one another to make sure no one uses the stream except to water cattle.").

capacities—to overburden the freshness and healthfulness of the air, then no trouble arises from the air being a commons, owned or regulated by none. Once such conditions change—once fresh and healthy air in fact becomes a *scarce* commodity that can be overburdened into nonhealthfulness—then this third sort of "property ownership" fails. And so pure commons ownership is in a sense nonownership, useful (as an intellectual construct) only in circumstances in which ownership regimes are simply unnecessary, while to the extent informal rules develop governing its use, and these informal rules are enforced, it comes that much to resemble private or government-owned (or -regulated) property.

As a practical matter, then, there exist only two potential forms of ownership and control of property: private ownership and government ownership. As a historical fact, moreover, there has really, in the whole of human history, been only one sustained and sustainable ownership regime: one of mixed private and government ownership (or control: A privately owned factory that must attend to a system of government-mandated regulations is for all practical purposes partly privately owned and partly government owned). Despite almost unbelievable effusions of blood and infliction of misery over decades, no government has ever been able wholly to stamp out private property (whatever the regime may have called it) from its polity for very long, nor even the transmission of that property at the "owner's" demise, per the owner's wishes.[3] And neither, outside of novels a bit hazy on the mechanics of the proposition,[4] has any society of purely private property ownership of any size or longevity woven its way into history's annals.

And so there will, in every society, exist together some private and some government ownership and control of property. Historically, the Anglo-American tradition has been to favor private ownership and control, with the United States from its founding until approximately the turn of the twentieth century perhaps representing the zenith of that bent.

---

3. *See, e.g.,* John N. Hazard, *Soviet Property Law,* 30 Cornell L. Rev. 466, 482 (1945) (Inheritance reintroduced into the Soviet legal code during the New Economic Policy of the Lenin years; limits on inheritance later revoked.).

4. *See, e.g.,* Ayn Rand, *Atlas Shrugged* (1957).

2. Mixed Solutions and the American Preference for Freedom of Descent

Likewise, the Anglo-American tradition has been to recognize (at least in commoners; the English aristocracy found itself bound—until fairly long into the twentieth century—by ancient restrictions on the passage of its landed estates) a broad right in property owners to transmit their property (at death or otherwise) as and to whom they choose—a tradition that exists to this day.

"In one form or another, the right to pass on property – to one's family in particular—has been part of the Anglo-American legal system since feudal times." So proclaimed the Supreme Court in Hodel v. Irving, 481 U.S. 704 (1987), a case in which the Court deemed unconstitutional a federal law providing for mandatory escheat of certain interests in Indian land.

Hodel implicated the Indian Land Acts of the late nineteenth century. These divided the tribes' reservations into individual allotments for Indians and unallotted lands for non-Indian settlements. As the allotted lands descended to future generations, each individual's ownership interest was divided equally among his or her heirs. By the 1930s, each parcel was held by a host of heirs, each with an increasingly (and sometimes vanishingly) small fraction of an interest, while each heir typically had many fractional interests in a host of different parcels. The multitude of interest holders for each parcel created two problems. First, all of those interest holders had to agree to develop the land. As a result, the land was typically leased to non-Indian ranchers and farmers, which defeated the Acts' original purpose of encouraging Indian settlement on those lands. Second, the extremely fractionated ownership of a given parcel— in one instance, each parcel of land owned by a tribe had an average of *196* owners—led to many owners making less than a dollar per year from their ownership interest in that parcel. In fact, due to the multitude of owners, the Department of the Interior incurred administrative costs significantly higher than the value of the land to manage each parcel.

To solve those problems, Congress passed the Indian Land Consolidation Act of 1983.[5] Section 207 of the Act stripped interest

---

5. Indian Land Consolidation Act of 1983, Pub. L. No. 97-459, 96 Stat. 2515 (later amended). Should you find yourself practicing trusts & estates law in this arena, you might also wish to be aware of the American Indian Probate Reform Act of 2004, which represents a further congressional attempt to deal with the problem of fractionalized inheritances.

holders of the right to pass fractionated interests to their descendants by will or intestacy if the interest did not exceed two percent of the parcel's total acreage and had generated less than $100 in profit in the year prior to the owner's death. Instead, those fractionated interests escheated (i.e., became forfeit) to the tribe.

Three prospective heirs who lost their rights to some of their ancestors' fractionated interests successfully challenged Section 207. The Court recognized that a person's right to pass on his or her property at death was itself a valuable property right (even though the property being passed on may not be particularly valuable itself). It held that Section 207 amounted to a complete abolition of that right with respect to the fractional interests escheated by the 1983 Act. *Hodel* represents a powerful recognition of the right to descent, especially considering that the interests in play were almost insignificantly small.

Of course, it is also true that this right of descent has *usually* not, since the Wilson Administration anyway, been complete for all decedents and grantors of gifts. Parties who by wealth, failure of planning, or other considerations are brought under estate tax obligations will find their right to pass their property to those of their choosing significantly curtailed by application of the federal (and in some jurisdictions, state) tax that goes either by the moniker of "estate tax" or "death tax," largely depending upon the political and intellectual affiliations of the speaker. It would be useless here to predict what the size and contours of this tax will be at the time when you read these lines, as its details change nearly constantly and once recently—for the single year of 2010—disappeared altogether.

Moreover, as we will consider at some length in the next section, there are a few other limitations on gift and devise: most particularly, an obligation to provide for one's surviving spouse (or a preexisting system in community-property states that renders such obligations unnecessary).

Despite these limitations, property owners are essentially free to give away their property as they wish, their grants limited by whatever restrictions those owners may desire.[6] There are, of course, different ways that a decedent's property *could* be distributed, and some people would prefer some alternative method, because they view decedent

---

6. One decreasingly relevant—and increasingly state-specific—limitation on grantor autonomy not to be considered further in this text is the Rule Against Perpetuities. *See, e.g.,* Scott Andrew Shepard, *Which the Deader Hand? A Counter to the American Law Institute's Proposed Revival of Dying Perpetuities Rules,* 86 Tul. L. Rev. 559, 567 (2012). Excerpts of this article, describing the ways in which the rule against perpetuities has been limited in various states, are available on the web site for this textbook.

control over present property interests as "the dead hand of the past" reaching inefficiently and unjustly from the grave to enforce the deads' necessarily incomplete visions of the future upon generations still living and perhaps as yet not even born.

But what are the options to permitting "dead hand" control? Neither the United States nor any modern nation is going to elect to bury the property of the dead with the decedents, as did Egypt for its Pharaohs (though not, of course, for those who were buried alive with the Pharaoh). Neither are we going to burn the property to the ground and sow salt into the decedent's lands. Nor yet shall we, *Hunger Games*-style, create an ultimate commons tragedy by throwing the property of decedents open to private seizure by the swiftest and the strongest. Thus, again, we are left with the fundamental fact of property law: There are really only two methods of holding and controlling property—private ownership and government ownerships—and 100 percent of the time, the regime is partially mixed.

In some continental European countries, such as France (and therefore also in the United State's outpost of the Code Napoleon, Louisiana[7]), balance between private control and government control is weighed somewhat more heavily in favor of state intervention. In those jurisdictions decedents are not permitted, for instance, wholly to disinherit their offspring, while in the remainder of the American states, such a result is entirely permissible (as the *Shapira* case will shortly demonstrate in significant detail). Some states do more to limit the reach of the dead hand, some less. But few, these days, do much.

3. (A Few, Narrow) Limits on Transfer

What limits remain, then—both in theory and in fact?

a. The Historical, Common-Law Tradition

One area in which the common-law took, at least nominally and sometimes actively, a very strong public policy stance was against ancestral attempts to deny heirs—especially women—the opportunity to marry.

---

7. When reading, in this text, a phrase like "the rule in the United States," the better part of wisdom might counsel adding, *sub silentio*, "except, maybe, for Louisiana," where many of these rules are uniquely different.

MADDOX v. MADDOX'S ADM'R.

52 Va. (11 Gratt.) 804 (1854).

The testator, who was a member of the Society of Friends, departed this life in the year 1834. By a codicil to his will, . . . after certain specific bequests, he directs the proceeds of his estate . . . to be disposed of as follows: One-third for the benefit of his father during his natural life; one other third to be applied to the payment of a bond due his brother Thomas Maddox . . . ; and the interest of the remaining third to go to his brother William G. Maddox during his natural life. . . . At the death of his brother William, the third "loaned" to him to be given to his [William's] daughter Ann Maria Maddox, "during her single life, and forever, if her conduct should be orderly, and she remain a member of Friends Society." The codicil concluded with the following clause: "Furthermore, at the closing of all the above things, I wish to give and bequeath all the remaining part of my estate to my nearest relations that may be then living, and that shall be at that time members of the Society of Friends."

After the death of the testator, and during the life time of her father, Ann Maria Maddox married the appellee Thomas Tiller, who was not a member of the Society of Friends, and thereby, according to the rules and discipline of the society, forfeited her right to membership. . . .

As Mrs. Tiller is claiming the benefit of the bequest in remainder to her after the death of her father, we are called upon in this state of the case, to pass on the validity and effect of the . . . bequest [to Mrs. Ann Maria Tiller, *nee* Maddox] in this codicil.

As by the rules of the Society of Friends, a member who married out of the society thereby forfeited his membership, the effect of the bequest of the third in remainder to Ann Maria Maddox, was to restrict her to marriage with a member of the society. Upon her marriage, the estate given to her "during her single life," would, according to the terms of the codicil, be determined; and if she married a person who was not a member of the society, she herself ceased to be a member, and was thus excluded from further enjoyment of the estate. The question then, as it respects the bequest of the third in remainder to Ann Maria Maddox, is as to the validity of such a restraint upon marriage under the circumstances disclosed in this case.

It will not be questioned that marriages of a suitable and proper character, founded on the mutual affection of the parties, and made upon free choice, are of the greatest importance to the best interests of society, and should be by all proper means promoted and encouraged.

The purity of the marriage relation and the happiness of the parties will, to a great extent, depend upon their suitableness the one for the other, and the entire freedom of choice which has led to their union. . . . Hence not only should all positive prohibitions of marriage be rendered nugatory, but all unjust and improper restrictions upon it should be removed, and all undue influences in determining the choice of the parties should be carefully suppressed. Accordingly, in the civil law all conditions annexed to gifts and legacies which went to restrain marriages generally, were deemed inconsistent with public policy, and held void. . . . This doctrine has been introduced into the English law with certain modifications, suggested by a disposition to preserve to parents a just control and influence with their children, and the means of protecting youthful persons against the said consequences of hasty, unsuitable or ill assorted marriages. Conditions, therefore, in restraint of marriage, annexed to gifts and legacies, are allowed when they are reasonable in themselves, and do not unduly restrict a just and proper freedom of choice. But where a condition is in restraint of marriage generally, it is deemed to be contrary to public policy, at war with sound morality, and directly violative of the true economy of social and domestic life. Hence, such a condition will be held utterly void. . . .

[I]n those cases in which restraints of a partial character may be imposed on marriage, as in respect of time, place or person, they must be such only as are just, fair and reasonable. Where they are of so rigid a character, or made so dependent on peculiar circumstances, as to operate a virtual . . . restraint on marriage, or unreasonably restrict the party in the choice of marriage, they will be ineffectual and utterly disregarded. . . . Judge Story lays it down, that restraints in respect of time, place or person, may be so framed as to operate a virtual prohibition upon marriage, or at least upon its most important and valuable objects; and he illustrates by a condition that a child should not marry till fifty years of age; or should not marry any person inhabiting in the same town, county or state; or should not marry any person that was a clergyman, a physician, or a lawyer, or any person except of a particular trade or employment; all of which, he tells us, would be deemed mere evasions of the law. . . .

Following these principles. . . , and looking to the facts in proof in the cause, I cannot avoid coming to the conclusion, that the condition imposed by the bequest of the third in remainder to Ann Maria Maddox, which in effect forbade her to marry any other than a member of the Society of Friends, was an undue and unreasonable restraint upon the choice of marriage, and ought to be disregarded. It is in proof, that when she became marriageable, the number of Quakers in the county of Hanover, in which she resided, and the vicinity, was small, and that it had been since diminishing. There were not within the circle of her association, more than five or six marriageable male members of the society, according to one of the witnesses, or three or four, according to another; and the probability is, as stated by one of the witnesses, the restriction imposed by the condition would have operated a virtual prohibition of her marrying. To say there were members of the society residing in other counties, is no answer to the objection. She certainly could not be expected, if she had the means, which it seems she had not, to go abroad in search of a helpmate; and to subject her to the doubtful chance of being sought in marriage by a stranger, would operate a restraint upon it far more stringent than those which are repudiated in the cases and illustrations which I have already cited. . . .

Nowhere can the policy of repudiating all unnecessary restraints upon freedom of choice in marriage apply with more force than among a free people, with institutions like ours. . . .

I think the Circuit court did right in treating the restrictions in the codicil as inoperative and void: and I am therefore of opinion to affirm the decree.

b. Honored in the Modern Breach?

The protections afforded to Miss Maddox were arguably a matter of life or death—or at least the difference between the pursuit of genuine happiness and a guarantee of penury and misery. Do you see why?

How have matters—and the court's fundamental conception of the role and meaning of a conditional ancestral bequest (whether by will or by trust)—changed between the *Maddox* case and *Shapira,* which follows?

SHAPIRA v. UNION NAT'L BANK

315 N.E.2d 825 (Ohio Ct. Com. Pl. 1974).

This is an action for a declaratory judgment and the construction of the will of David Shapira, M. D., who died April 13, 1973, a resident of this county. By agreement of the parties, the case has been submitted upon the pleadings and the exhibit.

The portions of the will in controversy are as follows:

Item VIII. All the rest, residue and remainder of my estate, real and personal, of every kind and description and wheresoever situated, which I may own or have the right to dispose of at the time of my decease, I give, devise and bequeath to my three (3) beloved children, to wit: Ruth Shapira Aharoni, of Tel Aviv, Israel, or wherever she may reside at the time of my death; to my son Daniel Jacob Shapira, and to my son Mark Benjamin Simon Shapira in equal shares, with the following qualifications: . . .

(b) My son Daniel Jacob Shapira should receive his share of the bequest only, if he is married at the time of my death to a Jewish girl whose both parents were Jewish. In the event that at the time of my death he is not married to a Jewish girl whose both parents were Jewish, then his share of this bequest should be kept by my executor for a period of not longer than seven (7) years and if my said son Daniel Jacob gets married within the seven-year period to a Jewish girl whose both parents were Jewish, my executor is hereby instructed to turn over his share of my bequest to him. In the event, however, that my said son Daniel Jacob is unmarried within the seven (7) years after my death to a Jewish girl whose both parents were Jewish, or if he is married to a non-Jewish girl, then his share of my estate, as provided in item 8 above should go to The State of Israel, absolutely.

The provision for the testator's other son Mark, is conditioned substantially similarly. Daniel Jacob Shapira, the plaintiff, alleges that the condition upon his inheritance is unconstitutional, contrary to public policy and unenforceable because of its unreasonableness, and that he should be given his bequest free of the restriction. Daniel is 21 years of age, unmarried and a student at Youngstown State University. . . .

Constitutionality

Plaintiff's argument that the condition in question violates constitutional safeguards is based upon the premise that the right to marry is protected by the Fourteenth Amendment to the Constitution of the United States. . . . In its opinion [in Loving v. Virginia, 388 U.S. 1 (1967),] the United States Supreme Court made the following statements. . . .

The freedom to marry has long been recognized as one of the vital personal rights essential to the orderly pursuit of happiness by free men.

Marriage is one of the 'basic civil rights of man,' fundamental to our very existence and survival. . . . The Fourteenth Amendment requires that the freedom of choice to marry not be restricted by invidious racial discriminations. Under our Constitution, the freedom to marry, or not marry, a person of another race resides with the individual and cannot be infringed by the State.

From the foregoing, it appears clear, as plaintiff contends, that the right to marry is constitutionally protected from restrictive state legislative action. Plaintiff submits, then, that under the doctrine of Shelley v. Kraemer (1948), 334 U.S. 1, the constitutional protection of the Fourteenth Amendment is extended from direct state legislative action to the enforcement by state judicial proceedings of private provisions restricting the right to marry. Plaintiff contends that a judgment of this court upholding the condition restricting marriage would, under Shelley v. Kraemer, constitute state action prohibited by the Fourteenth Amendment as much as a state statute.

In Shelley v. Kraemer the United States Supreme Court held that the action of the states to which the Fourteenth Amendment has reference includes action of state courts and state judicial officials. Prior to this decision the court had invalidated city ordinances which denied blacks the right to live in white neighborhoods. In Shelley v. Kraemer owners of neighboring properties sought to enjoin blacks from occupying properties which they had bought, but which were subjected to privately executed restrictions against use or occupation by any persons except those of the Caucasian race. Chief Justice Vinson noted, in the course of his opinion . . . : "These are cases in which the purposes of the agreements were secured only by judicial enforcement by state courts of the restrictive terms of the agreements."

In the case at bar, this court is not being asked to enforce any restriction upon Daniel Jacob Shapira's constitutional right to marry. Rather, this court is being asked to enforce the testator's restriction upon his son's inheritance. If the facts and circumstances of this case were such that the aid of this court were sought to enjoin Daniel's marrying a non-Jewish girl, then the doctrine of Shelley v. Kraemer would be applicable, but not, it is believed, upon the facts as they are. . . .

Basically, the right to receive property by will is a creature of the law, and is not a natural right or one guaranteed or protected by either the Ohio or the United States constitution. . . . It is a fundamental rule of law in Ohio that a testator may legally entirely disinherit his children. . . . This would seem to demonstrate that, from a constitutional standpoint, a testator may restrict a child's inheritance. The court concludes, therefore, that the upholding and enforcement of the provisions of Dr. Shapira's will conditioning the bequests to his sons upon their marrying Jewish girls does not offend the Constitution of Ohio or of the United States. . . .

Public Policy

The condition that Daniel's share should be "turned over to him if he should marry a Jewish girl whose both parents were Jewish" constitutes a partial restraint upon marriage. If the condition were that the beneficiary not marry anyone, the restraint would be general or total, and, at least in the case of a first marriage, would be held to be contrary to public policy and void. A partial restraint of marriage which imposes only reasonable restrictions is valid, and not contrary to public policy. . . . The great weight of authority in the United States is that gifts conditioned upon the beneficiary's marrying within a particular religious class or faith are reasonable. . . .

Plaintiff contends, however, that in Ohio a condition such as the one in this case is void as against the public policy of this state. In Ohio, as elsewhere, a testator may not attach a condition to a gift which is in violation of public policy. . . . There can be no question about the soundness of plaintiff's position that the public policy of Ohio favors freedom of religion and that it is guaranteed by Section 7, Article I of the Ohio Constitution, providing that "all men have a natural and indefeasible right to worship Almighty God according to the dictates of their own conscience." Plaintiff's position that the free choice of religious practice cannot be circumscribed or controlled by contract is substantiated by Hackett v. Hackett (C. A. Lucas 1958), 78 Ohio Law Abs. 485, 150 N. E. 2d 431. This case held that a covenant in a separation agreement, incorporated in a divorce decree, that the mother would rear a daughter in the Roman Catholic faith was unenforceable. However, the controversial condition in the case at bar is a partial restraint upon marriage and not a covenant to restrain the freedom of religious practice; and, of course, this court is not being asked to hold the plaintiff in contempt for failing to marry a Jewish girl of Jewish parentage.

Counsel contends that if "Dr. David Shapira, during his life, had tried to impose upon his son those restrictions set out in his Will he would have violated the public policy of Ohio as shown in Hackett v. Hackett. The public policy is equally violated by the restrictions Dr. Shapira has placed on his son by his Will." This would be true, by analogy, if Dr. Shapira, in his lifetime, had tried to force his son to marry a Jewish girl as the condition of a completed gift. But it is not true that if Dr. Shapira had agreed to make his son an inter-vivos gift if he married a Jewish girl within seven years, that his son could have forced him to make the gift free of the condition. . . .

In arguing for the applicability of the Maddox v. Maddox [excerpted above—Ed.] test of reasonableness to the case at bar, counsel for the plaintiff asserts that the number of eligible Jewish females in this county would be an extremely small minority of the total population especially as compared with the comparatively much greater number in New York, whence have come many of the cases comprising the weight of authority upholding the validity of such clauses. There are no census figures in evidence. While this court could probably take judicial notice of the fact that the Jewish community is a minor, though important segment of our total local population, nevertheless the court is by no means justified in judicial knowledge that there is an insufficient number of eligible young ladies of Jewish parentage in this area from which Daniel would have a reasonable latitude of choice. And of course, Daniel is not at all confined in his choice to residents of this county, which is a very different circumstance in this day of travel by plane and freeway and communication by telephone, from the horse and buggy days of the 1854 Maddox v. Maddox decision. Consequently, the decision does not appear to be an appropriate yardstick of reasonableness under modern living conditions.

Plaintiff's counsel contends that the Shapira will falls within the principle of Fineman v. Central National Bank (1961), 87 Ohio Law Abs. 236, 175 N. E. 2d 837, 18 O. O. 2d 33, holding that the public policy of Ohio does not countenance a bequest or devise conditioned on the beneficiary's obtaining a separation or divorce from his wife. Counsel argues that the Shapira condition would encourage the beneficiary to marry a qualified girl just to receive the bequest, and then to divorce her afterward. This possibility seems too remote to be a pertinent application of the policy against bequests conditioned upon divorce. Most other authorities agree with Fineman v. Bank that as a general proposition, a testamentary gift effective only on condition that the recipient divorce or separate from his or her spouse is against public policy and invalid. . . . But no authorities have been found extending the principle to support plaintiff's position. Indeed, in measuring the reasonableness of the condition in question, both the father and the court should be able to assume that the son's motive would be proper. And surely the son should not gain the advantage of the avoidance of the condition by the possibility of his own impropriety.

Finally, counsel urges that the Shapira condition tends to pressure Daniel, by the reward of money, to marry within seven years without opportunity for mature reflection, and jeopardizes his college education. It seems to the court, on the contrary, that the seven year time limit would be a most reasonable grace period, and one which would give the son ample opportunity for exhaustive reflection and fulfillment of the condition without constraint or oppression. Daniel is no more being "blackmailed into a marriage by immediate financial gain," as suggested by counsel, than would be the beneficiary of a living gift or conveyance upon consideration of a future marriage – an arrangement which has long been sanctioned by the courts of this state. . . .

In the opinion of this court, the provision made by the testator for the benefit of the State of Israel upon breach or failure of the condition is most significant [in that] it demonstrates the depth of the testator's conviction. His purpose was not merely a negative one designed to punish his son for not carrying out his wishes. His unmistakable testamentary plan was that his possessions be used to encourage the preservation of the Jewish faith and blood, hopefully through his sons, but, if not, then through the State of Israel. Whether this judgment was wise is not for this court to determine. But it is the duty of this court to honor the testator's intention within the limitations of law and of public policy. The prerogative granted to a testator by the laws of this state to dispose of his estate according to his conscience is entitled to as much judicial protection and enforcement as the prerogative of a beneficiary to receive an inheritance.

It is the conclusion of this court that public policy should not, and does not preclude the fulfillment of Dr. Shapira's purpose, and that in accordance with the weight of authority in this country, the conditions contained in his will are reasonable restrictions upon marriage, and valid.

QUESTIONS AND ANALYSIS

What to make of these two cases? They *can* be reconciled, largely in the way that the *Shapira* court purports to. Under the "reconciling" reading, the difference between *Maddox* and *Shapira* is essentially one of travel technology and the relative emancipation of young men in the 1970s as compared to young ladies of the 1850s. *Shapira* came out the way it did because son Daniel had easy access to destinations, like New York and Chicago, in which significant numbers of women lived, both of whose parents were Jewish. Not only could he travel to those cities, but he could move to them, spend money in them, introduce himself to qualifying women living there, and even propose to them. As a result, even taking the legal conclusions and presumptions of *Maddox* as still fully operative, *Shapira* comes out the other way.

There is, though, also a discordant way of reading the pair. Note that the *Maddox* court ignored one choice that was available to Miss Maddox but that she wished to avoid: She could marry (as she did) and by the election of marrying whom she wished, forego the one-third portion of her uncle's estate to which she was otherwise entitled. This was certainly a theoretically and practically available result, the latter witnessed by the fact that Maddox had in fact married before the Virginia Supreme Court's decision issued. The *Shapira* court, though, very intently contemplated this option. There is no sense that the court is withholding its final determination until it is found that Daniel Shapira can actually find a woman to fall in love with and make his wife, whether in or beyond Ohio, who fits his father's specifications. The court is not concerned about whether Daniel might already be in love with—or later fall in love with—a non-Jewish woman, or a man, or no one at all. Rather, the underlying position of the *Shapira* case is that Daniel's father has left him a choice: You may either marry a Jewish girl and get the trust fund, or go—and pay—your own way. Either way, though, concludes the *Shapira* court, what Dr. Shapira had offered Daniel was a tantalizing offer, though one bounded by conditions. Daniel could accept the offer—and the conditions—or reject both. But what Dr. Shapira had done did not constrain Daniel's life in any material way.

It is marginally diverting to consider which of these readings is more plausible (as well as whether it constitutes a logical error to set up such a dilemma). But in more than one sense, the answer is entirely academic. All young adult American citizens these days enjoy the freedom of travel, of resettlement, and of social interaction afforded to Daniel 40 years ago. As a result, whether *Shapira* represents a recognition of social change only or a shift in doctrine, the odds are very high indeed that any modern case testing the common-law restraints on marriage will come out as *Shapira* did and not in practical accord with *Maddox*.

c. The Real Remaining (Quasi-)Limitations

With the common-law concerns about inhibiting marriage largely vitiated or swept aside at modern law, almost no restrains on descent and devise remain.[8] The only significant one, an absolute restraint against beggaring surviving spouses, is considered in significant detail in the next section.

---

8. One minor issue: the common law still frowns upon discouragements of marriage, which include a discouragement that could arise, from, say, a decedent's trust which provides for his surviving spouse out of his own separate assets (more about which anon) "for so long as she remains single." Even this restraint has devolved into one of semantics, however. Should the provision be written to provide for the surviving spouse "for any period of single-income living, as before any remarriage," then it would be likely to stand.

PART II

BACKSTOP DEFAULTS, MANDATORY OBLIGATIONS, AND GENERAL PREDICATES

This part of the text explores default rules that apply to distribute a decedent's estate in cases in which the decedent failed to express his intentions in a legally cognizable form, such as a will or a trust. This is, by and large, the law of instestacy. It also considers mandatory rules and general principles that will inform the later, focused, study on the will and trust forms.

A. INTESTACY AND THE "STIRPII"

1. Intestacy: A Genuine, Good-Faith Default Construct

In crafting the laws of intestacy, legislatures have almost universally attempted to write law that seeks (with a very few but important exceptions, which will be considered extensively *infra*) only to provide default rules that model what the average citizen would have wanted had that citizen stated a preference. These intestacy laws provide the rules for how to distribute the estate of a decedent who has failed to prepare a will, trust, or other substitute disposing of some or all of her property.[1] In this realm the guiding question has been (again, with a

---

1. "Testate" means, as a first-order matter (especially in this course) "possessed of a will." Thus, one who dies testate is one who dies with a valid will in place. "In-" means "not," so that "intestate" means "not possessed of a will." Beyond that, though,

couple of vital exceptions): "What would the decedent have wished done with her property if she had written out a will?"

Intestacy law represents the legislatures' attempts to answer that question in the way that the majority—or at least plurality—of citizens of the jurisdiction would have answered it.

Intestacy presumes that if a decedent had left instructions about what to do with her estate, she would have wanted to leave her assets to the nearest of her kin for whom she had (or with whom she shared) some responsibility, and then to her nearest kin of any sort. A quick-and-dirty way of remembering the basic rule of representation is "over, down, up, out, down, repeat." Intestate assets pass first "over" to one's surviving spouse, if any.

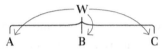

If none, then the assets pass "down," to one's issue, or to the descendants of one's issue.

If none, then the assets pass back "up," to one's parents if they survive.

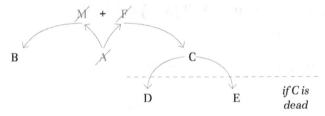

If they do not, then they pass "out" again, to one's surviving siblings and/or their descendants by representation.

If none, then "up" again, to one's grandparents. As they have likely passed, then this "up" is followed quickly by another "out" and "down," to one's aunts and uncles, and then to cousins and their descendants (cousins once removed, twice removed, and so on). After that, states follow one of two different courses. In some states, the process continues, up to great-grandparents and then out and down through second and third cousins. Other states, considering these distant relatives

---

the Latin root "test" means proof or evidence, so that a testament, while narrowly a will (a valid proof of intent for property at decease), is more broadly a proof or evidence of any sort. Hence the recurrence of the root word in terms such as attestation and testimony.

"laughing heirs," (i.e., heirs who would, upon hearing of their inheritance, laugh at their good luck rather than sorrowing for their loss), cut off the process at the grand-parentelic level and thereafter "escheat" (i.e., forfeit) the estate to the state's treasury.

Intestacy law and the need for it raises an interesting initial question: Why doesn't everyone prepare end-of-life instructions for their stuff, be it by trust or by will or otherwise? A number of potentially valid answers propose themselves. Do you have a will? A trust? If not, why not? Do you think most of your fellow students do? Which ones do and which don't? Do you think most of your professors do? Why or why not? Do these ruminations suggest to you that legislatures are both wise and just to write intestacy statutes that anticipate citizens' desires rather than enforcing the legislatures' "public-policy" will in this context, or do you demur? What would be the practical consequences of doing otherwise?

2. Intestate Distribution by Representation: Three Systems

Of the three methods that follow, the modern (or American) *per stirpes* system is used in the majority of the several states. The question of which rule constitutes the majority rule is not here—and seldom will be—of much interest or pedagogical value; of course you'd look up the rule that applied in any given state instead of simply presuming that the majority rule[2] applied there, in any context. The distinction that is of pedagogical interest in this narrow area, and for the vast majority of this semester, is the distinction between the traditional rule and the modern-trend rule. Understanding how and why various rules have developed over time usually provides both a deeper understanding of the general concept in play and a more reliable recall of what happened when (i.e., which is the traditional rule, and which is the modern trend).

English (or traditional) *per stirpes* arose in a country and an era in which most wealth came in the form of land and in which large land holdings frequently carried with them both vital badges of nobility and the political and social power that accompanied such noble status. Consequently, the "lines of the house," as it were—particularly the line of the eldest male—mattered intensely, even if the whole of the first generation of descendants of the decedent died before the family patriarch. In narrative terms, if Earl A and Countess B have children X, Y, and Z, then

---

2. Or the current Restatement of a particular subject. Remember that Restatements are not always even an assertion of a majority view; sometimes they are instead the statement by the author of the author's preferred policy position. Be very careful about citing them as authority rather than merely using them as a research option.

each of those children represents a "line" of A and B's house (or family). Under traditional (particularly medieval and early-modern, but stretching, as noted above, in some form into the twentieth century) English law, the line of the house that mattered most was the line of the first male progeny to survive into adulthood, and then the first male heir to himself have surviving male heirs. Thus, the traditional English rules of descent required division of the estate of A and B at the first generation, always.

The United States, from their first days as British colonial outposts, abjured noble titles and heritable power—at least heritable political power, at least *de jure*. It thus mattered far less in the colonies *cum* states that inheritance strictly follow first-generation lineage. As a result, American (or modern) *per stirpes*[3] makes a single change from its English forebear: If the first generation of descendants all predecease the ancestor-decedent, that generation is ignored, with the first division of assets occurring at the first generation from which at least one living taker remains. Otherwise, American and English *per stirpes* are indistinguishable. By narrative again, presume Mr. and Mrs. AB, of Sloughers Low, Delaware, produced children X, Y, and Z, each of whom in turn have at least one child, but then all of whom are killed before their parents die. Under the American *per stirpes* system, the first-generation, all dead, would be ignored, with division beginning at the second generation (assuming that some members of that generation were alive upon the death of Mr. and Mrs. AB, their grandparents).

The most modern innovation in this area of the law of decedents' estates is that of the Uniform Probate Code's (hereinafter UPC) method of making a common pool and equal redistribution at every generation.[4] The animating theory of this common-pool method is

---

3. This is also sometimes referred to as *per capita* with representation.

4. Unif. Prob. Code §2-106 (Unif. Law Comm'n 2014). The relevant text:

2 . . . (b) [Decedent's Descendants.] If, under Section 2-103(a)(1), a decedent's intestate estate or a part thereof passes "by representation" to the decedent's descendants, the estate or part thereof is divided into as many equal shares as there are (i) surviving descendants in the generation nearest to the decedent which contains one or more surviving descendants and (ii) deceased descendants in the same generation who left surviving descendants, if any. Each surviving descendant in the nearest generation is allocated one share. The remaining shares, if any, are combined and then divided in the same manner among the surviving descendants of the deceased descendants as if the surviving descendants who were allocated a share and their surviving descendants had predeceased the decedent.

(c) [Descendants of Parents or Grandparents.] If, under Section 2-103(a)(3) or (4), a decedent's intestate estate or a part thereof passes "by representation" to

that in the modern era, ancestor decedents would prefer the rule of "equally near, equally dear." This is to say that the UPC authors presume that, for instance, a grandmother who dies without having made a will would prefer that each of her living children take the same portion of her estate, and likewise that each of her grandchildren who take by representation similarly take the same portion of the estate, regardless of how many children were produced by that "line of the house," even if that means that the line in question actually receives, *in toto*, a greater portion of the estate than do other lines, including, potentially, lines still represented by her living children.[5]

As these developments, especially the UPC method, may initially seem somewhat confusing, further examples of each form of estate division by representation are considered below. For these examples, presume the following:

Model family tree. A and B, deceased, matri- and patriarch of the line, with children C, D, E, and F. Thereafter:

C has child G
D has children H and I
E has children J, K, and L

---

the descendants of the decedent's deceased parents or either of them or to the descendants of the decedent's deceased paternal or maternal grandparents or either of them, the estate or part thereof is divided into as many equal shares as there are (i) surviving descendants in the generation nearest the deceased parents or either of them, or the deceased grandparents or either of them, that contains one or more surviving descendants and (ii) deceased descendants in the same generation who left surviving descendants, if any. Each surviving descendant in the nearest generation is allocated one share. The remaining shares, if any, are combined and then divided in the same manner among the surviving descendants of the deceased descendants as if the surviving descendants who were allocated a share and their surviving descendants had predeceased the decedent.

A hotch pot is perhaps best understood as a medieval crock pot, or as a forerunner of the term hodgepodge. The hotch pot is just the common pool of assets that remain after some assets have been paid out; here, that payment occurs generationally.

5. Do you find the vital presumption (i.e., "equally near, equally dear") of the UPC's division method compelling? It appears that most states do not, as the majority American rule remains that of American *per-stirpes* division. When polled, most American citizens prefer the American rule as well. Interestingly, most *lawyers* when similarly polled prefer the English rule. Can you formulate some theory as to why these preferences might differ—and why both groups reject the UPC method? This intellectual exercise is valuable as a means of digging into the distinctions between these three systems—and between the three constituencies that favor each—even though (and perhaps *because*) there's no particularly good way of determining with any certainty the truth of any such theory, however thoroughly considered and developed.

F has no children.First, as a useful exercise, draw the family tree of the family just described here (or, you know, wherever you'd like, really):

All of the examples that follow will be based upon this family tree.

a. English (or Traditional) Per Stirpes

Under this rule, the estate is divided equally amongst all "living" lines at the first generation, even if all members of that generation have died before the relevant distribution occurs.[6]

Thus, in our family tree above, and assuming that all of the grandchildren are living, the decision tree is:

(a) Is F living or dead? If F is living, then the estate is divided by four, with each of C, D, E, and F getting a quarter share. (See Figure 1 below.). If F is dead, the estate is divided by three, regardless of the whether the other three children are living or have died. (See Figure 2 below.) Do you see why?

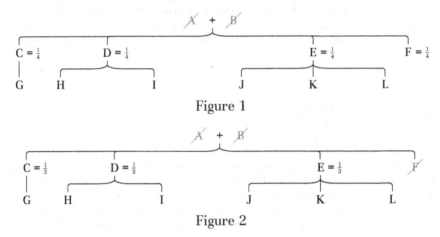

Figure 1

Figure 2

_____

6. "Living lines" here mean lines in which either (a) the relevant child is still alive, or (b) the relevant child has passed, but leaves still-living descendants able to take "by representation" from their dead "intermediate ancestors."

(b) Are any of the other three children dead? If they live, they keep their shares, and their children cannot take by representation.[7] (See Figures 1 and 2, which presume that all of children C, D, and E have survived their parents.) For each (if any) who has died, the children equally divide that parent's share. (See Figure 3 for what would happen if all members of the first generation have died. Note that because the children have different numbers of their own children, those children (the grandchildren of A+B) will inherit different amounts of their grandparents' estate, because the granchildren are equally dividing *their own parents'* equal shares.)

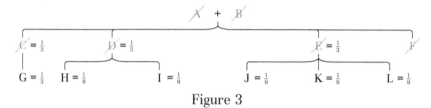

Figure 3

b. Modern (or American) Per Stirpes

As noted above, the only difference between English and modern *per stirpes* is this: If the whole first generation is dead (i.e., all the children of the dead estate owner), then the estate is not divided at that first level, but instead is divided at the grandchildren level (or, technically, at the first level at which a living descendant appears, but in reality that almost always means the grandchildren level). So:

(a) Are all of the children dead? If so, do not divide at that level. Go down to the next one and divide equally. (See figure b(a).)

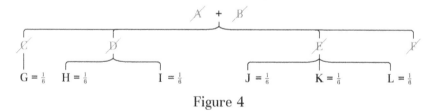

Figure 4

(b) If some children remain, is F one of them? If so, then division occurs at the children level, and the split is four ways. (See Figure 5, which assumes that all four children live, and then Figure 6, which

---

7. Note what "by representation" means here. If C has died, but G survives him, then G is said to "represent" (or stand in the place of) C in the process of distribution, so that G takes C's distribution "by representation." Similarly, if E has died, leaving children J, K, and L, then those three children *collectively* represent E, and so each takes an equal portion of E's distribution from the estate.

assumes, by way of example, that D has died, but that F still lives.) If not, then the split is three ways.

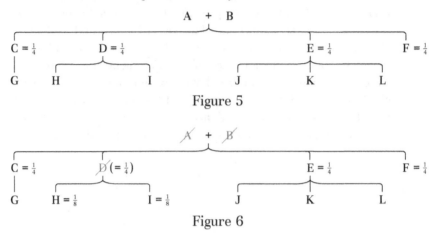

Figure 5

Figure 6

(c) Proceed as under traditional *per stirpes*.

c. The UPC System

The only difference between modern *per stirpes* and the UPC System is that each time those still alive in any given generation are "paid out," the remaining fraction of the estate is not passed through the dead of that generation directly; instead, all that remains is thrown back into a common pool, and divided equally amongst the living (and not already paid) lines of the next generation, but all that is not paid out in that generation then again returns to the hotch pot for yet another division. Thus:

(a) Are all the children dead? If so, see (a) under modern *per stirpes*.
(b) If some of the children remain, is F one of them? Either way, see (b) under modern *per stirpes*.
(c) How many children do remain? However many it may be, pay out to the living children (i.e., if only F remains, he takes a fourth; if only C remains, she takes a third).
(d) Take whatever is left and put it back in the hotch pot. Go down to the next level. Divide equally amongst all living grandchildren whose parents have not been paid (as, per the example above, none of the grandchildren has children). (Figure 7 assumes, by way of example, that C and E are dead, but that D and F live. Note that each of the grandchildren who take by representation through C and E get the same share of their grandparents' estates ($\frac{1}{8}$ th, or the $\frac{1}{2}$ of the estate that was left divided four ways). Note that this also means, however, that E's children, in aggregate, get three times as much of the total estate than does C's loan child.)

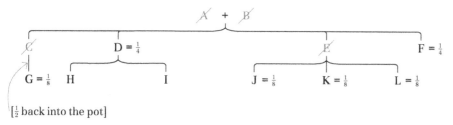

$[\frac{1}{2}$ back into the pot]

Figure 7

(e) If there are more than one dead grandchild who themselves had children, then the re-gathering and re-dividing process would occur again. (If there were only one dead grandchild with children, then those children (the -great-grandchildren) would just divide that parent's portion. (If you don't see why, draw it out.))

d. Example

Consider the following example, which is designed to illustrate the distinctions between, and continuities among, the three different types of division. Try to work out each of the diagrams and distributions yourself before viewing the figures below.

Here's the family: A + B have had children C, D, E, F, G, and H. C has had children I, J, and K. E has had child L. F has had children M and N. H has had children O and P. D and G have had no children. J has children Q and R. L has child S. O has child T. No other descendants have children.

Here is the initial family tree:

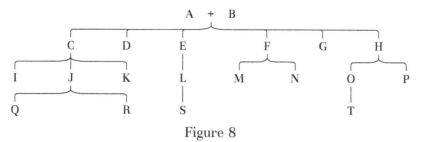

Figure 8

Throughout the rest of the examples, presume that A + B have died.

Next, assume that D, E, and F are dead. How would the distribution play out at the first generation Under English *per stirpes*? Modern? The UPC? Because some members of the first generation are still alive, English and Modern *per stirpes* will be the same. Because we are not looking yet at the second generation, the UPC method does not yet differ.

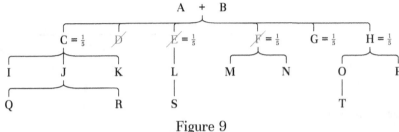

Figure 9

Each of the surviving children take one-fifth, as do the lines of each of the decedent children who are survived, and who therefore are "represented" in the distribution. D is dead without issue, so his line goes dry.

Now consider distribution to the third generation. Again, there will be no difference between English and modern *per stirpes*, as that distinction only occurs, if at all, at the first generation. So for both English and modern *per stirpes*, E's full one-fifth share descends to E's lone surviving child, L, while F's one-fifth share is divided equally between F's two children, so that M and N each take one-tenth of the estate.

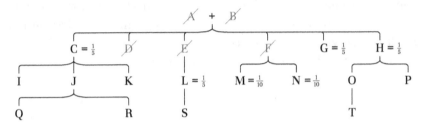

Figure 10

Compare this result to the UPC result. Under the UPC, C, G, and H, the surviving children, each take one-fifth. This leaves two-fifths undistributed. This two-fifths is put back into the common pool for division at the next generation. At the next generation, there are three descendants, each "equally near, equally dear" to A + B, the property owners. These three descendants totally represent the dead of the previous generation (i.e., there is no one in this generation who has died arid left representing descendants). As a result, the whole of the common pool is divided equally at this generation, so that each of L, M and N take one-third of two-fifths, or $\frac{2}{15}$ths each.

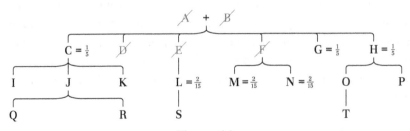

Figure 11

Now, draw the only diagram that could result in a difference between English and modern *per stirpes* by the end of the first generation.

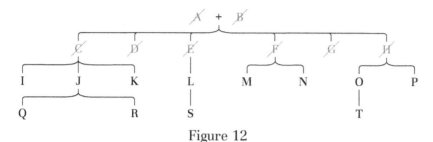

Figure 12

Of course, English and modern *per stirpes* can only have different outcomes if the whole first generation is dead. What are those results?
For English *per stirpes*:

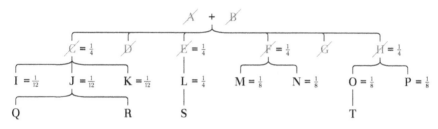

Figure 13

For modern *per stirpes*:

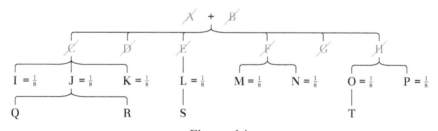

Figure 14

Finally, for a finale, work out the next diagram using all three different systems:

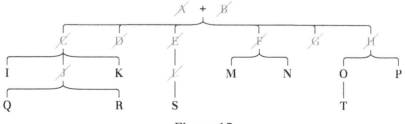

Figure 15

You should get a slightly different result with correct application of each system.

e. Comparative Distinctions and Aide-Mémoire

Another way to think about the distinctions between these methods and something to keep in mind if you attempt to work up your own hypotheticals as practice (not a bad way to study this subject): In order to devise an example that successfully illustrates all three of these methods distinctly (i.e., one that demonstrates the difference between each of the three), you must follow a pair of rules. For there to be a distinction between English and modern *per stirpes*, the whole first generation must be dead. For there to be a distinction between modern *per stirpes* and the UPC System, the first generation at which there are living members must have more than one dead member, and at least two of the dead members must themselves leave behind at least one but not the same number of children.

Otherwise (i.e., if, for English vs. modern *per stirpes* (a) someone is still alive in the first generation; or, for modern *per stirpes* as opposed to the hotch pot, (b) only one member of the first represented generation is dead, or (c) more than one member of the first represented generation is dead, but either one of them has no children or they both have the same number of children), the differences won't manifest themselves. Do you see why?

B. BIRTH AND CHILDREN

1. Law and Ethics Coping with Medical Advances in Birth Technology

What becomes of children born (or, given modern technology, even *conceived*) after the death of one—and, before long, perhaps both—of the parents? These children are all in some sense "posthumous," in that their birth (or conception) post-dates the demise of a parent. Because law, social norms, and technology all shift—sometimes sporadically, sometimes connectedly, but inevitably—over time, both the nature of posthumousness and the ramifications of the designation have changed significantly in the last half century.

a. Posthumous Children (the Common-Law Conception)

"Posthumous children" is a common-law "term of art" of ancient provenance, one that long predates virtually any medical advances this side of midwifery. Given those medical constraints, children could *only* be posthumous (by more than a couple of minutes, anyway) to the child's father, and even then could only (if nonpretextually applied) be born, at most, nine months' posthumous to the father's demise.

Death came regularly to our ancestors while they were still well within their child-creating years. Perhaps the paradigm case for posthumous death arose when a war-time military leave led to an amorous but brief visit between husband and wife, leaving the wife newly expectant when she received from the front the awful news of her husband's death in battle.

Now arises the question: is that child, born after the death of his father, the offspring of that predeceased warrior pa? In a biological sense, the answer is "of course." The law, though, is not always as straightforward as biology, nor are the facts always quite as clear as those sketched out above.

Moreover, the law sometimes establishes unique incentives (or penalties) not necessarily derived from nature. For centuries, the laws relating to a child's patrimony constituted just such a deviation. It mattered desperately under law whether a child was born in wedlock or in what was then unkindly labeled "bastardy" (and then later, as a softening effort, "illegitimacy.")[8] At modern law, as a constitutional imperative, no distinction may be drawn between children born within wedlock and those born without ("nonmarital children" being the preferred term today). Nonmarital children could not inherit family titles (and thus they were cut off from much of the stock of landed wealth and political power) and were often shunned by polite society.[9]

The posthumous-child rule worked to keep children born after their fathers' decease from falling into this shadow-child category. It declared (and declares, though the matter is of less relevance today) that such children were as a matter of law born *in* wedlock, despite the technical

---

8. Historically, such children have sometimes in polite society been referred as "natural" children–a rather charming locution, even if the tacit implications of the term seem rather odd.

9. So regular was this result that the habit grew up of illegitimate sons of English royalty—by their illegitimacy cut off from any lawful access to the crown—taking on the surname "FitzRoy," which was an English derivation of the French term "fils du roi," or "son of the king."

fact that their mothers were of necessity no longer actually married to their (dead) fathers at the time of their births. Moreover, it created a presumption—sometimes a presumption irrebuttable even by the clearest of evidence—that *any* child born of a mother within nine months of the mother's late husband's death was legally the child of the dead husband and thus fully legitimate under the laws of the time.[10]

b. Posthumously Conceived Children

Posthumously *conceived*—as opposed to posthumously *born*—children are still, as a matter of common-sense, definition "posthumous children," but they do not fit into the centuries' old legal term-of-art usage of posthumous children. They are a distinctly new category, the technology to permit conception of children after the death of one (or presumably both) of the parents only having arisen in the 1980s and shed its novelties, scientific uncertainties, and profound controversiality within the last few decades.

Posthumously *conceived* children create some unique public policy questions that did not append to "posthumous children," at least one of which receives airing in the following case.

ASTRUE v. CAPATO

132 S. Ct. 2021 (2012).

Justice Ginsburg delivered the [unanimous] opinion of the Court.

Karen and Robert Capato married in 1999. Robert died of cancer less than three years later. With the help of *in vitro* fertilization, Karen gave birth to twins 18 months after her husband's death. Karen's application for Social Security survivors benefits for the twins, which the Social Security Administration (SSA) denied, prompted this litigation. The technology that made the twins' conception and birth possible, it is safe to say, was not contemplated by Congress when the relevant provisions of the Social Security Act (Act) originated (1939) or were amended to read as they now do (1965).

Karen Capato, respondent here, relies on the Act's initial definition of "child" in 42 U.S.C. §416(e): "'[C]hild' means . . . the child or legally adopted child of an [insured] individual." Robert was an

---

10. *See, e.g.,* Unif. Parentage Act (Unif. L. Comm'n 2002) §204(a)(2) (children born within 300 days of the father's death considered the legitimate child of the deceased father).

insured individual, and the twins, it is uncontested, are the biological children of Karen and Robert. That satisfies the Act's terms, and no further inquiry is in order, Karen maintains. The SSA, however, identifies subsequent provisions, §§416(h)(2) and (h)(3)(C), as critical, and reads them to entitle biological children to benefits only if they qualify for inheritance from the decedent under state intestacy law, or satisfy one of the statutory alternatives to that requirement.

We conclude that the SSA's reading is better attuned to the statute's text and its design to benefit primarily those supported by the deceased wage earner in his or her lifetime. . . .

I

Karen Capato married Robert Capato in May 1999. Shortly thereafter, Robert was diagnosed with esophageal cancer and was told that the chemotherapy he required might render him sterile. Because the couple wanted children, Robert, before undergoing chemotherapy, deposited his semen in a sperm bank, where it was frozen and stored. . . .

Robert's health deteriorated in late 2001, and he died in Florida, where he and Karen then resided, in March 2002. . . . Shortly after Robert's death, Karen began in vitro fertilization using her husband's frozen sperm. She conceived in January 2003 and gave birth to twins in September 2003, 18 months after Robert's death.

Karen Capato claimed survivors insurance benefits on behalf of the twins. The SSA denied her application, and the U.S. District Court for the District of New Jersey affirmed the agency's decision. . . . In accord with the SSA's construction of the statute, the District Court determined that the twins would qualify for benefits only if, as §416(h)(2)(A) specifies, they could inherit from the deceased wage earner under state intestacy law. Robert Capato died domiciled in Florida, the court found. Under that State's law, the court noted, a child born posthumously may inherit through intestate succession only if conceived during the decedent's lifetime. . . .

The Court of Appeals for the Third Circuit reversed. Under §416(e), the appellate court concluded, "the undisputed biological children of a deceased wage earner and his widow" qualify for survivors benefits without regard to state intestacy law. . . . Courts of Appeals have divided on the statutory interpretation question this case presents. . . . To resolve the conflict, we granted the Commissioner's petition for a writ of certiorari. . . .

II

Congress amended the Social Security Act in 1939 to provide a monthly benefit for designated surviving family members of a deceased insured wage earner. "Child's insurance benefits" are among the Act's family-protective measures. 42 U.S.C. §402(d). An applicant qualifies for such benefits if she meets the Act's definition of "child," is unmarried, is below specified age limits (18 or 19) or is under a disability which began prior to age 22 and was dependent on the insured at the time of the insured's death. §402(d)(1).

To resolve this case, we must decide whether the Capato twins rank as "child[ren]" under the Act's definitional provisions. Section 402(d) provides that "[e]very child (as defined in section 416(e) of this title)" of a deceased insured individual "shall be entitled to a child's insurance benefit." Section 416(e), in turn, states: "The term 'child' means (1) the child or legally adopted child of an individual, (2) a stepchild [under certain circumstances], and (3) . . . the grandchild or step-grandchild of an individual or his spouse [who meets certain conditions]."

The word "child," we note, appears twice in §416(e)'s opening sentence: initially in the prefatory phrase, "[t]he term 'child' means . . . ," and, immediately thereafter, in subsection (e)(1) ("child or legally adopted child"), delineating the first of three beneficiary categories. . . .

A subsequent definitional provision further addresses the term "child." Under the heading "Determination of family status," §416(h)(2)(A) provides: "In determining whether an applicant is the child or parent of [an] insured individual for purposes of this subchapter, the Commissioner of Social Security shall apply [the intestacy law of the insured individual's domiciliary State]." . . .

The SSA has interpreted these provisions in regulations adopted through notice-and-comment rulemaking. The regulations state that an applicant may be entitled to benefits "as a natural child, legally adopted child, stepchild, grandchild, step-grandchild, or equitably adopted child." . . . Defining "[w]ho is the insured's natural child," . . . the regulations closely track 42 U.S.C. §§416(h)(2) and (h)(3). They state that an applicant may qualify for insurance benefits as a "natural child" by meeting any of four conditions: (1) the applicant "could inherit the insured's personal property as his or her natural child under State inheritance laws"; (2) the applicant is "the insured's natural child and [his or her parents] went through a ceremony which would have resulted in a valid marriage between them except for a legal impediment"; (3) before death, the insured acknowledged in writing his or her parentage of the applicant, was decreed by a court to be the applicant's parent, or was ordered by a court to contribute to the applicant's support; or (4) other evidence shows that the insured is the applicant's "natural father or mother" and was either living with, or contributing to the support of, the applicant. . . .

As the SSA reads the statute, 42 U.S.C. §416(h) governs the meaning of "child" in §416(e)(1). In other words, §416(h) is a gateway through which all applicants for insurance benefits as a "child" must pass. *See Beeler*[v. *Astrue*], 651 F.3d[954,] 960 [(8th Cir. 2011)] ("The regulations make clear that the SSA interprets the Act to mean that the provisions of §416(h) are the exclusive means by which an applicant can establish 'child' status under §416(e) as a natural child.").

III

Karen Capato argues, and the Third Circuit held, that §416(h), far from supplying the governing law, is irrelevant in this case. Instead, the Court of Appeals determined, §416(e) alone is dispositive of the controversy. . . . Under §416(e), "child" means "child of an [insured] individual," and the Capato twins, the Third Circuit observed, clearly fit that definition: They are undeniably the children of Robert Capato, the insured wage earner, and his widow, Karen Capato. Section 416(h) comes into play, the court reasoned, only when "a claimant's status as a deceased wage-earner's child is in doubt." . . . That limitation, the court suggested, is evident from §416(h)'s caption: "Determination of family status." Here, "there is no family status to determine," the court said, . . . so §416(h) has no role to play.

In short, while the SSA regards §416(h) as completing §416(e)'s sparse definition of "child," the Third Circuit considered each subsection to control different situations: §416(h) governs when a child's family status needs to be determined; §416(e), when it does not. When is there no need to determine a child's family status? The answer that the Third Circuit found plain: whenever the claimant is "the biological child of a married couple.". . .

We point out, first, some conspicuous flaws in the Third Circuit's and respondent Karen Capato's reading of the Act's provisions, and then explain why we find the SSA's interpretation persuasive.

A

Nothing in §416(e)'s tautological definition (" 'child' means . . . the child . . . of an individual") suggests that Congress understood the word "child" to refer only to the children of married parents. The dictionary definitions offered by respondent are not so confined. See Webster's New International Dictionary 465 (2d ed. 1934) (defining "child" as, inter alia, "[i]n Law, legitimate offspring; also, sometimes, esp. in wills, an adopted child, or an illegitimate offspring, or any direct descendant, as a grandchild, as the intention may appear"); Merriam-Webster's Collegiate Dictionary 214 (11th ed. 2003) ("child" means "son or daughter," or "descendant"). See also Restatement (Third) of Property §2.5(1) (1998) ("[a]n individual is the child of his or her genetic parents," and that may be so "whether or not [the parents] are married to each other"). Moreover, elsewhere in the Act, Congress expressly limited the category of children covered to offspring of a marital union. See §402(d)(3)(A) (referring to the "legitimate . . . child" of an individual). Other contemporaneous statutes similarly differentiate child of a marriage ("legitimate child") from the unmodified term "child." See, e.g., Servicemen's Dependents Allowance Act of 1942, ch. 443, §120, 56 Stat. 385 (defining "child" to include "legitimate child," "child legally adopted," and, under certain conditions, "stepchild" and "illegitimate child" (internal quotation marks omitted)).

Nor does §416(e) indicate that Congress intended "biological" parentage to be prerequisite to "child" status under that provision. As the SSA points out, "[i]n 1939, there was no such thing as a scientifically proven biological relationship between a child and a father, which is . . . part of the reason that the word 'biological' appears nowhere in the Act." [. . .] Notably, a biological parent is not necessarily a child's parent under law. Ordinarily, "a parent-child relationship does not exist between an adoptee and the adoptee's genetic parents." Uniform Probate Code §2-119(a), 8 U. L. A. 55 (Supp. 2011) (amended 2008). Moreover, laws directly addressing use of today's assisted reproduction technology do not make biological parentage a universally determinative criterion. . . .

We note, in addition, that marriage does not ever and always make the parentage of a child certain, nor does the absence of marriage necessarily mean that a child's parentage is uncertain. An unmarried couple can agree that a child is theirs, while the parentage of a child born during a marriage may be uncertain. . . .

Finally, it is far from obvious that Karen Capato's proposed definition –biological child of married parents," . . . would cover the posthumously conceived Capato twins. Under Florida law, a marriage ends upon the death of a spouse. . . . If that law applies, rather than a court-declared preemptive federal law, the Capato twins, conceived after the death of their father, would not qualify as "marital" children.

B

Resisting the importation of words not found in §416(e)–"child" means "the biological child of married parents," . . . the SSA finds a key textual cue in §416(h)(2)(A)'s opening instruction: "In determining whether an applicant is the child . . . of [an] insured individual for purposes of this subchapter," the Commissioner shall apply state intestacy law. (Emphasis added.) . . . The "subchapter" to which §416(h) refers is Subchapter II of the Act, which spans §§401 through 434. Section 416(h)'s reference to "this subchapter" thus includes both §§402(d) and 416(e). . . .

The original version of today's §416(h) was similarly drafted. It provided that, "[i]n determining whether an applicant is the . . . child . . . of [an] insured individual for purposes of sections 401-409 of this title, the Board shall apply [state intestacy law]." 42 U. S. C. §409(m) (1940 ed.) (emphasis added). Sections 401-409 embraced §§402(c) and 409(k), the statutory predecessors of 42 U. S. C. §§402(d) and 416(e) (2006 ed.), respectively.

Reference to state law to determine an applicant's status as a "child" is anything but anomalous. Quite the opposite. The Act commonly refers to state law on matters of family status. . . .

Indeed, as originally enacted, a single provision mandated the use of state intestacy law for "determining whether an applicant is the wife, widow, child, or parent of [an] insured individual." 42 U. S. C. §409(m) (1940 ed.). All wife, widow, child, and parent applicants thus had to satisfy the same criterion. To be sure, children born during their parents' marriage would have readily qualified under the 1939 formulation because of their eligibility to inherit under state law. But requiring all "child" applicants to qualify under state intestacy law installed a simple test, one that ensured benefits for persons plainly within the legislators' contemplation, while avoiding congressional entanglement in the traditional state-law realm of family relations.

Just as the Act generally refers to state law to determine whether an applicant qualifies as a wife, widow, husband, widower, 42 U. S. C. §416(h)(1) (2006 ed.), child or parent, §416(h)(2)(A), so in several sections (§§416(b), (c), (e)(2), (f), (g)), the Act sets duration-of-relationship limitations. . . . Time limits also qualify the statutes of several States that accord inheritance rights to posthumously conceived children. . . . No time constraints attend the Third Circuit's ruling in this case, under which the biological child of married parents is eligible for survivors benefits, no matter the length of time between the father's death and the child's conception and birth. See Tr. of Oral Arg. 36-37 (counsel for Karen Capato acknowledged that, under the preemptive federal rule he advocated, and the Third Circuit adopted, a child born four years after her father's death would be eligible for benefits).

The paths to receipt of benefits laid out in the Act and regulations, we must not forget, proceed from Congress' perception of the core purpose of the legislation. The aim was not to create a program "generally benefiting needy persons"; it was, more particularly, to "provide . . . dependent members of [a wage earner's] family with protection against the hardship occasioned by [the] loss of [the insured's] earnings." . . . We have recognized that "where state intestacy law provides that a child may take personal property from a father's estate, it may reasonably be thought that the child will more likely be dependent during the parent's life and at his death." ... Reliance on state intestacy law to determine who is a "child" thus serves the Act's driving objective. . . .

IV

As we have explained, §416(e)(1)'s statement, "[t]he term 'child' means . . . the child ... of an individual," is a definition of scant utility without aid from neighboring provisions.... That aid is supplied by §416(h)(2)(A), which completes the definition of "child" "for purposes of th[e] subchapter" that includes §416(e)(1). Under the completed definition, which the SSA employs, §416(h)(2)(A) refers to state law to determine the status of a posthumously conceived child. . . .

V

Tragic circumstances—Robert Capato's death before he and his wife could raise a family—gave rise to this case. But the law Congress enacted calls for resolution of Karen Capato's application for child's insurance benefits by reference to state intestacy law. We cannot replace that reference by creating a uniform federal rule the statute's text scarcely supports. . . .

For the reasons stated, the judgment of the Court of Appeals for the Third Circuit is reversed, and the case is remanded for further proceedings consistent with this opinion.

It is so ordered.

* * *

As the Court notes, some states have made *ad hoc* judgment calls about how long after the death of a parent the use of that parent's genetic materials may result in a legally recognized child of that parent. So has the UPC. Per §2-120(k), "[i]f, under this section, an individual is a parent of a child of assisted reproduction who is conceived after the individual's death, the child is treated as in gestation at the individual's death for purposes of Section 2-104(a)(2) if the child is: (1) in utero not later than 36 months after the individual's death; or (2) born not later than 45 months after the individual's death." In other words, the UPC simply extends the legal fiction of the common-law posthumous child (i.e., that a child in gestation at the death of its father is not nonmarital even though the marriage had necessarily ended upon the death of the father) into the world of modern reproductive technology by pretending that gestation that starts within three years of a parent's death had actually begun during that decedent parent's life.

c. Surrogacy

Surrogacy technology has created a panoply of relationships between participants in the life-giving and child-rearing process that could hardly have been credited beyond the environs of science fiction just a few generations ago. The very definitions that the UPC must deploy predicate to explaining its rules for dealing with such situations indicate the relatively novelty and complexity of the process. Per UPC § 2-120(a):

> (1) "Birth mother" means a woman, other than a gestational carrier under Section 2-121, who gives birth to a child of assisted reproduction. The term is not limited to a woman who is the child's genetic mother.
>
> (2) "Child of assisted reproduction" means a child conceived by means of assisted reproduction by a woman other than a gestational carrier under Section 2-121.
>
> (3) "Third-party donor" means an individual who produces eggs or sperm used for assisted reproduction, whether or not for consideration. The term does not include:
>
> > (A) a husband who provides sperm, or a wife who provides eggs, that are used for assisted reproduction by the wife;
> >
> > (B) the birth mother of a child of assisted reproduction; or
> >
> > (C) an individual who has been determined under subsection (e) or (f) to have a parent-child relationship with a child of assisted reproduction.

The rules that follow these definitions significantly bend toward sanctioning self-selected families and honoring the agreements made by the parties in the process of organizing their desired family form. Third-party donors are absolved of responsibility for children created from the matter of their donations.[11] As seen above, parenthood is defined by the desire and agreement of the relevant parties as to who the parents should be, not by the provision of materials or the act of gestation. The UPC, at 2-120, *et seq.*, deals with additional complications, such as withdrawal of consent by various parties or the divorce of the designated, intended parents.

Of course, a significant number of states have not adopted the UPC's surrogacy provisions, and some retain legal provisions that render the surrogacy process relatively uncertain and risky if undertaken there. And the very nature of the undertaking adds significant layers of human feeling, empathy, and drama that render this a situation in which those who embark on the process are wise to do so in a jurisdiction where late-stage vacillation and other complications are legally discouraged.

2. Law and Ethics Coping with Sociological Change

In case you've missed it, the times, they are a'changin.' As they change, so the law must–late or soon–change too to accommodate social developments. While we will see specific legal adaptations in response to social change, particularly in the areas of separate property and trust law, here are some examples of changes that affect the whole field.

a. Nonmarital Children

As recognized above, no legal distinction is—or constitutionally may— be made between children born in or out of wedlock at modern law. Children born of an unmarried mother and father, or by artificial insemination, or in any configuration of blended family that would have been—perhaps literally, but surely figuratively—inconceivable to most of our grandparents (but which feature prominently in hit sitcoms in the 2010s) face no legal, civic, or even very many social handicaps in most quarters.

One unique issue does necessarily arise in the case of some non-marital births: identifying the father. (The mother for various and sundry reasons is usually obvious except in those cases in which the

---

11. *See* UPC §2-120(b).

"substitute" parents are highly invested and easily identified. Think, for instance, of a case in which two dads use an anonymously "donated" egg from a third party to the marriage, and then a surrogate *fourth* party to carry the baby. These are motivated parents, and while the biological mom is legally unidentifiable, the parties who intend to rear the child are very much on hand.)

Of course, a DNA test can identify the father with a high degree of confidence (though with less certainty than the general public, tutored by the endless array of *CSI and Law & Order* cop-and-court shows of the last decades, tends to believe). It is not, however, entirely necessary. Rather, any behavior that tends reasonably to demonstrate that a man acted the part of a father for a nonmarital child will help to support a claim of paternity. Obviously the most conclusive demonstration includes helping to raise and support the child and acknowledging paternity, but any combination of these will provide some evidence. The general standard is this: If a man has "acted broadly as a father would act" in some way or another, then a presumption of paternity can arise.[12]

---

12. *See, e.g.,* Unif. Parentage Act (Unif. L. Comm'n 2002) §204(a):

A man is presumed to be the father of a child if:

(1) he and the mother of the child are married to each other and the child is born during the marriage;

(2) he and the mother of the child were married to each other and the child is born within 300 days after the marriage is terminated by death, annulment, declaration of invalidity, or divorce [or after a decree of separation];

(3) before the birth of the child, he and the mother of the child married each other in apparent compliance with law, even if the attempted marriage is or could be declared invalid, and the child is born during the invalid marriage or within 300 days after its termination by death, annulment, declaration of invalidity, or divorce [or after a decree of separation];

(4) after the birth of the child, he and the mother of the child married each other in apparent compliance with law, whether or not the marriage is or could be declared invalid, and he voluntarily asserted his paternity of the child, and:

(A) the assertion is in a record filed with [state agency maintaining birth records];

(B) he agreed to be and is named as the child's father on the child's birth certificate; or

(C) he promised in a record to support the child as his own; or

(5) for the first two years of the child's life, he resided in the same household with the child and openly held out the child as his own.

b. Adoption

"A creature of statute." While adoption existed at Roman and continental law,[13] the English common law, interested as it was in protecting the blood lines in which political power resided, never recognized it. In fact, Britain did not formally recognize adoption in any form until 1926.

American legislatures moved far more quickly than their British parliamentary cousins to recognize adoption, but here as there the common law provided no aid. Adoption, as the rote recital—included as a matter of course in the opinions deciding a vast array of adoption cases—intones, "is a creature of statute" alone. In other words, the legislature must act in order for adoption to be recognized, and adoption *is* recognized (in theory) exactly and only to the extent to which the legislation specifies.

"A branch of only one tree." Nevertheless, American courts are by nature, training, and disposition very much common-law courts in their patterns of thinking and acting, even in this era of extensive codification and regulation. And common-law courts tend to think by analogy and metaphor. The metaphor that the common-law courts developed in this context was one of a branch growing out of a tree. Stretching this metaphor to a fare-thee-well, and certainly past horticultural coherence, the courts concluded—sometimes in the very teeth of statutory dictates to the contrary—that a branch can stem from only one tree.[14] This is to say that when an adoption occurred, the child (or branch, in the metaphor), is cut from the original tree entirely and spliced, apparently,[15] onto the new tree, severing all ties to the old tree, er, family. Or, a little less ponderously: Once a child is adopted into a different family, that child *and all her descendants* are forever

---

13. "Perhaps no settlor in 1650 could have *anticipated exactly* some of these developments (though it is worth noting, for instance, that anyone in 1650 with even a passing knowledge of the Roman imperial dynasty—a thing that Shakespeare demonstrates was generally available—had some sense of the institution of adoption, and that while the English system largely rejected formal adoption, the institution was contemporaneously alive and well on the European continent.)" Scott Andrew Shepard, *Which the Deader Hand? A Counter to the American Law Institute's Proposed Revival of Dying Perpetuities Rules,* 86 Tul. L. Rev. 559, 600 (2012) (citing Leo Albert Huard, *The Law of Adoption: Ancient and Modern,* 9 Vand. L. Rev. 743, 745-47 (1956)) (other citations omitted).

14. *See, e.g., In re Brockmire,* 424 S.W.3d 445 (Mo. 2014). (An expurgated version of this case is available on the web page for this textbook.)

15. This, it turns out, is actually horticulturally possible.

cut off from the biological parents.[16] Relevantly, this meant that for intestate and general generational distribution purposes, adopted children are under traditional common law treated fully as part of their adoptive families and in no way as part of their birth families.

An example here is fairly straightforward. Assume that Alice is put up for adoption by her mother Bernice. Bernice has a brother, Eric, who dies intestate. Eric and Brenda's parents have died, and Eric has no spouse or children, but he does have three nieces and nephews, including Alice. But since Alice has been adopted out of her birth mother's family, Alice takes nothing from Eric, whether or not he knows of her current situation, and even if Bernice has died. Eric's estate is divided amongst his remaining niece and nephew.

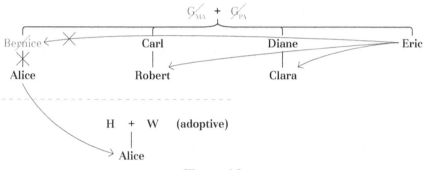

Figure 16

Note that while this summary captures the traditional development of the law of adoption in most states, it is not universally applicable. In a small minority of jurisdictions adopted children are treated as members of both families, while in a few more the decree of adoption may stipulate that the child continues to be a member of the birth as well as the adoptive family.

The UPC Innovation —stepparent adoption and intertwining trees. This state of things, though, sometimes leads to unfortunate results. Imagine, for instance, that husband and wife have a couple of children. Husband's and wife's respective parents are close with their grandchildren and love them very much. When the children are eight and three, however, mom dies. Dad is left to care for the children alone—a feat he manages in the months after his wife's death

---

16. *In re Brockmire*, 424 S.W.3d 445 (Mo. 2014).

only with nearly constant assistance and support from both sets of grandparents.

Eventually, dad starts dating again, and before too long marries a wonderful new woman, wife2. Contrary to the scarifying "fairy tales" of our collective youths, this stepmom turns out to be a great mom as well as a caring helpmeet; the kids rapidly grow to love her, and even their natural mother's (i.e., wife1's) parents recognize—however mistily, at times—that she is good for the kids, for their former son-in-law, for the family in general. And so W2 formally adopts the children.

Would you expect, under these circumstances, that upon W2's adoption of the children, W1's parents (the kids' biological grandparents) would be cut from their lives, and would themselves stop loving these kids as members of their own family? This seems, in this scenario, highly unlikely. *Of course* these grandparents are going to continue to love these grandchildren as their own—perhaps more even than they otherwise would have, insofar as the kids will exhibit mannerisms and personality traits and features that remind them of their mourned and beloved daughter, taken by accident long before her time. And since we have posited here not a wicked stepmother of horrifying late-medieval Teutonic imagination, but rather a caring and loving step- and adoptive-mother, we need not worry that W2 will for some inexplicable reason cut the grandparents off from their lost daughter's progeny. Sure, things might get a bit awkward, or wistful, from time to time, but three sets of grandparents are in these circumstances almost surely better than two.

It follows, then, that if the birth mother's parents, or other surviving members of her family, were to die intestate, they would almost surely wish these grandchildren to share in their estate along with the rest of their descendants and, as their mother is dead, they will surely take their mother's intestate share by representation—unless the "branch of only one tree" metaphor slashes down to cut them off.

The UPC's revision to the "branch of one tree" rule is designed explicitly and narrowly to deal with exactly this situation. At section 2-119(a), the code provides that, with some exceptions, "[a] parent-child relationship does not exist between an adoptee and the adoptee's genetic parents." The exceptions allow the adoptee to inherit from one or both genetic parents when adopted by a stepparent or a relative of a genetic parent, but the relationship is a one-way street; the nonadopting genetic parent(s) and their respective families cannot inherit from the adoptee. Thus, in the scenario sketched out above, the grandkids would still inherit from W1's parents, but those grandparents would not inherit from the grandkids (assuming, of course, that anyone who dies does so intestate).[17] The figure below illustrates the UPC rule for inheritance by children who have been adopted by a step-parent.

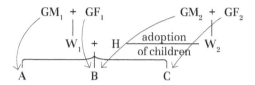

*Both sets of maternal grandparents
remain intestate ancestors.*

Figure 17

i. Equitable (or Virtual) Adoption

Adoption, as noted, is possible only where a legislature has authorized it by statute. And as with all statutory creations, there are some administrative hoops that must be jumped through before an adoption is recognized by the law (for our purposes, before it will be recognized after someone dies). Equitable adoption doctrine deals with the scenario that arises when a person brings a child into her family and treats the kid exactly as she would treat her own flesh and blood. For whatever reason, the administrative hoops never got jumped through properly—or at all—and when "mom" passes, the poor kid finds himself not on the list of heirs. That seems terribly unjust, doesn't it? Hence, equity (sometimes) steps in.

LUNA v. ESTATE OF RODRIGUEZ

906 S.W.2d 576 (Tex. Ct. App. 1995).

This appeal arises from an action to declare heirship in the estate of Henry E. Rodriguez. Appellant Christopher Luna appeals from a

---

17. *See, e.g.,* UPC §2-119:

(c) [Individual Adopted by Relative of Genetic Parent.] A parent-child relationship exists between both genetic parents and an individual who is adopted by a relative of a genetic parent, or by the spouse or surviving spouse of a relative of a genetic parent, but only for the purpose of the right of the adoptee or a descendant of the adoptee to inherit from or through either genetic parent.

(d) [Individual Adopted after Death of Both Genetic Parents.] A parent-child relationship exists between both genetic parents and an individual who is adopted after the death of both genetic parents, but only for the purpose of the right of the adoptee or a descendant of the adoptee to inherit through either genetic parent.

summary judgment granted in favor of appellees Hilario Rodriguez, Kay Williams Rodriguez, and the Estate of Henry E. Rodriguez. At issue is whether Christopher is decedent Henry Rodriguez's son by equitable adoption. We will reverse the trial court's judgment and remand the cause for further proceedings. . . .

Christopher is the biological son of Alfred and Mary Helen Luna; his parents divorced when he was only three years old. Following the divorce, Mary Helen was awarded custody of Christopher by court order; the record does not reveal that Alfred's parental rights have ever been terminated. Mary Helen married Henry Rodriguez, and both she and Christopher began living with him on approximately Christopher's sixth birthday. Christopher alleges that sometime before or during this marriage, his mother and Henry orally agreed, but not in the presence of any witnesses, that Henry would adopt Christopher. Apparently, Christopher's mother notified Christopher's natural father of Henry's plan to adopt Christopher, but Christopher's father refused to consent to the adoption. A formal statutory adoption never took place. Christopher did not find out about Henry's alleged agreement to adopt him until after Henry's death.

Christopher lived in his mother and Henry's home for seventeen years. During that time, Henry, as breadwinner for the household, paid Christopher's tuition and other school expenses through high school and college. Christopher was reared, cared for, and clothed by Henry and his mother. In turn, Christopher performed the normal chores of a son, such as mowing the grass, taking out trash, and cleaning up dog litter. Christopher called Henry "dad," and Henry called Christopher "son." While Christopher never assumed the Rodriguez surname, Henry held out Christopher to his friends as his own son, and Christopher was known in the community as Henry's son. As an adult and even after his mother's death, Christopher maintained a relationship with Henry, calling him on Father's Day and inviting him to his home on holidays like Thanksgiving and Christmas.

Christopher had a distant relationship with his biological father. As a child, he had no contact with his father; as an adult, he has spoken to him only once or twice. . . .

Henry died intestate and childless on December 26, 1991.[18] Christopher subsequently filed an application for declaration of heirship alleging his status as Henry's equitably adopted son and naming as

---

18. [This is a particularly inapt situation in which to die intestate.—ED.]

respondents Hilario Rodriguez, Henry's brother, and Kay Rodriguez, Henry's second wife. . . .

The trial court granted Hilario's motion [for summary judgment], stating that Christopher's application failed to state a cause of action and that no genuine issues of material fact existed to support Christopher's application. The trial court thus declined to find that Henry equitably adopted Christopher. . . . Christopher appeals from the summary judgment. . . .

Christopher contends that the trial court erred in granting the motion for summary judgment, implicitly complaining the trial court erroneously concluded that Christopher's application for declaration of heirship failed to state a cause of action to establish an equitable adoption. . . .

I. Elements of Equitable Adoption by Estoppel

In the instant cause, we are charged with articulating the elements necessary to plead a cause of action to establish an equitable adoption and with determining whether Christopher's pleadings allege those elements. Courts apply the remedy of "equitable adoption," which in Texas is based on an estoppel theory,[1] when efforts to adopt are ineffective because of failure to strictly comply with statutory procedures or because, out of neglect or design, agreements to adopt are not performed. . . . As first explained by the Texas Supreme Court in 1934, a decree of equitable adoption by estoppel rests in equity:

> [When] one . . . takes a child into his home as his own, receiving the benefits accruing to him on account of that relation, assumes the duties and burdens incident thereto, and . . . where justice and good faith require it[,] the court will enforce the rights incident to the statutory relation of adoption. *The child having performed all the duties pertaining to that relation, the adopting parent will be estopped in equity from denying that he assumed the corresponding obligation.*

Cubley v. Barbee, 123 Tex. 411, 73 S.W.2d 72, 81 (Tex. 1934) (emphasis added). . . .

---

1. Many states invoke the equitable adoption remedy under a specific performance theory of recovery. See generally Note, *Equitable Adoption: They Took Him into Their Home and Called Him Fred,* 58 Va. L. Rev. 727, 730-32 (1972). The Texas Supreme Court, recognizing that many courts grant equitable adoption relief based on specific performance of a contract to adopt, has rejected the specific performance theory, stating "the real classification of the remedy is that of estoppel." . . .

The trial court and some courts of appeals appear to hold that the establishment of an adoption by estoppel requires the following: (1) proof of an agreement to adopt, (2) performance by the child, and (3) the child's reliance on the agreement to adopt or on the child's belief in its adoptive status.[2]. . . In addition to these three elements, the trial court also appeared to require proof of the date on which the agreement to adopt took place in order to establish an equitable adoption.

Undoubtedly, proof of an agreement to adopt is essential to establish an adoption by estoppel.[3] . . . Likewise, performance by the child to benefit the adopting parent is a necessary element.[4] . . . As summarized by the supreme court: "The doctrine of equity . . . rests upon the adoptive parent having received the benefits of the relation fully performed by the child." Jones v. Guy, 135 Tex. 398, 143 S.W.2d 906, 909 (Tex. 1940). Thus, a court will uphold the child's adoptive status when a natural parent delivers a child into the custody of others under an agreement between the parent and the custodians that the child will be adopted, and thereafter the custodians and child live in a relationship consistent with that of parent and child. . . .

Case law does not clearly establish reliance as a separate and necessary element of an adoption by estoppel. Under both *Cubley* and *Guy*, the remedy of adoption by estoppel is available when a child is induced to perform for the adoptive parents by the adoptive parents' representations about the child's adoptive status:

> [An estoppel operates] to preclude adoptive parents and their privies from asserting the invalidity of adoption proceedings, or, at least, the status of the adopted child, when, by performance upon the part of the child, the adoptive parents have received all the benefits and privileges accruing from such performance, and they by their representations induced such performance under the belief of the existence of the status of the adopted child.

Cubley, 73 S.W.2d at 79-80; see also *Guy*, 143 S.W.2d at 908. The *Cavanaugh* court, in setting forth the elements of an adoption by

---

2. By comparison, an equitable estoppel generally results when a person (1) detrimentally (2) relies on the (3) misrepresentation of another. . . .

3. The agreement to adopt must be between the adopting parent and the child or the child's representative, such as a natural parent or someone in loco parentis. . . . The agreement may be in writing . . . or oral. . . . Proof of the agreement does not require direct evidence; clear, convincing, and unequivocal circumstantial evidence as demonstrated by the acts, conduct, and admissions of the adopting parent is sufficient.

4. Later court opinions have referred to the child's "performance" as the child's conferring of affection and benefits on the adoptive parents.

estoppel, did not expressly require that a child be induced to perform or confer affection and benefits on the adoptive parent out of reliance on an agreement to adopt. Rather, the *Cavanaugh* court indicated that the child must confer affection and benefits while "acting under and by virtue" of the agreement to adopt: in the absence of other written adoption documentation, a child must plead and prove that its natural parent and the custodian agreed that the custodian would adopt the child; equity then may require the trial court "to decree an adoption by estoppel in favor of [the child] who, acting under and by virtue of such an agreement, confers affection and benefits upon the [adoptive parent].". . .

In *Cavanaugh*, the child requesting a declaration of equitable adoption did not learn that she was not the natural child of her alleged adoptive parents until she reached adulthood. . . . Thus, even though an agreement to adopt may have occurred, it would have been impossible for the child to prove that she relied on that agreement or representations based on it. The *Cavanaugh* court, while deciding the case against the claimant, did not do so on the ground of absence of reliance, but on the basis that the record contained some evidence in support of the trial court's finding that there was no agreement to adopt. . . . By not speaking in terms of reliance per se, *Cavanaugh* encompasses situations where a child may have no knowledge of an agreement to adopt, yet, by virtue of the agreement, the child is placed in a situation wholly consistent with that of natural parent and child and thus, believing the relationship to be one of parent and child, naturally confers affection and benefits on its adoptive parent or parents.

Under circumstances such as those in *Cavanaugh*, proof of an agreement to adopt may lead to an inference that the child has been led to believe the adoption has been completed. . . . In essence, the child acts upon the belief that the adoptive parent is its parent and lives in accord with a parent-child relationship. Proof of the agreement alone, without regard to any proof of reliance, may thus, in some cases, sufficiently establish the reliance element necessary to justify the estoppel remedy. . . .

A decree of equitable adoption is an equitable remedy. When clear, unequivocal, and convincing evidence of an agreement to adopt exists and the child has performed services for the adoptive parent even though the child had no knowledge of the agreement to adopt or its status as an adopted child, equity requires a decree of adoption by the court. We conclude that equity will act to decree an adoption by estoppel when the elements necessary to establish a cause of action for an equitable adoption by estoppel . . . are present: (1) the existence of an agreement to adopt and (2) performance by the child. A child subject to an equitable adoption acts in reliance on its belief in its "status" as a child, not necessarily in reliance on an agreement to adopt or on representations about adoptive status.

II. Christopher's Pleadings

The trial court ruled that Christopher's application failed to state a cause of action for adoption by estoppel because, among other things, it did not allege that Christopher conferred benefits on Henry out of reliance on an agreement to adopt or a statement that he was adopted. In light of our conclusion above, we hold that Christopher's application was not inadequate by failing to plead reliance on the agreement or on Henry's representations. The trial court also required Christopher to plead the date Henry and Mary Helen entered into an agreement to adopt him. We hold that pleading the date of the agreement to adopt is also unnecessary. Proof of the agreement can be by circumstantial evidence. . . . Circumstantial evidence may establish that an agreement to adopt took place without also establishing the exact date that agreement occurred. A plaintiff should not be required to plead what it does not have to prove. The function of a pleading is to define the issues at trial, not to state the evidence. . . .

The trial court additionally required Christopher to plead that the agreement to adopt him was made between Henry and both of Christopher's parents, rather than just his mother. However, the adopting parent's agreement to adopt can be with the child, the child's parents, or someone in loco parentis. . . . Where the child's natural parents have died or have abandoned the child, the agreement to adopt necessarily takes place between one other than the child's natural parents. . . . Moreover, when one natural parent abandons the child, an agreement with the other natural parent is sufficient. . . . In the instant cause, Christopher pleaded that for all intents and purposes his natural father abandoned him. Viewing Christopher's pleadings in a light most favorable to him, we hold that Christopher was not required to plead that Henry agreed with both of Christopher's parents in order to plead a cause of action for equitable adoption.

Christopher's application for declaration of heirship alleged the essential elements of an equitable adoption set out in *Cavanaugh*: that an agreement to adopt took place between Henry and Christopher's mother and that Christopher performed by conferring love, affection, companionship, and other benefits on Henry. Christopher's pleadings were not legally insufficient to establish a cause of action for equitable adoption. The trial court erred by concluding Christopher's application failed to state a cause of action. . . .

[W]e reverse the trial court's judgment and remand the cause to the trial court for a trial on the merits.

JOHNSON v. ROGERS
774 S.E.2d 647 (Ga. 2015).

Judges: BLACKWELL, Justice. All the Justices concur.

Lillian and Jimmie Lee Johnson were married for 37 years, and together, they raised her grandniece, Jessica Rogers. In 2005, Ms. Johnson made a will that included a number of bequests to Rogers.[1] Ms. Johnson died in 2011, and Mr. Johnson then sought to probate her will. Rogers filed a caveat, asserting that she had been adopted by Ms. Johnson after the will was made, which would entitle her to an intestate share of the estate under OCGA §53-4-48 (c). Although Rogers was unable to point to any statutory adoption by Ms. Johnson, she claimed nonetheless that she had been adopted pursuant to the equitable doctrine of "virtual adoption." The probate court agreed that Rogers was "virtually adopted" by Ms. Johnson after she made her will, and so, the probate court admitted the will to probate, but subject to Rogers taking an intestate share of the estate. Mr. Johnson appeals, and he argues that the doctrine of virtual adoption has no application in a case in which the decedent disposed of her entire estate by will. We agree, and for that reason, although we affirm the admission of the will to probate, we reverse the judgment that Rogers is entitled to an intestate share.

"Virtual adoption is an equitable remedy utilized when the conduct of the parties creates an implied adoption without a court order." Morgan v. Howard, 285 Ga. 512, 512 (1) (678 SE2d 882) (2009) (citation omitted). This Court first recognized the doctrine of virtual adoption in Crawford v. Wilson, 139 Ga. 654, 654 (78 SE 30) (1913), noting that "[a] parol obligation by a person to adopt the child of

---

1. Under the terms of the will, Ms. Johnson left her real property to Mr. Johnson, and she left a contingent, remainder interest in her real property to Rogers. Ms. Johnson left specific items of her personal property to Rogers and others. Ms. Johnson left her residuary estate to Mr. Johnson, and she gave Rogers a contingent interest in the residuary estate.

another as his own, . . . acted upon by all parties concerned for many years and during the obligor's life, may be enforced in equity upon the death of the obligor, by decreeing the child entitled as a child to the property of the obligor, undisposed of by will." As we recently explained, the doctrine of virtual adoption "is applied only after the death of the person who agreed to adopt the child . . . and when there has been no legal (statutory) adoption. The child, who is often an adult by that time, is allowed to invoke the doctrine of virtual adoption to avoid an unfair result from the application of intestacy statutes." Sanders v. Riley, 296 Ga. 693, 698 (2) (770 SE2d 570) (2015) (citation and punctuation omitted). Indeed, the purpose of virtual adoption is "[t]o correct the injustice that would result were the intestacy laws woodenly applied," and "[t]he courts have traditionally limited the doctrine to narrow circumstances, reasoning that the adoption statutes are in derogation of the common law and thus provide the exclusive means for [equitably] effecting an adoption or obtaining its benefits.". . .

To establish a virtual adoption, Georgia has long required at least some showing of an agreement between the natural and adoptive parents, a severance of the actual relationship of parent and child as between the child and the natural parents, the establishment of such a relationship between the child and the adoptive parents, and the intestacy of the adoptive parent. . . . "These elements, particularly the requirement of intestacy, limit the circumstances under which the doctrine may be applied." Lankford v. Wright, 347 N.C. 115, 489 SE2d 604, 607 (N.C. 1997). Although the Georgia courts have interpreted the equitable principle of virtual adoption "on numerous occasions, they have never extended it beyond the intestacy situation. . . . "As a result, this Court has previously decided that, where a will gives all of the real and personal property of the alleged adoptive parents to someone other than the alleged virtual adoptee, except for a certain specific bequest of personal property, there no longer remains in the estate any property subject to enforcement of the virtual adoption claim. . . .

This intestacy requirement is completely consistent with the law of equitable or virtual adoption in other states. "Almost exclusively, the application of the doctrine has been limited to intestate estates. It generally has not been applied to testate estates . . . but only to intestate estates where the decedent's intent is unknown." Estate of Seader, 2003 WY 119, 76 P3d 1236, 1241 (Wyo. 2003) (citations omitted). . . . Otherwise, "the result may negate both legislative and testamentary intent.". . . "The effect of a promise to adopt and the application of the principle of equitable adoption are relevant only when there is no contract to make a will and the adopted child claims under a statute of distribution." 7 Williston on Contracts §16:21 (4th ed.) (citations omitted).

In light of this longstanding and consistent authority in Georgia and other jurisdictions, only a clear legislative direction could abrogate the rule that virtual adoption requires intestacy.

The General Assembly properly can, of course, enact legislation that departs from the common law, but to the extent that statutory text can be as reasonably understood to conform to the common law as to depart from it, the courts usually presume that the legislature meant to adhere to the common law. . . .

The probate court acknowledged the settled understanding that virtual adoption requires intestacy, but that made sense, the probate court said, only for so long as the law provided that the adoption of a child subsequent to the making of a will without contemplation of the adoption revoked the antecedent will altogether, leaving the maker of the will intestate. Prior to 2002, the law did provide that a subsequent adoption would revoke a will, ... and during that time, the probate court said, questions of virtual adoption "frequently arose in the form of a caveat to a [w]ill," in cases in which a finding of virtual adoption would "result in intestacy." In 2002, however, OCGA §53-4-48 was amended, and as a result of that amendment, the law no longer provides for the revocation of an antecedent will upon the subsequent adoption of a child, and it now provides only that a later-adopted child is entitled to an intestate share of the estate. . . . The 2002 amendment, the probate court concluded, did away with the intestacy element of virtual adoption. We disagree.

Contrary to the analysis of the probate court, the doctrine of virtual adoption did not "frequently ar[i]se in the form of a caveat to a [w]ill" that could "result in intestacy." Virtual adoption cannot itself form the basis for a caveat or a finding of intestacy. Certainly, a person may allege and prove her virtual adoption in connection with a caveat, but only to show that she is an heir-at-law and has an interest in the estate so as to establish her standing to contest the probate of a will on a proper ground like mental incompetence or undue influence. . . . That proposition, however, is perfectly consistent with the rule that virtual adoption can arise only when the virtual parent dies intestate. If the caveat to the will is successful, then the requirement of intestacy has been met.

Nothing suggests that the 2002 amendment of OCGA §53-4-48 was intended to alter the law of virtual adoption in any way. The old law providing that a subsequent adoption would revoke an antecedent will was never applied to a virtual adoption, and there is no reason to think that OCGA §53-4-48, even as amended in 2002, is meant to apply to any "adoption" other than a statutory adoption. To the contrary, the very use of the term "adoption" in the statute suggests that it does not concern any "virtual adoption." Despite its name, virtual adoption "bears almost no relationship to a statutory legal adoption," as it "does not result in a legal adoption or the creation of a legal parent-child relationship.". . . Because "[v]irtual adoption is not adoption,". . . it does not come within the ordinary meaning of the term "adoption.". . . Moreover, OCGA §53-4-48 applies only if the adoption (like the marriage of the testator or the birth of her child) is in a certain temporal relationship to the making of the will. But virtual adoption is not something that is complete before or after a particular date during the life of the adoptive parent. See Sanders, 296 Ga. at 699 (2) ("Virtual adoption is a posthumous legal fiction, a name given to a status arising from and created by a contract where one takes and agrees to legally adopt the child of another, but fails to do so.") (citation and punctuation omitted); Morgan, 285 Ga. at 513 (3) (virtual adoptee "could not legally be considered virtually adopted prior to [the adoptive parent's] death and intestacy"). Finally, even since the 2002 amendment, this Court has continued to recognize that the intestacy of the adoptive parent is one of the elements required to prove virtual adoption. . . . Because OCGA §53-4-48 can be at least as reasonably understood to leave the common law of virtual adoption unchanged as to depart from it, we must presume that the General Assembly meant to adhere to the requirement of intestacy.

For these reasons,

[w]e decline to apply the doctrine of equitable adoption to affect the distribution of a testate estate. Equity should not be available to countermand clear legislative mandates. Adoption and probate are both statutory procedures, with formalities designed to ensure certainty. Where neither the applicable statutes nor the last will and testament are ambiguous, neither legislative intent nor testamentary intent depend upon resort to equity.

Seader, 76 P3d at 1248. The judgment of the probate court is affirmed to the extent that it admitted the will of Ms. Johnson to probate, but the judgment that Rogers is entitled to an intestate share of the estate is reversed.

Judgment affirmed in part and reversed in part. All the Justices concur.

QUESTIONS AND ANALYSIS

What do you make of all of this? Do you think equitable adoption makes sense as a common-law (well, common equity) theory? Does estoppel or specific performance make more sense as the underlying theory of equitable adoptions? If equitable adoption is found, what parties should be bound by the finding? In your mind, did either or both of these courts reach the right decision? Does it matter to the legal rationale of the Georgia court's *Johnson* decision that Rogers was expressly contemplated in Mrs. Johnson's will? Does it matter to your equitable evaluation of that decision (i.e., to your conclusion about whether the court had appropriately "done equity')?

It's worth pausing to consider what the *Luna* court is fairly obviously shadow-boxing against: the notion, which had been embraced in the equitable adoption theories of some states, that equity would arise only if the party seeking the ruling could prove not only that an *express* promise to adopt had been made *to the child,* but that the child had then behaved like a descendant of the promisor *in explicit reliance on the proven-up promise,* i.e., had specifically performed on the parent-child agreement and promise. But this theory led to all sorts of practical confusion and a fundamental narrowing and limitation of the effect of the doctrine. First, as noted by the court, many children brought into an adoptive family—whether adopted *de facto* or *de jure*—are never told, or at least not told when they are children, that they are not natural children of that family. If the children are not even aware that they are adopted (or "adopted") they can hardly prove that they were expressly promised that they *would be* adopted and that they behaved like children of their putative parents on the grounds of such a promise. But such children—not even aware that they were of a different biological family—are likely to have behaved (for good and for ill) *most* like natural children of the putative parents and to have relied most completely (emotionally, financially, etc.) on that filial relationship. Yet an equitable adoption theory based in specific performance on a provable and in-terms promise will always miss all of these children.

Likewise, children taken into other families to be raised are very often by definition going to be particularly vulnerable children, in any number of ways. If the child is parentless, any agreement to adopt, if it did happen, will likely have taken place between whoever is serving as guardian of the child and the putative adoptive parents, not between the parents and the child. One imagines a particularly spunky, *Annie*-like child negotiating for adoption directly with an adult but doesn't imagine it as too likely away from the silver screen. Instead, in the real world, one imagines vulnerable children who have finally found a home directed by loving adults who take to calling them their own and treating them as their own—and imagines the children responding with massive amounts of joy, relief, love, and perhaps no little trepidation about rocking the boat and ruining things and hence with no interest whatever in demanding a promise of formal *de jure* adoption.

Estoppel theory sidesteps many of these problems. As the *Luna* court suggests, the real issue under estoppel theory is whether the parents held themselves out as the putative adoptee's parents and received in return the love and affection and obedience (and, no doubt, the irritations and heartaches) with which children honor their parents. Under estoppel theory, *de facto* adoptive parents are, as the theory suggests, estopped from asserting (from the grave) to the court that these *de facto* adopted children are not in fact *de jure* adopted children, and so the court goes ahead and treats them as *de jure* adoptees. (Estoppel theory, at least as employed by the *Luna* court, thus does away with the need to prove the exchange of an express, in-terms promise to perform.)

Of course, as suggested earlier, *all* children can be excluded from a parent's patrimony (except in Louisiana). The category of "all children" clearly includes "possibly equitably adopted children." The issue actually addressed by the Georgia court is whether equitably adopted children can ever qualify as pretermitted children (discussed shortly *infra*), though the court never used that term as a description of the 2002 amendment, which otherwise clarifies that children adopted after the execution of the last valid will *should* be treated as pretermitted heirs, though the will should otherwise stand as valid.

The court concludes (in a holding that is dictum, in that it reaches further than necessary for the decision of this case) that equitable adoption can never be employed to prove post-execution adoption by any testate decedent; if the decedent has a will, equitable-adoption doctrine does not apply.

Equitable adoptions have often arisen in circumstances in which parents were sociologically less likely to be well versed in, or have access to, the facilities of law, including adoption lawyers. Should equitable adoption apply differently—doctrinally or practically—in cases in which the facts reveal the parties involved to hail from such backgrounds?

ii. Adult Adoption

Not only child adoption, but *adult* adoption, that is, adoption of adults by adults, has been known to western civilization since at least the Romans, for whom it developed into a primary means not only of wealth transmission but of imperial succession.[19] The English knew of adoption, but demurred; in fact, adoption of future rulers constituted the *sin qua non* of their refusal even to countenance adoption until a mere century ago.[20]

Again, the American states found themselves between these two poles. Some legislatures expressly permitted adult adoption; others expressly forbade it; others changed their minds on the subject. On one hand, testator freedom. On the other,well, consider the situation in which an adult adopts his or her spouse to render the spouse an heir of the adoptive spouse/parent's family. Is this a fraud upon the family? Also: wait, what? The adoptive spouse/parent?[21] That can't be good, right?

Consider:

IN RE TRUST CREATED BY BELGARD

829 P.2d 457 (Colo. App. 1991).

Judges: Opinion by Judge Pierce. Ruland and Dubofsky, JJ., concur.

Respondent, Robert Johnson, appeals a judgment of the probate court which construed the trust created by his mother to exclude his adopted wife as a remainderman. We affirm.

Settlor created an express trust in Illinois in 1956 (the Belgard Trust). After her death and the death of her husband, respondent received the net income from the trust as lifetime beneficiary. Under the terms of the trust, upon respondent's death, the trustee is instructed to:

> divide the trust estate into as many equal shares as shall be neces-
> sary to allot one share for each child of my said son then living and

---

19. *See, e.g., Hugh Lindsay, Adoption in the Roman World* (2007) (reviewed here); UNRV History (Roman Empire), Adoptive Succession.

20. Adoption was countenanced at British law by the Adoption of Children Act 1926, but adopted children in Britain only took as intestate heirs of their adoptive parents after enactment of the Adoption of Children Act 1949.

21. "Hi, everyone! Meet my Mom-Wife, Sue."
Everyone: "Um . . ."

one share for the then living descendants *per stirpes* of each child of my said son then deceased.

The trust agreement defines "child" and "descendant" to include "persons legally adopted by my said son. . . ."

Respondent has three sons from his first marriage, which ended in 1972. He remarried in 1973 and has no children from this marriage. Settlor died in 1975, and, in 1979, respondent adopted his adult wife. . . .

The probate court construed the trust as excluding respondent's current wife as a remainderman, finding that:

> What we really have conceptually here is [respondent] through the adoption attempting to cut his wife in to a role as a remainderman. And I don't think [the settlor] intended that. . . .

I.

Respondent contends that, since his wife is included within the express terms of the trust as a "person legally adopted" by him, the probate court erred in construing the trust to exclude his wife as a remainderman. He argues further . . . that the probate court's determination is contrary to the Colorado adoption statute.

Whether an adult who was adopted after the creation of a trust and after the death of the settlor may be considered a child within the meaning of a trust created by this third person who is a stranger to the adoption is a question of first impression in Colorado. We hold that the probate court correctly construed the trust at issue here to exclude the adopted wife as remainderman.

A.

The trust must be construed in accordance with the settlor's intent as discerned from the entire instrument. . . . Thus, an examination of the language of the trust document in consideration of the relevant circumstances and laws in effect at the time it was executed is not an impermissible review of extrinsic evidence, but is necessary to determine, according to the instrument, the class of "persons legally adopted" and entitled to take as remaindermen. . . . Such examination here reveals that respondent's mother never considered, nor intended to include within the definition of a "child" adoptee, adult adoptees of the named beneficiaries as remaindermen under the trust.

The normal expectations of the settlor must be considered. . . . And, the trust instrument here does not indicate that the settlor considered the possibility of an adult adoptee seeking to take as a "child" under the trust. Moreover, at the time the trust was executed, Illinois did not recognize adult adoptions. . . .

Considering the circumstances at the time the trust was executed, and without a clear intent that the settlor intended to include an adult adoptee as a child under the trust, we conclude that the ordinary meaning of "child" as one's natural child should be invoked. . . .

Furthermore, the use of the phrase "persons legally adopted," rather than "children legally adopted" is not sufficient to defeat the common meaning under these circumstances. Language in the trust postponing distribution until each "child" reaches 21 years of age is further support for its common meaning. . . .

We acknowledge that it is the policy of the General Assembly to place adopted children on par with one's natural children. . . . However, this policy does not and should not extend to permit adult adoptions for the purpose of giving them an interest in property already specifically designated. . . .

To the extent an adoption statute violates a settlor's lawful intent or prevents property from passing in accordance with the stated wishes and to the detriment of the rightful heirs, it must give way to the expression of intent. . . .

Here, the probate court properly found that respondent was using the adult adoption statute to entitle his wife to a remainder of the trust estate contrary to the intent of the settlor as set forth in the instrument. Therefore, the probate court correctly excluded the adopted wife under the terms of the trust.

B.

We further conclude that the determination of the probate court is consistent with the Colorado Adoption Statute[, which] provides for the adoption of adults with the purpose of giving the adoptee the status of heir at law. As such, the adopted adult is entitled "to *inherit from the petitioner* any property in all respects as if such adopted person had been the petitioner's child born in lawful wedlock. . . . " (emphasis added) By definition, an heir is one who takes by descent and is entitled to a decedent's property under the laws of intestate succession. . . .

The adoption decree, therefore, pursuant to and incorporating the adoption statute, operates to grant the wife only the right to inherit through respondent, as his child, through intestacy. . . . The decree does not have the power to affect interests determined by an express disposition. . . .

Judgment affirmed.

* * *

iii. Historical Note: Adoption of Unmarriageable Partners

Before the advent of same-sex marriage—and more recently its national incorporation into constitutional doctrine,[22] adult adoption arose in a particularly poignant, but also potentially disturbing, context. Gay couples, legally forbidden to marry or (until 1999, in Vermont) enter into "marriage-light" civil unions resembling marriage, sometimes resorted to the expedient of adoption, usually of the poorer partner by the wealthier.

Now that same-sex marriage is legal nationwide, some of these aging, long-term couples want to formally tie the knot. The hitch: All states forbid one from marrying his/her "child," adopted or natural. And adoption—particularly adult adoption—is effectively irrevocable. Should this problem be redressed? If so, how? What problems may arise?

c. Pretermitted Children

Pretermitted children are those who are born after a will or trust has been written. Thus, for example, if a parent writes a will in 2018, and then is birthed of Child B in 2020, that child is pretermitted. On the other hand, if the parent had already borne Child A in 2016, before writing the 2018 will, Child A is not pretermitted, under the traditional (and literal) understanding of the concept. Pretermitted children are generally included by implication in any previously written end-of-life instruments wherever possible.

Some states have expanded the concept of pretermitted children to reach all descendants, while in others children actually living when the testamentary document is drawn can be treated as "pretermitted" if they are not *mentioned* in the will drawn while they are alive. The latter creates some trouble.

(1) For example, if child A is expressly disinherited, but dies, do his living children—not mentioned in the will one way or the other—take? Generally, no. The intent here seems pretty clear.

---

22. *See* Obergefell v. Hodges, 135 S. Ct. 2584 (2015).

(2) What if, instead, child A is mentioned only in passing. Child B isn't mentioned at all. Child A and B both die. Do Grandchildren A1 and A2 take? What about B1 and B2?

All of this can be avoided just by leaving the devises "to such of my descendants as survive me, *per stirpes.*" This is the right drafting move and probably the only safe-harbor for avoiding malpractice claims if you in practice are even passingly aware of additional blessings having been bestowed upon clients.

Consider this:

BENJAMIN v. BUTLER (IN RE ESTATE OF JACKSON)
194 P.3d 1269 (Okla. 2008).

Taylor, J.

We are presented with this question of first impression: whether the assets of a revocable inter vivos trust are subject to the provisions of Oklahoma's pretermitted heir statute. . . . We answer the question of first impression in the negative. . . .

I. FACTS

This appeal arises from a final decree in a probate proceeding of the estate of Walter Kinsley Jackson (Jackson). On August 18, 2003, Johnny C. Benjamin (Benjamin) filed a petition seeking to be named the personal representative of the estate of Jackson. In the petition, Benjamin alleged (1) Jackson died intestate, (2) Benjamin is Jackson's adult son,[1] and (3) Benjamin is Jackson's sole surviving heir at law. . . .

On September 3, 2003, the trial court found Jackson died intestate, found Benjamin to be Jackson's son and entitled to Letters of Administration, and found Benjamin to be Jackson's sole heir at law.

Benjamin brought an intra-probate proceeding against Robena Butler and Harris Butler (together, the Butlers), the co-trustees of a revocable inter vivos trust established by Jackson and his wife, who had predeceased him. In the intra-probate proceeding, Benjamin sought the removal of the Butlers as co-trustees with him named as trustee in their place, sought the disgorgement of any trust assets which had been disbursed, and sought a determination that he was Jackson's pretermitted heir and entitled to all the trust's assets. Benjamin's

---

1. Benjamin's delayed birth certificate shows his father as Kenneth Benjamin. At the time of Benjamin's birth, his mother was married to Kenneth Benjamin.

position hinged on the September 3, 2003 order's findings that he was Jackson's son and that he was Jackson's heir at law.

The Butlers filed a motion for summary judgment arguing that Benjamin had failed to produce evidence pursuant to title 84, section 215 that he is Jackson's son and heir at law and attaching Benjamin's birth certificate which shows Kenneth P. Benjamin to be his father. . . .

Benjamin then filed a motion for partial summary judgment in which, relying on Thomas v. Bank of Okla., N.A., 1984 OK 41, 684 P.2d 553, he argued that in the September 3, 2003 order, the trial court found him to be Jackson's son and Jackson's sole surviving heir at law; that the terms of title 84, section 132 applied to trusts, as well as wills; and that as Jackson's sole and pretermitted heir, he was entitled to all of the trust's assets. . . .

The trial court denied Benjamin's motion for partial summary judgment, finding that the terms of title 84, section 132 of the Oklahoma Statutes do not apply to a revocable inter vivos trust. . . .

Benjamin appealed asserting that he is Jackson's pretermitted heir; that the assets of the revocable inter vivos trusts are subject to the terms of title 84, section 132 of the Oklahoma Statutes; and that he is entitled to share in the trust assets. The Court of Civil Appeals affirmed the trial court's judgment, finding that even if Benjamin were Jackson's son, Oklahoma's pretermitted heir statute is inapplicable. This Court granted Benjamin's petition for writ of certiorari. . . .

IV. OKLAHOMA'S PRETERMITTED HEIR STATUTE

Disposing of property is an inalienable natural right throughout a person's lifetime. . . . However, the right to control disposition of property after death and the right of inheritance are statutory. . . . The Oklahoma Legislature has provided several means for disposing of one's property at death: one is by will, . . . and another is by trust. . . . In Oklahoma's pretermitted heir statute, the Legislature has also provided a statutory method of inheritance for children whom a testator fails to provide for or to name in a will. . . .

Here Benjamin invokes Oklahoma's pretermitted heir statute in his quest for a share of Jackson's assets and argues that it should be construed to extend to children omitted from revocable inter vivos trusts as well as wills. In construing a statute, our goal is to determine the Legislature's intent. . . . If the legislative intent is clear from a statute's plain and unambiguous language, this Court need not resort to rules of statutory construction. . . . When a statute's language is unambiguous, its words will be given their obvious and ordinary meaning and will be followed without additional inquiry. . . .

Oklahoma's pretermitted heir statute provides:

> When any testator omits to provide in his will for any of his children, or for the issue of any deceased child unless it appears that such omission was intentional, such child, or the issue of such child, must have the same share in the estate of the testator, as if he had died intestate, and succeeds thereto as provided in the preceding section.

84 O.S.2001, §132. This provision unambiguously pertains only to wills. It does not encompass a situation where a child is omitted from a trust, and we decline to extend its reach to revocable inter vivos trusts.[4]

Benjamin relies on Thomas v. Bank of Oklahoma, N.A., 1984 OK 41, 684 P.2d 553. In Thomas, the spouse had placed her separate property in a revocable inter vivos trust but had retained the right of complete control and dominion over the trust assets. This Court ruled that a spouse could not defeat a surviving spouse's share of an estate under title 84, section 44 of the 1981 Oklahoma Statutes by placing the estate assets in a revocable inter vivos trust with the deceased spouse retaining control of the assets while living. This Court found that such a trust was illusory as to the surviving spouse. Benjamin argues here for an extension of Thomas to children. He submits that children should be treated the same as surviving spouses in that they are forced heirs under Oklahoma's pretermitted heir statute. We disagree.

When Thomas was decided in 1984, the 1981 version of Oklahoma's forced heir statute found at title 84, section 44 was in effect. It prohibited a spouse from

> bequeath[ing] or devis[ing] away from the other [spouse] so much of the estate of the testator that the other spouse would receive less in value than would be obtained through succession by law; provided, however, that of the property not acquired by joint industry during coverture the testator be not required to devise or bequeath more than one half thereof in value to the surviving spouse.

---

4. For other cases reaching the same result based on pretermitted heir statutes similar to Oklahoma's see Kidwell v. Rhew, 268 S.W.3d 309, 371 Ark. 490, 2007 WL 3378399 (Ark. 2007); In re Estate of Cayo, 117 Wis. 2d 154, 342 N.W.2d 785 (Wis. Ct. App. 1983).

. . . Effective July 1, 1985, Oklahoma's forced heir statute was amended to prohibit a spouse from

> bequeath[ing] or devis[ing] away from the other so much of the estate of the testator that the other spouse would receive less in value than an undivided one-half (1/2) interest in the property acquired by the joint industry of the husband and wife during coverture.

. . . Title 84, section 44 of the 1981 statutes and its current counterpart, known as "forced heir" statutes, are limitations on a married person's power to dispose of his or her property. . . . The forced heir statute limits a spouse's power to disinherit the surviving spouse; the statute secures to a surviving spouse the right to elect a minimum statutory share in the deceased spouse's estate which is superior to other legatees and devisees . . . . A spouse may not disinherit a surviving spouse even with a clear expression of intent to do so. . . .

In contrast, Oklahoma's pretermitted heir statute. . . . is not a limitation on a testator's power to dispose of his or her property. [It] is an assurance that a child is not unintentionally omitted from a will. . . . The pretermitted heir statute does not secure a child with a minimum statutory share of a parent's estate upon the death of a parent. . . . Unlike a spouse, a testator can disinherit a child if the will shows a clear intent to do so. . . . Unlike section 44's forced heir provisions, section 132 is ineffective against a testator's bequest of a pittance to a child. . . . The limitation on a testator's power to disinherit a spouse, coupled with a testator's power to disinherit a child, prevents the extension of the Thomas decision to a child.

V. CONCLUSION. . .

[T]he trial court correctly found that the terms of Oklahoma's pretermitted heir statute do not extend to a revocable inter vivos trust. This decision left Benjamin with no claim to the trust assets. Because the trial court reached the correct result, we affirm. The Court of Civil Appeals' opinion is vacated, and the district court's judgment is affirmed.

* * *

ROBBINS v. JOHNSON

780 A.2d 1282 (N.H. 2001).

Dalianis, J. The plaintiffs, Pamela and Michael Robbins, are the daughter and adopted son of Elizabeth Robbins (Robbins). The defendants,

Bertha G. Johnson and Susan Wright, are Robbins' sister and niece. The plaintiffs appeal the orders of the Cheshire County Probate Court . . . denying their petition for declaratory judgment and related motion for reconsideration. This is the second appeal involving these parties. In the first appeal, we held that the plaintiffs were entitled to take under Robbins' will pursuant to the pretermitted heir statute, RSA 551:10 (1997). . . . The current appeal involves "The Elizabeth C. Robbins Revocable Trust." The probate court found that the trust was valid and nontestamentary. We affirm.

On appeal, the plaintiffs argue that the trust is a testamentary trust. They contend that if the trust is testamentary, the pretermitted heir statute applies to it because it is the functional equivalent of a will. . . .

The plaintiffs' focus upon whether the trust is testamentary or inter vivos is misplaced. Even if the trust is deemed inter vivos, it arguably still functions like a will because it provides for the distribution of property after Robbins' death. As the Restatement (Third) of Trusts §25 comment b (Tent. Draft No. 1, 1996) explains:

In proper usage today . . . the terms "testamentary" and "nontestamentary" (or "inter vivos") simply describe the means chosen to make disposition of property, not the legal characteristics of the disposition or the nature of the interests created. . . . Issues are obscured and litigation invited by confusing or unsound dicta often found in opinions that attempt to explain why something is or is not a present trust.

Thus, the central issue in this appeal is whether the pretermitted heir statute applies to the trust, regardless of its label.

RSA 551:10 provides as follows:

Every child born after the decease of the testator, and every child or issue of a child of the deceased not named or referred to in his will, and who is not a devisee or legatee, shall be entitled to the same portion of the estate, real and personal, as he would be if the deceased were intestate.

The statute creates a conclusive rule of law that a child who is neither named nor referred to in a will and is not a devisee or legatee of the will, nonetheless may take under the will, unless there is evidence in the will itself that the omission is intentional. . . .

We have not previously ruled that the pretermitted heir statute applies either to testamentary or inter vivos trusts, and we decline to do so here. "This court is the final arbiter of the intent of the legislature as expressed in the words of the statute." . . . "When construing the meaning of a statute, we first examine the language found in the statute, and where possible, we ascribe the plain and ordinary meanings of the words used." . . . The pretermitted heir statute, on its face, applies to "wills," not to trusts. "The statute does not contemplate a settlor's failure to provide for his or her . . . children in a trust." . . . We decline the plaintiff's invitation to construe the statute contrary to its plain meaning. . . .

The plaintiffs urge us to extend the statute to the trust at issue as a matter of policy. We note that trusts are not the only type of so-called will substitutes by which individuals pass property at death. Other will substitutes include payable on death accounts, transfer on death accounts, life insurance proceeds to a named beneficiary, and pension funds. We believe that the legislature should decide whether, as a matter of policy, it wishes to extend the pretermitted heir statute to will substitutes, such as the trust at issue. . . . Absent clear indication from the legislature that this is its intention, we decline to apply the statute to the trust.

Affirmed.

QUESTIONS AND ANALYSIS

There's a lot going on in these short cases. In both cases, an heir or heirs have gone unmentioned in a trust. In both cases, these children would have been treated as pretermitted heirs had the documents in question been wills. In both, they seek to have the pretermission rules applied to trust documents. In both they are denied.

The *Benjamin* court makes an interesting aside in its peroration. It says "[u]nlike section 44's forced heir provisions, section 132 is ineffective against a testator's bequest of a pittance to a child." This is true, and for the Oklahoma court, dispositive, as that court has framed the case as a question of whether the natural child of the settlor could force a share from the trust. It decided that the child cannot. But there is another way to frame this question, broadly the way the New Hampshire court framed it: as whether or not a pretermitted child can use the theory of pretermission to gain inclusion in the distributions from an instrument that makes distributions at or after death because the law presumes that, had the grantor had his or her children in mind at the time of executing the document, the grantor would have made a different distribution of his or her assets.

The New Hampshire court answers that question thus: "We believe that the legislature should decide whether, as a matter of policy, it wishes to extend the pretermitted heir statute to will substitutes, such as the trust at issue. . . . Absent clear indication from the legislature that this is its intention, we decline to apply the statute to the trust." A number of other courts have reached the same conclusion.

But whatever the relative merits of this conclusion, it is definitely not the only viable one. It is a bromide—but also a truth—that unlike wills law, which is very much a creature of statute, and of statutory detail, in any given jurisdiction, the trust is organically (though not exclusively) a product of the common-law. And so a judge considering whether a general doctrine should be applied to trusts would, at least *arguendo*, be justified in doing *common-law* reasoning—in applying a rule picked up somewhere else because it's a *good idea* to apply it in this new, common-law setting, unless one of two things is true: (1) there is a trust statute in the jurisdiction that forecloses such common-law reasoning-by-analogy, essentially transforming trust law in that jurisdiction to a rigorously statutory exercise; or (2) there is a provision in the wills act that forbids the courts from applying wills act provisions by analogy in other contexts. Neither of these courts undertook that kind of review.

d. Non-disinheritance

A negative will is one that intervenes in the intestate distribution only to exclude certain beneficiaries. Assume that Claire, a widow, has six kids. She leaves a will of only one sentence. "I . . . declare that my son Jackson will take nothing from my estate upon my death." Under traditional common law, such negative wills were forbidden, so disfavored were efforts to disinherit "natural" heirs. The modern trend is to permit them.

Nevertheless, it is still quite hard to disinherit a child without implying the potential existence of such a child. Say there were nonmarital child that the husband wished to keep the wife from having any inkling about.[23] Courts tend to require that blanket disinheritances at least mention the idea of such other children. (". . . any other heir of mine," held insufficiently explicit in In Estate of Robbins, 756 A.2d 602 (N.H. 2000).)

---

23. Note that upon the husband's death, the news is quite likely to get out anyway; this can be no more than a delaying tactic twinned with a hope that the wronged spouse also predeceases the cheat. Do you see why? If you were representing the husband/father in this situation, how might you minimize the chances of discovery?

So, for example, per Anna Nicole Smith's will: "[e]xcept as otherwise provided . . . I have intentionally omitted to provide for my spouse and other heirs, including future spouses and children and other descendants now living and those hereafter to be born." But for other ambiguous language in the will and the drafting attorney's testimony, this clause could very well have disinherited her daughter Dannielynn—who was born after this will had been executed, while both Anna Nicole and her first son, Danny, died of drug overdoses shortly after her birth. (We will hear more about Anna Nicole Smith, bizarrely enough, in a few pages.)

C. LOVE AND MARRIAGE

As has been alluded to above, the one (nearly; see pre- and post-nuptial agreements, *infra*) unavoidable mandatory rule that arises in this arena of law is the rule that a decedent spouse may not leave a surviving spouse to starve in the snow, penniless, while the decedent spouse (who, in these situations, must necessarily have been the primary bread winner or property owner) leaves all of his or her money to different beneficiaries.

Problems of disinheritance arose primarily—and with the highest potential for truly tragic consequences—in the era of the single-earner family. In such families—which were the norm until well into the 1970s—the earner was nearly always the husband, while the homemaker was the wife. This left significant opportunity for unenamored husbands in many states to leave, upon their deaths, surviving wives in bitter and miserable circumstances when their wills were read.

In most if not all states, some provision has always been made—or at least attempted—to provide for widows. Before the advent of Married Women's Property Acts, English-colonial states (and their progeny) developed systems of dower, of mandatory or presumed tenancy by the entirety, and other partial protections[24] that aimed at least to provide for widows (and for any minor children who survived their father) for the lives of the widows and until the sons' majorities and the daughters' marriages.

---

24. E.g., Homestead protections; "allowances" from the estate to keep the surviving spouse and dependent family afloat during the period of probate, etc..

Most of these protections, though, were fundamentally protections of *real* rather than *personal* property interests, and thus became increasingly less reliable as property began to take increasingly nonland forms. Moreover, the greater the employment of nonwill substitutes (such as trusts), the easier (for a time) it became for dispossessing husbands to leave their widows relatively destitute.

Not all states suffered from these historical problems of marital fairness, though, nor found themselves obliged to undertake nearly a century's worth of effort to keep their laws in line with changing economic and social norms. The community-property states have long espoused systems of marital-property division that preemptively coped with the modern notion of a marriage as a partnership of equal contributors, each member of which should enjoy full control at decease of an equal share of the earnings of the marital community during its tenure. The community-property system is considered first below. Attention then shifts to the "separate-property" states, which have found themselves obliged to engage in decades of legal reform in their attempts to emulate, so far as they may, the inherent methods of the community-property system.

1. Community Property Law

The western states long ago adopted, and since have developed, a system of property division between spouses (either at death or upon divorce) different than that in place in the rest of the Republic. The consensus amongst scholars in this area of the law has long been for the western system, called the "community-property" system: For generations courts, scholars, (some) legislatures, and the UPC authors, have attempted in various ways to reconfigure the marriage-property systems in the rest of the country (the "separate-property" states) to resemble community property so far as is possible. So analysis best begins with it, even though it remains the minority rule in the country.

Community-property law represents a centuries'-old attempt to solve the problem of equitable division of marital assets in a simple way. It has been adopted in the United States almost entirely—and almost exclusively—by the states that were at some point colonies of France or Spain.[25]

---

25. Washington State, though only very nominally and briefly an exclusive Spanish possession, nevertheless follows the community-property system. Idaho, the Spanish

The broad contours of the community-property system are described here. Each state, of course, follows its own unique variations.

a. The Marital Community

The idea of the "marital [financial] community" animates the community-property system. While the original purposes of the system were somewhat different, a satisfactory modern justification for the marital community arises from notions of privacy, intimacy, the valid consent of free and equal adults, and judicial modesty. All marriages are unique,[26] but most share the same central characteristics: two adults have voluntarily agreed—as a matter of law, as a fact before the world—to share their lives, their troubles, their times when richer and when poorer, together. *How* they elect to make this arrangement work, though, is almost wholly a matter for their consideration alone and can and does differ quite substantially from the paths taken by other couples. Both spouses might work, or one, or perhaps neither. They may have children "naturally," or by adoption, or might raise their stepchildren, or their neighbors' children,[27] or matching golden retrievers, or not so much as a tomato plant. They may own many houses or one, or may rent, may live together or separately, may . . . yeah, fair enough; you get the idea.

The response of community-property law to all of these possibilities is: eh, whatever. Not really any of our business. We're simply going to assume—barring evidence to the contrary—that you two adults have mutually and voluntarily and knowingly agreed to whatever it is you have going on, that you're mutually satisfied with the arrangement, and—this is the key—are mutual contributors (in toto) to the arrangement.

"Mutual contributors" here obviously does not mean "equal breadwinners," a proposition which is almost never going to be entirely true.

---

and French claims upon which were effectively fanciful, also adopted community property. Colorado, with a similarly nebulous colonial history, did not. The community property states are Arizona, California, Idaho, Louisiana, Nevada, New Mexico, Texas, Washington, and Wisconsin, an "eastern" state that adopted community property. The other states follow the separate-property rules. American territories and the Commonwealth of Puerto Rico that were colonized by the Spanish also follow community-property rules. Oregon is the single west-coast state that follows separate-property law.

26. This should *not*, of course, be taken as a paraphrase of Leo Tolstoy's "Happy families are all alike; every unhappy family is unhappy in its own way." *Anna Karenina*, Ch. 1, l. 1.

27. Presumably with their neighbors' consent.

Rather it means that the law assumes that if two freely consenting adults of sound mind join and remain together in marriage, then it more or less *must* be (or at least is constructively treated as though it were) true that both parties are—when all of the different ways and means of contributing to the marriage and supporting one's spouse are considered—pitching in equally, and are receiving an equal set of benefits from the union.

This being the case, when the first of the spouses dies, that spouse, as a matter of theory and law, is *automatically and instantly* the owner of half of the marital-community's assets, while the surviving spouse is likewise and entirely the owner of the other half of those assets. The marital-community's assets, of course, are called "community (or marital) property."

Hence, upon the death of the first spouse, that decedent spouse may grant, by will, trust, or any other vehicle, his share[28] of the community property, but no more—because he owns no more. And he may give *all* of that half, without interference by his surviving spouse, to whomever he might wish. (Of course, were he to die partially or wholly intestate, the laws of intestacy would distribute any property he had not otherwise granted away, usually to the surviving spouse.) Meanwhile, his surviving spouse becomes sole owner of the other half of the marital property the moment he drops dead, leaving him no opportunity to grant that property out from under her.

b. Marital Property

This explanation leads necessarily to consideration of the content of community property: What counts as community property and what does not?

The theory is elegant. All property held by either party at the moment of matrimony (i.e., the property that has been earned or received as a gift when the parties were single) remains the property of the relevant individual owner. We will for purposes of convenience in this discussion call this property "individual property," (though note

---

28. I say "his" because men tend, statistically and historically, to marry later, to marry younger wives, and to die earlier—with the result that there are a great many more widows filling the caselaw and the imaginations of legislatures and common-law judges than there are widowers.

that it is commonly —to the deep confusion of many, many students stepping into this arena for the first time—called "separate property").[29]

Once the nuptial bans are read, however, a new *de facto* legal entity arises: the married couple *qua* couple (i.e., the "marital community"). From the moment of marriage onward, *all income earned by either spouse, and any gifts made to the couple*, are treated as marital property. The individual spouses, of course, still exist as independent legal entities, and gifts made explicitly to only one spouse or the other are added to that spouse's individual property. Barring a prenuptial (or occasionally a postnuptial) agreement to the contrary, however, *all income earned* by either spouse during the course of the marriage automatically becomes part of the couple's community property.

When deciding whether some specific piece of property is, at the time of the first-dying spouse's demise, community or individual property, the vital rule of thumb is this: Courts have a significant preference for finding community property rather than individual property. This preference is not sufficient to defeat plain fact. Property that has always been individual property, has not changed form, and has not been in any way intermingled with the marital community's property will remain individual property.

Thus, for instance, imagine that H1 (whom we'll call Maverick) received from his parents (whether upon their deaths or otherwise; it doesn't matter) a beach house, owned in fee simple absolute and unencumbered by a mortgage. He also received a cash bequest of $200,000. Maverick retains the deed to the mortgage in his name alone and pays the property taxes on the house from the cash bequest, which he also keeps in a bank account in his sole name (i.e., the account is not amended to become a joint checking account by adding H2 (whom we'll call Iceman) to the account). When repairs are required on the house, Maverick pays for those repairs out of the bequest account or by selling or encumbering other individual property. Assume further that Maverick has kept good records of these transactions. In this

---

29. This terminology (i.e., "separate property") is deeply unfortunate for the novitiate student of the community-property state vs. separate-property state distinction. Note carefully: The community-property system has a separate-property component. For ease of basic understanding, I have elected above to call this separate property "individual property," which has the same "human-being" meaning, but is not the common legal term of art. I have made this election because otherwise students quite reasonably tend to get confused between separate property as a component of the community-property system, and the entirely distinct separate-property *system*. This "cheat" is, I think, highly valuable to the newcomer, but I add this note to make sure that I do not, by advancing understanding now, set the stage for confusion later on.

scenario, the court would rightly and easily conclude that the whole of this property—the beach house and whatever remains of the bequest—has entirely remained individual property throughout the whole of the marriage and so remains wholly within Maverick's estate (or otherwise within Maverick's entire ownership and control) at the time of the first spouse's death. If Maverick dies first, he will be able to grant that property by will or by testamentary trust—or may already have granted it away in an already established and active *inter vivos* trust. If Maverick elects to grant the individual property to someone other than Iceman, Iceman will have no (legal) ground for objection. Meanwhile, if Iceman dies first, his estate will not include any portion of the value of the beach house or the bequest account. Because of the First Rule of Property Law,[30] any attempt by Iceman to make a grant of that property would of course simply be void—exactly as though Iceman had attempted to make a bequest of the Pentagon.

The very detail of this example, though, should illustrate and prefigure the various and sundry ways that the presumption in favor of community over individual property can work itself out.

One means of exercising the presumption is through the application of the "commingling" rules. Commingling occurs when individual property and community property are, as it were, jumbled together. This can happen in an almost infinite variety of ways. Imagine, for instance, that Maverick used the couple's joint checking account to pay for the maintenance, upkeep, and taxes on the beach house. Or that Maverick and Iceman, having started a family, decide (again, using community funds) to add a second story to the structure. Contrariwise, should they turn out instead not to be the family type, they might instead install a pool, sauna, and volleyball court behind the house using marital funds. All of this would constitute commingling of individual with community assets.

Now, the rule is *not* that as soon as any commingling occurs, the whole of the individual property commingled automatically becomes community property. This is where the record keeping comes in. Assuming that Maverick (or his trustee or executor) can prove how much of the value of the beach house as renovated and how much of the past maintenance and upkeep (including taxes) at the time of the first husband's death were attributable to his individual assets and how much were attributable to the community inputs, then the value of the

---

30. "You can't grant what you don't own."

beach house would be divided accordingly. This demonstration of the relative value of the relevant inputs is called "tracing."

A concrete example is no doubt in order. Building out the previous hypothetical, while keeping things simple, assume that Maverick could demonstrate the following at the time of Iceman's passing:

Total value of beach house at Iceman's death: $1,000,000.

Value of house on date of marriage: $700,000 (individual property of Maverick).

General appreciation of comparable properties (both real appreciation and that arising as a result of inflation[31]) over period between marriage and Iceman's death: 10 percent.

Assume further that Maverick knows that "some" amount of the taxes, improvement, upkeep, etc., funds came from his individual property, but that most of it had come from community property and that he really can't prove the details beyond these vague memories.

There has certainly, here, been extensive commingling, and Maverick hasn't kept exacting (or perhaps niggling[32]) records and receipts of individual expenditures (though this method, too, would constitute effective tracing). He can, though, make out a reasonable, if rough, case for the proportion of the present value of the beach house that is attributable to separate property:

$700,000 (value of individual property at marriage) + $70,000 (the appreciation over the period of the marriage that is attributable to the individual-property base).

Maverick might thus reasonably claim that about $770,000 of the present value of the property remains his individual property.[33]

---

31. See the discussion of real and nominal inflation and the time value of money, *infra* at Part III.B.2.a.iii.

32. It might be rather a strain on a marriage for one spouse to keep constant and meticulous records of how every tube of caulk used at the beach house had been paid for. This might counsel in favor of permitting the commingling to occur, though it may instead suggest that whenever one or both members of a couple hold significant individual assets at the time of engagement, a prenuptial agreement should be (properly and carefully) negotiated. Of course, that creates its own dampening of animal spirits. But perhaps better soon than late. *Cf.* William Wordsworth, "The World is too Much With Us" (1802) *in Poems, in Two Volumes* (1807) ("The world is too much with us; late and soon,/ Getting and spending, we lay waste our powers; . . .").

33. Yes, for the accounting and finance majors in the room, this is certainly a simplification, one that ignores issues of depreciation, for instance. But your colleagues have no interest in making this *more* complicated and including *more* numbers for no good purpose. So just roll with it.

It follows, then, that, using the background presumption in favor of community property, $230,000 worth of the value of the beach house will be attributed to the community. Remember, though, that this does *not* mean that $230,000 in total value (not necessarily from the beach house *per se*, of course; the court wouldn't grant the pool and sauna to Iceman, but the house and front yard to Maverick) gets shifted to *Iceman*; rather it gets shifted (or, more properly, attributed) to *the community*. Then the community property is divided equally upon the death of the first spouse (in this case, Iceman).

As a result, when all the computations have been made, Maverick will retain, both as preserved (and reasonably proven) individual property and as his half of the marital community's interest in the beach house, $770,000 + $115,000 (i.e., $230,000/2), or $885,000 worth of value in the beach house, while $115,000 worth of the value of that house will be apportioned to Iceman. (Assuming that the couple, at the time of Iceman's death, had liquid assets of more than $230,000, it is likely that Maverick would elect to satisfy this interest by apportioning his half of those liquid assets to Iceman's estate, but that consideration gets us further into the weeds than we need here wander.)

Next, consider individual gifts made during the marriage. Again, the default presumption in favor of the community is only a presumption; it can be defeated by evidence that the gift in question was meant for one of the members of the couple rather than to both. Imagine, then, that Iceman's Uncle Bert—having himself been a rock-solid and bone-deep Marine—never much cared for Maverick. Hence, in his will, which he executed (and which therefore surely became operative) after Maverick and Iceman had married, he granted "to my nephew Iceman in his sole capacity," 500 shares of PBNCS Corp. Iceman will unquestionably take this grant as individual property; if he does not co-mingle it or make of it a gift to the marital community (an action known formally as "transmutation"[34]), then these shares will remain his individual property upon the death of the first of the spouses.

Assume instead, though, that Ernie, also Iceman's uncle, has made a habit of joining his nephew and nephew-in-law for Christmas. Most Christmases Ernie bought each of the guys his own present, but one

---

34. Transmutation can, in theory anyway, also work in the opposite direction, with community property being transmuted into individual property of one or the other of the spouses by their joint agreement. As such transmutation really constitutes either a unilateral gift from the grantor spouse to the grantee, or a form of postnuptial agreement, there is no need to linger long over the possibility.

Christmas he arrived with only a single present, wrapped but unlabeled. On Christmas morning he handed the present to Iceman, who was sitting closest to the tree, and who unwrapped it. The present was a solid-gold replica of the jet that both Maverick and Iceman had flown when they met in the service many years before. The couple mounts the present—worth about $500,000 on the day Iceman dies—on the mantelpiece of their marital home.

Here, it is simply not clear whether the gift was meant to be for both spouses or just for Iceman. The hypothetical detailed above permits inferences in both directions, but none is particularly definitive. Those inclined to fight (or embellish) the hypo could certainly add all sorts of additional details to push the proposition further in one direction or the other. Sticking only to the facts provided, though, the courts are in this instance—if called upon to decide—likely to find this gift to be a gift not to Iceman singly but to the couple, and thus to the marital community. And so it becomes community property, with the value of the artifact divided as a matter of law at the moment of Iceman's death.

What about liabilities? While—and in part because—the law in individual community property states differs more widely regarding accounting for individual and community liabilities than with regard to assets, let it simply be asserted—as a wholly acknowledged over-simplification for purposes of pedagogical effect—that liabilities are divided according to the same rules as assets.

2. Separate-Property Law

The preceding explication of community-property law may have seemed a bit complicated but remember: Community property is generally considered the easy and elegant solution to the issue of division of marital assets at the death of the first spouse. Strap up your boots, because this next bit is by comparison going to be rather a slog.

As noted above, the traditional, common-law rules providing for widows[35] had grown both complex and inapposite by the turn of the twentieth century. Courts and legislatures began to adapt accordingly. As became clear in the 1970s and early '80s, most legal scholars and

---

35. The common law provided primarily for widows, though curtesy existed for the protection of widowers whose wives' families had provided the foundation of the family's assets.

uniform law authors working in this field wished more or less wholly to adopt the community-property system described above for separate-property states. Their efforts, though, were successful in only one state: Wisconsin. All other separate-property states have maintained fidelity to the separate-property structure, at least in name, and in actual fact to varying degrees. Nevertheless, all of the pressure—and reform, especially as led by the UPC—has been in the direction of making the separate-property system rules for division of property at decease of the first spouse resemble the community-property system as closely as practically possible.

What follows is a somewhat simplified (especially in its chronology), and fairly brief, history of the development of this area of law in the separate-property states since the replacement of the ancient rules of dower and curtesy.

Picture it: Levittown, Anystate (in the eastern two-thirds of the country, anyway), 1947. A newly demobilized serviceman (let's call him Ward) has come home to marry his high-school sweetheart, June, after years of separation while he fought back the Nazi menace and she riveted sheet-metal for the hulls of Liberty Ships and saved lint, rubber, and cooking fat while occasionally finding that she'd exchanged scarce meat ration coupons at the butcher's for what turned out to be horse meat. Ward and June marry, and move—using the mutual savings that each had collected during the war, when there was little for either of them to buy—into one of the new identikit suburbs springing up in what would become the "collar counties" surrounding most of the cities of the country. They have, together, enough money to make a significant down-payment; June has a bit of hers left over, which she puts aside in a bank account of her own—"pin money" in the idiom of the day.[36]

Ward heads down to the city every day from the 'burbs to work at Grumthrop-Norrin, building advanced technologies that over the years contribute to the development of the U2[37] and the Apollo series of rockets.[38] Because he's smack dab in the middle of the Greatest

---

36. For a fuller understanding of the context of the times under discussion, dissolve into a grainy and sometimes distorted (especially if there's a thunderstorm somewhere in the viewing area) black-and-white, and recall our old friend Hugh Beaumont in that lovely archetype of the era for which the foundational facts of many of these laws and rules were drafted or devised, *Leave It to Beaver*, playing, of course, that Father Figure for the Eisenhower Era, Ward Cleaver.

37. No, not the band.

38. Yup. Those rockets.

Generation, he can manage all of this while also managing daily three-martini lunches. At one of those lunches, he meets—and falls for—a loud but endlessly entertaining redhead named Lucy. This being the '50s and '60s, they are of course required by law to start an affair.

The affair continues for decades, while June raises two boys—first in Levittown, then in a much larger house (complete with den, of course) in an older and fancier suburb. Though she did her part for the war, she, like so many of her peers of that generation, never works outside of the home again. Of course, she *does* work; with his job and his after-work activities, Ward's not exactly around to help much with what was in those days called "homemaking." And so, while the house in Levittown, and then the bigger house, are held by the couple jointly as Tenants by the Entirety, most everything else is titled in Ward's name. So the family capital is largely his as a matter of law. June never gave this a second thought, though Ward was nearly a decade older than she, and though he did smoke an *awful* lot. June supposed—without ever thinking about it very much—that she would outlive him, but she never for a moment imagined that she would be anything other than the primary—if not the sole—beneficiary of his will.

Well, June was wrong. Let us imagine that Ward not only fell for Lucy but wished upon his death to leave his estate to her. What will become of June, whose pin money has grown slowly to the (not-insignificant at the time) sum of $6,230, but who otherwise can claim actual title to little but her pearls and her Electrolux?

The answer, it turns out, depends upon how far along in the community-property envying process the relevant state has gotten by the time Ward dies, along with Ward's (and his lawyer's) cleverness in putting together Ward's decedent-distribution scheme.

First, though, a couple of initial details. Remembering the First Rule of Property, we can establish a minimum baseline for what June will take under any circumstances. First, she will not be thrown absolutely and immediately out into the snow: The marital home, held by the couple as Tenants by the Entirety, will as a matter of law become hers in fee simple absolute the moment that Ward dies. Additionally, the property that had remained separately hers, remains hers of course; no state, however backward, lacked a Married Women's Property Act by the '60s. This, however, might prove of small consolation should she have no other defenses and so find the day after the will is read that she is vacuuming an empty house in her pearls and her high heels, and wondering how long $6,000-odd will last and whether there might still be a few old lawn chairs in the garage.

a. Pivot Number One: From Support Theory to Partnership Theory

The vehicle of surviving-spouse protection that arose to replace the increasingly unhelpful dower and curtesy was the *forced share*. The forced share permitted a surviving spouse who had been cut out (entirely or largely) from the decedent spouse's will to "force" a share out of that will.[39]

Legislatures and courts adopted the forced share for three reasons. First, as noted, dower and curtesy had become increasingly unfitted to the times. Second, the legislators (who were in this era largely, though not entirely, men) felt that it was *damned ungallant* not to provide for one's spouse for the remainder of her life, whatever else might have been going on beyond her gaze. Third, should the early decedent (who was, as we have seen, far more likely to be the husband, and so the breadwinner and property owner) wholly disoblige his surviving spouse, that spouse and his surviving minor children (if any) would almost certainly end up as wards of the public or as criminals of various sorts, in their need to keep body and soul together. This, for reasons of public economy and stability, was to be avoided.

And so the forced share. Note, though, the import of the theories that undergirded the first iterations of the forced share. There is no sense of the marriage as an equal partnership or of equal division of assets. Rather, the concerns were about *sufficient* provision to keep the widow and any minor children comfortable (or at least self-sufficient) *during the widow's lifetime*. And so the first forced shares permitted the surviving spouse to force up to one-third[40] of the decedent's estate for the life of the surviving spouse.

Social mores and legal and economic norms were changing fast, though, as the Eisenhower Era first burst into Camelot and then collapsed—in collective national horror after Dallas—into the Johnson and Nixon years. With the Kennedy era and the New Frontier came new frontiers in relations between the sexes and new conceptions of marriage and family. Couples were increasingly seen to be equal partners and their marriages to be compacts of mutual benefit rather than institutions by which men supported dependent wives and children. And so, as the decades rolled on, the forced share was, in many states, expanded from one-third of the decedent spouse's estate to one-half,

---

39. Alternatively, this is also sometime called the "elective share," in which case the survivor is said to "elect against the will."

40. Or in some cases merely a quarter.

and from a life-estate to fee simple absolute ownership for the surviving spouse.

So, in answer to the question above about June's prospects: It depends. Assuming that Ward passed the whole of his estate to Lucy in his will, then in addition to the house, June would be entitled to force from his estate either one-third of the value of his estate for life, or one-half of the estate in fee simple absolute, depending upon whether the state in question was by then employing the *support theory* of the forced share or the *partnership theory.*

b. Pivot Number Two: From the Traditional Forced Share to the Augmented Estate and the Augmented Share

Another issue arises. The "traditional" forced share allowed the surviving spouse to force that share—be it one-third under support theory or one-half under partnership theory—out of the decedent spouse's *estate,* which is to say, out of the assets that the decedent either passed expressly by will or allowed tacitly to fall into intestate distribution. As you already well know, however, other vehicles for distribution of property are also available to those contemplating their own demise and

---

LIFE INSURANCE

Life insurance is a perfect will substitute, in that it is revocable until the insured's death and the beneficiary can be changed until the same event. It comes in three forms:

(1) A *term life* insurance policy is a contract whereby the insurance company must pay the named beneficiary if the insured dies within the policy's stated term of years. But the insurance company owes nothing on death if the insured survives past the term. Effectively, term life is a bet that the insured will die within a certain period of years. If the insured lives longer, you lose the bet (and the insurance company wins).

(2) *Whole life* insurance combines an insurance policy with a savings plan. The owner must pay a set amount (in installments) to endow the policy. Once it is endowed, the owner owes nothing more and the amount paid is invested. If the investments yield dividends, the owner may save them or take them for personal use. A whole life policy can be "cashed out" or sold to another person (always at a discount, per the time value of money). The insurance company must pay the then-current owner (who will usually be the beneficiary) at the insured's death.

(3) A *universal life* policy is a whole life policy with greater flexibility or more investment options.

Regardless of type, the named beneficiary is the one who gets the dosh, whether in lump sum or annuity.

wishing to exercise dead-hand control. The most important of these is obviously the trust, but additional forms include life insurance, joint tenancies (with some party other than the surviving spouse), joint accounts (ditto), and other forms treated in sidebars and pull-boxes in this section.

To illustrate the point, let us return to the deeply counter-"factual" scenario of an ailing Ward who has long since fallen in love with Lucy and out of love with June, and who wishes to dispossess June in favor of Lucy.

Under the traditional forced share, Ward, if well advised by competent counsel, and if truly determined to dispossess June, could after all leave June with nothing but the marital home and her separate property, and defeat the forced share, merely by leaving all of his assets to Lucy by trust or other substitute method rather than passing them by will. Do you see how?

This loophole was more than vaguely problematic; passing assets by trust rather than by will is, as will be clearer and clearer as the semester progresses, simplicity itself. It is, and was rapidly recognized as, one of those exceptions that could eat up the rule and leave of the forced share nothing but an empty husk.

And so the separate-property states—as illustrated by a series of emendations to the UPC—were obliged to undertake a second evolution.

PENSIONS

Pension accounts, while normally used to save for retirement, allow the owner to name a death beneficiary. Contributions are often tax-deferred and pay out at a fixed retirement age. If the pensioner dies before retirement (or before all defined benefits are paid), the remainder is paid to the death beneficiary outside of probate.

(1) For a *defined-benefit* plan, the employer promises to pay an annuity to the holder on retirement—e.g., a set percentage of the average of the employee's top three years of wages. The annuity is paid every year for the rest of the pensioner's life (or for a term of years; it depends on the policy). Defined-benefit plans exist today almost only for some government employees and in most states and at the federal level either have been phased out or are on their way out.

(2) For a *defined-contribution* plan, the employee, employer, or both make contributions to the employee's personal pension fund. On retirement, the employee can make withdrawals from the fund, which she owns, essentially like a bank account; or, depending on the policy, is paid a certain portion of the amount that has been saved in that retiree's account, the amount established being designed actuarially to see the pensioner through till death.

This time they moved away from the traditional forced share to what is called the "augmented (forced) share." The augmented share takes into consideration not only the decedent spouse's estate, but also pulls into the pot effectively (but not exactly[41]) the whole of both the decedent's property *and* the survivor's property (including all of the assets described in the sidebars in this section). Then the total value of this pot is divided by two. If the survivor's estate is larger than half of the pot (i.e., the "divided-by-two" quotient) then the survivor may take nothing through the forced share. (Do you see why? If the survivor's estate is *smaller* than half the pot, then the survivor may claim by the forced share enough so that, upon forcing, the property of the surviving spouse equals in value the property remaining to the decedent spouse's distribution in all relevant forms. (Or, perhaps more clearly, if the devise to the survivor plus the survivor's own property is less than the quotient (half the pot), then the survivor can force enough additional property to make the values equal.)

c. Pivot Number Three: The Anna Nicole Smith Problem and the Table of Longevity

Does it surprise you that *all* of the property of both spouses goes into the augmented estate determination pot? It *is* very odd, if you view the separate-property state evolutions as efforts to emulate community property (as you should). But it's also inevitable. There is simply no concept of the "marital community" or "marital property" in the separate-property system (outside of limited property concepts such as the tenancy by the entirety). But as you already will have realized, this creates horrific problems of its own. Let's call the problems created by this circumstance the "Anna Nicole quandary" (or ANQ).

Anna Nicole Smith gained national attention in the early 1990s as a model whose placements included a spread in *Playboy* magazine. Shortly after her feature there, while she was in her mid-20s, she married J. Howard Marshall II, an 89-year-old billionaire oil tycoon. A little over a year after their marriage, Marshall died.

The ANQ addresses the May-December nature of Smith's marriage to Marshall. Marshall had earned billions before he married Smith.

---

41. "[T]he value of the augmented estate . . . consists of the sum of the values of all property . . . that constitute (1) the decedent's net probate estate; (2) the decedent's nonprobate transfers to others; (3) the decedent's nonprobate transfers to the surviving spouse; and (4) the surviving spouse's property and nonprobate transfers to others." UPC §2-203(a).

She had earned some wealth, but far, far less. Marshall certainly earned significant dividends and other income during their year-long marriage, but under the "unqualified" augmented share, in a separate property state, Smith would have been able to force from Marshall's estate half of *the whole of his lifetime's assets.* Collecting $1.5 billion after a year of marriage to a geriatric spouse strikes many people, including legislators and lawmakers, as odd, and (perhaps) unjustifiable. The ANQ does not arise under community-property law (do you see why?), but under separate-property-plus-the-augmented-share, it arises inevitably—unless a further evolution were to arise.

That evolution arrived, in what we will here call the "Table of Longevity."[42]

The Table of Longevity (of the relationship) is used thus: All of the assets of both spouses are put into the pot, as before. Then, as before, the augmented estate total is divided by two. Then, this new, smaller number is multiplied by the appropriate multiple from the table above, as determined by the length of the marriage.

Here's an example. Imagine that Sarah and James had been married for five years. To make this example simple, let's posit that Sarah and James always rented, maintained their own cars throughout their marriage, and never had a joint checking account. When James was hit by a bus in the sixth year of their marriage (i.e., after they had

Table of Longevity

If the Decedent and the Spouse Were Married to Each Other:	The Percentage Is:	If the Decedent and the Spouse Were Married to Each Other:	The Percentage Is:
Less than 1 year	3%	8 years but less than 9 years	48%
1 year but less than 2 years	6%	9 years but less than 10 years	54%
2 years but less than 3 years	12%	10 years but less than 11 years	60%
3 years but less than 4 years	18%	11 years but less than 12 years	68%
4 years but less than 5 years	24%	12 years but less than 13 years	76%
5 years but less than 6 years	30%	13 years but less than 14 years	84%
6 years but less than 7 years	36%	14 years but less than 15 years	92%
7 years but less than 8 years	42%	15 years or more	100%

---

42. UPC §2-203(b) (Alternative A).

BANK (AND RELATED) ACCOUNTS

(1) *Payable-on-death* accounts ("PODs") work just like normal bank accounts, but the account holder names a death beneficiary, who receives the account balance when the holder dies. The bank pays the beneficiary directly, which means the balance does not pass through probate.

(2) *Joint accounts*–whether savings or checking–come in two forms: standard and agency/convenience. In a standard account, all named account holders can make deposits or withdrawals. The account usually includes a right of survivorship. In an agency/convenience account, the depositor gives the other named person (the agent) the power to draw on the account for his (the depositor's) convenience. The agent cannot draw for other purposes and does not take the account balance at the depositor's death, unless the depositor makes the account POD.

The account's terms usually dictate which type (standard or convenience) it is. When the terms are unclear, the majority (Florida) rule presumes it is a standard account. This presumption is rebuttable by clear and convincing evidence. The minority (New York/UPC) rule presumes agency/convenience, with the same standard for rebutting the presumption.

celebrated their fifth wedding anniversary, but before they had celebrated their sixth), Sarah was worth, *in toto*, $400,000, while James was worth $600,000 in all forms. Thus, the augmented estate of the couple was $1,000,000. Now, imagine that James left all of his estate to his parents.

JOINT TENANCIES AND TOD DEEDS

In a joint tenancy (and tenancy by the entirety, in the jurisdictions that recognize it), all joint tenants have equal ownership rights in the property. For as long as a joint tenancy remains joint, i.e., until it is severed, each joint tenant enjoys a right of survivorship, which is to say that all remaining joint tenants absorb the interest of any decedent joint tenant upon death. (Joint tenancies can be severed unilaterally; tenancies by the entirety cannot.) The deceased's interest is automatically split among the surviving joint tenants. This continues until there is only one tenant left, who then exercises sole dominion over the property (usually taking it in fee simple absolute).

Compare transfer-on-death (TOD) deeds. These increasingly common and popular instruments leave the fee-simple interest in a property in the hands of the owner throughout her life, but upon her death transfer the fee in the property directly to the transferee named on the deed, thereby keeping the property out of the estate, out of probate, and causes it to pass without ever forming part of the *res* of any trust created, unless the trust is itself made the transferee.

As an initial matter, just eyeballing this scenario, will Sarah be able to force any share? Yes, because her assets are smaller than those of James. But how much?

But for the Table of Longevity, the answer would be simple: $100,000. This answer is reached by taking the total augmented-estate pot, dividing by two, and reaching a figure of $500,000, the equal share. Then the surviving spouse's holdings are subtracted from the equal share, to find out what the top-up value would be. $500,000 less $400,000 is $100,000.

With the addition of the Table of Longevity, however, this "top-up" number is then multiplied by the appropriate factor on the Table to determine the final forced-share award. For all marriages of 15 years or longer, the number is 100 percent, so the surviving spouse takes the whole top-up number. For Sarah, who had been married to James for 5 but less than 6 years, the number is 30 percent, or .30. So the final calculation is $100,000 x .3, which is $30,000. Sarah may force $30,000.

This final pivot brings the UPC's augmented (forced) share very close indeed to the community property model it has been seeking to emulate—perhaps as close as separate-property systems can be brought. Can you see how the Table of Longevity roughly tracks the theory of community property law? Can you think of any additional pivots that might prove valuable? Can you think of any scenarios in which a separate-property regime might be preferred to a community-property regime?

Why are there separate rules for ERISA, social-security, and related retirement, insurance, and subsidy programs?

3. The Three Pivots Reduced to Code

The heart of the present iteration of the graduated, augmented share appears in the UPC at §§2-203 to -207.

2-203(a) Subject to Section 2-208, the value of the augmented estate, to the extent provided in Sections 2-204, 2-205, 2-206, and 2-207, consists of the sum of the values of all property, whether real or personal; movable or immovable, tangible or intangible, wherever situated, that constitute:

(1) the decedent's net probate estate;

(2) the decedent's nonprobate transfers to others;

(3) the decedent's nonprobate transfers to the surviving spouse; and

(4) the surviving spouse's property and nonprobate transfers to others.

Alternative A

(b) The value of the marital-property portion of the augmented estate consists of the sum of the values of the four components of the augmented estate as determined under subsection (a) multiplied by the following percentage:

[The Table of Longevity appears here.]

Alternative B

(b) The value of the marital-property portion of the augmented estate equals the value of that portion of the augmented estate that would be marital property at the decedent's death under [the Model Marital Property Act] [copy in definition from Model Marital Property Act, including the presumption that all property is marital property] [copy in other definition chosen by the enacting state].

End of Alternatives

2-204. The value of the augmented estate includes the value of the decedent's probate estate, reduced by funeral and administration expenses, homestead allowance, family allowances, exempt property, and enforceable claims.

2-205. The value of the augmented estate includes the value of the decedent's nonprobate transfers to others, not included under Section 2-204, of any of the following types, in the amount provided respectively for each type of transfer:

(1) Property owned or owned in substance by the decedent immediately before death that passed outside probate at the decedent's death. Property included under this category consists of:

(A) Property over which the decedent alone, immediately before death, held a presently exercisable general power of appointment. The amount included is the value of the property subject to the power, to the extent the property passed at the decedent's death, by exercise, release, lapse, in default, or otherwise, to or for the benefit of any person other than the decedent's estate or surviving spouse.

(B) The decedent's fractional interest in property held by the decedent in joint tenancy with the right of survivorship. The amount included is the value of the decedent's fractional interest, to the extent the fractional interest passed by right of survivorship at the decedent's death to a surviving joint tenant other than the decedent's surviving spouse.

(C) The decedent's ownership interest in property or accounts held in POD, TOD, or co-ownership registration with the right of survivorship. The amount included is the value of the decedent's ownership interest, to the extent the decedent's ownership interest passed at the decedent's death to or for the benefit of any person other than the decedent's estate or surviving spouse.

(D) Proceeds of insurance, including accidental death benefits, on the life of the decedent, if the decedent owned the insurance policy immediately before death or if and to the extent the
decedent alone and immediately before death held a presently
exercisable general power of appointment over the policy or its
proceeds. The amount included is the value of the proceeds, to
the extent they were payable at the decedent's death to or for
the benefit of any person other than the decedent's estate or
surviving spouse.

(2) Property transferred in any of the following forms by the
decedent during marriage:

(A) Any irrevocable transfer in which the decedent retained
the right to the possession or enjoyment of, or to the income
from, the property if and to the extent the decedent's right
terminated at or continued beyond the decedent's death. The
amount included is the value of the fraction of the property to
which the decedent's right related, to the extent the fraction of
the property passed outside probate to or for the benefit of any
person other than the decedent's estate or surviving spouse.

(B) Any transfer in which the decedent created a power over
income or property, exercisable by the decedent alone or in con-
junction with any other person, or exercisable by a nonadverse
party, to or for the benefit of the decedent, creditors of the
decedent, the decedent's estate, or creditors of the decedent's
estate. The amount included with respect to a power over property is the value of the property subject to the power, and the
amount included with respect to a power over income is the
value of the property that produces or produced the income,
to the extent the power in either case was exercisable at the
decedent's death to or for the benefit of any person other than
the decedent's surviving spouse or to the extent the property
passed at the decedent's death, by exercise, release, lapse, in
default, or otherwise, to or for the benefit of any person other
than the decedent's estate or surviving spouse. If the power is
a power over both income and property and the preceding sentence produces different amounts, the amount included is the
greater amount.

(3) Property that passed during marriage and during the two-year
period next preceding the decedent's death as a result of a transfer
by the decedent if the transfer was of any of the following types:

(A) Any property that passed as a result of the termination of a right or interest in, or power over, property that
would have been included in the augmented estate under
paragraph (1) (A), (B), or (C), or under paragraph (2), if the

right, interest, or power had not terminated until the decedent's death. The amount included is the value of the property that would have been included under those paragraphs if the property were valued at the time the right, interest, or power terminated, and is included only to the extent the property passed upon termination to or for the benefit of any person other than the decedent or the decedent's estate, spouse, or surviving spouse. As used in this subparagraph, "termination," with respect to a right or interest in property, occurs when the right or interest terminated by the terms of the governing instrument or the decedent transferred or relinquished the right or interest, and, with respect to a power over property, occurs when the power terminated by exercise, release, lapse, default, or otherwise, but, with respect to a power described in paragraph (1)(A), "termination" occurs when the power terminated by exercise or release, but not otherwise.

(B) Any transfer of or relating to an insurance policy on the life of the decedent if the proceeds would have been included in the augmented estate under paragraph (1)(D) had the transfer not occurred. The amount included is the value of the insurance proceeds to the extent the proceeds were payable at the decedent's death to or for the benefit of any person other than the decedent's estate or surviving spouse.

(C) Any transfer of property, to the extent not otherwise included in the augmented estate, made to or for the benefit of a person other than the decedent's surviving spouse. The amount included is the value of the transferred property to the extent the transfers to any one donee in either of the two years exceeded [$12,000] [the amount excludable from taxable gifts under 26 U.S.C. Section 2503(b) [or its successor] on the date next preceding the date of the decedent's death].

Legislative Note: In paragraph (3)(C), use the first alternative in the brackets if the second alternative is considered an unlawful delegation of legislative power.

2-206. Excluding property passing to the surviving spouse under the federal Social Security system, the value of the augmented estate includes the value of the decedent's nonprobate transfers to the decedent's surviving spouse, which consist of all property that passed outside probate at the decedent's death from the decedent to the surviving spouse by reason of the decedent's death, including

(1) the decedent's fractional interest in property held as a joint tenant with the right of survivorship, to the extent that the decedent's fractional interest passed to the surviving spouse as surviving joint tenant,

(2) the decedent's ownership interest in property or accounts held in co-ownership registration with the right of survivorship, to the extent the decedent's ownership interest passed to the surviving spouse as surviving co-owner, and

(3) all other property that would have been included in the augmented estate under Section 2-205(1) or (2) had it passed to or for the benefit of a person other than the decedent's spouse, surviving spouse, the decedent, or the decedent's creditors, estate, or estate creditors.

2-207(a) [Included Property.] Except to the extent included in the augmented estate under Section 2-204 or 2-206, the value of the augmented estate includes the value of:

(1) property that was owned by the decedent's surviving spouse at the decedent's death, including

(A) the surviving spouse's fractional interest in property held in joint tenancy with the right of survivorship,

(B) the surviving spouse's ownership interest in property or accounts held in co-ownership registration with the right of survivorship, and

(C) property that passed to the surviving spouse by reason of the decedent's death, but not including the spouse's right to homestead allowance, family allowance, exempt property, or payments under the federal Social Security system; and

(2) property that would have been included in the surviving spouse's nonprobate transfers to others, other than the spouse's fractional and ownership interests included under subsection (a)(1) (A) or (B), had the spouse been the decedent.

(b) [Time of Valuation.] Property included under this section is valued at the decedent's death, taking the fact that the decedent predeceased the spouse into account, but, for purposes of subsection (a)(1)(A) and (B), the values of the spouse's fractional and ownership interests are determined immediately before the decedent's death if the decedent was then a joint tenant or a co-owner of the property or accounts. For purposes of subsection (a)(2), proceeds of insurance that would have been included in the spouse's nonprobate transfers to others under Section 2-205(1)(D) are not valued as if he [or she] were deceased.

(c) [Reduction for Enforceable Claims.] The value of property included under this section is reduced by enforceable claims against the surviving spouse.

4. Pre- and Postnuptial Agreements

Thus, as we have seen, the augmented share creeps ever closer to the division achieved by the community-property system, the purpose of which is to permit the courts to refuse to (or avoid) looking into the mechanics of a marriage to determine who did what for whom, when, and who should therefore get how much of what. Instead, the default presumption is that sentient adults who have married have created a partnership and are contributing equally to that partnership—to its bounty and its burdens, to its toil and its tears as to its glories and its gains—for however long it endures.

The human condition being what it is, however, the issue eventually escapes from the couple's grasp, as—in the general run of things[43]—one or the other of the pair (but usually the husband, especially historically) slips the surly bonds[44] and joins the choir invisible.[45] (And, of course, one or the other of the pair, or both together, may grow tired of the union and so dissolve it, but those considerations arise in a family law class, not in our fairly complete doctrinal focus on distribution in anticipation of—and accounting for the peculiarities of—death.)

Even this rare, mandatory, binding provision (i.e., that a descendant spouse leave something like half of the marital assets to the survivor, outright), however, is not really mandatory. It can be circumvented. "Prenups," (actually, prenuptials,[46] and sometimes even postnuptials) are, in truth, nothing more than a mutually agreed circumvention of the marital community or the forced or augmented share. The key, here, though, is that the circumvention of the default must be genuinely, knowingly, and mutually agreed by the parties to the incipient marriage.

The issue, then, is this: What is required to make the parties' mutual agreement genuine and knowing (or informed)? Generally,

---

43. We will consider the alternative to the general run of things shortly in our review of simultaneous death statutes.

44.

Oh, I have slipped the surly bonds of earth, . . .
and while with silent, lifting mind I've trod,
the high untrespassed sanctity of space
put out my hand and touched the face of God.

High Flight, John Gillespie, Magee, Jr., American volunteer in the Royal Canadian Air Force, killed in action over southern England on December 11th, 1941.

45. George Eliot, *The Choir Invisible* (a phrase seized for its own purposes by that shining redemption of the otherwise shudderingly dreadful 1970s, Monty Python, thus (script)).

46. As opposed to "nuptuals," which is how the word is universally pronounced, but which actually is not a word at all. An unquenchable need to raise fine details of this sort at occasions such as cocktail parties and skiing trips is what gives lawyers their universally recognized reputation for pure awesomeness.

separate and independent counsel for each party plus a reasonable accounting of assets[47] will provide an inference of fairness—a rebuttable presumption, but a fairly strong one.

The modern trend, even as it moves to strengthen and complete the augmented estate, is also toward allowing free and sentient fiancées to make whatever deal they might wish, without an independent review by the court to ensure "objective reasonableness," which was the traditional standard. The modern standard seeks merely to ensure that the indicia of independent and informed decision making are objectively reliable; there the inquiry ends. (In this sense, the modern trend standard of review of the provisions of prenups is broadly analogous to the business judgment rule.)

Postnuptials, though still pose a special problem or two. First, is there really consideration for such an agreement? Why is this a serious question? Moreover, even if there appears to be genuine consideration at the time of agreement to the postnuptial terms, can you see how the party initially seeking the postnup has—if the other party is badly advised, or incautious, or too trusting—a means of ensuring, essentially, that the consideration turns out to be a mirage?

5. Ex-Spousal Predecease

If spouses divorce, but one ex-spouse is still named in a will or trust of the other, the named ex- is treated as having predeceased the decedent unless there is strong indication that the decedent fully intended still to make a grant of some of his worldly possessions to the spouse whom he had divorced (or who had divorced him). (It's the same presumption of predecease mechanism employed, wryly enough, in the context of slayer statutes, considered *infra*.)

6. Pretermitted Spouses

Pretermitted spouses have much in common, unsurprisingly, with pretermitted heirs. They are spouses who are not included in a partner's

---

47. This accounting need not be exact; a general sense that a potential spouse is materially and significantly wealthier than oneself, within an order of magnitude or so, seems to be sufficient. *See, e.g.,* Reece v. Elliott, 208 S.W.3d 419 (Tenn. Ct. App. 2006).

end-of-life documents because documents were written before the marriage and were not revised thereafter.

In most states, pretermitted spouses are entitled to the share of their deceased spouse's estate that they would have taken had the deceased spouse died intestate.[48] The presumption of pretermission does not, of course, obviate the surviving spouse's forced-share rights in separate-property states or the survivor's interest in the survivor's own half of the marital estate in community-property states. Very often, though, the survivor's intestate share will far exceed any available forced share. Consider, for instance, a family composed of two spouses and two children of those spouses. One of the spouses dies after 20 years of marriage. You know now what the surviving spouse could force in a separate-property state (and, for that matter, in a community-property state: nothing, as community property doesn't require the concept of the forced share). Recall, though, that given these facts in both community and separate property states[49] the surviving spouse would under intestacy take the whole of the decedent spouse's property.

D. SHUFFLING OFF THE COIL (AND PLANNING FOR THE LAST DANCE)

1. Slayer Statutes

One automatic alternative to trusts and wills, as noted above, is the survivorship benefit that obtains to joint tenancies and tenancies by the entirety, the most common forms of ownership of the marital home (and, effectively, much of marital liquidity, in the form of joint checking and savings accounts).

---

48. *See, e.g.,* Fla. Stat. § 732.301:

When a person marries after making a will and the spouse survives the testator, the surviving spouse shall receive a share in the estate of the testator equal in value to that which the surviving spouse would have received if the testator had died intestate, unless:

(1) Provision has been made for, or waived by, the spouse by prenuptial or postnuptial agreement;

(2) The spouse is provided for in the will; or

(3) The will discloses an intention not to make provision for the spouse.

In a few states, wills drawn before a marriage are void.

49. Remember the silent refrain: except Louisiana.

These automatic effects raise a unique and disturbing possibility: that a spouse who *kills* his spouse might end up benefiting by the act—owning in fee simple absolute that which had been owned only in joint tenancy before the killing. Every state has taken some effort, usually by statute, to mitigate this sort of tragedy. "Slayer statutes" keep slaughtering spouses from benefiting from their actions by treating the killing spouse as though that spouse had predeceased the decedent spouse. Thus, if husband kills wife, the statute steps in to require the courts to behave as though husband actually died *before* wife did, so that the property held in joint tenancy flows from the putatively dead (but actually alive) husband to the putatively alive (but actually dead) wife. Initially a bit confusing, perhaps, but then rather elegant, no?

None of this is particularly controversial, in the case of actual murder or voluntary manslaughter. The only real policy question arises in determining how far down the "ladder of intentionality (or evil)" the slayer statute should reach. Most states apply these statutes to murderers and to the commission of voluntary manslaughter, but not to involuntary manslaughter or "mere" accidental killing. Is this the right place to draw the line? Should a husband who accidentally–if negligently–backs over his wife with the family sedan take the marital home? Should it matter whether the surviving accidental killer and the deceased spouse have minor children who require further rearing at the time of the death? Should other factors play a role?

Meanwhile, consider that in most cases (we hope) the slayer by murder or voluntary manslaughter will end up in jail, often for life. Thus, in many cases these statutes serve in effect to take the property from the slayer's heirs in order to hand it to the deceased spouse's heirs. In almost all cases, both of those parties will be innocent of any wrongdoing. Is it troubling as a matter of public policy that this transfer from one set of innocent parties to another equally innocent set occurs? Might it not be better for the slayer statutes to "sever" the joint tenancies, while still treating the slayer as having predeceased, so that both sets of heirs inherit some measure of the property? Why or why not?

2. Simultaneous Death

A more problematic, and in many cases, such as the one below, less culpable and more heart-rending problem arises with the issue of simultaneous death—of episodes in which both spouses die at or near the same time.

JANUS v. TARASEWICZ,

482 N.E.2d 418 (Ill. App. Ct. 1985).

Judges: JUSTICE O'CONNOR delivered the opinion of the court. BUCKLEY, P.J., and CAMPBELL, J., concur.

This nonjury declaratory judgment action arose out of the death of a husband and wife, Stanley and Theresa Janus, who died after ingesting Tylenol capsules which had been laced with cyanide by an unknown perpetrator prior to its sales in stores. Stanley Janus was pronounced dead shortly after he was admitted to the hospital. However, Theresa Janus was placed on life support systems for almost two days before being pronounced dead. Claiming that there was no sufficient evidence that Theresa Janus survived her husband, plaintiff Alojza Janus, Stanley's mother, brought this action for the proceeds of Stanley's $100,000 life insurance policy, which named Theresa as the primary beneficiary and plaintiff as the contingent beneficiary. Defendant Metropolitan Life Insurance Company paid the proceeds to defendant Jan Tarasewicz, Theresa's father and the administrator of her estate. The trial court found sufficient evidence that Theresa survived Stanley Janus. We affirm.

The facts of this case are particularly poignant and complex. Stanley and Theresa Janus had recently returned from their honeymoon when, on the evening of September 29, 1982, they gathered with other family members to mourn the death of Stanley's brother, Adam Janus, who had died earlier that day from what was later determined to be cyanide-laced Tylenol capsules. While the family was at Adam's home, Stanley and Theresa Janus unknowingly took some of the contaminated Tylenol. Soon afterwards, Stanley collapsed on the kitchen floor.

Theresa was still standing when Diane O'Sullivan, a registered nurse and a neighbor of Adam Janus, was called to the scene. Stanley's pulse was weak so she began cardiopulmonary resuscitation (CPR) on him. Within minutes, Theresa Janus began having seizures. After paramedic teams began arriving, Ms. O'Sullivan went into the living room to assist with Theresa. While she was working on Theresa, Ms. O'Sullivan could hear Stanley's "heavy and labored breathing." She believed that both Stanley and Theresa died before they were taken to the ambulance, but she could not tell who died first.

Ronald Mahon, a paramedic for the Arlington Heights fire department, arrived at approximately 5:45 p.m. He saw Theresa faint and go into a seizure. Her pupils did not respond to light but she was breathing on her own during the time that he worked on her. Mahon also assisted with Stanley, giving him drugs to stimulate heart contractions.

Mahon later prepared the paramedic's report on Stanley. One entry in the report shows that at 18:00 hours Stanley had "zero blood pressure, zero pulse, and zero respiration." However, Mahon stated that the times in the report were merely approximations. He was able to say that Stanley was in the ambulance en route to the hospital when his vital signs disappeared.

When paramedic Robert Lockhart arrived at 5:55 p.m., both victims were unconscious with nonreactive pupils. Theresa's seizures had ceased but she was in a decerebrate posture in which her arms and legs were rigidly extended and her arms were rotated inward toward her body, thus indicating severe neurological dysfunction. At that time, she was breathing only four or five times a minute and, shortly thereafter, she stopped breathing on her own altogether. Lockhart intubated them both by placing tubes down their tracheae to keep their passages open. Prior to being taken to the ambulance, they were put on "ambu-bags," which is a form of artificial respiration whereby the paramedic respirates the patient by squeezing a bag. Neither Stanley nor Theresa showed any signs of being able to breathe on their own while they were being transported to Northwest Community Hospital in Arlington Heights. However, Lockhart stated that when Theresa was turned over to the hospital personnel, she had a palpable pulse and blood pressure.

The medical director of the intensive care unit at the hospital, Dr. Thomas Kim, examined them when they arrived in the emergency room at approximately 6:30 p.m. Stanley had no blood pressure or pulse. An electrocardiogram detected electrical activity in Stanley Janus' heart, but there was no synchronization between his heart's electrical activity and its pumping activity. A temporary pacemaker was inserted in an unsuccessful attempt to resuscitate him. Because he never developed spontaneous blood pressure, pulse or signs of respiration, Stanley Janus was pronounced dead at 8:15 p.m. on September 29, 1982.

Like Stanley, Theresa Janus showed no visible vital signs when she was admitted to the emergency room. However, hospital personnel were able to get her heart beating on its own again, so they did not insert a pacemaker. They were also able to establish a measurable, though unsatisfactory, blood pressure. Theresa was taken off the "ambu-bag" and put on a mechanical respirator. In Dr. Kim's opinion, Theresa was in a deep coma with "very unstable vital signs" when she was moved to the intensive care unit at 9:30 p.m. on September 29, 1982.

While Theresa was in the intensive care unit, numerous entries in her hospital records indicated that she had fixed and dilated pupils. However, one entry made at 2:32 a.m. on September 30, 1982, indicated that a nurse apparently detected a minimal reaction to light in Theresa's right pupil but not in her left pupil.

On September 30, 1982, various tests were performed in order to assess Theresa's brain function. These tests included an electroenceph-alogram (EEG) to measure electrical activity in her brain and a cerebral blood flow test to determine whether there was any blood circulating in her brain. In addition, Theresa exhibited no gag or cord reflexes, no response to pain or other external stimuli. As a result of these tests, Theresa Janus was diagnosed as having sustained total brain death, her life support systems then were terminated, and she was pronounced dead at 1:15 p.m. on October 1, 1982.

Death certificates were issued for Stanley and Theresa Janus more than three weeks later by a medical examiner's physician who never examined them. The certificates listed Stanley Janus' date of death as September 29, 1982, and Theresa Janus' date of death as October 1, 1982. Concluding that Theresa survived Stanley, the Metropolitan Life Insurance Company paid the proceeds of Stanley's life insurance policy to the administrator of Theresa's estate.

On January 6, 1983, plaintiff brought the instant declaratory judgment action against the insurance company and the administrators of Stanley and Theresa's estates, claiming the proceeds of the insurance policy as the contingent beneficiary of the policy. . . .

During the trial, the court heard the testimony of Ms. O'Sullivan, the paramedics, and Dr. Kim. . . .

In addition, Dr. Kenneth Vatz, a neurologist on the hospital staff, was called as an expert witness by plaintiff. Although he never actually examined Theresa, he had originally read her EEG as part of hospital routine. Without having seen her other hospital records, his initial evaluation of her EEG was that it showed some minimal electrical activity of living brain cells in the frontal portion of Theresa's brain. After reading her records and reviewing the EEG, however, he stated that the electrical activity measured by the EEG was "very likely" the result of interference from surrounding equipment in the intensive care unit. He concluded that Theresa was brain dead at the time of her admission to the hospital but he could not give an opinion as to who died first.

The trial court also heard an evidence deposition of Dr. Joseph George Hanley, a neurosurgeon, who testified as an expert witness on behalf of the defendants. Based on his examination of their records, Dr. Hanley concluded that Stanley Janus died on September 29, 1982. He further concluded that Theresa Janus did not die until her vital signs disappeared on October 1, 1982. His conclusion that she did not die prior to that time was based on: (1) the observations by hospital personnel that Theresa Janus had spontaneous pulse and blood pressure which did not have to be artificially maintained; (2) the instance when Theresa Janus' right pupil allegedly reacted to light; and (3) Theresa's EEG which showed some brain function and which, in his opinion, could not have resulted from outside interference.

At the conclusion of the trial, the court held that the evidence was sufficient to show that Theresa survived Stanley, but the court was not prepared to say by how long she survived him. Plaintiff . . . appeal[s]. In essence, [her] main contention is that there is not sufficient evidence to prove that both victims did not suffer brain death prior to their arrival at the hospital on September 29, 1982.

Dual standards for determining when legal death occurs in Illinois were set forth in the case of In re Haymer (1983), 115 Ill. App. 3d 349, 450 N.E.2d 940. There, the court . . . stated that in most instances death could be determined in accordance with the common law standard which is based upon the irreversible cessation of circulatory and respiratory functions. . . . If these functions are artificially maintained, a brain death standard of death could be used if a person has sustained irreversible cessation of total brain function. . . . However, the court refused to establish criteria for determining brain death because it noted that the advent of new research and technologies would continue to change the tests used for determining cessation of brain function. . . . Instead, the court merely required that the diagnosis of death under either standard must be made in accordance with "usual and customary standards of medical practice.". . .

Regardless of which standard of death is applied, survivorship is a fact which must be proved by a preponderance of the evidence by the party whose claim depends on survivorship. . . . The operative provisions of the Illinois version of the Uniform Simultaneous Death Act provides in pertinent part:

> If the title to property or its devolution depends upon priority of death and there is no sufficient evidence that the persons have died otherwise than simultaneously and there is no other provision in the will, trust agreement, deed, contract of insurance or other governing instrument for distribution of the property different from the provisions of this Section:

(a) The property of each person shall be disposed of as if he had survived. . . .

(d) If the insured and the beneficiary of a policy of life or accident insurance have so died, the proceeds of the policy shall be distributed as if the insured had survived the beneficiary. Ill. Rev. Stat. 1981, ch. 110 1/2, par. 3 – 1.

In cases where the question of survivorship is determined by the testimony of lay witnesses, the burden of sufficient evidence may be met by evidence of a positive sign of life in one body and the absence of any such sign in the other. . . . In cases such as the instant case, where the death process is monitored by medical professionals, their testimony as to "the usual and customary standards of medical practice" will be highly relevant when considering what constitutes a positive sign of life and what constitutes a criteri[on] for determining death. . . . Although the use of sophisticated medical technology can also make it difficult to determine when death occurs, the context of this case does not require a determination as to the exact moment at which the decedents died. Rather, the trial court's task was to determine whether or not there was sufficient evidence that Theresa Janus survived her husband. Our task on review of this factually disputed case is to determine whether the trial court's finding was against the manifest weight of the evidence. . . . We hold that it was not.

In the case at bar, both victims arrived at the hospital with artificial respirators and no obvious vital signs. There is no dispute among the treating physicians and expert witnesses that Stanley Janus died in both a cardiopulmonary sense and a brain-death sense when his vital signs disappeared en route to the hospital and were never reestablished. He was pronounced dead at 8:15 p.m. on September 29, 1982, only after intensive procedures such as electro-shock, medication, and the insertion of a pacemaker failed to resuscitate him.

In contrast, these intensive procedures were not necessary with Theresa Janus, because hospital personnel were able to reestablish a spontaneous blood pressure and pulse which did not have to be artificially maintained by a pacemaker or medication. Once spontaneous circulation was restored in the emergency room, Theresa was put on a mechanical respirator and transferred to the intensive care unit. Clearly, efforts to preserve Theresa Janus' life continued after more intensive efforts on Stanley's behalf had failed.

It is argued that the significance of Theresa Janus' cardiopulmonary functions, as a sign of life, was rendered ambiguous by the use of artificial respiration. In particular, reliance is placed upon expert testimony that a person can be brain dead and still have a spontaneous pulse and blood pressure which is indirectly maintained by artificial respiration. The fact remains, however, that Dr. Kim, an intensive care specialist who treated Theresa, testified that her condition in the emergency room did not warrant a diagnosis of brain death. In his opinion, Theresa Janus did not suffer irreversible brain death until much later, when extensive treatment failed to preserve her brain function and vital signs. This diagnosis was confirmed by a consulting neurologist after a battery of tests were performed to assess her brain function. . . . At trial, only Dr. Vatz disagreed with their finding, but even he admitted that the diagnosis and tests performed on Theresa Janus were in keeping with the usual and customary standards of medical practice.

There was also other evidence presented at trial which indicated that Theresa Janus was not brain dead on September 29, 1982. Theresa's EEG, taken on September 30, 1982, was not flat but rather it showed some delta waves of extremely low amplitude. Dr. Hanley concluded that Theresa's EEG taken on September 30 exhibited brain activity. Dr. Vatz disagreed. Since the trier of fact determines the credibility of expert witnesses and the weight to be given to their testimony . . . , the trial court in this case could have reasonably given greater weight to Dr. Hanley's opinion than to Dr. Vatz'. In addition, there is evidence that Theresa's pupil reacted to light on one occasion. It is argued that this evidence merely represents the subjective impression of a hospital staff member which is not corroborated by any other instance where Theresa's pupils reacted to light. However, this argument goes to the weight of this evidence and not to its admissibility. While these additional pieces of neurological data were by no means conclusive, they were competent evidence which tended to support the trial court's finding, and which also tended to disprove the contention that these tests merely verified that brain death had already taken place.

In support of the contention that Theresa Janus did not survive Stanley Janus, evidence was presented which showed that only Theresa Janus suffered seizures and exhibited a decerebrate posture shortly after ingesting the poisoned Tylenol. However, evidence that persons with these symptoms tend to die very quickly does not prove that Theresa Janus did not in fact survive Stanley Janus. . . .

In conclusion, we believe that the record clearly established that the treating physicians' diagnoses of death with respect to Stanley and Theresa Janus were made in accordance with "the usual and customary standards of medical practice." Stanley Janus was diagnosed as having sustained irreversible cessation of circulatory and respiratory functions on September 29, 1982. These same physicians concluded that Theresa Janus' condition on that date did not warrant a diagnosis of death, and, therefore, they continued their efforts to preserve her life. Their conclusion that Theresa Janus did not die until October 1, 1982, was based on various factors including the restoration of certain of her vital signs as well as other neurological evidence. The trial court found that these facts and circumstances constituted sufficient evidence that Theresa Janus survived her husband. It was not necessary to determine the exact moment at which Theresa died or by how long she survived him, and the trial court properly declined to do so. Viewing the record in its entirety, we cannot say that the trial court's finding of sufficient evidence of Theresa's survivorship was against the manifest weight of the evidence. . . .

Accordingly, there being sufficient evidence that Theresa Janus survived Stanley Janus, the judgment of the circuit court of Cook County is affirmed.

QUESTIONS AND ANALYSIS

This is a fascinating case. The human drama is intense. The newlyweds are just back from their honeymoon when they are called upon to attend a funeral of a family member who died mysteriously; both members of the couple suffer headaches and take extra-strength Tylenol at the house of the dead uncle. As it happens, the Tylenol has been laced with cyanide and was the cause of death of the uncle, though no one had yet realized this fact. The Tylenol ends up killing both of the newlyweds, but Stanley dies before being placed on life support, while Theresa is placed on life support. Perhaps as a result of this artificial assistance, but perhaps naturally, Theresa is judged by the courts to have survived some unspecified period longer than her new husband.

Not surprisingly, this human drama captured national headlines and massive attention–more than a little bit propelled by the fact that Theresa, Stanley, and the uncle were not the only victims of the poisoning, and the whole country wondered about the Tylenol in its own medicine chest. The nation-wide response was fevered and intense. It resulted in a complete redesign of how over-the-counter medicine was packaged in the United States, leading to the present circumstance in which older patients often find it impossible to open their medications.

The conclusion that Stanley predeceased Theresa by some period triggered significant legal consequences in this case. As the decision suggests, Illinois had adopted one of the first generation of simultaneous-death statutes, under which the parties were considered to have died at the same time *but only if there was no compelling evidence that one party survived the other for any time at all.* These first-generation statutes led to exactly the sort of deeply mordant and unedifying spectacle that arose in *Janus*, with experts called in to argue about just what constituted death in an increasingly (by then-current standards) technologically and medically sophisticated world (with issues of brain death and heart death and the "meaning" of artificial assistance in respiration and blood-flow all arising, and none having very obvious answers).

It appears that everything in the *Janus* case conspired to make the situation as awful as possible. One initial point worth considering: Why is this a case at all? The technical answer is that if the parties died at the same time or there wasn't evidence to the contrary, then Theresa would be treated as having pre-deceased Stanley under the Simultaneous Death statute, and so Stanley's parents would have taken the payout from the life-insurance policy. Because Theresa was judged to have survived Stanley, Theresa's parents took through her. (Theresa survived to take from Stanley; the payout entered her estate; then her parents took her estate upon her death.) As a practical matter, it's a case because the two living parties—the antagonistic sets of parents—couldn't find it in themselves to do, if not absolutely the *right* thing, then surely the decorous and agreeable thing, and split the money. This would have avoided lawsuit and all the ugliness that the lawsuit entailed. And $100,000 was a lot of money in 1982; split, it still would have gone a long way toward providing for the collective parents' old age.

If the couple had been longer married, this case would have been far less likely to end up in court. Had the couple had children, the human tragedy of the situation would have been even greater, but the life-insurance policy would have descended to the children of the couple. Had they been long married, and so known and beloved by each family, then some sort of accord would have presumably been easier to reach. But because they were newlyweds, and because these entanglements had not developed, a financial war between bereaved and grieving parents resulted, to the ultimate aggregate enrichment of lawyers and experts, and the overall impoverishment—economically and spiritually, of the families as a whole.

That this represented a fairly horrifying outcome was not lost on legislators, who in the years after this case moved in most states to adopt a second generation of Simultaneous Death statutes. This second generation specified that simultaneous death would be presumed unless the party propounding survival could demonstrate that the surviving party had outlived the first decedent by a period of 120 hours (i.e., 5 days). This modification has helped to obviate some of the ugliest examinations and contentions of the sort that appeared in *Janus*. (Note: Some states have extended the period beyond five days and have added the provision that if the parties die as a result of the same event, they should be treated as having died simultaneously. This latter provision opens its own can of interpretive worms.)

UNIFORM SIMULTANEOUS DEATH ACT (1993). . .

Section 2. Requirement of Surivival By 120 Hours Under Probate Code.

Except as provided in Section 6, if the title to property, the devolution of property, the right to elect an interest in property, or the right to exempt property, homestead or family allowance depends upon an individual's survivorship of the death of another individual, an individual who is not established by clear and convincing evidence to have survived the other individual by 120 hours is deemed to have predeceased the other individual. This section does not apply if its application would result in a taking of intestate estate by the state.

Section 3. Requirement of Survival by 120 Hours Under Governing Instruments. Except as provided in Section 6, for purposes of a provision of a governing instrument that relates to an individual surviving an event, including the death of another individual, an individual who is not established by clear and convincing evidence to have survived the event by 120 hours is deemed to have predeceased the event.

Section 4. Co-owner with Right of Survivorship; Requirement of Survival by 120 Hours. Except as provided in Section 6, if (i) it is not established by clear and convincing evidence that one of two co-owners with right of survivorship survived the other co-owner by 120 hours, one-half of the property passes as if one had survived by 120 hours and one-half as if the other had survived by 120 hours and (ii) there are more than two co-owners and it is not established by clear and convincing evidence that at least one of them survived the others by 120 hours, the property passes in the proportion that one bears to the whole number of co-owners.

Section 5. Evidence of Death or Status. In addition to the rules of evidence in courts of general jurisdiction, the following rules relating to a determination of death and status apply:

(1) Death occurs when an individual [is determined to be dead under the Uniform Determination of Death Act (1978/1980)] [has sustained either (i) irreversible cessation of circulatory and respiratory functions or (ii) irreversible cessation of all functions of the entire brain, including the brain stem. A determination of death must be made in accordance with accepted medical standards].

(2) A certified or authenticated copy of a death certificate purporting to be issued by an official or agency of the place where the death purportedly occurred is prima facie evidence of the fact, place, date, and time of death and the identity of the decedent.

(3) A certified or authenticated copy of any record or report of a governmental agency, domestic or foreign, that an individual is missing, detained, dead, or alive is prima facie evidence of the status and of the dates, circumstances, and places disclosed by the record or report.

(4) In the absence of prima facie evidence of death under paragraph (2) or (3), the fact of death may be established by clear and convincing evidence, including circumstantial evidence.

(5) An individual whose death is not established under the preceding paragraphs who is absent for a continuous period of five years, during which he [or she] has not been heard from, and whose absence is not satisfactorily explained after diligent search or inquiry, is presumed to be dead. His [or her] death is presumed to have occurred at the end of the period unless there is sufficient evidence for determining that death occurred earlier.

(6) In the absence of evidence disputing the time of death stipulated on a document described in paragraph (2) or (3), a document described in paragraph (2) or (3) that states a time of death 120 hours or more after the time of death of another individual, however the time of death of the other individual is determined, establishes by clear and convincing evidence that the individual survived the other individual by 120 hours.

Section 6. Exceptions. Survival by 120 hours is not required if: (1) the governing instrument contains language dealing explicitly with simultaneous deaths or deaths in a common disaster and that language is operable under the facts of the case;

(2) the governing instrument expressly indicates that an individual is not required to survive an event, including the death of another individual, by any specified period or expressly requires the individual to survive the event for a specified period; but survival of the event or the specified period must be established by clear and convincing evidence;. . .

3. Law and Ethics Coping with Medical Advance in Life Extensions

These instruments/provisions of law/doctrines are designed to assist those who are contemplating eternity and attempting to prepare for the necessities and inconveniences that attend it. One option: Wing it and hope your next-of-kin turns out to be wise, capable, interested, etc. The other options permit parties to convey their desires and to establish instructions to guide those next of kin. This latter option can involve, and be assisted by:

a. Power of Attorney

A Power of Attorney is an instrument that grants to some delegate the power to do certain things that one otherwise (but for the grant of the power) must do for oneself. Often it is employed as a convenience. For end-of-life considerations, a *Durable* Power of Attorney (DPoA) must be used, because durable powers survive the incapacity of the grantor while an ordinary power expires upon the grantor's incapacity—or just when it's needed, in this context. The default rule is that a power of attorney is not durable unless it expressly states that it survives incapacity. The agent given authority is called the attorney in fact (AiF).

The exercise of authority under a DPoA broadly follows the same rules and fiduciary obligations that append to trustees and so will be discussed in great detail in Part III of this text. Per that structure, an act could be within the agent's power but disloyal or imprudent. In other words, a court could rule that the AiF had been granted the power to do something by the grantor of the durable power, but that the AiF had acted without the grantor's best interests in mind, or had acted negligently, and so could be held liable for having acted.

Compare this with the older rule: An AiF (or a trustee) only had authority to do what the principal (or settlor) explicitly authorized her to do but no authority to do anything not explicitly delegated or in any way foreclosed. On the other hand, these agents could not be held liable for any actions that they had been authorized to perform, regardless of their level of care, or their ultimate motivation.

Even under the newer model, some powers either require explicit authorization or are viewed with deep suspicion (e.g., changing an estate plan materially).

b. Advance Directives

The three most common forms of advance directive are: Living Wills, Health Care Proxies, and Directions for Bodily Disposal.

Regardless of the kind of advance directive, it can take one of three substantive forms: (1) instructional directives (e.g., living wills, usually; DNRs), stating what the patient wants done in the event of mental incompetence or with his body after death, (2) proxy directives, delegating power to an agent to make health care decisions for the principal in the event of incompetence, and (3) hybrids that delegate power to an agent to act within guidelines established by the principal.

There are two common standards of duty/review of the agent's actions:

- *Substituted judgment: What would the power grantor have done?*
- *Best interests: What decision was in the best interest of the power grantor?*

Advance directives raise ticklish questions. How good are healthy people at forecasting, while they are healthy, about what they will want done once they become incapacitated? Does it matter whether they are good at such analysis? Which is more important: an individual's feelings when he effects a directive, or his feelings when incapacity draws closer? If his opinions or desires change, ought we to expect him to take responsibility to change his directives? Does it make sense to talk about peoples' "desires" *after* they've lost capacity?

In the absence of an advance directive, the default rule is to take every measure to save the person's life. But polls show most people would prefer to "pull the plug." Should the default rule be switched?

c. Disposition of the Body

Instruments disposing of a decedent's body include very common documents, such as donor cards. (In many states, in fact, the donor "card" is merely a checkmark made on a form during a driver's license application.) More complex instruments are available.[50] Why can't you sell your carcass to the cadaver collectors, the glue factory, or UNOS[51]? Alternatively, why is the default *against* bodily donation instead of for it?

---

50. *See, e.g.,* Uniform Anatomical Gift Act.

51. UNOS, the United Network for Organ Sharing, is responsible for establishing the rules and priority lists for the distribution of donated organs.

d. Euthanasia and Assisted Suicide

In Washington v. Glucksberg, 521 U.S. 702 (1997), the Supreme Court held that, although there is a constitutionally protected right to refuse life-saving medical care, there is no such right for a person to have a doctor euthanize him or help him commit suicide. But it recognized that states may choose to legalize euthanasia or assisted suicide. For many years, Oregon was the only state to have done so,[52] though in recent years, additional states have moved in that direction.

If a DPoA includes an instruction authorizing or even demanding physician-assisted suicide, is it honored? Should it be?

---

52. *See* Or. Rev. Stat. §§127.800-897 (2013) (enacted in 1997).

PART III

THE LAW OF WILLS

A. INTRODUCTION TO THE LAW OF WILLS

We begin the pivot to the law of wills with a basic question: Whom does the law permit to execute a will? The hurdle here is that of mental capacity. What constitutes, and obviates, mental capacity? As a predicate question, though, why do we require a minimum threshold of free and rational cognition at all?

The requirement of mental capacity has at least three functions. The first two of these, the protective and preventative functions, pertain to the testator. As a protective mechanism, requiring mental capacity allows a testator to dispose of her property while she is entirely sane, with the assurance that her estate plan will be carried out even if she later becomes insane (even if she executes a new will while insane). Thus, the capacity requirement protects the lucid testator and her plans against the possibility of future debility. After all, the driving purpose of the law of wills is to carry out the wishes of the (now- deceased) testator, just as the law of trusts works to carry out the wishes of the settlor. By requiring mental capacity, the law ensures—as best it can—that the testator's *rational* wishes are carried out.

The capacity requirement also prevents the unscrupulous from exploiting senile or otherwise incompetent testators. It is an unfortunate reality that some people see the weak-minded, institutionalized, or elderly not as people worthy of respect, but as "marks" from whom fortunes can be drained. While those dishonorable sorts may still coerce, convince, or otherwise finagle a will out of an incompetent testator, the testator's incapacity invalidates the will and renders the rogue's efforts for naught.

A third function of the mental capacity requirement arises to protect the dignity and solemnity of the court system and of government proceedings generally. Wills are public documents, recorded in county offices. Probate and appellate courts are government entities conducting open proceedings. High profile or unique and unusual probate cases attract significant public attention, in part because they are so easily understood and dissected by the public, most of whose members will face distribution at death issues at various times during their own lives and will therefore have formed more definite opinions about the propriety of probate proceedings than they may have formed with regard to many other areas of law. Courts that blithely undertook to execute wills obviously the product of deranged or coerced minds would rapidly lose the respect of the public and perhaps not merely with regard to probate proceedings alone. The law may well often be "a ass—a idiot,"[1] as we students of its grand structure and its fine details may appreciate more than most, but it cannot afford to be a[n] ass, or to be seen to as such, in this very public and ecumenical field.

As you review the rules by which mental capacity is established or challenged, consider a few important structural details. First, note when the law uses objective rules for determining or precluding capacity and when it uses subjective norms. What are the benefits and drawbacks of each structural method? Why are they employed as they are? Does the law make the right call? Similarly, pay attention to the assignment of burdens of persuasion and proof. These initial dispositions of burden very often end up determining the outcome in these cases. Is this surprising? Can this insight be deployed usefully in fields beyond the present study?

---

1. Charles Dickens, *Oliver Twist* 489 (1970) (first published serially, 1837-39) ("If the law supposes that," said Mr. Bumble, . . . "the law is a ass—a idiot. If that's the eye of the law, the law is a bachelor; and the worst I wish the law is that his eye may be opened by experience—by experience.") Bachelors may make of this additional elucidation what they will.

B. MENTAL CAPACITY FOR TESTATION

(i.e., being of sound mind . . .)

Generally, there are two (or four, depending on how you organize them[2]) requirements to make a valid will. First, the testator must be of a minimum age. In most states and under UPC §2-501,[3] that age is 18, although Georgia's minimum age is 14.[4] Second, the testator:

> must be capable of knowing and understanding in a general way the nature and extent of his or her property, the natural objects of his or her bounty[5], and the disposition that he or she is making of that property, and must also be capable of relating these elements to one another and forming an orderly desire regarding the disposition of the property.

Restatement (Third) of Property: Wills and Other Donative Transfers §8.1(b) (2003).[6]

Even a generally mentally incapacitated person can make a valid will if the will is executed during a lucid interval during which he or she meets the standard for mental capacity.[7] Note though that most states have adopted specific ethical rules by which counsel must abide whenever representing clients of questionable capacity, even when the clients still enjoy periods of lucidity.

The test is of capability, not actual knowledge. A reasonable mistake will not invalidate a testament, nor militate against the testator's competence to make a will. Similarly, the threshold is not that of

---

2. This often turns out to be the case, and nicely illustrates why it is far wiser to learn the law as an organic, connected field than as a set of discrete, memorized factoids. Lists are for ReddaBuzzGawk, not (primarily) for serious study of the law.

3. Section 2-501 ". . . An individual 18 or more years of age who is of sound mind may make a will."

4. Ga. Code Ann. §53-4-10 (2015).

5. The natural objects of the testator's bounty generally are limited to her closest family members, whether related by blood or not. *See* Restatement (Third) of Property: Wills and Other Donative Transfers §8.1 cmt. c (2003). Of course, this requirement does not require the testator to devise her property to those people; she need only know who they are.

6. The Restatement (Third) of Property's formulation is representative of what many states require.

7. See, e.g., Schlueter v. Bowers, 994 P.2d 937, 940 (Wyo. 2000).

average intelligence—the ordinary "moron in a hurry"[8] gets to make a will, too. (A party needs less mental capacity to get married than to make a will, but less to make a will or will substitute than to make a contract or to give a gift or make out a deed.[9] Why?)

So the task becomes that of fleshing out these requirements. Just how "confused" or structurally outré must a would-be testator be before incapacity will be found?

In practical fact, the decision in these incapacity cases (as in several other areas) is very often dictated by the rule assigning the burdens of proof.[10] It is hard to demonstrate whether someone is fundamentally incapable, either situationally or structurally. Pirtle v. Tucker, 960 So. 2d 620 (Ala. 2006)[11] illustrates that point in applying the burdens in accordance with the majority rule.[12] In that case, two granddaughters challenged their grandfather's will, which had left everything to Grandpa's neighbor (who was not a member of the family). There, as in most states, the Grandpa as testator enjoyed an initial presumption that he was mentally capable of testacy. Thus, the contesting granddaughters bore the burden of proving incapacity by (under Alabama law) a preponderance of the evidence.[13]

The *Pirtle* contestants—the granddaughters—had significant evidence that could be interpreted to suggest that their grandfather lacked capacity. He was a hoarder who lived in a shed in his backyard, rather than in the house. He preferred to spend time in jail rather than pay fines for the trash in his yard. According to the neighbors, he also used his backyard as a vast and breezy water closet. Only two weeks before he executed the will, he was hospitalized for shortness of breath. The hospital

---

8. *See,* e.g., https://www.techdirt.com/articles/20060330/1829246.shtml, http://dictionary.sensagent.com/a%20moron%20in%20a%20hurry/en-en/. As these citations suggest, the standard explicitly applies in trademark cases in English court, but it works here by analogy.

9. *See e.g.,* Kunz v. Sylvain, 159 Conn. App. 730, 741 (2015) (quoting Deroy v. Estate of Baron, 43 A.3d 759, 762-63 (Conn. App. Ct. 2012)).

10. Or, if you prefer, the burden of persuasion and the burden of proof.

11. An expurgated version of this case is available on the web page for this textbook.

12. The UPC also adopts the majority rule in §3-407, which the Restatement (Third) of Property: Wills & Other Donative Transfers references in comment f to §8.1.

13. As noted below, some states adopt this standard of proof, while others require clear and convincing evidence of incapacity. Which do you think has a larger effect on the outcome of probate cases (and cases generally), the distribution of burdens or the required standard of evidence (particularly as between the preponderance of the evidence and the clear and convincing standards)? Why?

records for that stay indicated that he was "confused, disoriented, and noncooperative with hospital staff." Perhaps the most important piece of evidence was the neighbor's admission in early August that the testator had been "unable to make decisions for the past several months," a time that certainly could have encompassed the date the will was executed.

Discrete pieces of evidence favoring capacity were few. When the testator was discharged from the hospital the day before the will was executed, the hospital records described him as "alert, coherent, and well oriented to time." In addition, the accountant who notarized the will said the testator seemed normal on the day he executed the will. The court decided that "several months" (i.e., the time during which the testator had been confused and unable to make decisions, according to the neighbor) was an ambiguous term and the claim general, and that the contestants' evidence was not enough to rebut the presumption that the testator had capacity on the day he executed the will.

Note how thoroughly and often definitively the burden of proof affects the result in a case of this sort. How does one prove with requisite persuasive force that whatever incapacity can be demonstrated was (1) pervasive, (2) more-or-less present at the time of will execution, and (3) sufficiently debilitating to wrest from the testator the (natural, constitutional) right to distribute his property as he "wills"?[14] It's tough.

Now consider how the rhetorically slight shift from the majority to the minority rule (which still holds sway in New Hampshire[15]) affects the result. The minority rule also starts with the initial presumption of capacity. However, once the contestant produces *some* evidence[16] of incapacity, the burden shifts back to the proponent to prove capacity by a preponderance of the evidence. Consider this: Could *something* be offered as evidence to suggest that not quite every single one of *your* screws has always remained tight? If so, and if you then faced the minority rule's shifted burden—you had to prove that you were sane, against an effective presumption to the contrary—just how would you go about it?[17] This last consideration, plus just the general oddity of effectively presuming in many otherwise ordinary cases that a party

---

14. Note the particular salience of the term "will." The testator enacts a testament to make sure that *her will be done* after her demise, despite her having shuffled off the coil. Consider the equivalent relevant freightage of the term "trust."

15. In re Estate of Washburn, 690 A.2d 1024 (N.H. 1997).

16. Less than even a preponderance, mind you.

17. Do you think the neighbor/beneficiary/proponent in *Pirtle*, based on one set of discharge papers and the accountant's statement that Grandpa seemed "like a normal

is not of sound mind, and then demanding that the party prove his capacity,[18] explains the popularity of the majority position.

Another reason states tend to opt for the majority, constant presumption of capacity rule is as a reaction to an unexpected existential quirk in jury conduct illustrated by Wilson v. Lane, 614 S.E.2d 88 (Ga. 2005).[19] In that case, the testator's will divided her estate evenly among seventeen beneficiaries, sixteen of whom were blood relatives of hers, while the seventeenth had been a fast family friend who had nursed the testator in her failing years. One of the sixteen relative-beneficiaries challenged the will. The jury found that the testator lacked testamentary capacity. The trial court reversed the verdict, reasoning that there was no evidence that she was incapable. A host of witnesses, including the drafting attorney, had testified that the testator was sharp as a tack. The challenger presented no evidence that she was incapable of forming a rational desire about the disposition of her property; he only showed that she was eccentric and elderly.

Given the clarity of the evidence, why did the jury find for the challenger? Well, it appears that lay people (i.e., the nonlawyers who constitute juries) have a subconscious sense that—as a moral truth—family members are the natural beneficiaries of a testator's bounty. It follows from this premise that *any* nonfamily bequest by a testator tends to raise a suspicion (and sometimes even an "illicit" presumption) of some sort of incapacity in the jury's minds. Moreover, people generally—as we considered previously—don't care to contemplate death, particularly their own. So they don't contemplate it, either consciously (avoiding writing a will) or subconsciously. As a result, juries appear overwhelmingly to commiserate with the (living) *beneficiaries* whom the testator has "cheated" out of some portion of their patrimony, rather than with the (dead) testator, whom the jury, by the very presumption of incapacity, has cheated of his or her autonomy and dignity. You may be sure (or at least you may evaluate—for whatever you think it worth—this assurance) that if juries tended to empathize with

---

person," would be able to prove that the testator had capacity if the burden was on him to do so?

18. And of course, these being wills cases, the demand really isn't even that "testator prove his sanity," but that the proponents of the will prove the sanity of a dead person, at the time of the making of the relevant will, which will very often have been some significant time prior to the testator's death and separated in time by the testator's decline and dotage.

19. An expurgated version of this case is available on the web page for this textbook.

testators, this common tendency of juries to find incapacity to defeat "unnatural" bequests would be reversed.

C. METHODS OF CONTESTING/UNDERMINING/ CHALLENGING TESTATOR COMPETENCE

1. Insane Delusion

An insane delusion is a false conception of reality to which the testator adheres despite all evidence and reason to the contrary. The notion of an "insane delusion" is one of law, not of psychology, and is "grounded" in science in the same sort of way that the boundary between trespass and nuisance is.[20] In the majority of states, insane delusions are said to arise at law and to thwart testamentary capacity when someone generally exhibits the mental capacity to execute a will, but suffers from an objectively loony notion and that objectively loony belief causes the testator to make certain discrete disposition(s). In the remaining states, the test is whether there has been an "unnatural"[21] disposition and an insane delusion that *might* have caused the unnatural disposition. Effectively, this shifts the burden to the will's proponents to prove that the delusion didn't cause the disposition. Per the discussion about capacity just above, can you see why this syntactically minor distinction is likely to have a very significant practical effect?

---

20. This is to say, broadly, that the science of the time at which the concept of the insane delusion was developed may have supported the contours of the concept, but much or all of that settled scientific understanding (or jurists' notion of the then-settled scientific understanding) has been swept away by later scientific developments. (By way of comparison, the distinction between trespass and nuisance was originally that trespass involved the invasion of the property of another by a physical object, such as a baseball, while nuisance arose to deal with less concrete invasions, such as smoke pollution. This distinction made some sense in the seventeenth and eighteenth centuries and before, but makes none given modern scientific understandings. Nevertheless, it continues to carry material weight (pun not really intended) in the law of property. And remember: trusts and estates is a specialty area within the law of property.)

21. A disposition is unnatural when it bequeaths property to a beneficiary who is not one of "the natural objects of the testator's bounty." In normal English, it is a disposition that would not ordinarily be expected, given what we know about the testator. This is very much a "gut check" test.

Regardless of which test is followed, any dispositions found to be caused by insane delusions are struck. These dispositions can be discrete portions of a larger testamentary scheme or the whole disposition of an estate. Only, but all, of the distributions tainted by the insane delusion are struck, with the dispositions thus obviated descending to any secondary/backup specific takers, if any, then to any residuary takers, then to takers by intestacy. The rest of the will stands, if such a distinction can coherently be made. Some courts hold that if there is any evidence to support the testator's belief, the belief can't qualify as an insane delusion. The majority, though, hold that if a rational person could not believe what the testator believes under all the facts, then an insane delusion could be found.

There is, at least notionally, a hard core of "easy" insane delusion situations, in which the fact(s) about which the testator is deluded are objectively falsifiable propositions, so that the testator clings to an incorrect take on reality of such duration, breadth, magnitude, and relevance that it can reasonably be said to explain one or more devises that would—but-for the delusion—have flowed to other legatees. If, for example, a testator believed firmly that he was the father of some child actor the testator had in fact never met; nor had he met the child's mother; disposed of his estate by dividing it equally between his two actual children and the child actor; and had positively indicated that he had made this distribution based on his erroneous understanding of the world, the law would have little trouble in concluding that an insane delusion had arisen, and in acting accordingly. Few commentators would be troubled by the conclusion.

Problems, though, arise in less straightforward cases. One fairly obvious example of a hopeless morass (from the law's point of view) is the question of religion and religious (or quasi-religious—which very term opens its own can of worms (and words) and may defy noncontroversial definition) belief. Many atheists think sincere believers are all whackadoo purveyors of gibberish. Many sincere believers think that people who believe sincerely but differently are dangerous nut jobs. Many also think that atheists are neurotic, existential catastrophes. Who's to say, really? Such issues, at all events, do not lend themselves to consideration in a course of this sort. But note how any member of any of those groups might genuinely and deeply believe that everyone else suffers from an insane delusion. And this is about the most fundamental (from some points of view) of propositions. Consider how replete, then, is the full gamut of opportunity for fundamental disagreement to play out as delusional error.[22]

Professor Melanie Leslie argues that the insane delusion category and doctrine really arose as an excuse for judges to override testators' wishes with their own when such judges thought the testator's distributions ill-advised or broadly (but sanely) irrational. She says:

> [n]otwithstanding frequent declarations to the contrary, many courts are as committed to ensuring that testators devise their estates in accordance with prevailing normative views as they are to effectuating testamentary intent. Those courts impose upon testators a duty to provide for those whom the court views as having a superior moral claim to the testator's assets, usually a financially dependent spouse or persons related by blood to the testator. Wills that fail to provide for those individuals typically upheld only if the will's proponent can convince the fact-finder that the testator's deviation from normative values is morally justifiable. . . . Courts impose and enforce this moral duty to family through the covert manipulation of the doctrine. . . . At the end of the day, testamentary freedom exists for the vast majority of testators who happen to have the same sense of duty and moral obligation that the law implicitly imposes—but often not for those who hold non-conforming values.[23]

Does *Strittmater* confirm or undermine that proposition? Why or why not?

IN RE STRITTMATER

53 A.2d 205 (N.J. 1947)

Prior History:

On appeal from a decree of the Prerogative Court, advised by Vice-Ordinary Bigelow, who filed the following opinion:

---

22. Should you doubt this, try to think back to the last time you had a serious political or moral argument with someone who disagreed with you fundamentally. (This may have some in the form of actual human discussion, or perhaps more often these days on the arguably ersatz platform of "social media.") Did either you or your fellow discussant end the conversation thinking ill of the other's logical capacity? How many twitter "discussions" conclude with a tweet amiably declaring, "That's a good point well made, but I fear that I must respectfully disagree. Let's explore these ideas again soon, friend"? Exactly.

23. Melanie B. Leslie, *The Myth of Testamentary Freedom*, 38 Ariz. L. Rev. 235, 236-37 (1996). Do you think that juries and judges substitute their value systems to analyze when non-"natural" bequests should stand? Always? Just at the margins?

This is an appeal from a decree of the Essex County Orphans Court admitting to probate the will of Louisa F. Strittmater. Appellants challenge the decree on the ground that testatrix was insane.

The only medical witness was Dr. Sarah D. Smalley, a general practitioner who was Miss Strittmater's physician all her adult life. In her opinion, decedent suffered from paranoia of the Bleuler type of split personality. The factual evidence justifies the conclusion. But I regret not having had the benefit of an analysis of the data by a specialist in diseases of the brain.

The deceased never married. Born in 1896, she lived with her parents until their death about 1928, and seems to have had a normal childhood. She was devoted to both her parents and they to her. Her admiration and love of her parents persisted after their death to 1934, at least. Yet four years later she wrote: 'My father was a corrupt, vicious, and unintelligent savage, a typical specimen of the majority of his sex. Blast his wormstinking carcass and his whole damn breed.' And in 1943, she inscribed on a photograph of her mother 'That Moronic she-devil that was my mother.'

Numerous memoranda and comments written by decedent on the margins of books constitute the chief evidence of her mental condition. Most of them are dated in 1935, when she was 40 years old. But there are enough in later years to indicate no change in her condition. The master who heard the case in the court below, found that the proofs demonstrated 'incontrovertably her morbid aversion to men' and 'feminism to a neurotic extreme.' This characterization seems to me not strong enough. She regarded men as a class with an insane hatred. She looked forward to the day when women would bear children without the aid of men, and all males would be put to death at birth. Decedent's inward life, disclosed by what she wrote, found an occasional outlet such as the incident of the smashing of the clock, the killing of the pet kitten, vile language, &c. On the other hand – and I suppose this is the split personality – Miss Strittmater, in her dealings with her lawyer, Mr. Semel, over a period of several years, and with her bank, to cite only two examples, was entirely reasonable and normal.

Decedent, in 1925, became a member of the New Jersey branch of the National Women's Party. [24] From 1939 to 1941, and perhaps later, she worked as a volunteer one day a week in the New York office, filing

---

24. [The National Woman's Party (the judge got the spelling just slightly wrong) was the most radical of the leading organizations that lobbied for the Nineteenth Amendment to the U.S. Constitution.—ED.]

papers, &c. During this period, she spoke of leaving her estate to the Party. On October 31st, 1944, she executed her last will, carrying this intention into effect. A month later, December 6th, she died. Her only relatives were some cousins of whom she saw very little during the last few years of her life.

The question is whether Miss Strittmater's will is the product of her insanity. Her disease seems to have become well developed by 1936. In August of that year she wrote, 'It remains for feministic organizations like the National Women's Party, to make exposure of women's "protectors" and "lovers" for what their vicious and contemptible selves are.' She had been a member of the Women's Party for eleven years at that time, but the evidence does not show that she had taken great interest in it. I think it was her paranoic condition, especially her insane delusions about the male, that led her to leave her estate to the National Women's Party. The result is that the probate should be set aside."

PER CURIAM. The decree under review will be affirmed, for the reasons stated in the opinion of Vice-Ordinary Bigelow.

* * *

Strittmater compares interestingly with the case of Breeden v. Stone, 992 P.2d 1167 (Colo. 2000). In that case, a days'-long bender by the testator, Breeden, and a buddy resulted in someone getting killed by hit-and-run—either by the testator or his bingeing companion. Breeden and company keep partying, but then Breeden went home, barricaded himself in his house, and eventually killed himself. Before he did that, though, he wrote a holographic will in which he changed the dispositions made in a prior will from his extended family to his cocaine-dealer girlfriend. The question that arose was whether he made those changes under the influence of an insane delusion.

There was certainly some evidence in that case that the testator had some problems, but their scope, extent, and effect are harder to grasp. He was paranoid, thinking there were listening devices in his home and car, and assassination plots against him and his dogs. He believed that he was being watched by the government. (As was later determined, though, he actually *was* being watched by the government.)

Using an older standard for whether a delusion exists or not, (i.e., "a persistent belief in that which has no existence in fact, and which is adhered to against all evidence"[25]), the contestant has a duty both

---

25. That's a minority view these days.

to show that an insane delusion exists, and that the delusion was the material cause of the contested bequest. So was Breeden "insanely deluded?" Was he materially insanely deluded? What does that mean in this context? Why would a claim of general incapacity fail in this context? (Note: these two claims are not mutually exclusive, and can be alleged together, as here, or in the alternative.)[26]

2. Undue Influence

Restatement (Third) of Property: Wills and Other Donative Transfers §8.3 declares that "[a] donative transfer is procured by undue influence" if the influence exerted over the donor "overcame the donor's free will and caused the donor to make a donative transfer that the donor would not otherwise have made." Fair enough, but this definition creates two problems, one theoretical and one practical.

As a matter of theory, the definition does not explain what kind of influence should be considered "undue." As a practical matter, undue influence cases as defined here are very likely to occur when there are no witnesses to the influencing actions except for the party accused of undue influence and the now-dead, potentially influenced testator, and often there is no direct evidence of any kind. This practical problem once again renders the vector of the relevant evidentiary presumptions very, very important.

Thus, the two overriding concerns in this area are to get a "nose" for which influences qualify as undue in which circumstances and for whether and when a presumption of undue influence may arise.

R(3)P §8.3 comment e gives some basic guidance: "in the absence of direct evidence . . . circumstantial evidence is sufficient to raise an inference of undue influence if the contestant provides that (1) the donor was susceptible; (2) the alleged wrongdoer had opportunity; (3) alleged wrongdoer had a disposition to exert undue influence; and (4) there was a result appearing to be the effect of undue influence" (which will necessarily inculpate a motive consideration; the motive to unduly influence is to achieve the relevant result). But note—the notion of which influences are undue has still been left undefined. That must be sussed from the cases. So . . .

---

26. An expurgated version of this case is available on the web page for this textbook.

The Estate of Lakatosh, 441 Pa. Super. 133 (1995), the case of the creepy cretin of a charlatan "caregiver," provides a sad but not uncommon example of the "core" undue influence case, and yet more supernumerary proof that the world has a fulsome complement of horrible, horrible people. An old woman (Rose) in poor health is effectively cut off from her family, whom she rarely sees. A younger person (Roger) steps into the breach to run errands, help with chores, keep her company—and rob her blind. Roger rapidly became the only person in the world with whom she had regular contact. After some interval of this situation, Rose executed a power of attorney designating Roger as her agent and a will leaving all but $1,000 of her estate, then worth $268,000,[27] to Roger. The will was drafted by Roger's second cousin, to whom Roger had referred Rose on an unrelated legal matter. Ultimately, Roger left Rose living in filth while he, using his power of attorney, siphoned off more than $128,000 of Rose's assets, including $72,000 which flowed to his friend Patricia Fox, whom Rose didn't even know. Although Rose revoked the power of attorney in 1990, she died in 1993 without having revoked her will.

What does your "nose" tell you in this instance: Was there undue influence here? Why? The answer is harder to articulate than to feel. Do we *know* that Roger talked her into changing the will or making the power of attorney? Not for sure. Do we know *how*? Not really. What do we know? That he had the opportunity to exert influence; that he got results (power of attorney over the estate, being named the sole beneficiary of a will drawn by his cousin) that he would not have gotten if he had not interacted with Rose (i.e., he was not a "natural" beneficiary); that he treated her badly (which might be seen as a disposition to exert undue influence); and that she eventually revoked the power of attorney (but, oddly, not the will).[28]

Under Pennsylvania law, a contestant who alleges undue influence ordinarily has the burden of proof. However, a presumption of undue influence arises, and the burden to rebut that presumption is put on the proponent, if the contestant can show that the person who procured the will was in a confidential relationship with the testator and

---

27. This was in November of 1988, so after the last great inflation, but when one could still, in that part of the world, buy two cans of Coke and a candy bar for a buck.

28. Consider this detail as you read through the rest of this case discussion. We don't know from the opinion in the case when or under what circumstances Rose decided to revoke the power of attorney and in fact did do. How does this fact affect any determination about undue influence wielded over her? Is it a dispositive fact? (An expurgated version of the case itself appears on the textbook web page.)

that there are suspicious circumstances.[29] To trigger the presumption (in Pennsylvania, which here provides an example rather than the only applicable method) the contestant must show "by clear and convincing evidence [1] that there was a confidential relationship, [2] that the person enjoying such relationship received the bulk of the estate, and [3] that the decedent's intellect was weakened." These are all apparent here: There was a close and reliant relationship even before the power-of-attorney was established; Roger got the bulk of the estate; and the decedent's intellect was in fact weakened.[30]

The application of the presumption does not *per se* end the case. The presumption is rebuttable, so Roger (or any party against whom the inference arises) could have made some showing to defeat the presumption, either by demonstrating that he had not exerted influence, or by establishing that any influence exerted was not undue. How might he have made such an evidentiary showing? This is counterfactual in this instance, of course, but he could have (1) had Rose see independent counsel (not, as here, his cousin) to confirm her intentions and establish her full capacity and (2) he could have treated her with dignity. These efforts would have helped, but it is reasonable to conclude that where he (unrelated to her) was granted a power of attorney over Rose's estate and spent the bulk of that estate in her lifetime, he was always going to be treated at least with extreme suspicion and was unlikely to be able to rebut the presumption under almost any circumstances. At all events, he had no rebuttal to make here.

Lakatosh is a useful model not only because of the starkness of the facts, but because it illustrates anew the profound practical effect of the initial distribution of presumptions and burdens. If no presumption of undue influence arises, such that the burden to *prove* undue influence lies on the contestants, the likelihood of success in the contest

---

29. *See also* Restatement (Third) of Property: Wills and Other Donative Transfers §8.3 cmt. f. "Suspicious circumstances" are discussed in detail in comment h.

30. If you read the opinion on the web page, it appears plain the court took particular note of an audiotape of Rose's testamentary acts (i.e., her signing, etc., of the will), which it deemed to demonstrate how befuddled she was. Audio and videotapes (or other recordings) of testators can be tricky. While they can provide good proof of capacity in the case of an obviously hale, hearty, and sentient testator, they can in more marginal cases (i.e., the very cases in which concern about later proving the capacity of the testator are most likely to arise) turn traitor; for whatever reasons, such recordings have a tendency to magnify any frailties that the objects of the recordings do exhibit, particularly if handled by inexpert recorders. (Can you proffer some explanations for this interesting datum?)

generally low. What (absent Roger's utter disregard for his putative charge's most basic care and comfort) would have been the evidence that the powers granted to and assets flowing through Roger were not the consequence of Ms. Lakatosh's genuine gratitude to Roger for his company and services, other than the contested distributions themselves? On the other hand, once a presumption does arise, then the presumed wrongdoer faces the potentially equally challenging scramble for hard evidence of the state of mind of the decedent. The central inquiry and proximate determinant of result, then, is generally whether the burden-shifting presumption should be employed. As with the commonwealth court here, most states presume undue influence if there is a confidential relationship + suspicious circumstances. This can be seen as a reworking of, or an incorporation of, the susceptibility + opportunity + disposition + result test of the Restatement.

Note that "confidential relationship" does not (necessarily) mean a secret relationship, but rather just a close one in which the would-be wrongdoer has some special obligation to attend to the interests of the testator. The classic example of such relationships is a fiduciary relationship, but they also arise when the testator is uniquely reliant on the beneficiary or the beneficiary is dominant over the testator.

"Suspicious circumstance" determinations allow for significant employment of the old "gut feeling." All three of susceptibility + opportunity + disposition can come into play here if there is an "unnatural" result favoring the party that was in the confidential relationship with the testator. By the way, do you understand or recall what is here meant by an "unnatural" result?

Consider an example. Your grandmother, a widow, takes ill at the end of the spring semester. Because all your other relatives are working, you agree to forego a summer job to take care of her. During the summer she dies. In her will, she has left you the same 1/10th share that you would have been entitled to under the intestacy statutes. Does this raise a presumption of undue influence? What if, instead, she had left you, along with the rest of your siblings and collaterals, a 1/10th share of the residue of the will, but also left you a specific bequest of $10,000? How about one-half of her estate?

What additional considerations are relevant either to determining whether the presumption should arise, or, should it arise, to your efforts to defeat it? Will that evidence suffice? Note that once the presumption of undue influence arises, a grantee must "prove by clear, satisfactory and convincing evidence that the grantee acted in good faith throughout the transaction and the grantor acted freely, intelligently, and voluntarily."[31] Will this usually be a reasonably simple thing to demonstrate?

Having explored the hard core of the doctrine, let's consider some of its most problematic (or perhaps tendentious) applications: In re Will of Moses and In re Kaufman's Will. After you read these cases, ask yourself if they are rightly decided. Why or why not? What do these cases demonstrate, if anything, about the undue-influence doctrine and its power and limitations? Would these two cases come out the same way today? Can you come up with some examples of cases that might be decided in similar fashion today, while receiving similar review a half century hence? Harder: Can you think of some examples of cases in which you, as a deciding justice, would be tempted to be in the majority finding undue influence, but nevertheless expect that, come 2066 or so, law-students born in 2042 are likely to consider you a hopeless Neanderthal? Is all of this avoidable? Why or why not?

In re Will of Moses[32] takes us to Mississippi in the 1960s. The case's facts are fairly straightforward, although the Mississippi Supreme Court split 5-4 on whether those facts supported a finding of undue influence. The testator was Mrs. Fannie Moses, who died on February 6, 1967, leaving behind an estate worth $125,000.[33] Mrs. Moses was "a strong personality" who blazed her own trail. She spent her career managing commercial property in Jackson and a 480-acre farm, and she continued to be the active manager of these properties until she died.

Mrs. Moses' personal life was distinct. Her strong-willed nature caused her to butt heads with her sisters. She was married three times; each ended with the death of her husband.[34] As she aged, she suffered from heart trouble and breast cancer, which required a mastectomy. During the '60s she—like much of the rest of the country—drank rather a lot.

Mrs. Moses (along with her second husband) met and befriended Clarence Holland. Holland was an attorney who eventually—the record

31. Jackson v. Schrader, 676 N.W.2d 599, 605 (Iowa 2003).
32. 227 So. 2d 829 (Miss. 1969).
33. For convenience' sake, multiply any figure arising before 1945 by 20, any figure arising before 1973 by 12, any figure before 1983 by 7 or 8, and any figure arising before 1990 by 2 to get some sense of present values. This is a *very* loose and inexact method—a rough attempt very broadly to incorporate not only book inflation, but a sense of general equalized-standard-of-living purchasing power—but it gives a general sense.
34. There was no suggestion that she had played any role in these deaths.

is unclear as to precisely when—took her on as a client. Her third husband also eventually became a friend of Holland's. Soon after that last husband died, Moses and Holland began seeing one another almost daily. Holland, who was fifteen years younger than Mrs. Moses, continued as her attorney throughout their romance, which ended with her death.

When Mrs. Moses died, two wills were proffered to the probate court. Under the first will, dated December 23, 1957, her elder sister was the primary beneficiary. Mrs. Moses had once lived with that sister and had declared on several occasions her intent to make the sister her testamentary beneficiary. The second will, tendered by Holland and dated May 26, 1964, revoked all former wills and left almost all of Moses' estate to Holland. The beneficiaries of the 1957 will, led by Moses' elder sister, claimed that the 1964 will had resulted from Holland's exercise of undue influence over Moses.

The circumstances surrounding the drafting of the 1964 will were important to the analysis of both the majority and the dissent. Uncontestedly, Mrs. Moses did not have Holland draft her will. Rather, Moses employed the services of Dan Shell, an attorney who knew Holland professionally, but who had no further connection to Holland and was unaware of Moses' relationship with him. At their only meeting, Shell asked about Moses's property, marital background, and children. When he learned she had neither a husband nor children, Shell asked for more specific descriptions of her properties for tax purposes and determined what dispositions she wanted to make.

After the meeting, he prepared a draft of the will and sent it to Moses. She called him to correct a mistake he had made in a disposition. He rewrote the will and mailed it to her. She came in shortly thereafter and executed it. Two or three years later, she gave the will and several other documents to another attorney, W. R. Patterson, for safekeeping.

The majority concluded that the fact of the relationship between Holland and Moses was *itself* sufficient to raise a presumption of undue influence. It then wrote:

IN RE WILL OF MOSES
227 So. 2d 829 (Miss. 1969)

[The presumption of undue influence] could be overcome only by evidence that, in making the 1964 will, Mrs. Moses had acted upon the independent advice and counsel of one entirely devoted to her interest.

Appellant [Holland] takes the position that there was undisputed evidence that Mrs. Moses, in making the 1964 will, did, in fact, have such advice and counsel. He relies upon the testimony of the attorney in whose office that document was prepared[35] to support his assertion. . . .

The attorney's testimony supports the chancellor's finding that nowhere in the conversations with Mrs. Moses was there touched upon in any way the proposed testamentary disposition whereby preference was to be given a nonrelative to the exclusion of her blood relatives. There was no discussion of her relationship with Holland, nor as to who her legal heirs might be, nor as to their relationship to her, after it was discovered that she had neither a husband nor children.

It is clear from his own testimony that, in writing the will, the attorney-draftsman, did no more than write down, according to the forms of law, what Mrs. Moses told him. There was no meaningful independent advice or counsel touching upon the area in question and it is manifest that the role of the attorney in writing the will, as it relates to the present issue, was little more than that of scrivener. The chancellor was justified in holding that this did not meet the burden nor overcome the presumption.

In Croft v. Alder, 237 Miss. 713, 724, 115 So.2d 683, 686 (1959), . . . [t]his Court said:

> [T]he law watches with the greatest jealously transactions between persons in confidential relations and will not permit them to stand, unless the circumstances demonstrate the fullest deliberation on the part of the testator and the most abundant good faith on the part of the beneficiary. Hence the law presumes the existence of undue influence, and such dealings are prima facie void, and will be so held "unless the guardian show by clearest proof" that he took no advantage over the testator, and the cestui's act was a result of his own volition and upon the fullest deliberation. . . .

From its very nature, evidence to show undue influence must be largely circumstantial. Undue influence is an intangible thing, which only rarely is susceptible of direct or positive proof. As was stated in Jamison v. Jamison, 1909, 96 Miss. 288, 51 So. 130, "the only positive and affirmative proof required is of facts and circumstances from which the undue influence may be reasonably inferred." . . .

---

35. [That is, Dan Shell.–Ed.]

In Jamison v. Jamison, 1909, 96 Miss. 288, 298, 51 So. 130, 131, it was said:

The difficulty is also enhanced by the fact, universally recognized, that he who seeks to use undue influence does so in privacy. He seldom uses brute force or open threats to terrorize his intended victim, and if he does he is careful that no witnesses are about to take note of and testify to the fact. He observes, too, the same precautions if he seeks by cajolery, flattery, or other methods to obtain power and control over the will of another, and direct it improperly to the accomplishment of the purpose which he desires. Subscribing witnesses are called to attest the execution of wills, and testify as to the testamentary capacity of the testator, and the circumstances attending the immediate execution of the instrument; but they are not called upon to testify as to the antecedent agencies by which the execution of the paper was secured, even if they had any knowledge of them, which they seldom have. . . .

In Croft, supra, this Court quoted the rule . . . as follows: . . .

Although the mere existence of confidential relations between a testator and a beneficiary under his will does not raise a presumption that the beneficiary exercised undue influence over the testator, . . . such consequence follows where the beneficiary "has been actively concerned in some way with the preparation or execution of the will, or where the relationship is coupled with some suspicious circumstances, such as mental infirmity of the testator;" . . .

Holland, of course, did not personally participate in the actual preparation or execution of the will. If he had, under the circumstances in evidence, unquestionably the will could not stand. It may be assumed that Holland, as a lawyer, knew this. . . .

[U]ndue influence will be presumed where the beneficiary "has been actively concerned in some way with the preparation or execution of the will, or where the relationship is coupled with some suspicious circumstances, such as mental infirmity of the testator."

Undue influence operates upon the will as well as upon the mind. It is not dependent upon a lack of testamentary capacity.

The chancellor's finding that the will was the product of Holland's undue influence is not inconsistent with his conclusion that "Her (Mrs. Moses') mind was capable of understanding the essential matters necessary to the execution of her will on May 26, 1964, at the time of such execution." A weak or infirm mind may, of course, be more easily over persuaded. In the case under review, Mrs. Moses was in ill health, she was an alcoholic, and was an aging woman infatuated with a young lover, 15 years her junior, who was also her lawyer. If this combination of circumstances cannot be said to support the view that Mrs. Moses suffered from a "weakness or infirmity" of mind, vis-a-vis Holland, it was hardly calculated to enhance her power of will where he was concerned. . . .

The sexual morality of the personal relationship is not an issue. However, the intimate nature of this relationship is relevant to the present inquiry to the extent that its existence, under the circumstances, warranted an inference of undue influence, extending and augmenting that which flowed from the attorney-client relationship. . . .

The rule laid down in Croft, supra, would have little, if any, practical worth, if, under circumstances such as those established in this case, it could be nullified by a mere showing that the beneficiary was not physically present when the will was prepared and executed.

The rule that where a fiduciary relationship has been established, a presumption of undue influence arises, is not limited to holographs, nor confined to wills otherwise prepared by the testator himself. It encompasses with equal force wills written for the testator by a third person. There is no sound reason supporting the view that a testator, whose will has become subservient to the undue influence of another, is purged of the effects of that influence merely because the desired testamentary document is prepared by an attorney who knows nothing of the antecedent circumstances. . . .

[I]t cannot be said that the chancellor was manifestly wrong in finding that Holland occupied a dual fiduciary relationship with respect to Mrs. Moses, both conventional and actual, attended by suspicious circumstances as set forth in his opinion, which gave rise to a presumption of undue influence in the production of the 1964 will, nor that he was manifestly wrong in finding that this presumption was not overcome by "clearest proof" that in making and executing the will Mrs. Moses acted upon her "own volition and upon the fullest deliberation," or upon independent advice and counsel of one wholly devoted to her interest. . . .

So, the majority found that the relationship itself raised a presumption of undue influence, largely because it was both a fiduciary relationship (attorney-client) and a sexual one. The burden then fell on Holland to rebut that presumption. His efforts to do so did not impress the majority.

The dissenting justices, naturally, disagreed with both propositions. They believed that the relationship between Holland and Moses was not enough to raise a presumption of undue influence under Mississippi law (specifically, the *Croft* decision cited by the majority). But even if it did, the dissenters were satisfied with Holland's efforts to rebut the presumption. Their opinion follows:

I am unable to agree with the majority of the Court that Mrs. Moses should not be allowed to dispose of her property as she so clearly intended.

Since 1848 it has been the law of this state that every person twenty-one years of age, male or female, married or unmarried, being of sound and disposing mind, has the power by last will and testament or codicil in writing to dispose of all of his or her worldly possessions as he or she sees fit. . . .

No matter what the form of the instrument, if it represented the free, voluntary and knowledgeable act of the testator or testatrix it was a good will, and the directions of the will should be followed. We said in Gillis v. Smith, 114 Miss. 665, 75 So. 451 (1917):

> A man of sound mind may execute a will or a deed from any sort of motive satisfactory to him, whether that motive be love, affection, gratitude, partiality, prejudice, or even a whim or caprice. . . .

Mrs. Fannie T. Moses was 54 years of age when she executed her last will and testament on May 26, 1964, leaving most of her considerable estate to Clarence H. Holland, her good friend, but a man fifteen years her junior. She had been married three times, and each of these marriages was dissolved by the death of her husband. Holland's friendship with Mrs. Moses dated back to the days of her second husband, Robert L. Dickson. He was also a friend of her third husband, Walter Moses. . . .

The chancellor found that she was of sound and disposing mind and memory on May 26, 1964, when she executed her last will and testament, and I think he was correct in this finding.

The chancellor found that there was a confidential relationship between Mrs. Moses and Holland, who had acted as her attorney in the past, and who was, in addition, a close and intimate friend, and that because of this relationship and some suspicious circumstances a presumption of undue influence arose. . . .

There is no proof in this voluminous record that Holland ever did or said anything to Mrs. Moses about devising her property to anybody, much less him. It is conceded that in the absence of the presumption of undue influence that there is no basis to support a finding that Holland exercised undue influence over Mrs. Moses. This being true, the first question to be decided is whether the presumption of undue influence arises under the circumstances of this case.

It is my opinion that the presumption did not arise. The fact, alone, that a confidential relationship existed between Holland and Mrs. Moses is not sufficient to give rise to the presumption of undue influence in a will case. We said in Croft, supra:

> Such consequence follows where the beneficiary 'has been actively concerned in some way with the preparation or execution of the will, or where the relationship is coupled with some suspicious circumstances, such as mental infirmity of the testator;' or where the beneficiary in the confidential relation was active directly in preparing the will or procuring its execution, and obtained under it a substantial benefit. . . .

It was not contended in this case that Holland was in any way actively concerned with the preparation or execution of the will. Appellees rely solely upon the finding of the chancellor that there were suspicious circumstances. However, the suspicious circumstances listed by the chancellor in his opinion had nothing whatsoever to do with the preparation or execution of the will. These were remote antecedent circumstances having to do with the meretricious relationship of the parties, and the fact that at times Mrs. Moses drank to excess and could be termed an alcoholic, but there is no proof in this long record that her use of alcohol affected her will power or her ability to look after her extensive real estate holdings. It is common knowledge that many persons who could be termed alcoholics, own, operate and manage large business enterprises with success. The fact that she chose to leave most of her property to the man she loved in preference to her sisters and brother is not such an unnatural disposition of her property as to render it invalid. . . .

In this case, there were no suspicious circumstances surrounding the preparation or execution of the will, and in my opinion the chancellor was wrong in so holding. However, even if it be conceded that the presumption of undue influence did arise, this presumption was overcome by clear and convincing evidence of good faith, full knowledge and independent consent and advice.

When she got ready to make her will she called Honorable Dan H. Shell for an appointment. Shell did not know her, although he remembered that he had handled a land transaction for her third husband, Walter Moses, some years before. Shell had been in the active practice of law in Jackson since 1945; he was an experienced attorney with a large and varied practice.

The chancellor hearing this case said of him in his written opinion:

Mr. Dan H. Shell is a highly reputable attorney. His integrity is unquestioned. This Court believes Mr. Shell's testimony, and finds that the circumstances surrounding the drawing of the instrument dated May 26, 1964, are exactly as he stated them from the witness stand. He testified that Mrs. Moses gave him the impression that she knew exactly what she was doing, and that there was no indication of outside influence. . . .

The majority was indeed hard put to find fault with [Shell's] actions on behalf of his client. It is easy for us who are removed from the active practice of law to criticize our brethren who are "on the firing line." The question is, did he do all that was reasonably required of him to represent his client in the preparation of her will. He was not required to be perfect, nor was he required to meet a standard of exact precision. He ascertained that Mrs. Moses was competent to make a will; he satisfied himself that she was acting of her own free will and accord, and that she was disposing of her property exactly as she wished and intended. No more is required. . . .

Shell was asked the direct question:

Q. Now in connection with the drawing of this will, what did Clarence Holland have to do with that?
He answered:
A. Not one thing on earth.
Shell was asked:
Q. From that time up until the time of her death, did you ever discuss the matter with him?
A. About his being a devisee under the will, or even writing a will?
Q. Yes.
He answered:
A. No. That was none of his business, as far as I was concerned. It was confidential between Mrs. Moses and myself.

In the majority opinion there are extensive quotations from Croft v. Alder, 237 Miss. 713, 115 So.2d 683 (1959) . . . . In Croft the Court was very careful to define and limit the suspicious circumstances that must exist, in addition to the confidential relationship, to even raise the presumption of undue influence. The specific examples listed were where the beneficiary actively participated in the preparation of the will, actually drafted it, or assisted in its execution. . . .

Mrs. Moses was 54 years old (Alder was 87) when she executed her will. She went alone to the law office of an independent, capable and experienced attorney. She herself told him how she wanted to devise her property. This was on March 31, 1964. After she had pointed out an error in the first draft to Mr. Shell he corrected and rewrote the will and mailed it to her on May 21, 1964. She went alone to his office on May 26, 1964, and signed her last will in the presence of two disinterested witnesses. Almost two months had elapsed between her first conference with Shell and the actual execution of the will.

There is not one iota of testimony in this voluminous record that Clarence Holland even knew of this will, much less that he participated in the preparation or execution of it. The evidence is all to the contrary. The evidence is undisputed that she executed her last will after the fullest deliberation, with full knowledge of what she was doing, and with the independent consent and advice of an experienced and competent attorney whose sole purpose was to advise with her and prepare her will exactly as she wanted it. . . .

What else could she have done? She met all the tests that this Court and other courts have carefully outlined and delineated. The majority opinion says that this still was not enough, that there were "suspicious circumstances" and "antecedent agencies", but even these were not connected in any shape, form or fashion with the preparation or execution of her will. They had to do with her love life and her drinking habits and propensities.

It would appear that the new procedure will be to fine-tooth comb all the events of a person's life and if, in the mind of the judge on the bench at that particular time, there are any "suspicious circumstances" or "antecedent agencies" in that person's life even though they are in nowise connected with the preparation or execution of that person's will, such last will and testament will be set aside and held for naught. . . .

If full knowledge, deliberate and voluntary action, and independent consent and advice have not been proved in this case, then they just cannot be proved. We should be bound by the uncontradicted testimony in the record; we should not go completely outside the record and guess, speculate and surmise as to what happened.

I think that the judgment of the lower court should be reversed and the last will and testament of Fannie T. Moses executed on May 26, 1964, admitted to probate in solemn form.

* * *

As you can see, the main difference between the majority and dissent opinions in *Moses* is their interpretation of the effect of the relationship between Holland and Moses. Was the relationship sufficient to raise a presumption of undue influence? If it was, did Holland have his claws so deep in Moses that the circumstances surrounding the challenged will could not rebut that presumption? Or did the majority disapprove of the extramarital relationship—or perhaps of some other aspects of the situation—so strongly that Holland never had a chance?

Will of Moses is far from the only case in which judges may have cloaked personal moral judgments in the language of undue influence. In re Will of Kaufmann[36] provides another potential example. Like *Moses*, the *Kaufmann* court rendered a split decision, finding undue influence by a 3-2 margin.

Kaufmann plunges us into the family affairs of the rich, famous and— by early-'60s' lights—scandalous. The decedent, Robert D. Kaufmann, was a scion of the family behind the Kay Jewelers company;[37] his father had launched the business, in which his three sons—Joel, Aron, and Robert—had inherited equal interests. When Robert died in 1959, he was a millionaire with a substantial income; his method of disposing of his fortune launched this case.

Robert had not troubled himself with financial or business affairs in his formative years. For most of his life, he was content to let his brother Joel handle his affairs, which Joel did free of charge.[38] This turned out well for Robert, who amassed a large fortune and substantial income without any effort of his own.

Up through 1947, Robert lived with Joel in Washington D.C. and became very fond of his two nephews, Richard and Lee.[39] But in late 1947 or early 1948, at 34, Robert moved to New York City to live independently. In rapid succession, Robert found his own apartment and met Walter Weiss, a man of 39.

Weiss was a nonpracticing attorney; little else is revealed about him by the case. In any event, shortly after they met, Robert retained Weiss as his "financial advisor and business consultant" in exchange for $10,000 annually (which Robert paid diligently until he died).[40] Soon thereafter, Robert transferred his financial records and accounts from Washington—where family employees had kept them at no expense—to

---

36. 247 N.Y.S.2d 664 (N.Y. App. Div. 1964).

37. You've likely heard the commercials, the tagline of which for decades has been "every kiss begins with Kay" diamonds. Given this case, are the commercials in perhaps even worse taste than originally suspected? Or perhaps a bit of Freudian acknowledgement? The world may never know.

38. Aron doesn't factor into this drama much. He was an invalid, and presumably Joel handled his affairs too. Joel, as you'll see later, did yeoman service for his brothers, and—to hear the majority tell the story—never really received recognition for it.

39. Joel's boys.

40. The majority finds it quite ominous—and germane—that Weiss drafted this employment agreement, which also gave Weiss the unilateral right to revoke it. Consider as you read further whether this baleful attention is warranted, and why or why not?

New York, and the dynamic duo established offices as financial consultants. Robert was the money behind the office and Weiss the brains. But over their ten-year partnership, they earned no fees and made only one investment, in a garage-construction enterprise headed by Weiss's brother that ended in a total loss.

But the relationship between Robert and Weiss was not primarily focused on the business. Weiss moved into Robert's apartment in 1949, and they lived together until Robert's death. Weiss took charge of maintaining the house and managing the help. The two men weren't homebodies; they traveled quite extensively in the '50s, mostly on Robert's dime.[41] And Robert continued to give Weiss more influence in his life. He gave Weiss drawing power on all his bank accounts, made him his attorney-in-fact, and made him either primary or secondary beneficiary on life insurance accounts worth $100,000.

The rest of the family was not enamored of Weiss, or of Robert's ever-closer relationship with him. Despite Weiss' best efforts to ingratiate himself, the rest of the Kaufmanns rejected him. Joel and Weiss particularly disliked one another. Their distaste came to a head in late 1953, when a dispute arose regarding a merger of Kay Jewelers with the Fairfax Company. On Weiss's advice, Robert objected to the merger and sought an appraisal of his shares. The dispute ended when Robert was bought out for $70,000 more than he would have made under the objected-to arrangement.

Despite his family's feelings toward Weiss, Robert clearly relied heavily on him, and continued to give Weiss an ever-increasing share in his estate. This process began when Robert wrote his first will in 1950. The 1950 will bestowed most of his estate on family, friends, and charities, leaving to Weiss only the stock in the garage-construction enterprise and a cancellation of any debts he owed to Robert.

In 1951 Robert executed a new will that increased Weiss's share in his estate to over $500,000 and made him one of three executors. Robert also drafted and signed a letter explaining why he had devised a substantial portion of the estate to someone outside the family. According to the letter, Robert's outlook on life had been "approaching the nadir" when he met Weiss;[42] he had been tremendously unhappy, emotional, and afraid. Per the remainder of the letter:

---

41. During discovery, Weiss claimed he paid his share of travel expenses, but the majority dismisses that claim because there is "no evidence other than his declaration on that score."

42. The letter claims that Robert met Weiss in 1946, when the record indicates that they met in 1948. Keep this discrepancy in mind, as the majority finds it important.

Walter gave me the courage to start something which slowly but eventually permitted me to supply for myself everything my life had heretofore lacked: an outlet for my long-latent but strong creative ability in painting[,]. . . a balanced, healthy sex life which before had been spotty, furtive and destructive; an ability to reorientate myself to actual life and to face it calmly and realistically. All of this adds up to Peace of Mind—and what a delight, what a relief after so many wasted, dark, groping, fumbling immature years to be reborn and become adult!

I am eternally grateful to my dearest friend—best pal, Walter A. Weiss. What could be more wonderful than a fruitful, contented life and who more deserving of gratitude now, in the form of an inheritance, than the person who helped most in securing that life? I cannot believe my family could be anything else but glad and happy for my own comfortable self-determination and contentment and equally grateful to the friend who made it possible.

Love to you all,

Bob

In 1952, Robert executed another document, which gave Weiss medical power of attorney, exclusive power over his corporeal remains, and the authority to make all funeral arrangements. The document gave Weiss authority to act as "though he were [Robert's] nearest relative" and declared "that his instructions and consents shall be controlling, regardless of who may object to them." This document, along with the 1951 letter, accompanied all of Robert's subsequent wills.

Those wills continued to give Weiss more authority and a greater share in Robert's estate, at the expense of Robert's family. By 1958, Weiss was effectively the sole beneficiary and executor of Robert's estate. Robert died in 1959, soon after executing this final will, in a fire at his Key West home that began while he slept, having taken prescription sleeping aids. Walter introduced the 1958 will for probate, which led to the following decision:

IN RE WILL OF KAUFMANN

247 N.Y.S.2d 664 (N.Y. App. Div. 1964)

[Majority] Opinion

. . . It cannot be doubted that prior to 1948 Robert was dependent on Joel in financial matters; that Robert was not involved in decision making; he had shown no interest in such involvement; that he was warmly attached to his family and had no serious differences with them. . . .

Shortly after taking up with Weiss, Robert's financial records were transferred from Washington to New York; Robert employed Weiss as financial adviser, and they launched the venture of financial consultants. . . . There is no evidence of any particular qualifications on the part of Weiss in financial matters; there is no suggestion of any practical reason for assuming the burden and expense of the maintenance of records in New York and the transaction of business away from the center of the family financial activities in Washington. There is no realistic expectancy of any demand for the services of either Robert or Weiss as financial consultants. On the other hand, these activities may have served to inspire Robert with a false feeling of accomplishment and independence. . . .

If Weiss successfully persuaded Robert that he was achieving independence when, in fact, Weiss was extending and exploiting Robert's dependence and estranging Robert from his family, then he violated his undertaking and the issue is presented whether the instrument offered for probate is a product of the breach of faith. . . .

The letter of 1951 fixes the year 1946 as the year of meeting between Robert and Weiss. The record evidence is that this event occurred in 1948. The anticipation of their meeting by more than one year is significant in that it was during 1947 and before Robert met Weiss that Robert took up and commenced his career in art. . . .

The 1951 letter is not based on reality. Robert had become aware of his desire to paint, had received instruction and had started painting prior to his meeting with Weiss. The will of 1950 provides for a bequest of $ 2,500 to Leo Steppat "my art teacher". Weiss had nothing to do with Robert's creative ability in painting. In attributing to Weiss the "start [of] something which slowly but eventually permitted me to supply for myself everything my life had heretofore lacked: an outlet for my long-latent but strong creative ability in painting", the letter is not in accord with the record. . . .

The letter refers to the "courage" acquired from Weiss "to supply for myself [. . .] a balanced, healthy sex life which before had been spotty, furtive and destructive". The implication is that Weiss in some fashion was identified with Robert's sex life. . . .

To the extent that the letter implies or suggests a marked improvement of a previously disoriented and fearful personality, it is again at odds with reality as will appear.

Assuming, however, the content of the letter, it completely fails to explain the extent of the testamentary gift to Weiss tantamount to over a half million dollars. . . .

The emotional base reflected in the letter of June 13, 1951 is gratitude utterly unreal, highly exaggerated and pitched to a state of fervor and ecstasy. . . .

Robert was endowed with a good mind, sensitivity, artistic ability and generous disposition. He earnestly sought independence. However, he had no prior experience in assuming responsibility; all decisions had been made for him. He sought help and direction to satisfy his drive for independence. He turned to Weiss for that help. Weiss acknowledges he was originally retained by Robert "to represent him and to handle his affairs and to help him be independent so that he could take his affairs unto himself."

The arrangement was not one of master and servant or principal and agent; it was a confidential relationship more in the nature of teacher and pupil in the area of finance with specific application to the resources and assets of Robert. It had a very ominous inception. The agreement dated June 15, 1948 prepared by Weiss, a lawyer by training, obligated Robert for one year, provided for annual compensation of $ 10,000, . . . and was terminable at the option of Weiss on one week's notice . . . . This one-sided agreement may, perhaps, be justified on the premise that Weiss was entitled to make the best bargain and was not then under any legal obligation to protect Robert. Weiss' attitude did not augur well for the qualities of fairness and loyalty required on his part to achieve Robert's desire for the capacity to be independent in matters of business.

The record is barren of evidence of Weiss' prior training or experience as a financial advisor or business consultant. We know that apart from his intrusion upon the various enterprises of the Kaufmann family the two proposals he espoused were dismal failures and caused Robert substantial losses and expenses. The Multi-Deck business involved a loss of $ 120,000. The partnership formed by Weiss and Robert to conduct the business of business consultants and advisors never acquired a client and resulted in much expense to Robert. . . .

Weiss and Robert lived together from 1949 to the date of Robert's death. Robert gave Weiss his unbounded confidence and trust. Weiss exploited Robert, induced him to transfer to him the stewardship formerly exercised by Joel, increased Robert's need for dependency, prevented and curtailed associations which threatened his absolute control of Robert and alienated him from his family. . . .

Weiss was responsible for the displacement of the attorneys who prepared the 1950 will; he introduced Robert to Garrison who prepared the instrument offered for probate. Weiss recommended the doctors who treated Robert; he employed all help who came in contact with Robert. Mail and telephone communications were routed through Weiss. Family mail at times was destroyed and did not reach Robert. Correspondence purporting to be from Robert was dictated by Weiss.

Weiss saw to it none other than himself took advantage of Robert. Weiss warned Mapson, Robert's companion on [a trip to Paris], not to take advantage of Robert during their stay in Paris in 1953. Finally, Weiss arrived in Paris unannounced and in the presence of Robert, who stood by mutely, told Mapson to remove himself. Robert attempted to maintain secretly his contact with Mapson in New York but was found out by Weiss who physically intervened. Again Robert submitted silently.

Anne McDonnell, the housekeeper and cook, testified Weiss was master of the household and brooked no interference from Robert. She also testified there were occasions when Weiss insisted that Robert sign papers without opportunity to read them and that Robert complied.

Watkins, a banker friend of Robert's father, testified he talked at length with Robert about the Fairfax matter. On one occasion Weiss was present and did all the talking while Robert was mute. On another occasion Watkins was alone with Robert and his only response was: "That's the way Walter [Weiss] wants it."

Robert perceptibly lost weight during the latter years, in part due to a low cholesterol diet. He became disinterested in his attire and appearance. After 1950 he received extensive psychiatric treatment, the nature of which does not appear.

In 1955 Robert complained of inability to sleep. His inability to sleep continued until his death. He took large quantities of pills for the condition. . . . He was unable to sleep without medication. On April 18, 1959, asleep at his home in Key West, Robert died in a fire which destroyed the house.

The record is replete with financial matters pertaining to Robert's interest in family investments. The suggestion is that Robert became estranged from his family because of financial matters. The jury could have found that Robert did not wish to be concerned with matters of business; that the differences based thereon were introduced by Weiss for the purpose of causing a breach between Robert and his family.

Significant is the unconcern with which Robert accepted the loss of $120,000 in the Multi-Deck venture promoted by Weiss. . . . The Fairfax matter in the final analysis involved considerably less than Multi-Deck. If Robert was affected by monetary considerations, then his continued reliance on Weiss after 1956 in the light of the Multi-Deck debacle is unexplained.

Robert and Weiss lived lavishly, travelled and entertained extensively. Despite the scale of living, which would appear to have been at the expense of Robert, and the ill-advised, financial ventures, he left an estate of over one million dollars.

Also significant are the provisions for members of Robert's family, his friends, his art teacher, his father's secretary and organizations in the wills of Robert prior to 1958 during the pendency of the Fairfax litigation. Other than Joel, none of the omitted beneficiaries were identified with the Fairfax litigation.

The record demonstrates overwhelmingly that Robert retained until his untimely death great affection for his nephews, warmth toward and, at times, to the evident chagrin of Weiss, considerable concern for the health and good opinion of Joel. . . .

The record becomes clear if it is viewed in the light of a skillfully executed plan by Weiss to gain the confidence of Robert, displace Joel as manager of his financial affairs, assume control of Robert's bank accounts, safe-deposit box, household and property as if it were his. The only impediment against completely relieving Robert of his worldly goods was the circumstance that his investments in the main were closely tied in with those of Joel and his brother Aron. To overtly seize Robert's property would risk a challenge by his family. So long as Robert was under his control and influence, Weiss was assured of a life of ease and luxury. He, therefore, need only direct Robert toward making him his principal beneficiary in the event of his death. This he could do without the knowledge of the family. The result was to be substantiated by written declarations of Robert assigning reasons for the unnatural disposition.

On June 13, 1951 Robert purported to explain the will of that day with substantial provisions for Weiss on the basis of gratitude. In June, 1952 Weiss was made beneficiary as to the bulk of Robert's life insurance. The latter transaction is unsupported by any written explanation by Robert. In June, 1958 the ultimate testamentary disposition to Weiss is explained by the writing of Robert on the basis of the Fairfax suit. . . .

One may make testamentary disposition of his worldly goods as he pleases. The motives and vagaries or morality of the testator are not determinative provided the will is the free and voluntary disposition of the testator and is not the product of deceit. There are two principal categories of undue influence in the law of wills, the forms of which are circumscribed only by the ingenuity and resourcefulness of man. One class is the gross, obvious and palpable type of undue influence which does not destroy the intent or will of the testator but prevents it from being exercised by force and threats of harm to the testator or those close to him.[43] The other class is the insidious, subtle and impalpable kind which subverts the intent or will of the testator, internalizes within the mind of the testator the desire to do that which is not his intent but the intent and end of another. . . .

We are concerned with the testamentary mind, intent and purpose of Robert on June 19, 1958, when the instrument offered for probate was executed. To what extent Weiss affected Robert's mind and whether, if at all, he influenced his testamentary intent can only be determined upon a close examination of the interaction between the two over the course of the period between 1948 and the time of death, April 18, 1959. When the influence, if any, is ascertained, we can then address ourselves to the question whether it was within legally permissible bounds or exceeded them and was therefore undue influence.

The weight of the evidence is that in 1948 Robert was 34, educated, unmarried, personable, wealthy, interested in art, and otherwise not particularly occupied. Prior to 1948 he had lived with his brother Joel in Washington; he was particularly fond of Joel's two children, Lee and Richard, who were his only nephews. His immediate family consisted of his brothers Joel and Aron. Aron was unmarried and an invalid. Joel had assumed the burden of managing the family fortune. . . . Robert enjoyed a substantial income; he had no business responsibilities and no expense so far as the conduct of his financial affairs. . . . He had no experience or training in affairs of business or finance. For reasons which do not appear, Robert at this time was possessed of the desire to act independently in business matters. Robert employed Weiss for the purpose of advising him in financial matters so that he could proceed independently. . . .

Weiss exploited the arrangement to advance his own selfish interests.

Appellant [Weiss] does not seriously urge that the change of the life insurance beneficiaries, the various gifts and the prior wills may not have been influenced by Weiss. He strenuously urges that the evidence fails to show he influenced the will of June 19, 1958.

---

43. [Just as an aside, is the majority talking about a form of undue influence here, or duress?—ED.]

The first of the four wills in which provision is made for Weiss is dated June 13, 1951. The letter signed by Robert the same day is cogent evidence of his complete domination by Weiss. Its exposure, implications and distortions can be understood only as an attempt to justify what is obviously unnatural and utterly inconsistent with reality and what the record establishes was the warm and close relation between Robert and his family. Apart from the content of the letter, two significant factors are present: a change from the attorneys who prepared the 1950 will and the substantial provisions for Weiss. The letter came into existence long before the Fairfax affair and evidences the presence of forces operating on Robert's mind in favor of Weiss to the detriment of Robert's family. The same forces continued to operate with ever-increasing potency to the date of Robert's death and at all times in favor of Weiss and against Robert's family and ultimately against his friends and persons who had served him faithfully. . . .

The record enabled the jury to find that the instrument of June 19, 1958 was the end result of an unnatural, insidious influence operating on a weak-willed, trusting, inexperienced Robert whose natural warm family attachment had been attenuated by false accusations against Joel, subtle flattery suggesting an independence he had not realized and which, in fact, Weiss had stultified, and planting in Robert's mind the conviction that Joel and other members of the family were resentful of and obstructing his drive for independence.

The fact that the instrument offered for probate was prepared by reputable, competent attorneys is a relevant circumstance but does not preclude a finding that the undue influence here involved was active, potent and unaffected by the interposition of independent counsel. . . .

If Weiss was in Europe at the times he became beneficiary of the life insurance policies and at the times when the four wills were executed in which he is named, and Robert was living in New York near or with his family, much of the argument made by counsel for appellant would be compelling. . . . "[T]here are certain cases in which the law indulges in the presumption that undue influence has been used, and those cases are . . . a will . . . of . . . a ward in favor of his guardian, or any person in favor of his priest or religious adviser, or where other close confidential relationships exist." [Marx v. McGlynn, 88 N.Y. 357.]

Here, the circumstances spell out a confidential relation between proponent and the decedent which gave rise to an obligation on the part of the proponent-devisee to offer an explanation. The language of this court in Matter of Satterlee (281 App. Div. 251, 254) is apropos: "Surely, in the light of the unusual setting and the highly fiduciary relationship which proponent had assumed toward decedent, it was incumbent on him to come forward and explain his becoming the principal beneficiary under her will.". . .

The record overwhelmingly sustains the verdict on undue influence on the basis of the charge made.

The decree denying probate of the instrument dated June 19, 1958 should be affirmed, with costs to respondents payable out of the estate.. . .

[Dissenting Opinion]

It is elementary that the statutory right of a competent person to dispose of his property as he wishes may not be thwarted by disappointed relatives nor by jurors who think that the testator used bad judgment or was misled.

Undue influence is a fact which must be proved by the contestant and not merely assumed to exist. . . . Like any other fact, it may be proved by substantial evidence but the circumstances must lead to it not only by fair inference but as a necessary conclusion. To avoid the will of a competent testator on the ground of undue influence, the contestant must show facts entirely inconsistent with the hypothesis of the execution of the will by any means other than undue influence. . . .

A mere showing of opportunity and even of a motive to exercise undue influence does not justify a submission of that issue to the jury, unless there is in addition evidence that such influence was actually utilized. . . .

The verdict in this case rests upon surmise, suspicion, conjecture and moral indignation and resentment, not upon the legally required proof of undue influence; and it cannot stand.

The record shows that the testator was intelligent and generally healthy. The evidence that he lost weight was explained by his doctor who said that he had placed him upon a no-fat diet. True, the testator was not wholly like other people. He had little zest for business, which fact set him apart from his family. He had artistic ability, and particularly loved to paint. So did Weiss. They had common interests. Testator felt and said that he had uncommon ability as a painter and that some day he would be known for his artistic work. In this, he was not wholly wrong, for it appears that eighty museums have accepted his work for permanent display.

The record is replete with evidence of the friendly relation, indeed love and affection, that existed between testator and Weiss for a decade. There is no substantial evidence that their relationship was not one of mutual esteem and self-respect. The isolated incidents of testator bowing to Weiss' wishes on certain occasions over this period fall far short of conclusively pointing to a subserviency, when viewed in the light of all the evidence. True, testator relied upon Weiss in business and administrative matters, but that is not to say that testator was not essentially in command. There is evidence that at times testator made his own business decisions. The fact that Weiss advised testator in his business dealings with his brothers is not inconsistent with his position as testator's financial advisor. Moreover, the record shows that under the proposed Fairfax deal testator's brother Joel was to be paid more per share than the testator, which the testator did not like, and that by reason of testator's lawsuit against his brother, testator collected about $ 70,000 more than he had been offered. Certainly, that affords no ground for suspicion of Weiss. The testator did not overlook his nephews; and the evidence shows that in 1955 at a time when he changed his will the testator had spent considerable money refurbishing Aunt Birdie's apartment; and chided his brothers with reference to their lack of concern for her. Substantial evidence also shows that for years prior to his death testator acted normally in his outward relations toward Weiss and other people in Weiss' presence. And within a few weeks of his death, in Key West, Florida, when Weiss wanted to return to New York City testator declined to do so at the time, and Weiss came on to New York alone. Such conduct on the part of the testator by no means permits of "a necessary conclusion" that the testator was dominated by Weiss. Although testator placed confidence in Weiss, the relationship was not that of attorney and client, and Weiss had no part, directly at least, in the preparation and execution of these wills. . . .

The letter written by testator on June 13, 1951 . . . and placed with his will of that date, and later reviewed with his attorney and placed with later wills, shows the regard which testator had for Weiss. This letter appears to lay bare the fact and prove the suspicion which members of testator's family had of the intimate relationship which existed between the two men. . . .

The issue in this case is not what were the morals of these men, nor whether testator led a normal life. . . . The issue is, does the propounded instrument represent the intrinsic wishes and will of the testator, or was it the product of the command of Weiss which the testator did not really want to follow, but was unable to resist?...

Every act of the testator from. . . . June 13, 1951, to the time of his death was consistent with what he expressed in that letter. Contestants' argument that Weiss induced testator to write said letter . . . to build a case for leaving his estate to Weiss, does not ring true. It is not reasonable that the letter would have contained the candid statement about sex, if it were written for such ulterior motive. It is true that contestants claim that at every stage testator was dominated by Weiss; but the period of time alone negates that claim. . . . The record shows that for years testator had business differences with his brother Joel; and it shows also that he rarely saw his relatives in the years in question. In the meantime his attachment for Weiss apparently grew; and testator openly proclaimed his friendship for Weiss. In [the letter] testator expressed for the eventual information of his relatives why he wished to leave his assets to Weiss. As far as the motive is concerned the relationship may be likened to that of one who has a mistress. Morals aside, upon the facts in this case "Proof of the circumstance that the will was an unnatural one is lacking." . . . [T]he moral law may not be substituted for the law of wills; and it should not be overlooked that difficult cases tend to make bad law. Undoubtedly the testator was influenced, but the evidence in this case is entirely consistent with the complete lack of undue influence. Yet, because of the suspicious circumstances involved, the majority of this court as well as the court below would deny him his legal right to dispose of his property as he has chosen to do. . . .

The decree appealed from should therefore be reversed, with costs to all parties appearing separately and filing briefs, payable out of the estate, and the matter remitted to the Surrogate's Court with directions to admit the will to probate.[44]

---

44. [This unhappy saga did not end with this case. The result of the decision above was to render invalid, by reason of undue influence, the *final* of Robert's wills, the one that had left everything to Weiss. The will prior to that would still have left about half of his estate to Weiss. Robert's brother Joel planned to contest *that* will, too, on the same grounds, because even that will would have given a significant amount of Kay Jewelers (and other family business) stock to Weiss and would have put him on the board of the company – a result that Joel wished very much to avoid. And so Joel prepared further battle. All this warring was costly, both to the contestants and to the estate itself, which found itself obliged to participate in the struggle. To fund the estate's participation in the second suit, the executor of the estate found himself obliged to petition the court for permission to sell some of the estate's Kay Jewelers stock. The court approved and set a minimum price for the stock. Joel was the only bidder, and so the stock sold for the minimum price—which all parties appeared to agree was less than the market price. Then Joel resold the stock to the company (of which he was president) at something like market price, recouping in the transaction a significant portion of his personal expenses in the cost of contesting the will against Weiss in the first trial. Weiss, who owned some Kay stock independently, filed a shareholder's derivative suit, challenging the sale by Joel to the company at a higher price as a breach of Joel's fiduciary duty

QUESTIONS & ANALYSIS

What is to be made of this case? Do you think it likely that the case would come out the same way today? Why or why not? If you have strong feelings about the outcome in the case, take the opportunity to polish your advocacy skills by trying to build the opponent's case. Which facts work best in constructing that case? Which worked for or against that case in 1964 but would play no role today? Do you see any facts that seemed to support one of the opinions that would likely support the *opposite* conclusion today? Relatedly, why is a case on specific facts similar to these unlikely to arise anymore?

Weiss and Kaufmann really did make some fairly basic mistakes that provide the majority some plausible footing for its theory: that the wily Weiss was taking advantage of the weak-willed Kaufmann. The failure to get independent counsel from the start was a serious one. The total loss of the parking-structure investment was surely unfortunate, and the clientless financial-services firm is strange. Beyond that, though, doesn't most of this case read like the case of a married couple: some arguments (and perhaps some straying) in the relationship; trouble with the in-laws and a sense by those in-laws that the marriage partner might be somewhat overbearing, etc.? To the extent that this is true, is this case really an expression of the court's dislike of the couple's sexuality? Is the decision of the court a sort of drawn-out enactment of historical stereotypes of gays as either conniving or weak-willed? Or is it an honest attempt by the court to enact the morality inherent in the law of the time (remembering that gay sex was everywhere illegal in the United States in the 1950s and 1960s, and remained so in New York into the 1970s)? Or is it both?

It seems fairly reasonable to conclude that were these two men to meet today, they would marry. (They would, at least, have the option.) If they were married, would their relationship serve as (implicit, anyway) evidence of the impropriety of their relationship, or, as it were, the "undueness" of Weiss' influence over Kaufmann? Certainly not. Even were the two merely a long-time unmarried couple today, it

---

to the company, claiming that he should have transferred it to the company at the purchase price, while bearing the costs of the will contest by himself. This addendum to the saga, and its denouement, may be found at Weiss v. Kay Jewelry Stores, 470 F.2d 1259 (D.C. Cir. 1972).—ED.]

seems highly unlikely that the Kaufmann family would even consider bringing this case against Weiss.

Avoiding Undue-Influence and Related "Interference" Contests. One thing to keep in mind is the problem of attorneys drafting wills for their family members (and, more broadly, of attorneys drafting wills in which they are to be beneficiaries). In many states, an attorney not related to the testator is barred from taking a bequest under a will that he has drawn for a client. Do you see why? Attorneys who draw up wills for their relatives also face suspicion, and a presumption of undue influence, if their bequests under the instrument are larger than (1) what similarly situated and distant relatives receive, or (2) what they would have received by intestacy. Drafting a will for a relative is a classic conflict of interest and a common pitfall.

Somewhat relatedly, why is it a bad idea to include lots of details about the motivations for actions in a will?

Another thing to consider is the no-contest clause (also called an *in terrorem* clause). A no-contest clause "sets a trap" (really, it creates a weighted alternative, but it will feel like a trap to the beneficiary) for disappointed beneficiaries by mandating the forfeiture of any dispositions to a person who challenges the will. Here's an example:

> Article IV. To Jack, a sum of $10,000. But should Jack contest this will or any part of it, this gift shall be void, and Jack will inherit nothing.

The inclusion of such a no-contest clause will not *by itself* guarantee that Jack will not contest the will. He may still contest, of course, and if he is successful in proving, for example, that the testator's volition had been undermined by the undue influence of a third party, the whole will (or all parts arising as a result of the undue influence) will be declared void. (By way of reinforcement, what happens if the court reaches this conclusion and throws out the will?) This will have the effect of invalidating the no-contest clause as well.

If, on the other hand, the challenge to the will fails, the no-contest clause will, like the rest of the will, remain in effect, with the result that Jack will not only be burdened with the costs of sustaining the challenge to the will but will also lose the $10,000 bequest. In other words, a no-contest clause does not *ensure* that there will be no contest, but does diminish the likelihood of a contest by, in effect, raising the cost of that challenge.

In fact, the cost of the challenge is raised by exactly the amount that the beneficiary has been left so long as the beneficiary does not contest the will. (So, in our example above, the gift-plus-no-contest-clause combination has raised the cost to Jack of contesting the will by $10,000.) The gift twinned with the no contest clause, by the way, is called the "bait" of the clause, as in the bait of a trap.

It follows from all of this that one of the stupidest things a trusts and estates practitioner can do, one that would almost surely carry malpractice liability, is to include an *unbaited* no-contest clause in a will. Can you see why? You might think that no practitioner could possibly make so obvious and serious an error, but you would be wrong. Look back at *Pirtle*.[45] Grandpa included a no-contest clause in his will, targeted specifically at his granddaughters,[46] but as he didn't leave *anything* to his granddaughters, they were hardly dissuaded from launching their challenge.

3. Duress

At some point, the level of physical coercion or threat involved in undue influence crosses an indistinct line and becomes duress. Duress occurs "if the wrongdoer threatens to perform or does perform a wrongful act[47] that coerced the donor into making a donative transfer that the donor would not otherwise have made."[48] The difference between undue influence and duress is that duress is triggered by a reasonably discrete *act*—either the threat of or performance of a wrongful act—that causes the disposition.

Effectively, duress is a subset of undue influence, but the influencing occurs not by trick but by trigger (as it were). The evidence to prove duress generally must consist of some "smoking gun" proof of the threat or act. Duress cases are thus rare and are either easy or

---

45. *See supra* at 11.

46. The clause read "[s]hould either of the granddaughters contest this will they shall be automatically removed as a legal heir." Food for thought: are *in terrorem* clauses universally enforced? What would be the policy reasons for *not* enforcing them, as a general proposition?

47. Comment i to R3d §8.3 defines a wrongful act as one that "is criminal or is one that the wrongdoer had no right to do." Interestingly, if the wrongdoer has a right to do the act, it is not duress, but conceivably could be undue influence.

48. Restatement (Third) of Property: Wills & Other Donative Transfers §8.3(c).

impossible to prove. Compare the evidence needed to prove duress with that needed to prove undue influence. Undue influence is much easier to prove absent that perfect duress evidence, so most potential duress challenges are often won on undue-influence grounds. Undue influence cases may well include threats of duress, which are themselves probably a type of duress, but wander ye not through that valley dark and drear: Just plead 'em both and let the judge figure out which one to apply.

4. Fraud

Fraud occurs when the testator is deceived by a deliberate misrepresentation and does that which he would not have done had the misrepresentation not been made.[49] A finding of fraud requires demonstration of intent to deceive and purposeful influence on the testator; an innocent or negligent misrepresentation is not fraud.[50] In fact, silence generally is not fraud either. It is not fraudulent to fail to disclose a material fact unless the alleged wrongdoer was in a confidential relationship with the donor.[51]

If fraud is found, the portions of the will tainted by the fraud are invalid; the remainder of the will stands unless fraud permeates the whole. A court can "create"[52] a constructive trust (equitable diversion of certain devises) to both probate the will and ensure that fraud-tinged dispositions are not made.

There are two types of fraud in probate contests: fraud in the inducement and fraud in the execution. It matters very little that you be able to distinguish between these two types of fraud, be it on a trusts and estates exam, in pleadings, or even in that most artificial

---

49. *See id.* §8.3(d).

50. *See id.* §8.3(d), cmt. k.

51. *See id.* §8.3(d), cmt. j.

52. Or, more properly, as discussed in the trusts section, "declare." As will be made clearer there, a "constructive trust," along with a "resulting trust," is not really a trust at all. Rather, these two "trusts" are simply somewhat confusing labels for convenient judicial or practical facts. A constructive trust is really just a judicial declaration that while X improperly maintains control over certain assets, X must hold them for the sole purpose of delivering them to Y, lest X face court sanction. Meanwhile, a resulting trust is merely a judicial declaration that X for some reason finds herself in once-proper-but-no-longer-timely control over certain assets (at, for example, the winding up of an until-now-valid trust), which assets should now be delivered to the possession and ownership of Y.

setting, the bar exam. But considering the distinction for a minute or two can help underscore the various ways in which fraud can arise.

Fraud in the inducement occurs when the wrongdoer commits fraud to get the testator to make dispositions[53] that the testator would not have otherwise made. The fraud must be a but-for factor causing the disposition. For example, a grandson promises to use Blackacre as a nature conservancy, in accordance with his grandmother's wishes. He always intends, however, to turn it into the Shooting Safari in Saugatuck, and, when his grandmother passes, he begins to do so. This is fraud in the inducement; he induced his grandmother to make a disposition by defrauding her. Note that the relevant fraudulent intent must obtain at the time of the inducement.[54] If a party simply changes his mind after the testator has made a gift (and certainly after she has died and can't do anything about it), then he may act according to his changed intent, even if "precatory language" in the will expressed grandma's wishes, so long as her wishes could not reasonably be construed as conditions.

Fraud in the execution occurs when the wrongdoer intentionally misrepresents the character or contents of the instrument signed by the testator, which instrument as signed (rather than as represented) does not in fact carry out the testator's intent. Once again, the fraud must be a but-for factor causing the disposition. For example, Grandma does not read English. Her grandson prepares a will for her—in English—saying that Blackacre was to go to him in fee simple absolute. She had intended that it pass to him on the condition that it be used as a nature conservancy. He tells her that the condition is included in the will, but it is not. For fraud in the execution to arise, the fraudulent act obviously must have been performed before or at the time of execution, and with the intent to defraud (though equitable remedies may be available for negligent acts which befoul the execution).

Like duress, fraud looks much like undue influence sometimes. The case of *Puckett v. Krida*, 1994 WL 475863, 1994 Tenn. App. LEXIS 502 (1994),[55] usefully illustrates this point. The opinion in the case first quotes approvingly from an earlier Tennessee opinion holding that the difference between fraud and undue influence is real, and that it arises

---

53. Those "dispositions" can range from including particular provisions, executing or revoking a will, or refraining from any of those things.

54. Or perhaps arise later and not be admitted to the still-extant testator.

55. The facts of which are largely irrelevant for our purposes.

from a consideration of the free-will *vel non* of the testator.[56] Almost directly afterward, though, the opinion quotes a different Tennessee source suggesting that the distinction between fraud and undue influence was for practical purposes illusory.[57] If faced with a fact pattern that clearly illustrates (or allows for a presumption of) foul play, and the foul play might reasonably be characterized in any of the three overlapping ways (undue influence, fraud, or duress), just plead all three of the highly related causes of action.

Consider this further example: H asks W to destroy his will. W destroys papers in an envelope that are ostensibly, but not actually, H's will. After H dies, W probates the supposedly destroyed will, which leaves her everything. Clearly (presuming that all of these facts are true and are competently proven up), something has gone wrong in a way that the law should recognize and correct, but many angels indeed could dance atop the pin designed to point out the "correct" cause of action. Can you make the case for fraud? For duress? For undue influence? For incapacity? More interestingly, could you come up with a set of facts that would place a case like this squarely at the intersection of these causes, such that they would (as is not yet the case here), all reasonably apply? If fraud (which is fairly clearly the best answer here—why not the others?), then is the fraud one of inducement or execution? In *Brazil v. Silva*, 185 P. 174 (Cal. 1919), on which the facts above are based, the court, wearing its at-law hat, decided that the case didn't quite fit into any of these categories, and that it therefore lacked authority to grant any legal relief; but then replaced the top hat of law with the slouch-kepi of equity, and decided in that capacity that after formally (or technically, if you prefer) distributing the estate to the wife, it would impose a constructive[58] trust on the proceeds dis-

---

56. "The two grounds of undue influence and fraud are closely related, but in the case of fraud the free agency of the testator remains, but he is misled into doing that which he otherwise would not have done." Union Planters Nat. Bank of Memphis v. Inman, 588 S.W.2d 757, 761-62 (Tenn. App. 1979).

57. "It is recognized . . . that undue influence may be grounded on false and fraudulent representations made to the testator and insofar as the present case is concerned, the distinction between the two grounds of attack is of no practical importance." Cude v. Culberson, 30 Tenn. App. 628, 209 S.W.2d 506, 521 (1947).

58. Remember: In the peculiar vocabulary of the law, "constructive" generally means "not a," such that, for example, a "constructive contract" is in fact an arrangement that is *not a contract* under the formal rules of contract, because some necessity is absent, but the court will for reasons of equity behave as though it were. The case is the same with constructive trusts: They *are not* trusts in the way in which the term is used in the law of trusts; rather, "constructive trust" is the term that a court uses when, *inter alia*, it must, at law, give or leave some collection of property (in whatever

tributed to her. To merit a constructive trust, however, the contestants had to prove their case by what we today would call "clear and convincing evidence" (the court said "clearly and satisfactorily"). Of course, the party that ultimately carries the burden of proof in any of these causes[59] also generally carries a clear-and-convincing burden.

5. Incontestable Wills and Malpractice Avoidance

A will is most likely to be challenged for lack of testamentary capacity and undue influence, which may—and probably will—be brought together. After having read all the preceding, you should have a good nose for what circumstances encourage a will contest. An unnatural disposition —cutting out a close relative or making some unexplained distinction between equally near family members—is the biggest red flag. Family members often expect an inheritance as a moral right; a testator who abjures this "duty" invites a challenge. As the preceding discussions illustrate, other possible warning markers include an eccentric testator; conditions on the bequest that beneficiaries may find offensive; gifts to unpopular[60] or unnatural devisees;[61] production of a late-in-life will that differs wildly from prior testamentary plans; or (not directly addressed but arising as a corollary from the issues considered above), conflicts between multiple or blended families. Any of these should flash a warning light signaling the need to prepare to neutralize challenges in advance.

So how do you plan to neutralize will contests? One initial move is to suggest that your testator-to-be use an *inter vivos* trust as his main instrument of disposition. As a theoretical matter, revocable trusts are every bit as subject to contests on lack-of-capacity and undue influence grounds as are wills. But that is as a theoretical matter only. In capacity

---

form) with A, but nevertheless insists that the sum be handed over to B, who, in equity, rightly should have the property (in order to rectify fraud and prevent unjust enrichment). Declaring a constructive trust makes A liable to court sanction should she do anything with the property other than handing it over to B. There are useful analogies between A's position and a trustee's, though they are incomplete, but the court is in no meaningful sense an analog to a settlor, and the other comparisons are equally weak. In the case above, the constructive trust was employed, in a sense, as its own quasi-cause-of-action, but it is best understood as an instrument for achieving an equitable remedy.

59. Duress, fraud, undue influence, or incapacity. *See* UPC §3-407.

60. Unpopular with the testator's family, that is. For example, a testator's mistress would probably be rather unpopular with his wife and leaving most of the estate to the "other woman" will almost certainly result in a challenge.

61. See *Wilson v. Lane, supra*, where the gift to *one* unrelated beneficiary out of *seventeen* resulted in a challenge.

and undue-influence cases there is usually a hidden question: did the donor really intend his dispositions after much thought, or does the will demonstrate the testator's intent only on the day of the will's execution? Because a will must be drawn (and altered) with attention to all the requisite formalities to be discussed in the next section, usually with the involvement of counsel, and because the will only "speaks" at the moment of the testator's death, with speech emitted only on the day of formalization, the capacity of the testator on that particular day becomes a matter of singular import. Trusts, on the other hand, are more easily formed and changed and less often need to involve counsel. Moreover, *infer vivos* trusts are considered "active" from the moment of their making. As a result, the longer a trust continues, the greater the probability that a jury will find the grantor really intended it, and that it was not a product of ephemeral influence, and thus the less willing the court will be to declare the trust—and everything that has been done by it during the testator's life—invalid. Longevity can be achieved either by keeping the trust secret from beneficiaries, or by letting them know that if they challenge during the settlor's life, they'll be cut out.

Regardless of the instrument used, counsel can also ask that the testator hand-write a letter to the lawyer indicating her desired dispositions. The lawyer can then respond in writing, explaining the consequences to the testator's family of such a plan of disposition and asking for a letter explaining the testator's reasoning. Once the lawyer gets that letter, all three will be saved in the client's file.[62] A video-recorded explanation can work if the testator is in good health, but video tape and other non-film recording methods, especially in these days of 4K, super-high-def, 60-inch concave 3D televisions—tends to magnify the frailties (physical, vocal, and other) of the elderly or infirm. The testator also can hold a witnessed family meeting where the testator tells everyone what's up and explains his reasoning for it. This last, of course, carries with it a special potential drawback: It makes the family aware of any "negative" dispositions during the testator's life, potentially opening a tall can of unpleasantness as a declining-days draught for the testator. This is an implication of this final strategy that a good counsel will think through expressly with her client.

Finally, of course, the lawyer needs to take special caution to get the formalities right. We turn now to those.

---

62. This suggests a broader practice suggestion: Conduct as much business as possible in writing. After a telephone or in-person conversation, send a written memorandum confirming everything that was said. Contemporaneous written evidence is *great* evidence in practice.

D. WILL FORMALITIES

1. The Formalities Considered

Once we have assured ourselves that the testator has capacity and is executing a will of his own free will, we arrive at the third important question: Did the execution of the will satisfy the jurisdiction's formal Will's Act requirements? A court will only admit a will to probate if it complies with the jurisdiction's testamentary formalities. The relative rigidity of enforcement of these requirements has in part led to increased reliance in recent decades on will substitutes—such as trusts, life insurance, and others discussed in detail throughout this text—in order to get around the strict probate requirements.

Although jurisdictions differ in the fine details, there are three formalities[63] that are generally required:

1. The will must be in writing;
2. The will must be signed by the testator; and
3. The testator's signature must be attested to by competent witnesses.[64]

a. Writing Requirement

The writing requirement is the most straightforward of the three formal requirements. A will is valid—anywhere—only if it is written (whether handwritten or machine-generated), almost always (for now) *on paper.* At present, only Nevada recognizes electronic/digital wills, though the subject is receiving additional attention as life drifts further and further into pixilation. The Florida legislature recently passed an Electronic Wills Act, only to see the governor veto it on the not-irrelevant ground that remote electronic notarization, which would have been permitted under the act, would not have provided much in the way of protection for testators. The Uniform Law Commission (as well as the Colorado

---

63. It's awkward, but perhaps useful, to refer to the formalities as "the elements of a valid will."

64. UPC §2-502 adopts the least common denominator for each of the three main formalities, and it requires no others. As discussed below, it does not require the witnesses to be present at the same time, and it allows them to sign "within a reasonable time" after witnessing the testator's signature. Further, in a break with prior law, as revised in 2008 (and still true as of this book's publication) the UPC allows for *notarization* as a complete substitute for *attestation* by two witnesses. Most states, though, have not yet mellowed that far. UPC §2-502 (1990, rev. 2008).

bar) have also begun to address the issue, organizing committees to draft model legislation to address—and very likely to liberalize the rules around—more digital forms of documentation for this ethereal age.

Despite these (perhaps belated) nods to modernity, no state recognizes video wills. As we have already considered, though, audio or video recordings of one sort or another can accompany a will and provide evidence of (or against) competence.

Meanwhile, there remains one minor addendum to this simplest of requirements. Arising more as a rule of evidence than as a feature of the law of wills, but something that the bar examiners like to trot out: In some states, and at common law, the final—though spoken—dispositions made by a party who is both dying forthwith *and is aware that he is dying forthwith,* and who then actually dies forthwith, are honored if they are witnessed by two disinterested witnesses whom the soon-decedent has specifically asked to witness his dying bequests, insofar as they grant personal rather than real property. This is called a nuncupative will. Given that every rule of law has an exception somewhere, let the sheer number and weight of the limitations and qualifications built into this rule stand as a demonstration of the near water-tightness of the writing requirement.

b. Signature Requirement

All states and the UPC require that the testator sign the will.[65] "Signature" is a fairly flexible term. Most courts prefer the testator's full name, but a mark, abbreviation, or nickname can suffice as long as the testator intends it to serve as his signature. The signature requirement provides evidence of finality, which distinguishes the will from the testator's notes or drafts. By signing, the testator demonstrates that he intends *this* document to serve as his will.

Under common law, a testator is not forbidden to make a will when he is "reasonably incapable" of making a signature (or mark, etc.).[66] In that case, the testator's signature can be replaced by that of another, provided that other signs the will at the testator's direction, in his presence, and on his behalf. The UPC dispenses with the "reasonably incapable requirement," and accepts the signature of another person, who must sign "in the testator's conscious presence and by the testator's direction."[67]

The final nuance of the signature requirement involves the signature's placement on the document. The old common-law "subscription"

---

65. *See, e.g.,* UPC §2-502(a)(2) and cmt. a.

66. Consider, for example, a paralyzed testator who is still mentally vigorous.

67. *See* UPC §2-502(a)(2).

rule required the testator to sign at the foot or end of the document for it to be valid. Most states and the UPC have abandoned the subscription requirement.[68] But if a state requires subscription, failure to subscribe can be handled in three ways: (1) the entire document is invalid; (2) the place where the signature appears is treated as the end of the will, with everything before the signature treated as a valid will and everything following it invalid; or (3) the place where the signature appears is treated as the end of the will, with everything before the signature treated as a valid will and everything following it treated as an addition to the will (and so potentially valid as a codicil, or perhaps saved by one of the material compliance theories discussed below).

c. Attestation Requirement

The purpose of the attestation requirement is to identify those who can testify in the probate proceedings that the testator duly executed the will. The most basic way to satisfy the requirement is to have the witnesses sign a witness block on the will.

An example of a (signature and) attestation block:

I, Testator, sign this will on this 15th day of Movember, 2020

_____

(Testator)

Signed and declared by Testator on this 15th Day of Movember, 2020 to be his/her will, in our presence [depending on state: in his/her presence and in the presence of one another:

_____

(Witness One, as Witness)

_____

(Witness Two, as Witness)

Such a witness block does the job of identifying witnesses for the future, but raises a problem: what if the signing witnesses cannot be found when the will is probated? They may have changed addresses or phone numbers, forgotten the events of the (potentially long-ago) execution, or even predeceased the testator.

---

68. *See, e.g.,* UPC §2-502(a)(2). *But see* N.Y. Est. Powers & Trusts Law §3-2.1(a)(1)(B) (Consol. 1974) (requiring subscription and invalidating all text after the testator's signature).

Thankfully, this problem is not insoluble. Remember, the point of identifying witnesses is so that they can provide evidence at the probate proceeding regarding what they observed when the testator executed the will. There are two ways to secure this evidence without needing to call those people to testify during probate. Neither of these methods is *required* by any state, but it is borderline malpractice not to use one when drafting a client's will.

The first method is to include an attestation affidavit, in addition to the standard witness block. An attestation clause is a sworn affidavit describing what the witness saw under penalty of perjury. Put differently, it is a sworn statement that the will has been duly executed. Under most rules of evidence, a sworn statement is admissible when the witness is unavailable or unable to remember the events in question. Thus, the attestation clause allows the will to be admitted to probate even though the attesting witnesses may be dead, forgetful, or unable to be located.

An example of an attestation affidavit:

State/Commonwealth of _____
_____ County

Each of the undersigned, each on his/her oaths, swears or affirms that the above witnessing signature is his or her own. We swear or affirm that at the time of signing this will, the Testator was over the age of [usually 18] years and, in our individual and joint opinions, of sound mind, memory and understanding and not under restraint or in any respect incompetent to execute a will.

This will was executed as the single document attached hereto.

Each of us knew Testator when the will was executed and we have sworn or affirmed this affidavit at his/her request.

_____
(Witness One)
Address

_____
(Witness Two)
Address

Sworn/Affirmed to before me this 15th day of Movember, 2020.

_____
(Notary Public)   (Notary Public Seal)

Because the attestation affidavit is separate from the witness block, the witness must sign in two different places. First, he must sign the witness block, affirming that he was present and saw the testator sign the will. Then he must sign the attestation clause, setting forth his affidavit describing what he saw. This may seem trivial, but it is very important to make sure the witness signs in both places. If the witness forgets one of those signatures, then there are problems when probate rolls around. The first option is that the will won't be properly attested, because the witness forgot to sign the witness block. That means the will doesn't satisfy the formalities and can't be admitted to probate. The second option is that the witness didn't sign the attestation clause, which means there is no sworn statement of what he saw at the execution. Thus the witness *must* be called to testify at the probate proceeding. These simple mistakes can happen and ruin a testator's carefully crafted estate plan.

The second method—the self-proving affidavit—is designed to eliminate the possibility of a failure to sign twice, with its attendant, potentially disastrous, consequences. The self-proving affidavit combines the witness block and attestation clause into a single block, which requires only one signature. Care must be taken to ensure that the self-proving affidavit contains the language appropriate to both the witness block and the attestation clause. Once the prudent estate-planning attorney has created (or borrowed[69]) a satisfactory self-proving affidavit, she can use it as a standard template in all wills she drafts for her clients. Thus, care only need be taken once (in drafting) rather than every time a will is executed. Fewer *ab initio* creations can mean fewer opportunities for mistakes, which can mean less potential malpractice liability.

Regardless of whether the will contains a witness block, attestation clause, or self-proving affidavit, under the traditional rules: (1)

---

69. One of the fundamental errors (there are far more than one, but this is a big one) that young attorneys—especially those who hang a shingle on their own, but also those who go into a practice but lack the confidence or the wisdom to "bother" the people they work with—can make is to try to (as the cliché goes) "re-invent the wheel," designing anew language for provisions that have been deployed thousands or millions of times by previous practitioners. This error arises from noble premises and instincts, including a desire to do one's own work and not to plagiarize. But practice is not a law review article, and imitation can often be the sincerest source of wisdom. This is not a suggestion merely to borrow boilerplate *ad hoc* and without careful review and appropriate revision of the borrowed language. But (as this footnote is a festive of clichés already) practice can often make something much closer to perfect than can novice eagerness and fastidiousness.

the witness needed to be in the room watching the testator until the testator has signed the will, (2) the witnesses could sign only after the testator had signed, and (3) the witnesses' signatures were valid only if they signed in the testator's presence. The rationale for the first two of these rules seems fairly obvious: after all, the witness is by her signature affirming that she *witnessed* the testator signing the will itself; for the witness to sign first would render the attestation itself a lie.

English and early American law required that the *testator* remain in the room watching as the witnesses signed the will and that the witnesses remain in the room watching as one another signed the will. The rationale for this appears to have been additional sureties of propriety, though the value is somewhat attenuated. A failure of all of the parties to remain in the room and alertly watch the proceedings resulted in a failure of the attestation formality and thus of the will itself.

Most jurisdictions have moved away from the traditional rules regarding both the order of signatures and the "in the testator's presence" rule, ignoring the technical deficiency that the first rule-relaxation creates. Regarding the order of signing, the modern trend is that the order does not matter if all parties sign as part of a single transaction. As for presence, the traditional rule is utterly dead; no state requires the witness' and testator's absolute, unblinking attention for the entirety of the execution ceremony. Three tests have replaced the traditional rule: the line of sight test, the conscious presence test, and the UPC test.

Under the line of sight test, the testator is "present" if the testator would be able to see the witness were he to look.[70] The testator need not actually see the witness sign. Under the conscious presence test, the testator is present if the testator comprehends—through sight, hearing, or general consciousness of events—that the witness is in the act of signing. Does this seem like the same test in different words? Consider this scenario: The testator signs, then goes into the next room to get coffee for the witnesses. He can't see the witnesses but could hear them were they to speak. Under the line of sight test, the testator couldn't see the witnesses if he looked; he would see the kitchen wall. But under the conscious presence test, he could comprehend that the witness was signing by listening to the pen scratching

---

70. For a blind testator, the test is whether he would have been able to see the witnesses if he had sight.

on the paper if he had listened for it or from the general facts of the situation. So there is a difference between the two.

UPC §2-502(a)(3) sets up a third test. Under the UPC, the witnesses must sign the will "within a reasonable time" of seeing either (1) the testator signing the will or (2) the testator acknowledging his signature or the will itself. Notably, the UPC doesn't care where the testator is when the witness signs.

The UPC also allows for notarization as a substitute for attestation by witnesses. Notarized wills will be covered in more detail later, but for now, know that the attestation requirement is satisfied if the testator acknowledges the will "before a notary public or other individual authorized by law to take acknowledgements." [71]

There's one more question to answer: Who may properly serve as witnesses? Consider: The testator's will leaves everything to his business partner and a local charity, and nothing to his only son (the testator's lovely wife having died several years ago). What problems do you foresee if the partner and a member of the charity's board of trustees sign as witnesses? At the very least, the son will be leveling claims of undue influence and/or duress. What if the partner's spouse is a witness instead of the partner herself?

An obvious conflict of interest arises when a witness—or his or her spouse—takes under the will. Witnesses are supposed to ensure that the testator bequeathed freely and competently. If the witness doesn't take under the will, the witness can, as an initial presumption, be assumed to be honest in the act of witnessing, because the witness has nothing at stake in being dishonest. If the witness does take, this cannot be the case; the concern necessarily arises that the witness may have coerced, fraudulently included, or otherwise inappropriately influenced her bequest.

There are four possible answers to the question of what to do when a witness is interested (that is, is a devisee under the will): (1) hold the witness's signature invalid, (2) invalidate the bequests to that witness so as to make him disinterested, (3) give the witness what he would naturally have taken in intestacy only (or what he would have taken in a prior, competent will), or (4) waive the formality by calling the error "harmless" or finding substantial compliance. [72]

---

71. UPC §2-502(a)(3)(B).

72. The harmless error and substantial compliance doctrines are considered in detail in the "Policing of Compliance with the Formalities" section, *infra*.

The first of these answers was the traditional rule. An interested party was completely invalid as a witness, which usually left the will one witness short of the requirement and thus void.[73] This was rather harsh, in effect punishing a lay testator for executing her will at home by invalidating it when her closest kin (and likeliest beneficiaries) witnessed her signature.

In response to the harshness of this initial rule there arose the "purging" doctrine, with the purpose of saving wills despite the interested witness's involvement. Purging doctrine allows the interested party to be a valid witness, with varying consequences for the interested party depending on the jurisdiction.

One method of purging is to invalidate all bequests to the interested witness. Under "complete" purging, the interested witness takes nothing. The property bequeathed to him generally falls into the residue. In the absence of a residuary clause, that property passes through intestacy unless otherwise disposed of in the will. As of this writing, complete purging is a minority rule among jurisdictions.

Another method of purging is the more nuanced "relative" purging. Any bequests (or portions of bequests) in the witnessed document that exceed what the interested witness would have taken prior to the witnessed document's execution are purged. Thus, if the interested party witnessed the testator's only will, additional bequests over the witness' intestate share are purged. If he witnessed only the testator's second will, additional bequests over his share under the first will are purged. Naturally, no purging occurs if the interested witness receives *less* under the witnessed document than he would have in its absence. Can you see why, given the reason for the purging doctrine? Relative purging is the rule in most jurisdictions.

Consider a few scenarios. Assume first that T (a widower) has three children, A, B and Ralph. Now assume that T writes a will that leaves half of T's estate to child A, with the other half divided between B and Ralph. A is one witness of T's will; neighbor Z is another. Under relative purging, what will A take? What will happen to the portion of the bequest to A not received by A? What would happen in a state employing "complete" purging?

By comparison, imagine instead that T left, in the will that A attested, one-third of the estate to each of the three children? What would A take this time under relative purging?

---

73. No jurisdiction follows the traditional rule any longer. It has been replaced by one of the purging doctrines discussed.

The UPC takes a third approach in §2-505. In the comment to that section, the drafters note that requiring disinterested witnesses "has not succeeded in preventing fraud and undue influence."[74] Accordingly, the UPC allows for interested witnesses, and will not purge any bequests to those witnesses (or, at least, will not purge them on the grounds of interestedness), believing that this will "not increase appreciably the opportunity for fraud or undue influence." This is not a surprising outcome given that the UPC has already loosened the rules regarding attestation.[75] To take the UPC's logic a step farther, why do we need witnesses at all? If we accept the UPC drafters' logic, witnesses—whether interested or not—provide little or no protection against fraud, undue influence, or duress.[76] So the formality of attestation would appear to serve no purpose. However, attestation remains a formality in most jurisdictions, and even the UPC would still require notarization as an attestation substitute.[77]

What do you make of these various positions? Do you accept the UPC's logic? The reasonability of relative purging? Are you a stickler for the rules, and prefer complete purging? Why do you take the position that you do?

2. The Functions Performed by the Formalities

Why are these formalities (or elements) required, and why have they been (at least until the last few decades) enforced so rigorously? One answer: the formalities have been required in order to ensure, so far as possible, that the actual, considered, interpretable will of the newly dead is being respected and fulfilled.[78] This overarching purpose can be divvied into discrete functions. According to leading scholars in

---

74. As a matter of public policy and statutory construction, is this the right question to ask? The nearly right question? Irrelevant? Is it complicated?

75. By allowing witnesses to sign without having seen the testator sign the will at all, or by allowing for notarized wills.

76. *See* James Lindgren, *The Fall of Formalism*, 55 Alb. L. Rev. 1009, 1024-30 (1991-92).

77. Note that *executors*, who get paid for their services, are not considered interested witnesses.

78. The dead, unable to tell tales, also have a difficult time suing if their wishes are tinkered with, misunderstood, or ignored.

the field, there are four[79]: (1) the Channeling function, (2) the Ritual function, (3) the Evidentiary function, and (4) the Protective function.

Channeling. Human beings are idiosyncratic, unique, and complex beings. We all have our own ways of doing things that almost certainly differ from those of others. That's all well and good when it comes to how we brush our teeth or arrange the cabinets, but it is less helpful when judges are trying to figure out if the document you left behind is a will. Wills can pass incredible amounts of money and property, making proper interpretation and administration vital; this process is greatly eased if each testator's intentions are stated in regularized and coherent ways. After all, the substance of wills cannot be standardized (because we all have different stuff and different ideas on how to distribute said stuff); therefore, the *form* must be standardized as much as possible so judges don't have to puzzle too hard to determine if a document is a will and, if so, what it was meant to achieve. They can just focus on divvying up the dosh.

Ritual. One of the important attributes of a will is that it is not effective until death. The testator isn't giving up any of his property when he writes the will, so there is a concern that the testator might not be putting enough thought into what he's doing when he drafts and signs it. The formalities lend a sense of *gravitas* to execution and impress on the testator the seriousness of what he's doing. (This sense of ritual, the theory goes, is actually enhanced by forcing the testator into a lawyer's office; the act of making an appointment, spiffing up in suit and tie, and heading downtown to do a little expensive business, it's thought, rather concentrates the mind.) Presumably, this will cause him to sign only the document that truly reflects his intentions, which necessarily means he will put appropriate and adequate thought into the matter. The act of signing the will during the ceremony also shows fairly concretely that the document is not just a preliminary draft.

Evidentiary. Perhaps the most obvious purpose of the formalities is to give evidence of the testator's intent. The whole purpose of wills law is to give effect to the testator's intent, but there must be some consistently reliable and reasonably permanent means of ensuring that the evidence exists (hence, the writing requirement: Memories fade, after

---

79. Ashbel G. Gulliver & Catherine J. Tilson, *Classification of Gratuitous Transfers*, 51 Yale L.J. 1 (1941-42) (ritual, evidentiary, and protective functions); John H. Langbein, *Substantial Compliance with the Wills Act*, 88 Harv. L. Rev. 489 (1974-75) (discussing the other three and adding the channeling function).

all, so the witnesses may not be the most reliable source of evidence). After all, the testator won't be able to testify on the matter.

Protective. The final purpose purportedly performed by the formalities is to protect the testator against nefarious external influences[80] at the time of execution. Gulliver, Tilson, and Langbein make persuasive critiques of the formalities' protective power in their respective articles. Perhaps their two most persuasive points are that: (1) determined rogues won't be deterred—or really, inconvenienced much at all—by the formalities; and (2) fraud, undue influence, and the like can be, and have been, proven regardless of due execution and attestation. A plausible argument can be made that the formalities are about as good at protecting against these things as an antivirus is at protecting against tiger attacks. Nevertheless, this is a longstanding justification for the formalities.

Do these work? In other words, are these formalities good at their functions? Are they the right functions? Are the formalities the most efficient method of achieving these functions? The most just? Being efficient with what? Just on what metric of justice? Are your answers transcendent or context-dependent? What are the relevant contexts and considerations?

While these questions can prove interesting should there be time to go into them, the conversation will be better informed by consideration of the treatment of the formalities over the centuries. For most of those centuries, the ecumenical historical rule was: Stick to the formalities exactly or be denied probate. Lately, though, things have begun to change.

3. Policing of Compliance with the Formalities

Traditionally, courts admitted a will to probate only if the formalities had been strictly complied with. The would-be beneficiaries bore the burden of proving compliance and suffered the loss if a technical failure of the formalities arose. This unyielding rule was fairly universal and still remains the rule in the majority of jurisdictions.

In recent years (well, recent in terms of property law), the law in some jurisdictions has started to move away from strict adherence to numerous formalities, both by lessening the number of formalities and by relaxing the strictness of observation. There are both

---

80. Undue influence, duress, etc.

testator-regarding and drafter-regarding explanations for this shift. The drafter-regarding consideration can be summed up in three words: increasing malpractice liability.

The testator-regarding consideration requires more discussion. Many scholars have come to think that the formalities are too onerous, and out-of-step with the way other modern things are done and that they in the aggregate serve to impede the doing of the testator's intent more often than they effectuate that intent.[81] What explains this conclusion?

Consider Professor Lindgren's objections to the formalities.[82] According to Lindgren, the law of wills is based on a fear that people "might improvidently give away their property at death." The law assumes that testators are "so weak, old, feeble, and subject to pressure" that we cannot trust their "seriously intended statements about their property." It gives no weight to a testator's attempt to orally dispose of his property and accepts written statements only if they have been witnessed by two people, who must sign in the testator's presence. In contrast, contract law presumes that people "know their own mind" and their statements can be relied on, whether oral or written. No witnesses are necessary for contracting. Yet a person can convey large sums of money by contract, as much as or more than he could by a will.

Is this objection well taken? Is it really startling that two-party, mutually agreed, consideration-justified contracts between living parties might be honored with fewer concerns about formalities than gratuitous bequests usually made (or claimed to be made) by people now dead, with no supporting evidence of a bargained-for exchange, and often made by people in their declining days? After all, parties to a contract are usually around when litigation comes up. They can testify to their intent and the circumstances surrounding agreement. Testators can't, for obvious reasons. The whole point of wills law is to give effect to a dead person's "will" regarding his property, which the testator cannot give direct evidence of. Compliance with the formalities could be seen as indicia of the testator's intent, although Lindgren has a thing to say about this as well.

---

81. *See e.g.*, James Lindgren, *The Fall of Formalism*, 55 Alb. L. Rev. 1009 (1991-92); Jane B. Baron, *Gifts, Bargains, & Form*, 64 Ind. L.J. 155 (Spring 1989). Excerpts from Professor Lindgren's article appear on the web page.

82. *See* Lindgren, previous footnote.

Lindgren notes that probate litigation typically centers on whether the technical niceties of the formalities were satisfied, rather than determining whether the testator intended the document to be his will.[83] If the whole purpose of wills law is to give effect to the testator's intent, then why does the law focus on whether he jumped through all the necessary hoops to execute a document according to formal rules? Under the strict compliance standard of enforcement, many wills executed without the slightest trace of fraud or undue influence are denied probate.[84] Lindgren argues that the real issue should be whether a testator—uncoerced and of right mind—intended a document to dispose of property at death, not whether he strictly complied with the formalities when writing it. Some states—though by no means a majority of them—agree with Lindgren (and others) and have moved away from the strict compliance standard.

The desire to give effect to the testator's intent is not the only factor motivating the modern trend away from strict compliance. The use of will substitutes—such as trusts, joint accounts, or the others discussed throughout this semester—in estate planning is expanding. Will substitutes have the same effect as wills, in that they dispose of a person's property at death, but do not require anything near the strict formalities that wills do.[85] This has given rise to the dual-track system of disposing of one's property at death, as discussed previously. In addition, improving indicia of reliability have made determining the testator's intent easier, fulfilling the purpose of the evidentiary and channeling functions.

On an entirely practical level, trusts have been successful at disposing of the settlor's property at death without a sudden flood of fraud and undue influence associated with their use. Accordingly, judges have become more comfortable with the use of testamentary trusts, despite their less formal nature. Finally, and—most importantly for your future—attorneys are potentially liable for malpractice to the beneficiaries of wills. As malpractice liability related to wills expands, attorneys look for alternative estate planning tools that lack the potential landmines associated with the formalities.

---

83. *See id.* at 1016.

84. *Id.* Jane Baron makes a similar point, noting that it is no secret that "in reality, formalities often defeat donative intent" in the law of wills. Jane Baron, *Gifts, Bargains, & Form,* 64 Ind. L.J. 155, 159 (Spring 1989).

85. The UPC's general trend, in fact, is to unify the law of probate and nonprobate transfers. Given that these are two paths to substantially the same end, the UPC drafters believe that the requirements for validity should be the same. *See* UPC §2-503 cmt.

These factors have resulted in[86] a broad (though not yet majority) trend toward adoption of either the substantial compliance doctrine or the harmless error rule. Both modern rules eschew strict compliance with the formalities, although they are based on different rationales. The substantial compliance doctrine is a functional approach, whereas the harmless error rule focuses on the testator's intent.

Under the substantial compliance doctrine, a court can forgive non-compliance with a formality if the court can conclude with confidence that—given the unique circumstances of the case—the functions of the formal rules have been achieved despite the technical failure. *In re Will of Ranney*, 589 A.2d 1339 (N.J. 1991) and John H. Langbein, *Substantial Compliance with the Wills Act*, 88 Harv. L. Rev. 489 (1975) provide the historical background of the doctrine, should you be interested in it. (Excerpts of each appear on the web page.)

The substantial compliance doctrine is the less radical of the two reformation doctrines, in that it attends centrally to the functions performed by the formalities. The test requires a minor (subjective) search into the testator's mind, rather than the easier, objective test of whether each formality was strictly complied with.

Here's an example. Suppose that the Commonwealth of Jefferson's probate code requires that testators "subscribe," that is, sign at the end of the will, else everything after the signature is invalid unless independently valid as a proper codicil. Now suppose that Madison Monroe, the testator, is handed a page out of order, and signs not the last page of the will but an earlier page, the printing on which had ended somewhat early in an effort to keep distinct paragraphs together on single pages. Suppose further that the witnesses had signed appropriately, having watched the testator sign but without realizing the failure to sign the *last* page of the will.

What result? Under the traditional rule, the "tough luck" rule, the will would have ended at the bottom of the page on which Monroe had signed, the rest of the bequests being ignored. Here, though, under these facts, a court applying the substantial compliance rule could allow the whole will to be probated. The judicial reasoning process would go like this:

(1) The purposes of requiring a subscription are to make sure that the testator intended every page submitted to probate to be counted as part of the will;

---

86. Or, have these factors been dictated by events? If so, which ones, and why?

(2) the totality of the evidence in this case indicates that while the sub-scription rule was not *technically* complied with, the action which did occur arose only from immaterial error, while it is clear that the testator read and approved every page that has been submit-ted to me for probate; and therefore

(3) the actions which did occur provide *substantial* compliance with the will requirements because they, along with extrinsic evidence, confirm that the functions underlying the formalities have been achieved in a satisfactory manner.

In other words, the step taken under substantial compliance is miti-gatory, but measured. The document under review must still constitute something that the testator intended to be her will, and while a trifling error in compliance with one of the formalities can be overlooked, it may be waived only if the court satisfies itself that the functions under-lying those formalities have been met: that is, that all the parts of the documents submitted for probate really were intended by the testator to be her will, as drawn in sound and free mind and body.

In contrast, the harmless error rule proves more radical; it discards both the formalities *and* their functions, in favor of focusing solely on the testator's reconstructed intent. As the UPC, at §2-503 explains:

[a]lthough a document or writing added upon a document was not executed in compliance with [the formalities], the document or writing is treated as if it had been executed in compliance with [them] if the proponent of the document or writing establishes by clear and convincing evidence that the decedent intended the docu-ment or writing to constitute:

(1) the decedent's will,

(2) a partial or complete revocation of the will,

(3) an addition to or an alteration of the will, or

(4) a partial or complete revival of his [or her] formerly revoked will or of a formerly revoked portion of the will.

Per this definition, the harmless error rule might initially seem little different than the substantial compliance rule. But because the rule is explicitly tethered neither to formalities nor functions, two fundamen-tal problems arise. The first is that it's unclear what meaning of "will" is being used. Does §2-503 mean the decedent's Will (as in, the formal document, i.e., the Last Will and Testament)? Or does it mean the decedent's "will," as in wishes or desires in a less formal sense—that is, the decedent's wishes about what happens to her stuff once she's gone?

The second, and more troublesome, problem is that there isn't much to tether a judge's analysis of the testator's intent except for the judge's own subjective analysis. Which leads us to the saga of Charles Kuralt's Last Ro[a]deo.

Charles Kuralt was a profoundly avuncular fellow who drove around the country in an R.V., stopping off to do the softest of soft-news features at various out-of-the-way, often rural locations steeped in good-living and old-time Americana, places found hither and yon "On the Road," for CBS Television. As it turns out, he was a little less lonely out on the road than it otherwise appeared. Rather, he had undertaken a long-term affair with a lady named Pat Shannon. During their relationship, he had built (or had had built, as it were) a log cabin for himself and for her in Montana, had supported her family, and had bought her a vacation house in Ireland.

Kuralt executed a holographic will[87] in 1989 devising his Montana property to Shannon. The holograph was unmistakably testamentary; it included the full date, his address and signature, spoke of "the event of my death," and "bequeath[ed]" property. Then Kuralt—without telling Shannon—made a new lawyer-drafted will in 1994, which contained the standard language revoking all prior wills, and leaving Kuralt's entire estate to his second (and then-current) wife Petie and their two children. Thanks to the revocation clause, this will revoked the 1989 will. Kuralt gave Shannon the Montana cabin and 20 acres outright in 1997 and then hid that gift by structuring it as a sale, but giving Shannon the purchase price. He planned later to convey 90 more acres to her the same way, but he died first.

Before dying, Kuralt wrote Shannon a letter from his hospital bed. After updating her on his health, he expressed his intent regarding those 90 acres. According to this letter he clearly intended that she inherit them, but he also clearly did not think he was writing a holographic will *in that very document*, saying "I'll have a lawyer visit the hospital [i.e., I will do that in the future] to be sure you inherit the rest of the place in MT. if it comes to that." He never had the lawyer visit, and died on July 4, 1997.

Now arises the question: Who takes the relevant 90 acres of Montana land? Shannon sought to have Kuralt's letter probated as a holographic codicil to his 1994 will. His executors, appointed under that 1994 will, opposed this proposition. The district court denied probate because the letter "clearly contemplates a separate testamentary

---

87. *See infra* at II.C.6.

instrument not yet in existence to accomplish the transfer of the Montana property" to Shannon. The Montana Supreme Court disagreed in In re Estate of Kuralt (Kuralt I), 981 P.2d 771 (Mont. 1999). The Supreme Court said the plain language of the letter indicated that "Kuralt desired that Shannon 'inherit' all of his property" in Montana. "The Court said that the language about having a lawyer come visit to ensure Shannon's inheritance was not enough to prove that Kuralt was contemplating a separate testamentary instrument to achieve that result. Thus, the Court determined, there was a genuine question of material fact as to whether Kuralt intended, given his state of serious illness, that the very letter" serve as a disposition. It justified this reading by looking to evidence outside the text of the letter itself; namely, the way the sham sale was conducted for the first 20 acres, plus testimony that Kuralt planned to convey the 90 acres to Shannon in the same manner.[88] Thus, the matter went back to the district court for trial.

On remand, the district court found that the letter *did* express Kuralt's intent to posthumously transfer those 90 acres to Shannon and thus was a valid holographic codicil. This despite the letter's plain language that Kuralt intended to make a new disposition in a future document. Do you buy this reasoning? The Montana Supreme Court did, in In re Estate of Kuralt (Kuralt II), 15 P.3d 931 (Mont. 2000).[89]

Is there any danger in following the Montana Supreme Court majority here? If so, what?

It may well be argued that the *Kuralt* case provides a nearly perfect demonstration of the dangers that arise from employing the harmless-error rule. While the Montana Supreme Court suggested, and the lower court then agreed, that the letter from Charles to Shannon might *itself* have been intended by *Charles himself* as a final will/ codicil, this result seems belied by the very words of the letter: that Charles intended to bring in a lawyer later to create such a legal result. What the Court seems rather to mean, especially given the extrinsic evidence upon which it relies, is that Charles *intended to give the*

---

88. The admission of extrinsic evidence was authorized by UPC §2-502(c), which states:

> [Extrinsic Evidence.] Intent that a document constitute the testator's will can be established by extrinsic evidence, including, for holographic wills, portions of the document that are not in the testator's handwriting.

Montana had adopted the Uniform Probate Code by the time this case came to court, which explains why they applied the UPC's rules.

89. An expurgated version of the case appears on the web page.

property to Shannon, when he had the chance, if he had the chance, i.e., that the letter shows that he *wished* to give the letter. But a wish is not a Will; or, alternatively, if a mere written wish *can* constitute a Will, then any writing can constitute a will.

Meanwhile, how sure are you that the court made the right call about Charles' actual, lower-case-w will (i.e., his competent, thoughtful intent)? He was seriously ill, in the hospital, when he wrote that letter. Might his thinking have been impaired? Might he have changed his mind before drawing a formal document and making a formal conveyance? Or if he were more convinced that it really would "come to that," (i.e., that he would die)? Finally, consider the totality of the circumstances. Does history provide any examples of boyfriends lying to their girlfriends? Of the dying saying comforting but untrue and unmeant things to their survivors? Of, ahem, *adulterers* expressing untruths?

The fear is that the harmless-error doctrine, whatever its intentions, in fact allows courts to label any documents they wish to be Wills *ex post*, based on the sheerest of speculation or substituted will and that the *Kuralt* case provides a perfect example of exactly that. If this is even remotely true, is the harmless-error doctrine one of fabled exceptions that defeats the rule? (This is not entirely true, of course, because even under the harmless-error rule there must be *some* writing to hang the analysis on, but on balance, and especially with the much more grounded substantial-compliance rule available, it does seem like an unnecessary stretch.)

There are some ways in which the formalities themselves have simply been relaxed. For example, and as noted above, the UPC and some states have adopted a "delayed attestation" rule, abolishing the requirement that witnesses sign in the same transaction as the testator. Under the UPC, witnesses must sign "within a reasonable time" of seeing the testator's signature or acknowledgement.[90] Note that the witness could sign *after* the testator's death under this standard. In contrast, California requires that the witnesses sign during the testator's lifetime but does not specify when during the testator's lifetime.[91]

---

90. UPC §2-502(a)(3)(A).

91. Cal. Prob. Code §6110(c)(1) (Deering 2008) ("Except as provided in paragraph (2), the will shall be witnessed by being signed, during the testator's lifetime, by at least two persons each of whom (A) being present at the same time, witnessed either the signing of the will or the testator's acknowledgment of the signature or of the will and (B) understand that the instrument they sign is the testator's will.").

New York offers a third alternative, requiring the witnesses to sign within thirty days after the testator.[92]

4. Notarized Wills

The UPC adds a twist to the attestation requirement by allowing the testator to acknowledge her will before a notary in lieu of having two witnesses sign.[93] The Code's drafters, in the comment to §2-502(a), put forth a twofold rationale for allowing notarized wills. First, allowing notarization promotes uniformity in estate planning. According to the drafters, it is "common practice" for other estate planning documents, such as powers of attorney, to be notarized. The comment suggests that it would "reduce confusion" if the same formalities were required for all estate planning documents. The other justification is to bring the law in line with lay expectations. The drafters suggest that most, or all, lay people expect that notarization will make a will valid, and the law should conform with those expectations.[94]

It should come as no surprise that the UPC recognizes notarized wills. The Code's primary purpose is to give effect to the testator's intent. The fact that the testator went to the trouble of taking his home-drawn will to a notary public is a pretty good sign that he intends to dispose of his property in this manner at death, no? Now, this does nothing to protect the testator against things like undue influence, duress, or fraud. In fact, there is nothing to stop someone from taking a forged identification to the notary's office and getting notarized a will that happens to leave a great deal of money to the forger. But those dangers are equally present—at least theoretically—with attested wills (though this assumes that the fraudster has the will attested by strangers, an unusual arrangement historically, and one that it is hoped would raise both the suspicions and the

---

92. N.Y. Est. Powers & Trusts Law §3-2.1(a)(4) (Consol. 1974) ("There shall be at least two attesting witnesses, who shall, within one thirty day period, both attest the testator's signature, as affixed or acknowledged in their presence, and at the request of the testator, sign their names and affix their residence addresses at the end of the will. There shall be a rebuttable presumption that the thirty day requirement of the preceding sentence has been fulfilled. The failure of a witness to affix his address shall not affect the validity of the will.")

93. *See* UPC §2-502(a)(3)(B).

94. *See also* Lawrence W. Waggoner, *The UPC Authorizes Notarized Wills*, 34 ACTEC J. 83 (2008) ("The public is accustomed to thinking that a document is made 'legal' by getting it notarized.").

guards of any parties approached to be witnesses). In any event, most states have not adopted the UPC's option for notarized wills.

5. Conditional Wills

A conditional will is a will that is drafted to be effective only if a particular event (specified in the will) occurs. For example, a will that says, "This is my will if I die on my trip to the South Pole" is very clearly a conditional will; it is effective only if the adventurous (or foolhardy) testator springs the mortal coil while venturing to the bottom of the earth.

The issue becomes less clear when the will says, "I am leaving to seek the Grail. It is entirely possible that I shall not return from this perilous quest. Should that be the case, I leave everything to my brethren of the Round Table. Except Lancelot, that self-righteous [redacted]. He got the girl, so he gets none of my stuff."[95] What if our poor, jealous knight returns from his quest—successfully or otherwise—and rejoins the court at Camelot, spends a few months recounting his adventures to anyone within earshot, and dies in a jousting accident? What then? Does the Table Round split his stuff among them?

In most courts, yes. Does this seem odd? The language certainly *seems* conditional; the second and third sentences make it sound like the will is meant to be effective only if the testator does not return from his quest for the Grail. He returned alive and died months later in an unrelated incident. But, absent a revocation, most courts will treat the purported condition as precatory language and will probate the will.[96] They manage this trick by treating the text as an introductory explanation of what caused the testator to reflect upon his mortality and not as a formal condition. (A minority of courts will find a condition rather than precatory language, and so the estate will fall into intestacy.)

Of course, if the will is superseded, then this issue doesn't come up. So *always* be sure to have your client revoke such a will as soon as possible after the purported condition lapses. It is not at all clear that malpractice liability would arise from a failure to remind a client to revoke such a will (that later became valid after the condition failed),

---

95. This may or may not be a direct quote from Malory.

96. For an early (and the seminal) example of this phenomenon, *see* Eaton v. Brown, 193 U.S. 411 (1904).

but good practice is not bounded by the extent of malpractice liability. Given the role of accident and indeterminacy in life, the best practice, even if just to avoid malpractice liability, is to aim to stay *well away* from the margins.

6. Holographic Wills

A holographic will is a document (1) written long-hand by the testator (2) that disposes of some of the testator's property (3) that the testator has signed. No other formalities are required.[97] The stereotypical[98] holographic will is one that the testator, suddenly confronted with imminent death, scrawls off and signs with his dying breath.[99] Just over half of the states permit holographic wills.[100]

For an illustrative example of a holographic will, consider Kimmel's Estate, 123 A. 405 (Pa. 1924). Here, the holographic will comes in the form of a letter from the decedent to his sons (the "Kimmel Bros."). It starts with a pretty standard discussion of the father's farm and the area weather. Then:

> *if I come I have some very valuable papers I want you to keep fore me so if enny thing hapens all the scock money in the 3 Bank liberty lones Post office stamps and my home on Horner St goes to George Darl and Irvin Kepp this letter lock it up it may help you out. . . .*
>
> *Father*

Father goes out, mails the letter, comes back, and drops dead.

What says the commonwealth: Are these lines a will? Yes. They satisfy the holographic will rules, in that they are a writing, written out

---

97. Are you sensing a trend here? Like most, if not all, of the relaxation doctrines we've discussed, holographic wills omit the attestation requirement. Why is the presence of witnesses deemed the least important of the formalities? What reasons can you come up with?

An interesting side note: Pennsylvania no longer requires attestation for wills. *See* 20 Pa. Cons. Stat. §2504 (repealed 1974). Thus, only writing and signature are necessary for a valid will. *See* 20 Pa. Cons. Stat. §2502 (2015). The net effect is that holographic wills are not a special category in the Commonwealth; they are as normal and valid as what other jurisdictions would consider "regular" wills.

98. Though likely not the modal.

99. Or, for an even more thrilling example, check out the Epic of Cecil Harris in the next few pages.

100. It should come as no surprise that the UPC, with its goal of giving effect to the testator's intent, authorizes holographic wills as long as "the signature and material portions of the document are in the testator's handwriting." UPC §2-502(b).

manually by the testator, that purport to dispose of property. What about the signature? "Father" is enough.

Reconsider the reasons or purposes of formalities. Does writing out a letter like this satisfy the ritual or cautionary function (i.e., you know you're making a will, giving away property) of the Wills Act? What about the channeling function (putting things in coherent, probatable terms)?[101] The evidentiary? The protective function? As with this example, holographic wills tend to be messy, ambiguous, and incomplete—and so hard to probate.

Meanwhile, imagine that an omitted brother believed that a friend of George, Darl, and Irvin had come over to Dad's house, held a pistol to his head, made him write out the letter, escorted him to the post office, and then taken him home and fed him hemlock. Would anything about this handwritten letter provide any evidence to prove this theory false?

So the holograph fulfills the evidentiary function, and something of the ritual function, almost accidentally,[102] but (almost) nothing of the protective function. Is this enough? There is a pretty clear intent to make a disposition here, even if Kimmel would not have thought that his note was "a will, *per se*." But what about generally? Is more gained or lost by admitting holographic wills?

What about accepting "Father" as a valid signature? Kimmel clearly meant "Father" as his signature in this circumstance. Would a Dad ever sign a letter to his kids "Mr. Leonidas P. Kimmel?"[103]

---

101. *See* Ashbel G. Gulliver & Catherine J. Tilson, *Classification of Gratuitous Transfers*, 51 Yale L.J. 1, 3 (1941) ("Does this [letter] indicate *finality of intention to transfer*, or rambling meditation about some future disposition. . . . Does this demonstrate a deliberate transfer, or was it merely a tentative draft of some contemplated instrument, or perhaps random scribbling?").

102. In the days before computers, tweeting, and Facebook, there was a certain ritual value in writing out a document by hand. How much more ritualistic does that act become now that those electronic communication styles are vastly more prevalent?

103. An X (or similar symbol) can also be a sufficient signature, for those whose illiteracy requires them to rely upon a "mark" rather than a full signature. What about a testator who writes out the words "I, John Smith . . ." in the body, but then doesn't sign again? Some courts require "subscription," while other courts will accept the signature/mark wherever it appears so long as it can establish intent of the testator to authenticate the document (per Williams v. Towle, 66 Cal. Rptr. 3d 34 (App. 2007): pages of block-letter written dispositions; court looked for "sufficient indicia of completeness from which to conclude that the name at the top was intended to be a mark of authentication").

If you were opposed to the notion of a holographic will before, does the following rather famous (by trusts and estates standards, anyway) story temper your views?

GEOFF ELLWAND, AN ANALYSIS OF CANADA'S MOST FAMOUS HOLOGRAPHIC WILL: HOW A SASKATCHEWAN FARMER SCRATCHED HIS WAY INTO LEGAL HISTORY
77 Sask. L. Rev. 1 (2014).

"In case I die in this mess I leave all to the wife."
Cecil Geo. Harris

I. INTRODUCTION

The rudimentary facts surrounding [the] will (reproduced in full above) . . . began on a Prairie farm, not far from Rosetown, Saskatchewan, shortly after lunch on Tuesday, June 8 of the same year. . . .

Harris, a fifty-six-year-old British-born Saskatchewan wheat farmer, decided to take his red Case tractor to a quarter section of land he owned, a few kilometres north of his homestead in the McGee district about an hour-and-a-half drive west of Saskatoon. He planned to do field work using a tilling device known as a one-way disc plough, or more commonly, a "one-way." . . .

Harris told his wife, Bessie May Harris, to expect him back around ten in the evening, about the time the Prairie light begins to fade in early June. He did not return as planned, however, so his wife went to the field where she knew he was working to check on him. She found her husband of ten years alive but in a desperate state. His left leg was wedged almost entirely under the left rear wheel of the family's tractor. The tractor had no tires, but rather metal wheels equipped with deep "V"-shaped lugs. Those lugs had cut into Harris's leg from his ankle to his hip. The Rosetown Eagle, the local weekly newspaper, later reported "the lugs caused severe lacerations and he suffered much loss of blood [and] . . . his leg is severely fractured."

Bessie Harris needed to find help to release her husband immediately. She ran to the nearest farmhouse. It was the home of George Whatley, a former business partner of Harris's. Whatley, apparently concluding he would need assistance to free Harris, drove immediately to get another neighbour, Dan Fullerton. . . .

Whatley, accompanied by his wife and Mrs. Harris, drove to the accident scene where they found Harris. He "had his left leg caught under the left rear wheel of the Case tractor and was jammed between the said tractor and the one-way." Meanwhile Fullerton was heading for the small community of McGee, about five kilometres away, for help. He went to the local baseball diamond where he found his teenage son, Nelson Fullerton, as well as fifteen-year-old Bob Hannay and Hannay's father. The two fathers and young Nelson Fullerton drove straight to the accident scene. In the meantime, Bob Hannay was told to go to the family farm to get the tractor, and then make his way to the accident as quickly as he could.

Hannay recollects arriving at the accident scene on his family's tractor and seeing Harris still trapped in a sitting position between the tractor and the one-way disc. "It was dark and there was a terrible lightning storm," Hannay remembers. Pelted by rain, the neighbours jacked up the tractor to release Harris. Once freed, Harris was put in the back of Dan Fullerton's car with the intention of driving him to the hospital in Rosetown. Hannay recalls the downpour had turned the rough concession roads leading to the fields into "'terrible mud, impossible to go through with a car,' so he had to use the tractor to tow the car all the way to Highway 7, the gravelled main road to Rosetown and [the route to] medical help."

It was well past midnight by the time Harris got to the hospital. While in his hospital bed, he told Whatley he had been conscious the whole time and estimated he was under the tractor for twelve hours. There is no record that he ever mentioned a will, perhaps because he anticipated he would recover and any mention of a will would seem irrelevant. The next day, June 10, Harris died a little more than thirty-six hours after his rescue . . . . A small stone tablet, flat in the grass, reading simply "Cecil George Harris 1892-1948" still marks his resting place. . . .

V. DISCOVERY OF THE WILL

Just hours before Harris died in hospital on the afternoon of Thursday, June 10, 1948, two neighbours, George Whatley, who had been instrumental in Harris's rescue, and Louis Large, were laying grasshopper poison near the scene of the accident. Louis Large, who had not been at the incident, began examining the tractor, which had not been moved since it had been raised to free Harris. In the course of that examination, Large found what appeared to be a handwritten will scratched into the paint on the left fender and alerted Whatley. . . . The next day, Whatley and some neighbours removed the fender from the tractor and, along with Bessie Harris, took it "to the office of W.S. Elliott of Rosetown, Saskatchewan, in whose possession I [Whatley] left the said fender." William Stanley Elliott was a First World War veteran and Saskatchewan native who, at fifty-five, was a very experienced lawyer and no doubt well versed in wills and estate law. . . .

Elliott retained the fender in his office, probably out of the understandable desire to protect it, and the writing on it, from any tampering or wear. . . . [O]n the very day he received the tractor fender, Monday, June 14, 1948, Elliott engaged a local professional photographer, Vernon Pope, to make a contemporaneous photographic record suitable for use in court. . . .

While there is no direct record of Elliott's thinking of how to manoeuvre the will through the court, we do have the case comment written for The Canadian Bar Review by his son William McBurney Elliott. In the case comment he writes that from their research into holograph wills they found that "the only similar case reported is Hodson v. Barnes." This is an English case with its own set of remarkable facts. It involves a will written by the pilot of a canal ship on an eggshell. It was "the first time in the records of the Court [that] writing on the shell of a hen's egg was propounded as a will." The eggshell will was only discovered by chance after the death of James Barnes. It was challenged and faced a number of difficulties, including the existence of a previous conventionally made will, and the fact Barnes had never mentioned the eggshell will to anyone nor indicated where important documents might be found upon his death. In addition, the will lacked clarity in its intent. In the end it was found that "the writing on the eggshell was not a testamentary disposition" and it was rejected by the English Court of Probate. It must be noted there is no indication in the judgment that the unusual surface upon which the alleged will was written had anything to do with its rejection. As noted above, unattested holograph wills are not normally acceptable to English courts. But, in Barnes, it was argued that even though Barnes was only a pilot on a canal, he sometimes worked in the tidal waters of the River Mersey, and thus was "at sea" under the meaning of the Wills Act, 1837. Therefore, the argument went, the handwritten will fell within the special provisions for soldiers *in expeditione* and sailors at sea. The court declined to embrace this proposition.

In spite of the rejection of the will in Barnes, Elliott seems to have used this English case as something of a guide in his bid to avoid the pitfalls that might lead to a similar failure of the fender will in the Saskatchewan courts. As in Barnes, the Harris will was entirely handwritten, only discovered after death, it had never been mentioned by the testator, and, like in Barnes, the will was written on a very unusual surface. . . .

VI. AUTHENTICITY OF THE HANDWRITING

The law governing holograph wills in Saskatchewan in 1948 was The Wills Act, which read at s. 6(2),

> A holograph will, wholly in the handwriting of the testator and signed by him, may be made without any further formality or any requirement as to the presence of or attestation or signature by any witness.

To fall squarely within the statutory requirements of The Wills Act, Elliott knew he had to provide solid evidence that the will was, in the words of the Act, "wholly in the handwriting of the testator." . . . [I]t is the handwriting, theoretically at least, that "guarantees" without independent witnesses that a will was actually prepared by the testator. He thus went to considerable lengths to provide the most compelling evidence possible that the will was in Harris's hand so this fundamental statutory requirement could be met.

He obtained several affidavits that touched on the authenticity of the handwriting, including one from Harris's bank manager in Rosetown, William James Garland. That affidavit included a signature card from the bank's files and a strong affirmative statement from Garland: "I say definitely from my experience of handwriting that the signature George Harris is the same handwriting as that on exhibit 'A' [the tractor fender]." The bank manager, presumably at the urging of Elliott, goes on to address an anomaly between the signature on the will and the signature that appears on the bank card. Clearly Elliott was mindful of the s. 6(2) provision in The Wills Act that a valid holograph will must be "wholly in the writing of the testator and signed by him."

Harris signed the bank's signature card Geo. Harris but on the will he used three names, Cecil Geo. Harris."[I]n my banking experiences," Garland swears in his affidavit, "it is often found that the customer does not use his full name, but only one name and this was the practise of the said deceased."

The bank manager's affidavit was powerful because it came from someone with a certain professional knowledge of handwriting and signatures, and Garland was entirely independent. But Elliott, aware that in order to grant the will letters of administration the court would have to accept a testament scratched on metal in rather large handwriting, did not intend to rely on just one affidavit to verify the handwriting. He had George Whatley, in his affidavit, specifically echo the wording of the The Wills Act and swear it was "wholly in the handwriting" of the deceased.

Whatley deposed,

14. That now produced and shown to me and marked as exhibit "B" to this my affidavit is the said tractor fender.

15. That I was at one time a partner of the said deceased, and have known him for over twenty years and am familiar with the handwriting of the said deceased.

16. That I have frequently seen the writing of the said deceased and after thorough examination of the writing on the said exhibit "B" I say that the said handwriting and signature is wholly in the handwriting of the said deceased.

As a former business partner of Harris and as a man of affairs, Whatley would have some significant credibility in assessing that the body of the will and the signature were indeed in Harris's hand.

Elliott also ensured in the affidavit he obtained from Harris's wife, Bessie May, that she specifically swore that both the body of the will and the signature were "wholly in the handwriting of my deceased husband," once again mirroring the wording of The Wills Act. But she was the sole beneficiary and the court may have found her testimony less than compelling. So perhaps still unsatisfied on this crucial point, Elliott took the extraordinary step of providing his own affidavit swearing to the authenticity of the writing: "I have done business for Cecil George Harris, and during the course of his business I have examined certain documents on which his signature is written." He goes on to depose,

1. THAT I have carefully examined the said documents and compared the handwriting on the said documents and signature with the handwriting and signature on the said exhibit "A" [the tractor fender] and in my opinion, the handwriting was done by the one and same person, namely the said deceased. . . .

Finally, Harris had fulfilled another statutory requirement in the preparation of his holograph will. He clearly placed his signature at the end and thus, unwittingly or perhaps intuitively, fully complied with s. 8 of The Wills Act, 1931:

Every will shall...be valid if the signature is so placed at or after or following or under or beside or opposite to the end of the will, [and] that it is apparent on the face of the will that the testator intended to give effect by the signature to the writing signed as his will. . . .

VIII. HOW DID HARRIS SCRATCH THE FENDER?

How Harris managed to scratch out his will on the fender was a matter of central importance. If the will was indeed written in Harris' hand, what did he use to mark the hard surface of the fender? What could a man trapped under a tractor wheel have available to accomplish the task? And furthermore, if he found something to write with, how could an immobilized man get access to the fender? . . .

On the night of Tuesday, June 8, Harris was rescued from under the tractor. He was transported to hospital in the manner detailed above. He was undressed at the hospital and his clothes were given to young Nelson Fullerton who then took them to his father's farmhouse. At some unspecified time afterwards, his father, Dan Fullerton, searched the clothing, "and in the right hand pocket of the trousers, located the knife." The knife was a typical pocket knife with a folding blade at one end and a belt punch at the other. . . . [T]he knife provided vital physical evidence of how the will could have been written. It was also an opportunity to gather additional testimonial evidence lending weight to the proposition that the will was written and signed by Harris. Consequently, Elliott was careful to ensure that several of those swearing affidavits made observations about the knife and their belief it was the instrument Harris used to write his will. . . .

> George Whatley deposed,
>
> 17. . . . [I]n my opinion this said knife which is marked as exhibit "A" was the instrument used to write the said writing as there is a sharp pointed belt punch on the said knife which could be used for the writing, and from my examination of the said belt punch blade there is indication it was used recently as it is clear, bright and shining and free from all dirt or rust.
>
> 18. That the said Deceased had access to the said knife and his physical condition was such when I discovered him on the evening of June 8th, 1948 that he was capable of using the said knife to write the said writings.

Louis Large, the discoverer of the will, swore in his affidavit that "in my opinion the writing on the said Case tractor fender, from its clearness and lack of rust, could only have been done a few days previous to the 10th day of June, A.D. 1948 [the day on which Large discovered the writing]." . . .

Another issue foreseen by Elliott regarding the writing of the will was the need for an explanation of how a man caught beneath a tractor's wheel was able to reach the fender. So, he had Whatley specifically depose that Harris was literally in a position to do just that:

5. [H]e was caught [in such a manner that] his right leg was free, and his body and his arms were free, so that he had the full use of his arms and was capable of using his arms and hands.

6. That the left rear fender was pressing against his body and was within easy reach of his hands.

"[I]n my opinion," Whatley further wrote in his affidavit, "the said deceased was reclining in such a position when I found him that he could write the said writings."

* * *

The next evolution of the holographic will is the pre-printed preprinted will. Remember that "holographic" means hand-written. That becomes important in the "modern" (i.e., beginning in the 1980s) era, when will forms became readily and cheaply available, allowing laypeople to draw up their wills without the intercession—or expense or expertise—of lawyers. (This is not, certainly these days, a rare phenomenon, given that the cost of distributing such "preprinted" forms has dropped essentially to nothing whatever.) While these will forms do allow those of modest means to put together a will without the expense of a lawyer's assistance, they also create opportunities for legal difficulty later[104] (though this difficulty largely stems from the law itself rather than from any fundamental inability reasonably to interpret the efforts of the layman).[105]

---

104. *See, e.g.,* Estate of Gonzalez, 855 A.2d 1146 (Me. 2004). Gonzalez filled in the blanks of a preprinted will form, but his attempted dispositions suffered from the problem that the form was signed, but not attested—or, more exactly, that one copy of the form *was* attested, but the testator wrote out the manuscript portions and signed a *different* copy of the same form. There arises here *some* opportunity for foul play or error, but is it clear that the space for nefariousness is materially larger here than in other similar situations, whether holographic or lawyer-overseen? A generation ago, the response might have been fairly clear: Include instructions on the top of the forms that the testator should first fill out the forms and then proceed to write out longhand the whole of the document, preprinted words and all. These days, though, one suspects that such an instruction would be met with the same fundamental incomprehension as an instruction to hitch the horses to the phaeton and lead them to the postern gate. Accepting these propositions *arguendo*, what if anything do they suggest in the way of appropriate reform of the law of wills?

105. This quandary leads to consideration of some very, very deep thoughts indeed, thoughts that should engage those of us specially entrusted with ensuring the just and equitable regularization of free people's lives far more than it does. How much of the law exists for the genuine furtherance of citizens' good? How much for the arrogation of power and dosh to those "called to the bar?" How much for similar arrogation to those "called" to "serve" the Republic in its legislatures, its executive mansions, and its ever-growing ranks of regulators? Ever and always, *cui bono*, both in theory and in practice.

The problem is rendered particularly poignant if we posit a (not uncommon) state that (a) has adopted neither substantial compliance nor harmless error and (b) permits holographic wills.[106] Then the question becomes: can the partly preprinted and partly handwritten instrument be probated as a holographic will?

What are the potential answers to this quandary?

(1) Probate the document if there is within the whole of that document enough handwritten text to demonstrate the testator's intentions and that she was the author of those intentions; and enough surrounding atmospherics (i.e., the preprinted bits, mostly) to demonstrate her intent that this be her will. This is largely where the UPC (1969 and 1990) was headed with its rule requiring only that "material provisions/portions" be in holograph.[107] It's easy to see how this could be (and was) misinterpreted, though. If all of the assertions of intention and of gift, etc., are printed, and the only manuscript words are an inventory of property and a list of names then, by a certain light, essentially all of the legally "material" words are preprinted.

(2) Consider only the handwritten words and probate the document only if these words alone create a coherent will. The problem here is an exacerbation of the preceding difficulty: The preprinted language is not mere surplusage. On the contrary, the preprinted language was intended to be integrated into the will, and this is the very reason why the testator used a preprinted will form—to absorb professional language.

(3) Unless there's a complete holographic writing that includes no printed text, the document cannot be considered a holographic will. This is the traditional rule.

Are there other potential answers to this quandary? What are they? What difficulties do they present—what are their unintended consequences? What rule would you pick, and why?

---

106. *See* comment to §2-502. About 10 states still require that the whole document be handwritten; slightly fewer either ignore the preprinted words or follow the modern trend; the rest don't allow holographs.

107. UPC §2-502(b) still requires only that "the signature and material portions of the document" be in the testator's handwriting. To help uphold the validity of preprinted wills, §2-502(c) allows the printed portions of the document to be admitted as extrinsic evidence to demonstrate the testator's intent.

7. Will Contracts

Clients may seek to write either a joint will[108] (one will for both members of the couple) or "matching (or mutual) wills" [109] and then a contract forbidding the survivor of the two from changing the will later. The thinking here is fairly obvious: The parties feel that they've joined their lives, that they've (likely) had children together, and that they want to decide—together and for all time—what should become of their joint assets. But these are bad ideas.

One of the beautiful things about contract law is that people can make a legally enforceable agreement to do just about anything.[110] The agreement to make a will, or not to revoke a will, is valid consideration for a contract.

In any such situation, the question arises as to whether the will(s) was/were genuinely executed pursuant to a contract not to revoke it/them. When the will is silent as to the existence of a contract, most states presume that there was no contract not to revoke. A minority of states follows the reverse presumption.

If such a contract exists, the law of wills does not forbid the surviving testator from revoking the will after the first has died. The disappointed (non-)beneficiary has no recourse under Wills law; the new will is going to be probated. The would-be beneficiary's only recourse is to sue the testator's estate for breach of contract. Proving a valid contract between two dead people is a tall order, which makes recovery difficult.

Another practical consideration: Sometimes the surviving spouse may long outlive the decedent. Sometimes the death will occur early enough in the lives of the first couple that the survivor will have a new relationship; a new spouse, even a new family. This creates obvious difficulties. What has the survivor promised: not to change the language of her will; or not to deprive her and her decedent spouse's

---

108. A joint will is one will executed by two people as the will of both. A joint will typically devises the entire estate of the first testator to die to the survivor of the pair. When the second testator dies, the estate is distributed according to a scheme that both testators desired. These are frequently executed between spouses because they are simple: Regardless of which spouse dies first, both would want the estate to go to the survivor, with distribution to their kids when the survivor dies.

109. Mutual wills are two separate wills with reciprocal provisions. That is, A's will bequeaths everything to B, but if B predeceases A, then everything to their kids. B's will does the same, except A is the beneficiary.

110. Within limits that you should recall from your contracts class.

beneficiaries of the portion of the estate that they had earned together during the decedent spouse's life? Should the decedent spouse's contract be permitted to force the surviving spouse to disinherit any future family? How does the forced share of the second spouse interact with the promise to the decedent spouse?

For these reasons, a wise attorney is well advised strongly to counsel clients not to undertake will contracts, joint wills, or mutual wills. If they refuse to listen, and should you elect still to represent them, then you should at least make sure to insert a clause expressly saying whether a contract not to revoke has been made while memorializing to them and to your files your reasoned and thoughtful efforts to attempt to dissuade them from their course.[111]

E. CHANGES FOLLOWING WILL EXECUTION

Things change; stuff happens. Relevantly for present purposes, this means that the provisions made in wills can grow stale after a will's execution. This staleness falls into two broad categories: changes in the availability of beneficiaries and changes in the availability of the goods bequeathed. The law of wills provides a pair of doctrines—lapse and ademption, respectively—to deal with each circumstance.

1. Lapse: Changes in Beneficiary Availability

Under common law, all gifts made by will are subject to an implicit requirement that the devisee survive the testator. A devise *lapses* (fails) when the devisee predeceases the testator, unless the testator provided otherwise (e.g., "Blackacre to A, but if A should predecease me, then to B").[112] The effect of lapse differs depending upon the type

---

111. As the trusts section makes clear, the flexibility, facility, and potentially *inter vivos* and testamentary nature of trusts make them a far better vehicle by which to achieve the goals sought by means of will contracts, joint wills, and mutual wills.

112. Technically, lapse occurs when the devisee lives when the will was properly formalized but dies before the testator. Devises to parties already dead at the time the will is formalized are *void*. No one, though, much notes nor long remembers this technical distinction.

of gift involved. Lapsed specific or general gifts[113] are fairly straightforward; they fall into the residue (or into intestacy if there is no residuary clause[114]).

For residuary gifts, two questions must be answered: (1) are there any surviving residuary taker; and (2) is the no-residue-of-a-residue rule in force in the relevant jurisdiction?[115] If there is one or more surviving residuary taker and the no-residue-of-a-residue rule has been abolished, then the lapsed gift is divided among the surviving residuary takers. If a residuary taker survives but the rule is still in force, the lapsed gift to the decedent falls into intestacy. If there is no surviving residuary taker, the entire residue falls into intestacy.

a. Anti-Lapse Statutes

State legislatures have generally recognized that strict application of these common-law lapse rules often failed to achieve the central purpose of default rules in this area of the law. The lapse rule, that is, failed in significant ways to conform with and carry out what would have been the wishes of testators, had the testators considered and addressed the question.[116] Most, therefore, have enacted "anti-lapse" statutes to modify the effects of the common-law rule.[117]

An anti-lapse statute usually applies when the predeceasing beneficiary was in a specified relationship to the testator and was survived by descendants who also survived the testator. Those surviving descendants step into the shoes of the deceased beneficiary and take that beneficiary's gift by representation.

---

113. Specific and general devises are defined when discussing ademption, *infra*.

114. There should always be a residuary clause. Do you see why?

115. The no residue of a residue rule is a common-law rule that applies when there is more than one residuary taker. When only a share of the residue lapses, under this rule, that share passes by intestacy to the testator's heirs rather than to the remaining residuary devisees. Most states and the UPC (at §2-604(b)) have rejected this rule. Consider why: If the testator devises his entire estate to two people, and one predeceases him, which result do you think is consistent with the testator's intent? That the remaining taker inherits everything or that the lapsed half passes to the testator's heirs through intestacy?

116. Recall, generally, the discussions *supra* about the purposes and aims of intestacy law.

117. "Anti-lapse" isn't *quite* the perfect name for these statutes. They do not work, where triggered, to *prevent* the lapse; they don't result in predeceasing devisees being dug up and the otherwise-lapsed gifts thrown in with them. Rather, these statutes act to *redirect* lapsed gifts to alternative takers, takers (generally heirs) who take the lapsed gifts "by representation" of their deceased devisee ancestors. This "taking by representation" should ring a bell or two.

An example: X writes a will. Y is X's sister. Y has three children: A, B, and C. Y lives when X's will is validly executed, but dies before X does. But for anti-lapse rules, X's gift to Y would lapse upon X's death, with the result that the gift would fall into the residue or into intestacy. With anti-lapse, however, the gift to Y descends by representation upon Y's descendants, A, B, and C, equally.

The purpose of anti-lapse statutes is to effect the presumed intent of the average testator. It is, for instance, presumed that most ancestors, predeceased by their descendants, would wish their gifts to pass through to their remoter descendants. In normal English, it is generally presumed that Grandma, having watched her beloved second child, Billy, die, would have preferred—had she thought about it—to pass Billy's share of the family farm along to his only son, Will, rather than allowing it to fall into the residue for the benefit of whomsoever the residual takers might be.

Cases involving close family—especially descendants—are fairly easy, and the states are essentially uniform in applying anti-lapse principles in these circumstances. Then, though, rises the question: how "far out" should the anti-lapse principle extend? How much taking by representation, and in which circumstances, will accurately reflect the unarticulated intent of the average incomplete testament? Here consensus breaks down. Some states limit the effect of anti-lapse principles to direct descendants,[118] others encompass all gifts to descendants of the testator's grandparents,[119] yet others to all relative-devisees,[120] and a few to all devisees, whether related to the testator or not.[121]

Food for thought: why do anti-lapse statutes, especially the most expansive of them, limit their effect to ensuring passage to the predeceasing beneficiary's *descendants* by representation? Why not let the gift pass to the beneficiary's own named devisees?[122] If childless Laura predeceases her mother, who had left her and her siblings equal shares of her estate, why should not Laura's lapsed gift pass to her

---

118. *See, e.g.,* Miss. Code Ann. §91-5-7.

119. *See, e.g.,* Idaho Code §15-2-605 (2015).

120. *See, e.g.,* Kan. Stat. Ann. §59-615 (2012).

121. *See, e.g.,* Iowa Code §633.273 (2015). Apparently there has been little empirical work in this area to determine what testators would want, had they considered the question. In ways that we have explored earlier in the semester, such empirical work might prove difficult, unreliable, incoherent, or some combination of all three.

122. Named in that beneficiary's will, that is.

surviving husband Dennis, to whom she had herself left the whole of her estate?[123]

Anti-lapse statutes are default rules; a testator who does not wish the jurisdiction's anti-lapse statute to apply can draft around it. The anti-lapse statute will not apply when the testator expresses a contrary intent. But how definite must the testator's expression be? The UPC takes the position that the anti-lapse statute "should be defeated only by a finding of intention that *directly contradicts* the substitute gift created by the statute."[124] As such, "mere" words of survivorship[125] are not sufficient to defeat the anti-lapse statute's application. What do you think about this rule? Are words of survivorship just boilerplate, or should courts presume that every word in a testator's will is there for a reason? Most states disagree with the UPC and consider words of survivorship sufficient in themselves to defeat the anti-lapse statute.

b. Class Gifts

Having discussed anti-lapse statutes, let's return to the basic, common-law lapse rule. A devise to a *class* of persons (a "class gift") is handled somewhat differently than a devise to an individual. When the testator makes a gift to a class, the *class* is considered to be the beneficiary, not each individual member. If a member of the class predeceases the testator, then the remaining class members still take the total gift, including the predeceasing member's share, rather than having that member's share lapse. As a result, no anti-lapse considerations ever arise.

Determining whether a gift is a class gift or not is both trickier and less technical than it sounds. The basic rule is that when the testator is "group-minded"[126] in making a gift to multiple persons, the gift is a class gift. The interesting question is how, precisely, to determine whether the testator was group-minded. The modern view (or perhaps the accidental modern trend) has tended toward a rules-based approach, turning factors that had been proxies for group-mindedness in earlier cases—such as use of a group label and dynamic shares—into necessary requirements for a class gift.

The Restatement (Third) of Property: Wills and Other Donative Transfers takes this approach in §§13.1 and 13.2. The key distinction

---

123. Consider other possible permutations as well.
124. Comment to UPC §2-603 (emphasis in original).
125. E.g., "Blackacre to Roland *if he survives me.*"
126. Yes, that is the actual term.

under the Restatement is whether the beneficiaries' identities and shares are subject to fluctuation (meaning class gift) or fixed (meaning not[127]). If the disposition's terms identify the beneficiaries only by a group label or term of relationship (e.g., "my nieces and nephews"), a rebuttable presumption arises that the disposition is a class gift.[128] But if the disposition identifies the beneficiaries by a group label or term of relationship *and* name and/or number (e.g., "to my three nieces, Shelby, Hailey, and Colby"), then the opposite presumption arises; that is, that the disposition is to beneficiaries whose shares and identities are fixed.[129] Ultimately, it's a question of the testator's intent.[130]

As you read through *Womack*, compare the court's logic with the Restatement's rule. Can you square the two?

STATE OF WOMACK
280 S.W.3d 317 (Tex. App. 2008).

Opinion

Appellants, Barbara Holladay, Richard H. Byrne, Michael V. Byrne, and James E. Byrne, Jr. (collectively "Byrne"), appeal from a judgment of the County Court at Law # 3 of Lubbock County, Texas, construing the will of Russell E. Womack, deceased. Through six issues, Byrne attacks the legal determination that the will of the deceased intended a class gift to "nieces and nephews" of Russell and his deceased wife, Beverly. . . . We affirm.

Factual and Procedural Background

Russell E. Womack was a successful businessman who had accumulated a sizeable estate by the time of his death. He was married to Beverly Womack, who predeceased him. Russell and Beverly did

---

127. Because such a gift is to individuals, not a class, a devise to any of those individuals who predeceases the testator will lapse, unless the anti-lapse statute applies.

128. The presumption can be rebutted by evidence that the testator intended fixed shares to fixed beneficiaries.

129. This presumption also is rebuttable, this time by evidence that the testator intended the beneficiaries to take as members of a group.

130. The advantage of bright-line rules—such as those the Restatement espouses—instead of the open standard of group mindedness is that rules may reduce litigation and lead to more predictable results. The disadvantage is that in any given case the rules may not be a good proxy for group mindedness. Hence the result may not reflect the intentions of the testator. This is another example of the tension between formalism and intent that arises so often in the law of wills.

not have children of their own, however, their respective siblings did have children. As a result, Russell wrote a holographic will that left his entire estate to his and Beverly's nieces and nephews.

The issue of the Womack estate was brought before the trial court as a "Combined Application For Identification Of Distributees, For Probate Of Will, For Appointment Of Independent Executor, And For Waiver Of Bond." Within this document was a request that the trial court determine the identities of the class of living nieces and nephews, as designated by the Womack will. . . .

The will was admitted to probate on May 10, 2006. . . . [O]n August 2, 2007, the trial court entered a judgment declaring the identity of the distributees under the Womack will. The court found that the will gave the entire estate to a certain group of persons, those being the nieces and nephews of Russell and Beverly Womack. The trial court found that the nieces and nephews of Russell [who remained distributees after the codicil noted below] were James E. Byrne, Jr., Barbara Holladay, Michael V. Byrne, Richard H. Byrne, Wes Womack, and Carolyn Victoria Cain. The trial court also found that the nieces and nephews of Beverly were Nancy Higginson, Debbie Cheadle, Arthur Cheadle, Camille Sawaya, Wayne Carson, and Raeanne Martin. The court further found, although there had been a dispute regarding the status of [Deah'dra Anne] Cummings, that dispute had been resolved by and between Cummings and those parties who had filed an objection and that the objection had been withdrawn. . . . [T]herefore, Cummings was to receive an equal share as a distributee under the Womack estate. The trial court proceeded to order the estate distributed in 13 equal parts to all nieces and nephews found by the court, to include Cummings. It is from this order that Byrne appeals.

Class Gift

Byrne's first three issues all deal with the subject of whether the will of Russell made a class gift to the nieces and nephews of Russell and Beverly. It is Byrne's contention that the will specifically provides that the estate is to be distributed to 12 distributees. We disagree.

The original holographic will, dated April 9, 1999, stated, in relevant part:

> I leave all of my estate to my nieces and nephews and to Beverly's nieces and nephews and to Basilio Coronado. The estate is to be divided into fifteen (15) equal shares and each niece & nephew & Basilio Coronado are to receive one (1) equal share.

Subsequently, on May 4, 2000, Russell wrote a holographic codicil to the will. In this codicil, Russell stated:

I Hereby delete from this will the following Persons:

1. Basilio Coronado
2. Finney Cheadle
3. Edward Cheadle

The codicil does not mention 12 equal shares nor does it otherwise try to limit the interpretation of the original will. It simply deletes three individuals from the list of distributees.

"It is a cardinal rule in the interpretation of wills that the intent of the testator is the object to be sought. . . ." No party to this case alleges that the will is ambiguous, therefore, the proof of intent is to be taken from a reading of the will as drafted without aid to extraneous sources. . . . In determining whether a gift is to be treated as a class gift or gifts to specifically named devisees, we look at the words used to describe the takers of the gift. . . . A class gift is a gift to several persons answering the same description so that one word describes them all. . . . The gift must be an aggregate sum to a body of persons uncertain at the time of the gift. . . .

In the case before the Court, the group originally consisted of the nieces and nephews of Russell and Beverly and Basilio Coronado. By the codicil, Coronado and two nephews were deleted. After the codicil, the aggregate sum to be given was the totality of the estate of Russell and the several persons designated to take were the aforementioned nieces and nephews. According to Byrne, this means that it is a specific gift to those twelve nieces and nephews of Russell and Beverly in equal shares. However, what makes this a class gift is that, at the time of execution of the will, the body of persons the gift was made to was uncertain. This uncertainty was due to not knowing which of the nieces and nephews would survive Russell. This uncertainty was not resolved until Russell's death. . . . The fact that the number "fifteen" was used in the original will means only that Russell was attempting to ensure that all received equal shares. Had he intended a gift to specific devisees, all Russell had to do was name them. As the will named one specific devisee, Basilio Coronado, we are guided by the fact that Russell did not specifically name the nieces and nephews. . . . Accordingly, we overrule Byrne's issues regarding the nature of the gift and find that the will left the estate to a class of distributees, as found by the trial court. . . .

[W]e affirm the judgment of the trial court.

QUESTIONS AND ANALYSIS

Note what is at stake in this case: whether Cummings, who was not, it appears, a wedlock-established niece of the decedent couple, nevertheless qualified as a "niece" who should take under the will. Specifically, the issue was whether Cummings qualified under Texas law as an adoptee-by-estoppel (equitable adoption). Because the will contestants failed to raise an objection to equitable adoption in the court below, they instead relied on appeal primarily on an argument that the testators had meant to grant shares of their estate to 15 people total, which is to say 14 nieces and nephews, plus Basilio Coronado. When, later, Basilio and two named nephews were excluded from the grant, the theory went, what remained was a grant to 12 nieces and nephews as individuals. Since including Cummings–the only questionable grantee–would have resulted in 13 takers, said contestants, the unavoidable conclusion was that the testators had meant to exclude Cummings. In other words, if the court had found a gift to 12 specific individuals, then the 12 "natural" nieces and nephews would have taken; if the grant was to all of the testators' nieces and nephews *as a class*, then all parties so certified by the court, as Cummings was here, would take an equal share. This raises the issue of a class gift in the following way: If the will left the estate to the class of "all of our nieces and nephews," and Cummings was in fact biologically a niece, then she would take.

The court here follows a formalist process. It notes that (1) the fourteen uncontested nieces and nephews were not listed uniquely in the will; while (2) the group-minded term "nieces and nephews" was used; and that (3) the class was still indeterminate at the time the will was executed because the death of one or more nieces or nephews would have decreased the size of the class. But isn't this third point both a makeweight and a (rare indeed) *literal and true* example of question-begging (rather than of question-raising, merely)? After all, if, as the court here concludes, the gift in the will was a class gift, then the fact of the gift having been a class gift *itself* determines that pre-deceasing beneficiaries will have been treated as though their gifts had lapsed without corrective application of an anti-lapse statute. On the other hand, if the gift had been found to be a gift to 15 (then later 15 minus 3) individual beneficiaries, then *that determination itself* would have resulted in application of the anti-lapse statute (at least with regard to those beneficiaries who had progeny). Is the court *really* saying that it had found a class gift here for the technical reason that when the gift was made, it was possible that some of the beneficiaries *might* have died before the testator and that those who had borne descendants may have additionally suffered the deaths of those descendants before they died? Or is it just reaching the conclusion it wants, and then working backward? Or something else?

Does such analysis best align with the underlying purpose of wills law: to attempt to recreate the intent of the—in this case holographic—testator as best as possible? The text of the will seems to suggest that the testator had a specific list of 15 (later 12) people in mind; might extrinsic-evidence analysis have demonstrated which 12 people the testator had in mind, and why? If so, then why not undertake it? Do the advantages of formality and ease of disposition outweigh the potential benefits of searching intent analysis here? If so, why here and not in other instances? Do the advantages of formal analysis dissipate here because the will is holographic rather than attorney-generated? Is it appropriate to follow a different set of (relaxed and more searching) rules when interpreting holographic wills than when interpreting attorney-generated wills? Why or why not?

c. Class Gifts and Anti-Lapse Statutes

Most states apply their anti-lapse statutes to class gifts, if the class members meet the statute's requirements. A gift to "my nieces and nephews" would almost certainly fall under the average anti-lapse statute. Thus, if any nieces or nephews predeceased the testator and had descendants who survived the testator, they would still be counted as class members; their surviving descendants would take their share by representation. But if the gift were to "my co-workers" as a class, then—in most states—any predeceasing co-workers would be ignored (i.e., the anti-lapse statute would not be applied); only those who survived the testator would divide the gift.

One question about which states differ is when the class to whom the gift has been given should close. In some jurisdictions, the class closes then the will is executed; in others, when the testator dies. This distinction will often make no difference, as when the class is of the testator's siblings and the state applies the anti-lapse statute to *all* gifts to siblings. In such a circumstance, the state's anti-lapse law will include all nieces and nephews of the testator as appropriate takers by representation of any predeceasing siblings, regardless of when they die. Here's a scenario in which it might matter, though. Imagine that the gift was to testator's co-workers. Imagine further that the will is executed and the testator dies, in one of the minority of jurisdictions that has extended the anti-lapse statute to apply to all grantees, regardless of relationship to the testator. Now suppose that a person was a co-worker when the will was executed but died before the testator. Should the anti-lapse statute apply to give a share of the gift to the pre-deceasing co-worker's descendants? Why or why not? Does your evaluation of this problem shed additional light on the question of the wisdom of extending anti-lapse statute beyond close kin? In what way?

2. Changes in the Testator's Estate

This discussion is the second facet of the stale will problem, the first half of which, just completed, dealt with the doctrines of lapse, anti-lapse, and the class gift. Then the question was: What is to be done when a beneficiary named in a stale will has passed before the testator. Here the focus shifts to doctrines that apply when there have been changes in what or how much property is owned or how it is held between execution and the testator's death.

a. Ademption by Extinction

Specific devises of real and personal property are subject to the doctrine of ademption by extinction when those items of property are no longer in the testator's estate at death. There are two theories of ademption—the identity theory and the intent theory—but before addressing those, we must define the kinds of devises a will can make.

There are four kinds of devise: specific, general, demonstrative, and residuary. A specific devise disposes of a particular item of the testator's property, rather than money (e.g., her wedding band). Only specific devises can be adeemed. The other three devises—general, demonstrative, and residuary—cannot be adeemed; they will be satisfied to the extent that they can be and will fail to the extent unsatisfied. A devise is general when the testator intends to confer a general benefit rather than giving a particular asset (e.g., $100,000 to A). If there is not enough liquid cash to satisfy a general devise, other assets will be sold to make up the difference. Demonstrative devises are a hybrid of specific and general devises; a demonstrative devise is a general devise that is payable from a specific source (e.g., $100,000 to Emily, to be paid from the proceeds of sale of my ranch in Texas). The executor must sell the Texas ranch to come up with the $100,000, but if the sale doesn't bring in enough money (or if the ranch is no longer in the estate at death), the executor must sell other property to make up the difference.[131] Finally, a residuary devise conveys the portion of the testator's estate not effectively devised by the rest of the will.

Again, only specific devises can be adeemed. Ademption occurs when a devised asset ceases to be part of the testator's estate between the will's execution and the testator's death. Money can always be raised by selling assets, and the beneficiary of money can receive as much of it as the estate can give (up to the amount of the gift). In contrast, specific items of property are either in the estate or they are not, which means those beneficiaries can either receive them or not. Ademption is a black-and-white doctrine; either the property is there for the beneficiary to take or it is not there and must fail. Having established that proposition, let us turn to the two theories of ademption.

i. Identity Theory

Under the traditional identity theory of ademption, a gift is extinguished if the specifically devised item is not in the testator's estate at death. Over the years, various exceptions (or corollaries) arose that in large part hollowed out the unforgiving identity theory, the most important of which is that the gift is adeemed only if the specifically devised item left the estate as a result of the testator's conscious action.[132] In the absence of evidence as to whose act created the absence, courts presume that the absence resulted from the testator's conscious action (and therefore, the gift is adeemed). The intent theory is an objective test: The item is not there, and that is either the result of the testator's conscious action or not, with no intent analysis generally required. (Note, though, that in states that have adopted the conscious action exception, courts are necessarily open to extrinsic evidence that the gift had been removed from the testator's estate by acts other than conscious acts of the testator.)

Another (or perhaps a subsidiary) way courts have sidled their way around the identity theory doctrine is by classifying an *inter vivos* transaction disposing of a specifically devised item as a "change in form" of ownership, rather than as a substantive removal of the specific

---

131. Demonstrative devises are thus not very meaningfully different than a general devise other than specifying the first source—not the *sole* source, mind you, just the first resort—that the executor must tap to raise the money.

132. *See, e.g.,* In re Estate of Anton, 731 N.W.2d 19 (Iowa 2007). *Anton* also states that when the testator knows about a transaction involving a specifically devised item and can change her will, but chooses not to, then the item's absence is considered the result of the testator's conscious action.

asset from the estate. "Perhaps subsidiary" because change of form situations usually arise when testator has been passive with regard to the change. Common examples of change of form arise when a specific gift has, by corporate action, been changed in accounting but remains unchanged in value. Imagine, for instance, that testator owns three hundred shares of Xrocks, Inc., and leaves these shares to Z. Xrocks merges with Kecca to become KX, Ltd., and issues new stock in the new corporation's name; testator's 300 shares of Xrocks is replaced by 500 shares of KX. This change is considered a change in form, and the new stock replaces the old in the will. Stock splits receive similar treatment.[133]

ii. Intent Theory

The exceptions that slowly developed to the identity theory were a movement away from what many courts considered the harsh effects of the identity theory's rigid application. In 1990, the UPC abandoned the identity theory entirely and adopted the *intent theory* in its place. Under the intent theory,[134] the beneficiary is entitled to a specifically devised gift's replacement item(s) if the testator had replaced it or to the gift's cash value if the beneficiary can prove that the testator did not intend the ademption of the devise. This is a fuzzier, more

---

133. For more, see *Increase, infra.*

134. *See* UPC §2-606(a):

A specific devisee has a right to specifically devised property in the testator's estate at the testator's death and to:

(1) any balance of the purchase price, together with any security agreement, owed by a purchaser at the testator's death by reason of sale of the property;

(2) any amount of a condemnation award for the taking of the property unpaid at death;

(3) any proceeds unpaid at death on fire or casualty insurance on or other recovery for injury to the property;

(4) any property owned by the testator at death and acquired as a result of foreclosure, or obtained in lieu of foreclosure, of the security interest for a specifically devised obligation;

(5) any real property or tangible personal property owned by the testator at death which the testator acquired as a replacement for specifically devised real property or tangible personal property; and

(6) if not covered by paragraphs (1) through (5), a pecuniary devise equal to the value as of its date of disposition of other specifically devised property disposed of during the testator's lifetime but only to the extent it is established that ademption would be inconsistent with the testator's manifested plan of distribution or that at the time the will was made, the date of disposition or otherwise, the testator did not intend ademption of the devise.

subjective analysis. The key to this analysis will often be whether the testator wanted the beneficiary to have *that specific thing named in the will* for reasons specific to the testator's relationship with the beneficiary or whether the testator wanted the beneficiary to have something from the estate, with the something in question best identified at the time of the will's execution by the specific thing named in the will, but subject to change after execution of the will without the change signifying the desire of the testator to deprive the beneficiary of taking any bequest. If the former, then the gift is adeemed. If the latter—if the testator just wanted the beneficiary to have something of that general type (e.g., a car for the grandkids)—then the gift is not adeemed, and the beneficiary gets the replacement or cash value, as appropriate.

iii. Effect of Ademption

If a devise is adeemed, it simply means that the devise is no longer operative and so the beneficiary takes nothing (as a result of that particular gift; the beneficiary may still take other gifts under the will that were not adeemed). But if the gift is not adeemed under the relevant theory, then the beneficiary gets the item's cash value in lieu of the item itself. Of course, the money must come from somewhere; if there is no cash available, other assets in the estate will be sold to raise the funds. Assets will be sold depending on where they fall in the distribution scheme. The first to be sold are any assets that would have fallen into intestacy. If that doesn't raise enough funds, then assets falling into the residue are next on the block. And if that still doesn't do the job, then assets that would have gone to general beneficiaries get tapped.

b. Ademption by Satisfaction

Ademption by satisfaction[135] occurs when the testator gives a gift to a named beneficiary after executing the will and the property given is of a similar nature to what the beneficiary is to receive under the will. Under common law, a rebuttable presumption arises that the gift is given as an advance on what the beneficiary is to receive under the will.[136] Posit for instance that Tom had devised $100,000 to each of his

---

135. This doctrine is called "advancements" in the intestacy context.

136. By nature, this doctrine usually applies to general devises. When specific property is given to the named beneficiary *inter vivos*, then it would be adeemed by extinction when probate rolled along because the specifically devised item would no longer be in the estate.

six children. Thad, the youngest, asks his father Tom for $50,000 for a down-payment for his first house. Tom concurs. Under the common law, this gift would presumptively constitute a satisfaction of half of the $100,000 testamentary gift, so that Thad would only receive the remaining $50,000 upon his father's demise unless he could rebut the presumption.

The UPC has added to the common law's requirement in a way that radically restricts this doctrine's application. Under §2-609(a), the gift is adeemed "only if (i) the will provides for deduction of the gift, (ii) the testator declared in a contemporaneous writing that the gift is in satisfaction of the devise . . . , or (iii) the devisee acknowledged in writing that the gift is in satisfaction of the devise. . . ." The modern trend here is to treat *inter vivos* gifts as gifts, not advances on the will.

One example of satisfaction in action is Yivo Institute v. Zaleski, 874 A.2d 411 (Md. 2005). The court found ademption by satisfaction of a specific bequest of shares of stock worth about $100,000 when the testator wrote the will. The testator had previously signed an agreement promising to donate $100,000 to the devisee, a charity, by will or by lifetime transfer. A couple years later, the testator donated stock worth $99,997.69, plus wrote an additional check for $2.31, to bring his total lifetime gifts to the charity to exactly $100,000.

c. Increase

What happens when a testator devises 100 shares of stock to a beneficiary and sometime between execution and death, the company splits its stock two to one? Does the beneficiary take 100 shares of stock or 200? Under the doctrine of increase the answer is 200, because the 200 shares (post split) represents the same proportional share of ownership as did the 100 shares originally devised. When a company's stock splits, or the company merges, or spins off a subsidiary, a devise of shares made before those corporate developments occurred should result in a gift of the equivalent amount of the company's assets following the split, merger, or spin-off because the change is merely one of form, not substance. In other words, the beneficiary receives the economic equivalent of the devise, as long as that equivalent can be traced from the original gift.

The issuance of stock dividends is notably absent from the corporate developments discussed above. Some courts treat those differently, concluding that they are more analogous to a cash dividend than to a stock split. Cash dividends have always been denied to the beneficiary of the stock shares, and those courts see no reason that the beneficiary should get one form of dividend and be denied the other. The UPC[137] and Restatement,[138] in contrast, recognize that a stock dividend is designed to maintain the shareholder's proportionate ownership and give those dividends to the beneficiary.

d. Exoneration

Exoneration, if it applies, results in the nonspecific gift assets of an estate being used to pay off any mortgages or liens that encumber specific gifts.[139] The traditional, now minority, common-law rule presumed that exoneration applied absent contrary language in the will. The modern trend (and majority) presumes otherwise; the beneficiary will take the gift encumbered by the lien.[140] (The bank holding the mortgage or lien may well call it in upon the death of the debtor, leaving the grantee with the options of re-encumbering the property under her own name, owing the estate for having satisfied the debt, or having to sell the property to meet the obligation.)

e. Abatement

Abatement occurs when the estate doesn't have enough assets to satisfy all of the testator's devises and debts. Under those circumstances, some gifts must be reduced ("abated"). Typically, property that would

---

137. *See* UPC §2-605(a):

If a testator executes a will that devises securities and the testator then owned securities that meet the description in the will, the devise includes additional securities owned by the testator at death to the extent the additional securities were acquired by the testator after the will was executed as a result of the testator's ownership of the described securities and are securities of any of the following types:

(1) securities of the same organization acquired by reason of action initiated by the organization or any successor, related, or acquiring organization, excluding any acquired by exercise of purchase options;
(2) securities of another organization acquired as a result of a merger, consolidation, reorganization, or other distribution by the organization or any successor, related, or acquiring organization; or
(3) securities of the same organization acquired as a result of a plan of reinvestment.

138. *See* Restatement (Third) of Property: Wills and Other Donative Transfers §5.3.

139. The choice of which assets to sell in order to pay off the lien follows the same scheme as that when ademption by extinction does not apply.

140. *See, e.g.,* UPC §2-607 ("A specific devise passes subject to any mortgage interest existing at the date of death, without right of exoneration, regardless of a general directive in the will to pay debts.").

pass by intestacy abates first, followed by the residue. General devises come next, and lastly, specific and demonstrative devises. Within each category, the gifts are reduced *pro rata.*

Of course, the testator can prescribe her own abatement plan in the will, if this default structure does not suit her desires. The UPC also allows for the court to alter the default abatement plan "as may be found necessary to give effect to the [presumed] intent of the testator" when the default plan would defeat "the testamentary plan or the express or implied purpose of the devise."[141] Under what circumstances would a court take advantage of that power? Can you craft such a scenario?

F. INTERPRETING A WILL

The final wills law issue to address is the question of interpreting a valid, up-to-date will. The following doctrines assist these efforts.

1. Incorporation

Before we begin interpreting a will, we need to identify its components. There are three doctrines that define the documents that compose the testator's will: integration, republication by codicil, and incorporation by reference.

a. Integration

The typical will is comprised of more than one sheet of paper. A paper is part of the will ("integrated" into the will) if it is present at the time of execution and intended to be part of the will.[142]

It is usually obvious which documents are intended to be part of the will, because they are physically connected, numbered, and display an internal coherence of language. A prudent attorney will ensure all

---

141. UPC §3-902(b) ("If the will expresses an order of abatement, or if the testamentary plan or the express or implied purpose of the devise would be defeated by the order of abatement stated in subsection (a), the shares of the distributees abate as may be found necessary to give effect to the intention of the testator.").

142. The Restatement (Third) of Property: Wills and Other Donative Transfers §3.5 sums it up nicely.

of these before the testator signs and should have the testator initial each page for identification purposes. If the document in question (or some part of it) lacks any of these attributes, it likely won't be integrated.[143] Where integration fails, the court must rely on intent analysis, as guided by these integration doctrines.

Note that integration matters only if the document in question does not qualify as a will in its own right. If it does, then different issues arise.[144]

b. Republication by Codicil

Publication is the testator's indication to all and sundry that he intends a certain document to be his will. A will is "published" (in this legal, term of art sense[145]) when it is originally executed. But as time goes on and things happen, life events can turn the will—or parts of it—stale and outdated.[146]

Republication by codicil is a way of refreshing old wills. A codicil is an amendment to a will that must be executed with testamentary formalities.[147] Under the republication by codicil doctrine, a will is presumptively treated as re-executed ("republished") on the date its most recent valid codicil was executed.[148] This presumption can be rebutted by showing that treating the will as republished on that date is inconsistent with the testator's intent.

Republication not only indicates that the earlier will is still in force to the extent not altered by the codicil but can also have other effects. It can come in handy to cure defects in wills, such as potential

---

143. For an example of a case where a document is not physically connected, there is no numbering scheme, and the two pages in question (it was an allegedly two-page will) fail to refer to each other at all, *see* Estate of Rigsby, 843 P.2d 856 (Okla. App. 1992).

144. The key such question: Does this document revoke the earlier one or is it a codicil?

145. By contrast, a will is *recorded* by (usually) the county of the testator's final residence, when probate proceedings begin.

146. Things such as the birth of children that—logically—are not included in the old will (*see* pretermitted children, *supra*).

147. Codicils can be holographic if the state recognizes holographic wills.

148. Restatement (Third) of Property: Wills and Other Donative Transfers §3.4. The codicil need not expressly republish the will for this presumption to apply, but it is good practice to expressly republish if the testator wants it republished (or expressly state that it is *not* republished, if appropriate).

incorporation by reference problems (considered below), or to bring a formerly pretermitted child within the will's dispositions.[149]

Pretermission is one area to consider carefully to determine if a finding of republication would actually serve to carry out the testator's presumed intent. Consider the following example:

> In 1965, Winston has one kid, Brandon. In 1967, Bruce executes a will, which mentions Brandon *by name*. In '69, Winston has another child, Shannon. In '72, Bruce executes a codicil, which leaves his old philosophy books to his friend Dan and does not mention either of his kids in any fashion. In '73, Bruce dies an untimely death.

Would republishing Bruce's will carry out his intent[150] under these circumstances? The effect of republication would be that Shannon is no longer pretermitted (because the will would be considered as executed after her birth). This would cut her out entirely. If we presume that Bruce's intent is to provide for both of his children, then republication should and would not apply. Shannon would have to make this argument in a probate challenge to the presumption of republication, but all other things being equal, she should prevail.

Another effect of republication is to revive a formerly revoked will.[151] But only a validly executed former will can be republished; a testator cannot, by republication, validly publish a prior failed will.

c. Incorporation by Reference

Incorporation by reference doctrine allows extrinsic evidence to identify the beneficiaries of, or property passing under, a will. Under the traditional (and still majority) doctrine,[152] a writing may be incorporated into a will by reference if it satisfies three criteria: (1) it must be "in existence when [the] will is executed," (2) the will must manifest

---

149. Here's a thought problem for you. T executes a will, and one of his witnesses is also a beneficiary. Later, he executes a codicil, using two different witnesses, both of whom are disinterested. What is the effect on the disposition to the beneficiary witness of the will?

150. Presumed intent, obviously. He, like all other testators, is no longer around to answer the question.

151. For example, T publishes Will 1. A few years later, he publishes Will 2, expressly revoking Will 1. And a month before he dies, he executes a codicil to Will 1. By republishing Will 1 as of the codicil date, it would be the last validly executed will on the day he dies.

152. Captured in UPC §2-510 ("A writing in existence when a will is executed may be incorporated by reference if the language of the will manifests this intent and describes the writing sufficiently to permit its identification.").

an intent to incorporate it, and (3) the will must "describe[] the writing sufficiently to permit its identification."

Note which important requirement is missing here; the incorporated document need not independently satisfy the testamentary formalities. The doctrine treats the incorporated matter as though it is covered by the formalities of the execution, but prohibits the testator from making later revisions (or reserving the power to do so) without subsequent testamentary formalities. The requirement that the document exist when the will is executed also prevents the testator from referencing a document that he plans to create later;[153] once the will is executed, the incorporated document is frozen in time (much like the will itself).

The UPC adds a modern twist to the doctrine in §2-513, which has not been widely adopted. Section 2-513 permits incorporation of documents not yet in existence, as long as they are signed, only dispose of personal property, and describe the property and devisees with reasonable certainty.[154] Of course, the will must manifest intent to incorporate the document, but the sample clause—which the UPC drafters consider a sufficient manifestation—says "I [the testator] *might* leave a written statement or list disposing of items of tangible personal property" (emphasis added). Should the testator's mere recognition of the possibility that she will write such a list be a sufficient manifestation of intent to incorporate it?

Consider the implications of the UPC's new doctrine. The incorporated document need not comply with testamentary formalities. It need not have independent significance (discussed next). It may be created or modified at will after the will's execution, so it's not covered by the formalities of the will's execution, as a traditionally incorporated document is. The only conceivable protection that applies to the incorporated document is the testator's signature. The comment to §2-513 says that this new doctrine is "part of the broader policy of effectuating

---

153. If the testator wishes to incorporate a document he knows he must write later, then republication by codicil becomes a very handy tool. Think about it.

154. *See* UPC §2-513 ("Whether or not the provisions relating to holographic wills apply, a will may refer to a written statement or list to dispose of items of tangible personal property not otherwise specifically disposed of by the will, other than money. To be admissible under this section as evidence of the intended disposition, the writing must be signed by the testator and must describe the items and the devisees with reasonable certainty. The writing may be referred to as one to be in existence at the time of the testator's death; it may be prepared before or after the execution of the will; it may be altered by the testator after its preparation; and it may be a writing that has no significance apart from its effect on the dispositions made by the will.").

a testator's intent and of relaxing formalities of execution." But consider how far this stretches. The testator can dispose of *all* her personal property (except money) by a simple list, protected only by her signature. That could be a substantial portion of her estate; after all, there is no maximum value that can pass under this section. Do you think this policy is wise? How well does it fulfill the functions that the formalities purportedly perform, *especially* the protective function?

2. Acts of Independent Significance

The doctrine of acts of independent significance is another way for extrinsic evidence to identify the beneficiaries of, or property passing under, the will. The will may dispose of property by referring to acts or events that have some independent[155] significance, purpose, or effect other than to designate a beneficiary or bequest.[156] For example, the testator can leave "the car I own at my death" to "the person who is my secretary at my death."

These acts are considered trustworthy despite lacking testamentary formalities, and despite occurring later than the will's execution, because the testator is unlikely to be motived (to buy a new car, or to fire his secretary) just by the desire to reconfigure the practical distributions to be made from his already executed will. Surely it would be easier to have the will revised (or just an amendatory codicil added) than to for example make a car purchase or a hiring or firing decision. The effects that the testator's later actions have on the estate distribution are incidental to their real purpose.

Some courts, obviously not as captivated by the nuances of property law as we, have made a hash of this doctrine, but this is its coherent core.

3. Revocation and Related Details

Under traditional wills law, there were two ways to revoke a will, methods still universally recognized. The first is revocation by a subsequent

---

155. "Independent" from their effect on the will, that is.

156. This doctrine is embraced by UPC §2-512 ("A will may dispose of property by reference to acts and events that have significance apart from their effect upon the dispositions made by the will, whether they occur before or after the execution of the will or before or after the testator's death. The execution or revocation of another individual's will is such an event.").

writing. The testator can revoke his will by executing a subsequent writing with testamentary formalities that expressly revokes the prior will. States that apply the harmless error or substantial compliance doctrines will apply those doctrines to the subsequent writing as well. After all, it makes little sense to apply those forgiving doctrines to the will, which fails to comply with the formalities perfectly (or else those doctrines would not be implicated), but to require strict adherence to the formalities for a subsequent writing that would otherwise be "close enough" under the applicable doctrine.

The second way to revoke a will under traditional wills law is by physical act. A testator can revoke her will by destroying or obliterating it with intent to revoke or by directing another person to do so in her presence. Removing the testator's signature—for example, by tearing it off, lining through it, or removing the signature page—is sufficient to revoke the entire will. Traditionally, the act of revocation must "touch the words of the will." Charring the edges of the will, but not eliminating any of the words on the page, has historically not been good enough.

Now consider this situation. What if the testator crosses out one provision (say, deciding that cousin Ed shouldn't get Blackacre after all) and writes above it that Aunt Sue should take Blackacre instead? A holographic change like this is only a partial revocation of the will, not an entire one, and will only be valid if the change itself, standing alone, satisfies the requirements of a valid holographic will (and the state recognizes holographic wills, of course). If the change is not a valid holograph or the state does not recognize holographic wills the original language of the will controls.

Two presumptions apply in potential repeal by physical act situations. The proponent of the will bears the burden of rebutting each of these presumptions. Some states require clear and convincing evidence, while others only require a preponderance of the evidence.

The first presumption arises when there are multiple copies of the will, and the testator destroys or revokes the copy he possesses. A presumption arises that all duplicates are revoked also, even those not in the testator's possession. (Put another way: The presumption is that the testator intended to revoke the will upon destruction or revocation of the copy in his possession, regardless of whether there are other extant and undestroyed/revoked copies somewhere else.) This presumption can be rebutted by evidence that the testator did not intend to revoke the duplicates.

The second presumption arises when the testator has written a will and kept possession of it, but the will is not found among her possessions at death. In that case, a presumption arises that the testator destroyed—and thus revoked—the will. This presumption can be rebutted by evidence that the will's absence is not due to the testator destroying it.

If it is clear that a will has truly been *lost* (or accidentally destroyed, as opposed to missing and presumed purposely destroyed), or destroyed in a manner not compliant with the state's revocation statute, the will can be probated if its contents are proven by clear and convincing evidence. The proponent bears the burden of proving both of those propositions. Should the proponent fail, then intestacy (or a valid prior will) controls.

The UPC adds a third method of revocation in §2-507: cancellation. Cancellation is a writing on the will that states that the will is cancelled. Under traditional law, writing words of cancellation *over the words of the will* has been sufficient to cancel the entire will, but the UPC's innovation is to remove the requirement that the words of cancellation touch any of the will's words.[157]

A quasi method of revocation arises in the inconsistency doctrine. A well-written will that is intended to revoke one or more prior instruments will contain an express revocation clause. (Remember always the malpractice pitfalls that lie strewn about in this field.) If a subsequent will does not contain an express revocation clause, the inconsistency doctrine may be invoked. A subsequent will that disposes of the testator's entire estate would, by definition, be inconsistent with all parts of the prior will and revoke it entirely. In some jurisdictions, though, this— a subsequent will that disposes of the entire estate—can be difficult to achieve. There has been debate over the years about whether a residuary clause in a subsequent will trumps specific devises in previous wills; the now increasingly minority rule is that because specific bequests in a *single* will trump general or residuary bequests, specific bequests in *prior* wills overrule general or residuary bequests in *subsequent* wills as

---

157. *See* UPC §2-507(a)(2) ("A will or any part thereof is revoked . . . by performing a revocatory act on the will, if the testator performed the act with the intent and for the purpose of revoking the will or part or if another individual performed the act in the testator's conscious presence and by the testator's direction. For purposes of this paragraph, "revocatory act on the will" includes burning, tearing, canceling, obliterating, or destroying the will or any part of it. A burning, tearing, or canceling is a 'revocatory act on the will,' whether or not the burn, tear, or cancellation touched any of the words on the will.").

well. (This rule has the effect of turning the later will into a very long and involved, but not entirely complete, codicil. A codicil, as mentioned briefly before, is an addendum to a will, undertaken with testamentary formalities, that often appears at the bottom of the last page of a will. Supplementing a will with a short writing is a more efficient way to make minor changes to a will than executing a brand-new will. Codicils must comply with testamentary formalities to be valid. A codicil revokes the will it supplements to the extent that the codicil's dispositions are inconsistent with the will.)

The previous discussion relates to revocation based on a volitional act by the testator with intent to revoke the will. In some circumstances, states will presume partial revocation upon the occurrence of certain narrow and specific life events, even though the testator may not have any thought about the effect of these events on her testamentary dispositions. Specifically, states presume partial revocation upon divorce, under the theory that *the last person on earth* that a divorcee would wish her possessions to flow to would be her estranged former spouse. Any provisions for the former spouse in the testator's predivorce will are revoked upon divorce.

Note that this presumption only applies to a will executed before a divorce. Courts will not override the testator's disposition if she executes a new will after the divorce and decides to bestow property on her former spouse. Can you see why?

Marriage is another life event that will lead courts to revoke a will. A will executed before the testator's marriage will be revoked—completely or partially, depending on the jurisdiction—by the marriage. In the majority of states, an omitted spouse is given his intestate share, unless it appears from the will that the omission was intentional or that he is provided for in the will or by a will substitute with the intent that the transfer be in lieu of a testamentary provision. Note that this does not affect the spouse's eligibility to take a forced share in separate property states. The minority of states simply revokes the premarital will entirely upon the testator's marriage.

Finally, we look at a pair of doctrines that can, in some instances, revive prior wills if later wills for some reason failed of sufficient execution, and so could not be probated.

a. Dependent Relative Revocation

Testators who have executed valid wills, but who have then revoked those wills based on some belief that turns out to be false, may have preferred the old will to remain valid (i.e., unrevoked) if they had known the true state of things. Dependent Relative Revocation (DRR) allows a court to presume that the testator would have preferred the initial will to have remained valid under the circumstances and on that basis to revive the earlier, once valid, now revoked will (i.e., to treat the revocation of that will as "relative" because it was "dependent" upon the facts of the world actually being the way the testator incorrectly thought they were). Evidence that the testator would not have wanted the old will revived in any case is admissible to defeat the DRR presumption.

DRR can arise in two different situations. The first occurs when the testator revokes a prior (valid) will in favor of a new will but that new will turns out to be invalid. So, for example, say that John executed a will a few years ago, before he went into the service, splitting everything amongst his nieces and nephews. John has done his tour, acquired a few things, and the nieces and nephews have gotten older, started to go to school, meet significant others, and spread their wings. John decides to change his distribution plans somewhat. He writes up a will at home and gets it notarized. Happy with his new will, he consigns his old one to the flames. Unfortunately, John lives in a state that has not adopted notarization as a replacement for attestation.

DRR requires a mistaken belief; John's mistake here is believing that the new will was valid when he revoked the old one (i.e., he revoked the old will by burning (physical act) on the reliance that the new will was valid; it was not, because notarization is not recognized as a replacement for attestation in John's state). What DRR does here is to revive the *old* will unless it is demonstrated to the court that the testator (John) would have preferred intestacy to the revival of the old will.[158] In effect, the revocation is ineffective because a presumption arises that the testator would not have revoked the old will if he knew the truth (that the new will was invalid).[159] That presumption can be rebutted by evidence to the contrary.

---

158. Do you think DRR comes into effect in this hypo or does intestacy control?
159. As the court said in LaCroix v. Senecal, 99 A.2d 115 (Conn. 1953):

The gist of the doctrine [DRR] is that if a testator cancels or destroys a will with a present intention of making a new one immediately and as a substitute and the new will is not made or, if made, fails of effect for any reason, it will be presumed that the testator preferred the old will to intestacy, and the old one will be admitted to probate in the absence of evidence overcoming the presumption.

This "core" DRR scenario—where the new will is legally invalid—is universally accepted among states. The second scenario is not as universally accepted. As with the core scenario, the testator in this second situation revokes an old (valid) will in favor of a new will. Here, the new will is valid, but explicitly based on an error. The effect is slightly different. Instead of a presumption arising that the testator preferred the old will, the proponent must demonstrate to the court that the testator would have preferred the old will's dispositions to those of the new, had the testator not been in error.[160]

Here is an example. John writes a will in 1957 leaving his estate to his sister and youngest brother. In 1959 his brother, who had worked at the State Department, flees to the Soviet Union. Believing that his brother had defected, John revises his will. He revokes the previous will and writes a new, valid will leaving everything to his sister, which recites that "I leave nothing to my traitorous brother but my disgust that he would support that murderous and repressive regime." John dies in 1965. The brother comes home for his funeral. It turns out that the brother had been an American spy all along, and that the "defection" had been his cover. DRR saves the day by treating the second will as invalid (technically a legal fiction, of course) and probating the first one.

When reading the doctrine of revival (next), try to pinpoint how DRR and revival differ. Do curative doctrines kill off DRR? Why or why not? Do you see the importance of the question?

b. Revival

Revival is another softening doctrine that allows a court to probate a previously revoked will under certain circumstances. The typical revival scenario looks like this: The testator executes a will. Later, she executes a second will, which revokes the old one (expressly or by inconsistency). At some point after that, she revokes the second will and dies without having made a new will. The question here is whether the old will can be probated (is it "revived"?) or is the testator doomed to intestacy?

---

160. The proponent faces a difficult battle. Either the mistake must be recited in the new will's terms (as in the example) or the proponent must prove it by clear and convincing evidence.

The answer to that question depends on whether the second will revoked the first will entirely or only revoked parts of it. Partial revocation is an easier proposition to handle. Almost all states and the UPC[161] agree that when the second will is revoked, a presumption arises that the revoked dispositions in the first will are revived.

There are three schools of thought about what happens when the second will completely revoked the first. Most states and the UPC[162] presume that the first will remains revoked. This presumption can be rebutted by showing that the testator intended to revive the first will. That intent can be proven by the circumstances surrounding the second will's revocation or by the testator's contemporaneous or subsequent declarations that the first will is to take effect. In the comment to §2-509, the UPC drafters justify the presumption—and how it differs from partial revocation—because when the second will entirely revokes the first, the testator has no reason for believing that the first will has any continuing effect.[163] Contrast that with partial revocation, where the first will does have some continuing effect (and the presumption is the opposite).

The other two schools of thought are, naturally, minority positions. The more widely accepted of them will not revive the first will unless it is re-executed with testamentary formalities or republished by being referred to in a later, duly executed, testamentary document. In other words, "revival" is a bit of a misnomer. Effectively, the testator must properly execute a new will that happens to be *exactly* like the first in order to "revive" the first will.

The two rules described above share an underlying theory. They both understand a new will to be both a revoking document and a dispositive document. (In other words, the new will both revokes the old will and makes new dispositions.) They both give the will revoking effect when it is executed (that is, it revokes any prior wills as soon as it is executed) but withhold dispositive effect until the testator's death. The theory that underlies the third rule (followed by the fewest states) is different. Under this alternative theory, a will is not legally effective at all during the testator's life, not even to revoke prior wills. At death,

---

161. *See* UPC §2-509(b).

162. *See* UPC §2-509(a).

163. *See* UPC §2-509 cmt. ("The presumption against revival imposed by subsection (a) is justified because where Will #2 wholly revoked Will #1, the testator understood or should have understood that Will #1 had no continuing effect. Consequently, subsection (a) properly presumes that the testator's act of revoking Will #2 was not accompanied by an intent to revive Will #1.").

the valid will executed last in time is effective. Thus, the execution of the second will does nothing to the first while the testator lives. Should the testator decide to revoke the second will, then it drops out of contention to be the "valid will executed last in time." When the testator dies, the first will would be the most recently executed valid will, and would go to probate.

Do you understand the logic underlying each approach? What are the advantages of each? Which would you adopt?

4. Mistakes and Reformation

In this discussion of mistakes and reformation, we are not considering failures to conform to the Wills Act formalities. Rather, this discussion refers to the concomitant question of what the courts should and will do in the event of a mistake made in the substantive portions of the will, whether by the testator or by her counsel. As you will see, both the starting point and the developments in this area broadly conform to those we have already seen regarding the formalities. Remember that the core goal of the law of wills is to *do the testator's intent*.

The traditional rule should be unsurprising at this point: strict compliance with the text of the will. The traditional rule[164] presumed that the testator did what the testator intended to do and thus gave full effect to the will, based on the plain meaning of the words used. As long as the will was formally valid, it would be honored as written. The traditional rule is still, at least *de jure*, the majority rule.

Under the traditional rule, extrinsic evidence is not admissible to disturb the plain meaning of the words in the will. It is, however, admissible to resolve certain ambiguities in the text. That is, extrinsic evidence is not allowed to show that a clear gift was actually a mistake and that the testator intended to do something else. But with an ambiguous gift or where the words used lack a plain meaning, there is no choice but to look outside the will to figure out how to resolve the ambiguity.

There are two kinds of ambiguity (with one kind having two subflavors): patent and latent. A patent ambiguity is one that appears on the face of the will. For example, one clause leaves the testator's "one and only Nintendo" (which he got in 1985 as part of the initial North American release, so it's a collector's item) to his youngest

---

164. Also known as the "plain-meaning" rule.

nephew, while the very next clause leaves the very same Nintendo (here described as "my Nintendo, the only game console I have ever owned") to his granddaughter. This is a patent ambiguity because the will itself identifies it as the only Nintendo in the testator's estate, and it is being left to two different beneficiaries.[165] Under the traditional rule, extrinsic evidence is not admissible to clear up a patent ambiguity. The court is limited to the plain meaning of the will's text, even if as a result the devise must fail and the property pass by intestacy.

What is the basis for the traditional rule's hostility toward patent ambiguities? One explanation is that the patent ambiguity *is* apparent on the face of the will, which means that, presumably, the testator (or his attorney) saw the ambiguity when he wrote or reviewed the will before signing it and chose to leave it in. Remember, the cardinal rule of wills law is to give effect to the testator's intent, except where it violates some rule of law or public policy.[166] With a patent ambiguity, the court *can* determine the testator's intent from the plain meaning of the will: Give the same Nintendo to my nephew and to my granddaughter independently. But it is logically impossible to give the same Nintendo to two different people at once. The plain meaning of the text controls, and if the plain meaning leads to a logical impossibility, then the relevant devise(s) will fail. Courts are increasingly more receptive to using extrinsic evidence to resolve patent ambiguities rather than let the devise(s) fail.

On the other hand, extrinsic evidence is traditionally admissible to clarify latent ambiguities. A latent ambiguity is one that manifests only when the terms of the will are applied to the testator's estate or designated beneficiaries. Latent ambiguities come in two flavors: where the will clearly describes a person or thing and (1) two or more persons or things *exactly* fit that description or (2) no person or thing exactly fits the description, but two or more persons or things partially fit.[167]

An example of the first flavor of latent ambiguity arises when a devise is to "my cousin Jim," when the testator has two cousins named Jim. The second kind of latent ambiguity is more common. An example can be found in Ihl v. Oetting, 682 S.W.2d 865 (Mo. App. 1984),[168]

---

165. Another example, which may be easier to see, is when the testator leaves the "disposable portion of [his] estate" to one daughter, and in the next clause leaves "[his] entire estate" to his other daughter, as happened in *Succession of Neff*, 716 So. 2d 410 (La. App. 1998).

166. *See, e.g.*, McBride v. Sumrow, 181 S.W.3d 666 (Tenn. App. 2005).

167. *See, e.g.*, Phipps v. Barbera, 498 N.E.2d 411, 412 n.3 (Mass. App. 1986).

168. An expurgated version of the case appears on the web page.

where the testator left his home to "Mr. and Mrs. Wendell Richard Hess, . . . presently residing at No. 17 Barbara Circle." In 1979, when the will was executed, Wendell and his wife Glenda resided in marital bliss at No. 17 Barbara Circle. But that happy union ended shortly thereafter. Wendell divorced Glenda and they sold No. 17.

Wendell took Verna as the second Mrs. Hess some time before the testator died in 1983, and she tried to claim the "Mrs. Hess" portion of the devise, arguing that she was the only "Mrs. Wendell Richard Hess." But she didn't fit the second half of the description because she had never lived at No. 17 Barbara Circle. Glenda met the description of the Mrs. Hess residing at No. 17 in 1979, but no longer did in 1983. Thus, neither of them *exactly* fit the description in the will at the time of its excution. The court admitted extrinsic evidence on the matter, which showed that the testator intended Glenda to get (half of) the house. Regardless of which flavor of latent ambiguity arises, direct expressions of the testator's intent to the drafter (and *only* to the drafter) are admissible as part of the extrinsic evidence package.

The distinction between patent and latent ambiguities is becoming less relevant these days. Some courts have explicitly become increasingly receptive to admitting extrinsic evidence to resolve any ambiguity, whether patent or latent. The Restatement (Third) of Property: Wills and Other Donative Transfers[169] also endorses doing away with the distinction. Some other courts have recognized that their stance against reformation to correct innocent mistakes[170] might actually defeat the testator's intent, rather than carrying it out. Although the majority of courts facially stick with the traditional "no reformation" rule, careful examination of the cases reveals that they tend to admit extrinsic evidence to correct substantive mistakes in order to carry out the testator's actual intent. Essentially, courts are reforming wills without admitting what they are doing.

These courts do not want non-Wills Act approved speech or action effectively to "speak the Will" in the face of the will's clear text. This justification allows them purportedly to stick to the traditional rule while opening up a massive functional loophole. They permit objective evidence regarding real-world circumstances pertaining to some

---

169. Comment d to §11.2.

170. When a mistaken term is included as a result of an intentional wrongful act—fraud—then courts will reform the will to carry out the testator's actual intent. In light of that fact, refusing to carry out the testator's actual intent because the testator made an innocent mistake looks an awful lot like punishing the testator for messing up. Or punishing his drafting attorney, since this might very well result in a malpractice suit.

facially clear gifts and allow reformation on that basis (claiming the circumstances create an ambiguity), while still refusing to admit subjective evidence about the testator's intent, were that intent is said to differ from what the will clearly says. If this additional exception is permitted and combined with an elastic use of extrinsic evidence to create ambiguity, then the traditional rule—while still the *de jure* majority rule—is largely gone in fact.

Arnheiter v. Arnheiter, 125 A.2d 914 (N.J. Super. Ct. Ch. Div. 1956) is one example of that phenomenon. The testator ordered her executrix to sell her undivided one-half interest in "No. 304 Harrison Avenue, Harrison, New Jersey" and use the proceeds to establish trusts for each of her two nieces. But the testator owned no interest in No. 304; her undivided one-half interest was in No. 317 Harrison Avenue. The court facially stuck to the no reformation rule, saying that it "had no power to correct or reform" obvious mistakes in a will. But then it dredged up some Latin to justify ignoring the address number[171] and ordering the executrix to sell No. 317 instead. But in order to reach that conclusion, it had to consider extrinsic evidence (that the testator owned the described interest in different property), which is taboo under the traditional plain-meaning rule.

While the traditional rule is limping toward reformation, a minority of states have joined the UPC in the modern trend, which unabashedly allows reformation. Under UPC §2-805,

> [t]he court may reform the terms of a governing instrument, even if unambiguous, to conform the terms to the transferor's intention if it is proved by clear and convincing evidence what the transferor's intention was and that the terms of the governing instrument were affected by a mistake of fact or law, whether in expression or inducement.

The Restatement (Third) of Property: Wills and Other Donative Transfers §12.1 adopts the same standard for reforming wills to correct mistakes. The rationale for the modern trend is threefold:

---

171. The court applied the principle *falsa demonstratio non nocet* (meaning "mere erroneous description does not vitiate"). According to this principle, "Where a description of a thing or person consists of several particulars and all of them do not fit any one person or thing, less essential particulars may be rejected provided the remainder of the description clearly fits." The court decided that the address number was a less essential particular because the remainder of the description—street name, city, and state—clearly fit the description of property the testator actually owned.

(1) The purpose of the law of wills is to give effect to the testator's intent. By refusing to reform a will when a mistake occurs, the court allows the mistake to defeat the testator's intent, even if that intent can be proven. The Restatement recognizes that allowing even unambiguous wills to be challenged may cause an increase in challenges by potential beneficiaries looking to score a quick buck. That is why these challenges must meet a clear and convincing evidence standard to succeed.[172]

(2) The use of the nonprobate system for estate planning has increased by a factor of roughly 10,000,000[173] since the traditional rule achieved its universal status. The nonprobate donative documents[174] can all be reformed according to the standard now adopted by the UPC and Restatement for wills. The modern trend seeks to unify the law of the probate and nonprobate system for ease of estate planning.[175]

(3) The third reason is the desire to spare lawyers from needless malpractice liability for those mistakes.

---

172. *See* Restatement (Third) of Property: Wills and Other Donative Transfers §12.1, cmt. b.

173. This may be a bit off.

174. Trusts, life-insurance contracts, deeds of gift, etc.

175. *See* Restatement (Third) of Property: Wills and Other Donative Transfers §12.1, cmt. c.

PART IV

THE LAW OF TRUSTS

What follows in this introduction is only a quick, stage-setting overview of the law of trusts, though that law really is neither terribly complicated nor terribly tricky. We will put additional flesh on these bones in the coming weeks.

Trusts come in two flavors: (a) those created by a deed of trust in writing and (b) those created by a declaration of trust orally. Yes, trusts can be created orally—according to trust law, anyway. Other laws, including the Statute of Frauds or a state's Wills Act (or, as a general example, the Uniform Probate Code) may independently require a writing depending upon the content of the trust. More importantly, good sense and good lawyering require, in most instances, that the trust provisions be written into a deed of trust—however named—and that a copy of that trust document be delivered to an attorney, a trustee or some other neutral, attentive, disinterested party.[1]

Let's start with a brief consideration of the basic principles and parts of trusts law itself. Trust law developed in the common law as a way to subvert the Statute of Uses (the content of which need not delay us here) but since 2000 has been significantly influenced by the Uniform Trust Code (UTC), which has been adopted in about half of the states.[2] Trusts arise initially in equity, rather than at law.

---

1. Note the difference between "disinterested," as here, meaning "a non-beneficiary third party who has every reason to pay attention to proceedings for other reasons," and "uninterested," meaning "just doesn't care."

2. Keep in mind, though, a point raised in Part I: The trust is as fundamentally a creature of the common law—and, more, of common *equity*—as the will is wholly a

The Trust Triangle:
A Graphical Representation of the Beating Heart of the Matter

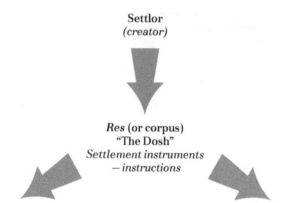

Settlor
(creator)

Res **(or corpus)**
"The Dosh"
*Settlement instruments
— instructions*

Trustee(s) — *legal* owner(s)
• Administers the *res*
• Has verifiable duties that
can be enforced
• Is usually paid
• Distribution of management
responsibilities (if divided)
between the trustee and
"trust protector" permitted

Beneficiaries — *equitable* owners
• Get the dosh
• May sue trustee for failure
of duties
• May not alter material
purposes of trust

You can use a trust to achieve anything that isn't independently illegal.[3] The fundamental characteristic of a trust is that it separates legal from beneficial (or equitable) ownership, which is to say it separates the burdens of ownership from the benefits. This usefully allows property to be held and managed in a pool, by a trustee, while the benefits shoot out to multiple parties, or to one party who lacks capacity or interest to manage it, or to one party at a time, but multiple parties *seriatim*. Trusts are often used as will substitutes (revocable trusts), will enhancements (testamentary trusts), for tax benefits (e.g., testamentary marital trusts), for incompetent people or minors (e.g., support trusts, supplemental trusts, supplemental support trusts), or to wall off the profligate while still giving them income at the trustees' discretion (discretionary trusts). Trusts can be used to achieve other purposes as desired, however, and so learning a list of trust types

creature of statute. Consider as this part unfolds the structural and practical implications of these facts.

3. A few very slight caveats to this broad assertion were considered earlier in the semester when we discussed the *Shapira* case.

provides limited value. (Learning various characteristics of trusts and trust forms,[4] though, is vital.)

There is a great deal of money held in the trust form. Though it will in no meaningful way be the subject of this course, it's worth knowing that the trust form really came into its own as a business form rather than as an exercise of dead-hand control or *inter vivos* personal wealth management. (The vast majority of the assets held in trust are still held as part of business activity.) This was perhaps particularly true in the United States. One evidence of that fact: In most developed countries, the laws that thwart private monopoly are often called some variation on "competition laws," or, not surprisingly "anti-monopoly laws." Do you know what they're called in the United States? Rather more to the point, do you know why?[5]

A. CREATING A VALID TRUST

These are the elements required for successful creation of a valid trust.

1. A settlor

The settlor is the property owner who decides to transfer his ownership interest to the trust and does so, either by declaration of trust (spoken) or deed of trust (written) (thereby "settling" the trust). The settlor, in the declaration or deed, sets the rules of the trust. Magic words are not required; the rule is not that one "must say 'trust'" for a trust to be formed.[6] A writing is not required by the law of trusts itself, though it is often otherwise necessary (because of the statute of frauds, various tax regulations, trust company rules, etc.), and is very much a good idea.[7] Settlors must beware, though, of language that could be interpreted as precatory rather than mandatory.

---

4. Meaning "forms of trusts," not "the forms one fills out when settling a trust."

5. This is not to say that trust law is limited to the American, or even the English-speaking, common-law tradition. Trust law arises on the continent and elsewhere as well.

6. *See, e.g.,* Lux v. Lux, 288 A.2d 701 (R.I. 1972).

7. It would almost certainly constitute malpractice *per se* in most circumstances not to advise a client very strongly to write down the client's preferred trust provisions

VAN DUYNE v. VAN DUYNE

14 N.J. Eq. 397 (N.J. Ch. 1862)

THE CHANCELLOR. The case depends upon the true construction of the second and third clauses of the will of Hiram Van Duyne, of the county of Morris. By the second clause of his will, the testator devised his homestead farm to his son James and his daughter Hetty, equally "to them, their heirs and assigns for ever, hoping and believing they will do justice hereafter to my grandson, Hiram Van Duyne, to the amount of one half of the said homestead farm." The third clause contains a devise in similar terms.

The bill claims that the terms of the devise create a trust in favor of Hiram Van Duyne, the grandson, for one half of the land devised in fee, to take effect upon the death of the devisees respectively. The legal position is, that a devise to A. in fee, hoping that he will hereafter do justice to B. to the amount of half of the land, is tantamount to a devise to A. of half the land, in trust for B. from and after the death of A.

This is not the natural import of the terms of the devise. No trust is declared. No condition is imposed. No injunction is laid upon the devisee. A mere hope and belief is expressed that the devisee will do justice to the grandson. It would have been natural for the testator, in case he had designed to create a trust or impose a condition upon the devisee, so to have declared. There is a clear and obvious distinction, which every man understands, between an injunction and an entreaty, between a condition imposed and a hope or belief expressed. The one imposes an obligation, the other rests in discretion. Compliance with the one is voluntary, with the other compulsory. The devise, it will be observed, is to the devisees in fee simple, "to them, their heirs and assigns for ever." The hope annexed to that gift, it is claimed, converts that estate *pro tanto* into an estate for life, with remainder in fee in trust for a third party. The testator certainly indicates no such intention. That is not the natural import of the terms used. . . .

No inference, I think, can be fairly drawn from the terms of this will that the testator designed to create a trust in favor of his grandson. If such had been the intention of the testator, he would have indicated such intention by terms more appropriate to that design. His failing to do so is the best evidence that he had no such intention. Such is the

---

in valid trust-deed form.

fair and reasonable conclusion to be drawn from the terms of the will itself. . . .

> [W]here the testator, by his will, disposes of part of his estate to another absolutely untrammelled by any condition, unaffected by any express trust, but accompanied by a hope or a confidence that he will dispose of the whole or a portion of it in a specified way, it seems very remarkable that the mere wish or hope should cancel the gift. . . . [H]ere, as elsewhere, the manifest intention of the testator is to be regarded, and unless he intends that the words should be imperative, they are not so. Unless it was intended to create a trust, none is created. "The real question in these cases always is, whether the wish, or desire, or recommendation that is expressed by the testator is meant to govern the conduct of the party to whom it is addressed, or whether it is merely an indication of that which he thinks would be a reasonable exercise of the discretion of the party, leaving it, however, to the party to exercise his own discretion. That is the real question. Williams v. Williams, 1 Simons N. S. 357.

It cannot be questioned that the earlier English authorities, adopting the principles of the Roman law, establish the rule, that words expressing hope, wish, expectation, confidence, or recommendation will create a trust as against a devisee or legatee.

But the current of authorities of late years has been against converting the legatee into a trustee. . . . A strong disposition has been manifested by the courts to limit rather than extend the doctrine of raising trusts upon words of recommendation, and as far as the authorities will allow, to give the words their natural and ordinary effect, unless it be clear that they are intended to be used in a peremptory sense. . . .

In Briggs v. Penny, 3 Mac N. & Gor. 546, the rule was laid down by Lord Chancellor Truro, as the result of the authorities, to be, that

> words accompanying a gift or bequest expressive of confidence or belief, or desire, or hope that a particular application will be made of such bequest, will be deemed to import a trust upon these conditions: first, they are to be so used as to exclude all option or discretion in the party who is to act, as to his acting according to them or not; secondly, the subject must be certain; and thirdly, the object expressed not too vague or indefinite to be enforced. Now it is obvious to remark that the mere expression of a hope, or wish, or belief, or request that the devisee will make a particular use of the property, does not naturally import a design to exclude the exercise of discretion by the donee, but to permit its exercise. The technical

rule of the English courts have, it is true, given them such effect; but it is directly opposed to their natural import and the sense in which they would be used and understood by every man of ordinary intelligence, independent of artificial rules of interpretation.. . . .

In conformity with this statement of the principle, the rule has been stated by a recent accurate elementary writer to be, "where a bequest is accompanied by words expressing a command, recommendation, entreaty, wish, or hope on the part of the testator that the donee will dispose of the property in favor of another, a trust will be created, if the words on the whole are sufficiently imperative and the trust and the object be sufficiently certain." Hill on Trustees 71 (ed. 1857).

A command certainly is sufficiently imperative. So a hope or wish may be, if addressed to an executor or trustee, the trust being created; or if coupled with other expressions indicating a clear intent that they shall operate as a command. But standing alone, and addressed to a legatee to whom property is given by the testator in terms importing an absolute gift, they are not imperative. A wish addressed to my agent, as to the mode of dealing with my property, is tantamount to a command; but a wish addressed to a third party, as to the mode of disposing of his own property, can amount but to a request, and nothing more. . . .

This conclusion receives strong support from the emphatic language of Justice Story regarding the principle of construction adopted in the earlier English decisions:

> This doctrine . . . of thus construing expressions of recommendation, confidence, hope, wish, and desire into positive and peremptory commands is not a little difficult to be maintained upon sound principles of interpretation of the actual intention of the testator. It can scarcely be presumed that every testator should not clearly understand the difference between such expressions and words of positive direction and command, and that in using the one, and omitting the other, he should not have a determinate end in view. It will be agreed on all sides, that where the intention of the testator is to leave the whole subject as a pure matter of discretion to the good will and pleasure of the party enjoying his confidence and favor, and where his expressions of desire are intended as mere moral suggestions to excite and aid that discretion, but not absolutely to control or govern it, there the language cannot and ought not to be held to create a trust. Now words of recommendation and other words precatory in their nature imply that very discretion, as contradistinguished from peremptory orders, and therefore ought to be so construed unless a different sense is irresistibly forced upon them by the context. 2 Story's Eq. Jur., §1069.

I am not aware that the subject has ever undergone judicial investigation in this state. . . . In the absence of any adjudicated case or any settled rule of construction, I feel at liberty to adopt such rule of construction as seems best calculated to effectuate the intention of the testator. I think there is nothing in the will indicating an intention to create a trust in favor of the complainant. The gift to the testator's children is absolute in its terms. The expression of a hope or belief as to the mode of disposing of the property created no qualification of the gift. There is nothing in the will indicating that the testator used the terms in any other than their natural and ordinary sense, or that he designed them to be imperative. On the contrary, the form of the expression seems to import directly the reverse, and that the disposition of the matter was to be left to the discretion of the devisees. The testator does not request, or even hope that the devisees will give the complainant one half of the real estate within one year after his death, or on the death of the devisees, or at any other time, or that they will do him justice by giving him half the farm. He hopes merely that they will hereafter do him justice to the amount of one half of the land. . . . The testator neither indicates the estate which the grandson is to receive, nor when he is to receive it, nor whether he is to have the land itself, or the value of the land in money. All this is obviously left to the discretion of the devisees. To convert the property into a trust fund would defeat the real design of the testator.

> The form of expression used in this will, and which is relied on as creating a trust, would not have been resorted to by any experienced scrivener for the purpose of creating a trust, nor would it have been adopted by any man *inops consilii* as a mode of making an absolute gift. . . .

No trust is created by the second and third clauses of the will in favor of the complainant. [The plaintiff] is not entitled to the relief prayed for.

* * *

CAHILL v. MONAHAN

155 A.2d 282 (N.J. Super. Ct. App. Div. 1959).

Judges: Goldmann, Conford and Freund. The opinion of the court was delivered by Goldmann, S.J.A.D.

Plaintiff appeals from an adverse judgment of the Chancery Division determining that the precatory language appearing in her father's will did not create a trust in her favor.

Testator married Laura Carverry in 1899. She died in 1922, leaving as survivors her husband and a daughter (plaintiff). In 1923 he married defendant, and the issue of that marriage was a daughter, Jeanne Monahan (now Ward). At the time of testator's death on June 24, 1950 plaintiff was 50 years old and her half-sister Jeanne 25. His will, prepared by an attorney and executed on January 10, 1941, is quite brief. After revoking all prior wills, it provided as follows:

> Second I give devise and bequeath all the rest of my property, whether the same be real or personal, or of whatsoever nature or wheresoever situate, or to which I may be entitled fully and completely, to my dearly beloved wife, Mary M. Monahan.
>
> Third It is my wish and desire that my dearly beloved wife always provide for my two beloved daughters Helen C. Cahill and Jeanne F. Monahan.

Defendant widow was appointed sole executrix. . . .

Plaintiff lived with her father and stepmother until she married Dr. Lawrence Cahill in 1928. The marriage was a failure, and when plaintiff separated from her husband in 1931 she returned to live in her father's home. Soon after the separation she turned to alcohol and the company of companions whom her father considered entirely unfit. He strongly condemned her drinking companions and way of life, but was unsuccessful in correcting her ways. Finally, in 1945 he had her committed to the House of Good Shepherd, in Morristown, N.J. Toward the end of her stay there he wrote her that there were some things he would have to insist on if she expected to be released and return home, since he was getting too old to put up with any more of her "depradations":

> First of all, I want to be sure that you are repentent for all of the wrongs you have done. There is no use for me to go into details telling you of them as you know them all yourself, and they are many and shameful. You must promise Almighty God that you will never associate with the low class of people you have been associating with.
>
> Your so-called friends who were the lowest type that anybody ever knew, only used you for the money you spent on them. Even with all of the money you had to spend you were always in debt. * * *
>
> You are now out of debt and have a nice tidy bank account to your credit; your jewelry is out of the pawn shop, and your income tax is paid. . . .

Don't be a fool all of your life. Try and improve your way of living. I am giving you a chance to regain your respectability, and I hope you will take advantage of it. . . .

In her reply plaintiff assured her father that she meant to lead an entirely different life and would do her best to make up for the heartaches and worries she had caused him. She said she no longer had a desire for drinking or smoking. She hoped she would be home shortly and have the opportunity of proving to him that she would stay away "from those who are not for my good."

Soon after this letter plaintiff was released in her father's custody and returned to live with him. Despite her resolutions she resumed her associations and drinking habits. Finally, her father put her out of the house after she had spent some four or five days over the Labor Day weekend with her companions, without communicating with him. Upon hearing of her father's action plaintiff said, "I am very glad to hear that." She went to live with one Van Brunt, and stayed with him until he died shortly after this action was instituted. The two moved from one cheap rooming house or hotel to another, plaintiff paying for the rent, food and other expenses, including alcoholic beverages. During all her years with Van Brunt he did not work, but looked to plaintiff for support. She spent a good deal of her time in saloons and in association with friends for whom she would purchase drinks.

In the period between her separation from her husband and her commitment to the home plaintiff had managed to spend whatever funds she had. . . . She also pawned her jewelry and incurred minor debts. (This explains the reference in her father's letter.) Following her release from the home she dissipated the bank account her father had built up for her, consisting of at least $ 1,500, as well as her weekly income.

After leaving her father's house in 1947 plaintiff never communicated with him for the rest of his life. Although she corresponded with defendant—her postcards closing with expressions of love—there was no note of affection for her father.

One more fact should be mentioned. Other than supplying plaintiff with a home under his own roof from 1931 to 1947, except for the eight months at the House of Good Shepherd, testator never gave plaintiff any money. Nor did he give her money or provide for her in any way after he put her out of his home. . . .

By her complaint plaintiff sought to compel the payment of monies allegedly due her under her father's will, to have defendant account for the distribution of the proceeds of the estate and, further, for an order determining what amount will constitute a proper sum to establish the care which plaintiff claims was intended under the provisions of the will. Defendant, by way of counterclaim, sought a judgment construing the will and advice concerning her duty under paragraph Third thereof. The pretrial order declared that the "basic issue" to be determined was the construction of paragraph Third—did it constitute a mandatory direction to defendant to provide for plaintiff? . . . The judgment under appeal construed testator's will as follows:

> 1. It was the intention of testator, as expressed in his will, to bequeath to the defendant, his wife, absolute and unconditional ownership and control of the residue of his estate.
> 2. It was not the intention of testator to create a trust or legal obligation in favor of plaintiff or Jean Monahan Ward, by his said will, and Paragraph Third of said will was intended merely as an admonition, not amounting to an imposition of a trust or mandatory direction.
> 3. It was not the intention of testator to impose upon defendant any legal obligation to supply money or funds to plaintiff under the circumstances revealed by the evidence herein. . . .

In his oral decision at the close of the testimony the trial judge found the "clue" to his determination "in the circumstances which existed at the time when this will was written [January 1941] and the circumstances that continued to exist up until the date of the testator's death in 1950." He said that the controlling reason for arriving at his conclusion that it was testator's intent to give the residue of his estate to his widow outright, and not to set up a trust in favor of one or both of his daughters, was testator's concern that "the one thing Helen Cahill must not have was money which would permit her to continue in the habits of her life that she had formed and to permit her to use that money in the support and maintenance . . . of persons whom the father manifestly believed were exerting upon her an influence which eventually resulted, to all intents and purposes, in ruining the lady's life."

Plaintiff's single contention is that the precatory language of paragraph Third created a trust in her favor. In this she relies solely on the opinion of this court in Bankers Trust Co. v. N.Y. Women's League for Animals, 23 N.J. Super. 170 (App. Div. 1952). She incidentally cites a line of cases (considered in the Bankers Trust case) which, it is asserted, establish it as "settled doctrine that unless a will indicates otherwise, the expression of a desire on the part of the testator that a bequest be applied to a particular purpose creates a trust."

Some reliance is also placed upon the language of the trial court in stating that it could carry out testator's intent only by construing the will "to be an outright gift to the widow with an admonition, not in any sense amounting to a trust, that in the event the situation arises, that the widow is bound morally to see that the daughter, Helen Cahill, and the other daughter, Jeanne M. Ward, are not in actual want . . . ." The argument that such an admonition is tantamount to creating a legal duty to provide for plaintiff is clearly without merit. The whole point of the so-called precatory trust doctrine is to distinguish those cases where the obligation is moral from those where it is legal.

We had occasion to review the precatory trust doctrine, particularly in its New Jersey aspect, in the Bankers Trust case, 23 N.J. Super., at pages 178-179. As was said there, the earlier view of the English and American courts was that if the testator expressed a desire that a certain disposition be made of the property passing under his will, this was sufficient, in the absence of peculiar circumstances, to create a trust. We noted that not only had the English courts overruled the doctrine established in their earlier cases, but the overwhelming majority of courts in the United States had adopted the more modern view, which is that mere precatory expressions do not in themselves carry the force of command; to determine whether the testator intended to impose enforceable duties, one must look to manifestations of interpretation contained in the will, construed under general principles. In the modern view the question is one of interpretation of a particular will—that of ascertaining the intention of the testator. . . .

In the Bankers Trust case the N.Y. Women's League for Animals had suggested that Marx v. Rice, 1 N.J. 574 (1949), had overturned the earlier English doctrine that had been followed by so many of our courts. . . . The testator in Marx gave his wife a general power of appointment. By a subsequent paragraph he "requested" the donee to make such donations as she might "deem proper" to such charitable institutions in Essex County, N.J., as she might select. The following language then appears in the will:. . .

and I do further request her in case she shall exercise the power of appointment by will which I have hereinabove given her, to include among the beneficiaries by her to be designated such of my own blood relations as she may deem worthy to be the recipients of her bounty.

The widow appointed part of the fund in favor of testator's blood relations. The contention on appeal was that the quoted provision was mandatory and converted what would otherwise be a general power into a power in trust for the collateral line of the donor, thereby prohibiting the donee from designating any beneficiaries who were not of that line. Our Supreme Court refused to interpret the will in this manner, stating

> "The word 'request' was not used here in a mandatory sense. It may be used as a command or an entreaty depending upon the context in which the word is inserted, and the circumstances attendant upon its use. However, the real test is whether or not the testator intends, by his language, to control the disposition of his property. . . . We conclude that here it was not so intended.". . .

There can be no question that the court in Marx considered the entire will and attendant circumstances in arriving at testator's intention. Although prior decisions of New Jersey courts were not referred to, the obvious import of the Marx decision was to depart from any pat formula which would establish a trust whenever the testator expressed a desire or request that a bequest be applied to a particular purpose. Instead, it emphasized anew the principle which underlies all cases involving the construction of wills: it is the testator's intent, as determined from the will as a whole and the surrounding circumstances— "the context in which the word is inserted, and the circumstances attendant upon its use"—which governs. . . .

We now consider the Marx case as clearly expressing the philosophy of the modern rule, requiring a case-by-case determination of the import of the precatory language without any presumption in favor of a trust arising therefrom. . . .

We hold, therefore, that where a testator uses language expressive of desire rather than of command, the question in each case is whether he intended to impose a legal duty upon the legatee to carry out the desired purpose, or whether he meant to leave the legatee free to carry it out or not as he should choose, even though testator hoped he would carry it out. In each case the court, in reaching its determination, will examine the whole of the will and deal with it in the light of all the circumstances. . . .

Our examination of the language of the present will in the light of the facts and circumstances surrounding its execution clearly demonstrates, as the trial court found, that testator did not intend to create a trust under paragraph Third. Before the will was drawn in 1941, testator had had ten years of experience with what he considered the wayward life led by his daughter. He bitterly opposed her addiction to alcohol, her companions, and the expenditure of all her substance on drink. In that period he gave her shelter, but no money. He knew in 1941, as well as he ever would, the weakness and proclivities of his daughter. The years which followed proved only too well that she had not changed her ways.

The facts and circumstances we look to are those which existed prior to and at the time of the making of the will. Our reference to what came after merely completes the picture and can only be considered as lending some color to the situation obtaining at the time the will was executed. We do not mean to imply that circumstances postdating the will may in themselves determine testator's intention at the time of execution.

Defense counsel places some stress on an analysis of earlier decisions which, it is contended, demonstrates that where it was held that a trust was created, testator's wish or desire was expressed either in the same sentence as the bequest or devise of the property to which the mandatory direction was to apply, or in the same paragraph; or it was made manifest by other clear language that it was testator's intent to impose the mandatory command and attach it to the property disposed of by him. By way of example, we are referred to the testamentary language in [several cases], where the clause expressing testator's "request" referred back to the property given her in an immediately preceding clause. The trial judge observed that the present will differs from the wills in those cases, in that the provision giving the residue of the estate to the widow outright was separate and apart from the provision which plaintiff contends sets up a mandatory trust.

The gift of the residue to testator's wife in paragraph Second is unquestionably an absolute one, without condition or proviso, and unburdened of any charge. It is only in paragraph Third that there is an expression of a distinctly separate thought: testator's "wish and desire" that his wife always provide for his two daughters. There is no reference to the preceding absolute gift. The very structure of the will contra-indicates the intention to erect a trust.

However that may be, there is an insurmountable obstacle to creating a mandatory trust here under any circumstances. Even the earlier cases required not only that the testator wish or desire something to be done, but what he wished or desired had to be specific both as to the subject matter of his bounty and the object thereof. A trust requires a specific *res*, and where there is no specific *res*, there can be no trust. . . . [The] testator designated no definite part or amount of his estate from which plaintiff was to derive a benefit. . . .

Testator's wish and desire that the widow provide for his daughter was not a sufficient identification of the trust *res* to warrant the imposition of a trust.

The judgment is affirmed.

* * *

Demonstrable Settlor Intent. A settlor must demonstrate an intention, provable to a court, to create a trust.[8] This intention can be demonstrated by, for instance, delivery of a deed of trust to a trustee or to some third party, by delivery of the *res* of the trust to the trustee or some third party, or by a provable (and not otherwise invalid) declaration of trust. This is not, however, a complete list. Suppose that a settlor were to type up and sign a document headed "Deed of Trust," which dealt coherently with a significant portion of her property and which she had signed. She then placed the document in an envelope, sealed the envelope, signed across the flap-edge, and placed the envelope in the top drawer of her home office desk, to which she kept a key. Were she later to die without having mentioned the trust to anyone and the envelope and the document then were found, her behavior and its evidence would create a strong presumption that she had fully intended to establish a trust, regardless of her failure to communicate the fact of its existence to any party before her demise. (And, again, this would very likely be true even if she had never actually used the word "trust" anywhere in the document, so long as the intent to form what the law recognizes as a trust were otherwise clear.)

2. Settlor Capacity

The capacity necessary to form a trust is essentially the same capacity requirement that pertains to wills.[9]

3. A Res or Corpus

The *res* (or *corpus*) center of the trust—specific, designated, segregable trust property. This property *must* be separately identifiable. Thus, for instance, settlement of a trust the *res* of which is "the $5,000

---

8. *See* UTC §402(a)(2).
9. *See supra* at Part II.B.

in my Lock Haven Savings & Loan passbook account" would be valid (or, really, would have been valid), while an attempt at making a trust that just designated "$5,000 of my wealth" as the intended *res* would fail.

This *res* requirement arises from the nature of the trust itself. The formation of a trust legally transfers title to the trust property from the settlor to the trustee, who becomes the legal owner, and the beneficiaries, who become the equitable owners. It simply doesn't make any practical sense—or, perhaps better put, creates far too many practical impossibilities—to say that "X, my trustee, owns some $5,000 sloshing around in my checking account." How would the trustee access those funds to fulfill her duties to the beneficiaries? How could the trust's funds (which are, remember, no longer owned by the settlor, but rather by the trustee for the benefit of the beneficiaries) be distinguished from the remaining funds in the checking account—which would remain in the ownership of the settlor? If the settlor contracted debts (or otherwise incurred liabilities) and at the time of the settlor's death, the debts overwhelmed the assets retained by the settlor, including the checking account, how could the probate court distinguish between assets to be paid out to creditors and assets to be delivered to the trust?[10] Hence, a trust *must* have an independent, identifiable *res*, the ownership of which passes to the trustee, or it fails. Meanwhile, the trust continues for so long as trust assets remain, and the trustee retains a duty toward the trust and the beneficiaries an interest in the trust assets, for that period. If a trust should run out of funds and lack any reasonable possibility of more funds arriving, then the trust "runs dry."

Pay special attention to this phrase in the previous sentence: "and lack any reasonable possibility of more funds arriving." That phrase raises the issue of "future income streams" as valid *reses* of trusts, an issue which lies at the heart of the following seminal case.

SPEELMAN v. PASCAL

178 N.E.2d 723 (N.Y. 1961).

Judges: Chief Judge Desmond. Judges Dye, Fuld, Froessel, Van Voorhis, Burke and Foster concur.

---

10. A duel between the executor and the trustee to settle the affair of honor—or better yet, a joust—might seem romantic, but these hearty measures have fallen sadly out of fashion (and legality) these past couple of centuries.

Gabriel Pascal, defendant's intestate who died in 1954, had been for many years a theatrical producer. In 1952 an English corporation named Gabriel Pascal Enterprises, Ltd., of whose 100 shares Gabriel Pascal owned 98, made an agreement . . . to prepare and produce a musical play to be based on [George Bernard] Shaw's play "Pygmalion" and a motion picture version of the musical play. The agreement . . . required the licensee corporation to pay the Shaw estate an initial advance and thereafter to pay the Shaw estate 3% of the gross receipts of the musical play and musical movie with a provision that the license was to terminate if within certain fixed periods the licensee did not arrange with Lerner and Loewe or other similarly well-known composers to write the musical play and arrange to produce it. Before Pascal's death in July, 1954, he had made a number of unsuccessful efforts to get the musical written and produced and it was not until after his death that arrangements were made, through a New York bank as temporary administrator of his estate, for the writing and production of the highly successful "My Fair Lady." Meanwhile, on February 22, 1954, at a time when the license from the Shaw estate still had two years to run, Gabriel Pascal, who died four and a half months later, wrote, signed and delivered to plaintiff a document as follows:

> Dear Miss Kingman
>
> This is to confirm to you our understanding that I give you from my shares of profits of the Pygmalion Musical stage version five per cent (5%) in England, and two per cent (2%) of my shares of profits in the United States. From the film version, five per cent (5%) from my profit shares all over the world.
>
> As soon as the contracts are signed, I will send a copy of this letter to my lawyer, Edwin Davies, in London, and he will confirm to you this arrangement in a legal form.
>
> This participation in my shares of profits is a present to you, in recognition for your loyal work for me as my Executive Secretary.
>
> Very sincerely yours,
>
> Gabriel Pascal . . .

The only real question is as to whether the 1954 letter above quoted operated to transfer to plaintiff an enforceable right to the described percentages of the royalties to accrue to Pascal on the production of a stage or film version of a musical play based on "Pygmalion". We see no reason why this letter does not have that effect. It is true that at the time of the delivery of the letter there was no musical stage or film play in existence but Pascal, who owned and was conducting negotiations to realize on the stage and film rights, could grant to another a share of the moneys to accrue from the use of those rights by others. There are many instances of courts enforcing assignments of rights to sums which were expected thereafter to become due to the assignor. A typical case is Field v. Mayor of New-York (6 N. Y. 179). One Bell, who had done much printing and similar work for the City of New York but had no present contract to do any more such work, gave an assignment in the amount of $ 1,500 of any moneys that might thereafter become due to Bell for such work. Bell did obtain such contracts or orders from the city and money became due to him therefor. This court held that while there was not at the time of the assignment any presently [enforceable] or even existing chose in action but merely a possibility that there would be such a chose of action, nevertheless there was a possibility of such which the parties expected to ripen into reality and which did afterwards ripen into reality and that, therefore, the assignment created an equitable title which the courts would enforce. A case similar to the present one in general outline is Central Trust Co. v. West India Improvement Co. (169 N. Y. 314) where the assignor had a right or concession from the Colony of Jamaica to build a railroad on that island and the courts upheld a mortgage given by the concession owner on any property that would be acquired by the concession owner in consideration of building the railroad if and when the railroad should be built. The Court of Appeals pointed out in Central Trust Co., at page 323, that the property as to which the mortgage was given had not yet come into existence at the time of the giving of the mortgage but that there was an expectation that such property, consisting of securities, would come into existence and accrue to the concession holder when and if the latter performed the underlying contract. This court held that the assignment would be recognized and enforced in equity. . . . [A]ll that need be established is "an intention that the title of the donor shall be presently divested and presently transferred.". . .

The judgment should be affirmed, with costs.

QUESTIONS AND ANALYSIS

In the *Pascal* case above, the court declares that

[t]he only real question is as to whether the 1954 letter above quoted operated to transfer to plaintiff an enforceable right to the

described percentages of the royalties to accrue to Pascal on the production of a stage or film version of a musical play based on "Pygmalion". We see no reason why this letter does not have that effect. It is true that at the time of the delivery of the letter there was no musical stage or film play in existence but Pascal, who owned and was conducting negotiations to realize on the stage and film rights, could grant to another a share of the moneys to accrue from the use of those rights by others.

This passage captures the heart of the matter. The play was not being performed when the trust was formed, and so as of the moment of formation there was no "present *res*." But there was an identifiable, "excludable" future income stream, one that could be fenced off: Either profits would arise from the play, or they would not. If profits did not arise (which was hardly a trifling possibility; most Broadway shows don't make any money, and at the time of trust formation it was not even clear that this would even become a *dud* Broadway show, much less a successful one), then the trust ran dry, and died stillborn. If profits did arise, however, then the trust—by its trustee—was from the first dollar of profit owner of either 2 or 5 percent of Pascal's share of it, depending on the provenance of the profit. But none of this caused any fuss for the court: A wait-and-see attitude did no damage to common-law, equitable trust theory or practice.

* * *

If the future income stream fails to materialize within a reasonable period or if facts conclusively demonstrate that the future income stream *will not materialize*, then the trust fails for want of a *res*. In this way, future income stream trusts serve essentially as supple, "tended" (by the trustee), modern-day equivalents of the contingent future interests that may have bedeviled your first-year property nightmares. Do you see why?

Trustee(s)

The trustee is (or the trustees are; a trust may be designed to be managed by plural trustees[11]) the party that carries the burdens of—that is,

---

11. If there are two trustees, the default rule requires unanimity in order for the trustees to act. With more than two trustees, majorities rule (at least under the majority and modern trend rules; at traditional common law, if there were more than one trustee, unanimity was always the default).

must administer—the trust. A trustee has three types of duty: invest-ment, administration, and distribution. A trust fails, or runs dry,[12] when none of these duties or burdens can be enforced against the trustee. Trustees often get paid for carrying this burden—as a default, they may claim "reasonable" fees for their services—although they can waive their right to payment. Individual trustees sometimes waive compensation, but corporate trustees—which are regulated by the state—generally do not.

A trustee owes a fiduciary duty to the settlor and the beneficiaries: The trustee must manage the *res* of the trust with fidelity to the trust instrument (the deed or declaration of trust) so as to satisfy the set-tlor's intent, and within the ambit of the settlor's instructions must act in the best interests of the beneficiaries. These fiduciary duties may be divided, and it is often wise to divide them. Investment and administrative duties may be vested in a corporate trust company, for instance, while a family friend (sometimes called a "trust protector") directs distribution or oversees the administrative trustees or changes provisions of the trust as directed by the settlement documents and as warranted under them. (These duties will be considered in greater detail below.)

Trusts, as the nearly obligatory judicial black-letter trope puts it, "will not fail for want of a trustee;" a court can and will appoint one and will appoint successors, even if the settlement documents provide no method for selecting successor trustees, unless the trust instrument explicitly makes the trusteeship "personal to the trustee." The trustee cannot be forced into the position; he must accept the duty freely—for reasons that will become clear when we examine the breadth and depth of the trustee's fiduciary obligations and the penalties that arise upon failure of a trustee to meet these expansive obligations. (In short, trustees who breach their very high fiduciary duties are held liable for the most possible damage they could plausibly have caused the trust *res* by their behavior—with all presumptions against them.)

A trust is not an independent legal entity (as a corporation is). The trustee sues and is sued (and acts in all other ways appropriate to her station) individually, but in her legal capacity as trustee rather than in her individual capacity. Any liabilities incurred by a trustee's actions are paid by the trust, unless the trustee fails of her fiduciary duties in a way that has decreased the remaining *res* of the trust or involves

---

12. These terms are not synonymous, exactly, but can be understood fairly interchangeably.

willful breach of duty. This "dual hat" status means that the trustee's personal creditors cannot get to trust assets to satisfy the trustee's debt. Trust assets are kept in a separate pocket, as it were.

Beneficiaries

These parties get the goodies: They hold the beneficial or equitable ownership of the trust. The beneficiaries can sue for breach of fiduciary duty by the trustee. If they win damages against the trustee personally, this gives them a personal judgment against the trustee, on par with trustees' other creditors; otherwise, their recovery comes from the trust *res* itself. Beneficiaries may also seek to replevy specific trust goods if the trustee improperly disposes of them, so long as they haven't been purchased by a *bona fide* purchaser for value (or good-faith purchaser for value), and on any resulting goods held by non-BFPVs. Without beneficiaries, a trustee's duties cannot be enforced, and the trust fails. (*Contra* charitable trusts, as discussed shortly.)

A single person can hold two—or even three—of these roles (i.e., settlor, trustee, and beneficiary), though if no one else has a beneficial stake, the trust merges into complete ownership again. As a useful test of your knowledge thus far, think through this proposition and make sure you understand it, and why it is true. If you don't understand, make sure to raise this issue during class discussion. This is a vital foundational moment.

B. COMMON TYPES OF TRUSTS AND THEIR IMPLICATIONS

As the preceding text indicated, the settlor's intent—as demonstrated in the trust instrument(s)—is the touchstone for interpreting and administering a trust. As we considered at length in Part I, almost no trust purposes are forbidden under modern law.[13] (Do you remember what the relevant boundaries are?)

---

13. Recall *Shapira* from Part I, *supra*.

Given the centrality of the settlor's intent as explicated in the trust documents—and the emotionally charged nature of end-of-life distributions of property, especially within families—careful and thoughtful drafting becomes absolutely vital to the wise and well-educated practitioner.

Because settlors enjoy such nearly boundless room for ingenuity, it is impossible to categorize all the various types of trusts that can arise. There are, however, some necessary "toggle switches," which is to say that all trusts fall necessarily into these categories: of A; not A; or partly A and partly not A. The first of these is the revocable/irrevocable toggle, considered next.

1. Revocable Trusts

Revocable trusts, which by their nature are always *inter vivos* trusts,[14] may in all American jurisdictions today effect a nonprobate transfer upon the death of the settlor in spite of a lack of testamentary formalities.[15] But particularly with regard to revocable trusts, the distinction

---

14. Do you see why?

15. This seemingly simple proposition caused decades of confusion and hesitation in the courts. The concern arose, essentially, out of fidelity to the old maxim *expressio unius est exclusio alterius* ("the expression of one thing excludes the possibility of another"). In other words, the courts worried for quite a long time about this problem: If the Wills Act requires certain formalities (discussed *supra* at Part III) for a testamentary transfer to be valid, how can we permit transfers at decease to be effected by any documents that lack those Wills Act formalities? *See, e.g.,* Restatement (Third) of Property: Wills and Other Donative Transfers §7.2, cmt. a. The courts—often with a push from frustrated legislatures—finally came effectively to the conclusion that while Wills Acts provided a way to transfer property at death, they need not provide the *only* means of doing so: American common and statutory law often provides many different means of achieving the same end. The Uniform Testamentary Additions to Trusts Acts (UTATA), universally adopted in some form or other, validates bequests to a trust even if the trust was not funded during the testator's lifetime. Thus you should not concern yourself with the issue of present funding of "complementary" trusts. UTATA appears at UPC §2-511.

The courts' long struggle with this problem may reasonably be understood, like that of the application of will's act presumptions and default rules to trust interpretation, as simple error: an example of a metaphor or canon of construction defeating thoughtful common-law adjudication; a misunderstanding by those courts about their roles and about the question properly before them. Unless a Probate Act were to include an explicit provision that specifies, for instance, that "the default rules and rules of construction contained in this Act may be applied only to Wills, but may not by common-law reasoning be applied by analogy to other instruments that perform similar functions," then exactly the sort of reasoning-by-analogy that fuels and informs

from a will, which must have such formalities, is thin indeed; typically the settlor not only retains, during his lifetime, the power to revoke the trust, but also, as a named beneficiary, has the right to income and principal, and, as the trustee, has management power over the property. Given this profound dominion over the trust property during the settlor's life, the trust looks an awful lot like a will, which is simply a declaration of intent that can be revoked or amended by the testator at any time; it also looks rather a lot like complete fee-simple-absolute ownership.

The primary example of a revocable trust in the estate planning context is a form that seems thus far not to have been named in trust-law literature, and so we will call it, for purposes of this text, a complementary trust. Generally, a complementary trust is a revocable *inter vivos* trust. This trust is conjoined with a pour-over will, a will written to dump anything from the estate not expressly contemplated in the complementary trust into that trust, thus avoiding the possibility of partial intestacy and ensuring a unified estate plan for the settlor.[16] (Under the circumstances, it would probably be more accurate to call the pour-over will a complement to the "primary" trust, but terms of art often survive long after their core sensibility has passed into history, and the pour-over trust has already been named.)

A helpful diagram:

---

the underlying logic and process of the common law should allow their application to trusts, etc. Legislatures simply did not mean, by specifying these construction rules in their Probate Acts, to preclude their application to will substitutes; the rules are in the probate codes because probate has historically been the primary mode of transfer on death. Similarly, unless a Probate Act states that "property may be passed, the trigger for passage being the death the owner, *only* by instrument designed in fidelity with this Act," then that Act should not be understood to forbid "testamentary" aspects of trusts, any more than they are read to make joint tenancies illegal in the relevant jurisdiction.

16. You can also make the complementary trust the beneficiary of a life insurance policy or other POD instrument. Essentially, the trust can be the final repository for most of the varied estate planning instruments, not just the pour-over will. It thus allows for convenient, efficient, and relatively inexpensive consolidated estate planning.

A Complementary Trust

Testator's Estate
- When the testator dies, his estate passes first through his will.

The (pour-over) Will
- The will is probated.
- Example Will: "The Grail to Arthur. All the rest and residue of my estate to Lancelot in his capacity as Trustee of the Round Table Trust."

The Trust
- The residuary estate passes to the trustee (in his official capacity), and into the trust itself, forming the *res*. The trustee must now administer the trust according to its terms.

In the majority of states, a trust of unspecified character—one that is not expressly either revocable or irrevocable—is treated as revocable. This follows the general intuition that a settlor should be able to revise her trust while she lives so long as she has not expressly denied herself that option. Under traditional law, and still in the minority of states, the reverse presumption is true: Unspecified trusts are considered irrevocable. This latter presumption arises from the very flimsiness of revocable trusts themselves. If a settlor can simply revoke the trust at any time—returning all the property to her own fee-simple-absolute ownership—then the trust fails (as will become clearer *infra*) to serve much effective purpose. The law thus presumes that a settlor who fails to specify the nature of the trust intended by his efforts to select the more effectual, meaningful vehicle—an irrevocable trust.

Note the effects and limitations of revocable trusts. They avoid probate for the assets held in trust (which is a public proceeding, while the details of a trust are not open to public scrutiny), can avoid ancillary probate (which arises when a testator owns real estate in another state than her state of domicile; the out-of-state real property is probated under an *in rem* probate proceeding in the state in which the real property is located), permit consolidated estate planning (if

233

nonprobate assets are poured into the trust as well, as per the diagram *supra*), and reduce the likelihood of a will contest. (This last is because trusts are usually drawn up long before a settlor's death, making claims of settlor incompetence at the time of trust drafting relatively unlikely. Meanwhile, a sentient trustee's present competence makes challenge to trust "performance" more difficult than challenge to a will.). A revocable trust though, as illustrated *infra*, won't fool creditors or the tax man.

The fragility of revocable trusts is illustrated by the helplessness of named beneficiaries during the period of revocability. Under UTC §603(a),[17] so long as the trust is revocable the "rights of the beneficiaries are subject to the control of, and the duties of the trustee are owed exclusively to, the settlor." This rule effectively treats wholly revocable trusts as will substitutes that are not meant to convey a present interest and denies nonsettlor beneficiaries any rights until the settlor dies.

Note, though, that

> [w]hen a person or entity different from the settlor removes property or money from a revocable trust, those withdrawals could conceivably be made without the settlor's knowledge or consent. In this situation, . . . after the death of the settlor, the beneficiaries of a revocable trust have standing to challenge pre-death withdrawals from the trust which are outside of the purposes authorized by the trust and which were not approved or ratified by the settlor personally or through a method contemplated through the trust instrument.[18]

Borrowing (or not) defaults and presumptions from Wills Acts. As we considered in Part I, the courts have grown fairly comfortable in borrowing Wills Act presumptions when interpreting trusts, particularly revocable (until death) complementary trusts that have essentially served as a will substitute. These include the forced/elective/augmented share, slayer rules, revocation of provisions favoring an ex-spouse upon the couple's divorce, creditor-rights provisions, and so forth. These provisions *should* (usually) presumptively apply,

---

17. *See also* Restatement (Third) of Trusts §74, cmt. e (2007), which takes the position that "the beneficiaries of a revocable trust cannot exercise the ordinary rights of trust beneficiaries as long as the settlor is legally competent and capable of understanding and evaluating information provided by the trustee. The settlor, who is almost always a beneficiary, exercises those rights on behalf of the other beneficiaries. The other beneficiaries can exercise their rights only when the settlor becomes legally incompetent."

18. Siegel v. Novak, 920 So. 2d 89, 95 (Fla. Dist. Ct. App. 2006).

because they are the product of centuries of experience in resolving problems in transfers on death and implementing the decedent's probable intent.[19]

2. Irrevocable Trusts

Irrevocable trusts are simply trusts that, once triggered, cannot be revoked. This is obviously true of "testamentary" or "will-substitute" trusts; any trust that is triggered by the death of the settlor can by definition not be revoked once activated, as the dead manifestly cannot revoke trusts. Irrevocable *inter vivos* trusts can also arise, though, in two pertinent ways. First, of course, any trust that declares itself irrevocable once triggered is irrevocable once triggered.[20] Second, at least in a minority of states, a trust that is silent as to whether it is revocable or irrevocable is treated as the latter by default.

3. Charitable Trusts

The rules for charitable trusts are in some important ways nearly the opposite of those for private trusts. The key to understanding charitable trusts: The assets that are transferred into the charitable trust to form its *res* are not taxed, and the income of the trust (and often its distributions) is not taxed. This is a huge advantage over noncharitable

---

19. Keep this category in mind as we continue to discuss trusts. Are there any such construction/interpretation rules or default presumptions that make sense in the wills context, but melt into gibberish, or fail of their function, when applied to trusts? Courts seem to think so, at least occasionally. Generally, for instance, the courts that understand the real question before them and their common-law roles nevertheless have not applied the rules regarding revocation of wills by physical act (*see supra*) to trusts, so a missing trust document in the settlor's possession at the settlor's death generally will not work a *sub silentio* revocation, the way it would under most probate acts. Whether more overt physical acts constitute a revocation depend on the terms of the trust and the relevant circumstances. What does this omission suggest: that something is different about trusts that justifies the exception, or that the presumption itself is either wrong or outdated, such that wise and thoughtful courts wish to cabin it so that it applies *only* where statute absolutely obliges them to employ it? (Underlying this whole discussion is the foundational distinction between statutory and common law and the restrictions and relative freedom for courts raised by each, respectively. Do you recall the distinction? Does it make sense to you? Are you comfortable with a legal regime that "sponsors" such a dual-track approach?)

20. *See* pretty much everywhere in this part (demonstrating the centrality of settlor intent).

trusts. If a settlor could avoid paying state and federal income tax, estate/death taxes, and the plethora of other taxes that descend from the various levels of government on businesses and individuals merely by employing the trust form and labeling the relevant trust "charitable"—well, wouldn't you?

The IRS, whatever you may individually think of its virtues *vel non*, is not a *stupid* organization. It does not permit the formation of "charitable" trusts, so called, for the purpose of distributing property to beneficiaries, tax free, to whom the settlor would have distributed those assets in all events. The IRS requires that the grants in charitable trusts be genuinely charitable (i.e., a gift to a class of strangers in recognition of some need or virtue of theirs, such as being among the homeless or the halt or lame or rather as being among the bright young things deserving scholarship support).[21]

Note well: the beneficiaries of a charitable trust must be selected from a "class of strangers." But an indeterminate class of strangers (e.g., the homeless of San Francisco; the Yoknapatawpha Law School Class of 2025) will find it difficult to bring an ill-acting trustee into court to enforce the fiduciary obligations of the trust, at least most of the time. Say, for instance, that the grant was "an $8000 bar study and support scholarship for the top five members (in g.p.a.) of the YLS class each graduating year." During the period between the computation of final grades and the distribution of the trust funds, there will be an identified class of beneficiaries who can sue to enforce the trustee's duties, but through the remaining, say, 345 days of any year, there is no one. *Astonishing* amounts of mischief can be achieved in 345 days. Meanwhile, in the "homeless of San Francisco" example suggested above, there may well never be any person who is entitled to, rather than merely eligible for, a grant at any given time. Hence, there are never any clearly identifiable beneficiaries in a position to enforce the trustee's fiduciary duties.

a. Enforcement of the Trustee's Duties

Normally, this would scupper the trust at the start. Our tax law and the goodness of the good-hearted commend charitable giving, however.

---

21. According to UTC §405(a), "[a] charitable trust may be created for the relief of poverty, the advancement of education or religion, the promotion of health, governmental or municipal purposes, or other purposes the achievement of which is beneficial to the community."

To avoid the absurdity of outlawing valuable and noble undertakings (i.e., charitable trusts), which are forbidden to have a clearly identifiable set of definitely entitled beneficiaries, exactly because they fail to have a clearly identifiable set of definitely entitled beneficiaries, state trust laws and the UTC generally substitute the relevant attorney general's office (or the office of some other public official) as a third-party enforcer.[22]

b. The Cy Pres Doctrine

Another quirk of doctrine applies particularly to charitable trusts. It is presumed—rebuttably but presumed in the absence of evidence to the contrary—that the highest purpose of a settlor of a charitable trust is to do charity, rather than to do only the exact charity specified in the trust documents. Thus, when faced with a charitable trust or trust provision that can no longer be performed according to the express terms of the provision, the court will prefer to reform the terms, with an eye toward continuing to do the settlor's will as far as possible while still doing charity. This reformation presumption is called the *cy pres* (Latin for "as near as possible") doctrine.

An example: An old professor makes a gift of $1 million, the income of the trust to be used to fund curriculum reform efforts at his law school *alma mater*. The trust goes into effect and is administered for the benefit of the law school for 20 years. At the 20-year mark, though, the law school merges with another nearby law school, the population of law school applicants having fallen significantly over that time. The new law school bears a different name than the pre-merger *alma mater*.

Here, the *cy pres* doctrine is fairly easy to apply. Yes, some reformation is necessary to permit the grant to transfer from the original *alma mater* to the merged school but—without evidence to the contrary—there's very little reason to suspect that the grantor would not have wanted exactly that reformation to have been permitted in the initial grant if he had thought about it when drafting the provision.

Consider a slightly more difficult case. This time, the *alma mater* does not merge, but completely shuts down, the university having decided that the school could no longer be run profitably and ethically

---

22. *See e.g.,* UTC §110(d) ("[(d) The [attorney general of this State] has the rights of a qualified beneficiary with respect to a charitable trust having its principal place of administration in this State.]").

given the decrease in law school attendance. Now what? Is it still clear that the settlor would have wanted the gift to continue, with a different beneficiary? If so, is it merely because of the presumption in favor of continued charitable giving? And even if so, how should the gift be reformed? To support curricular reform at the broader university? At a nearby law school? At the law school he had gone on to teach at? At law schools generally? Or would some other solution fit better? On what grounds? Could you put together a "brief" against any or all of these positions?

Note the collateral effect of the *cy pres* doctrine: It keeps more money in charitable giving of some sort, but at the expense of denying that money to the settlor's natural (intestate) heirs. Is this the right call in cases in which the object of the gift-over is not obvious? Why or why not?

4. Constructive/Resulting Trusts

These are not really trusts at all. They are things that judges say when they must make things happen and have no other tool with which to do it. If the beneficiaries of a valid trust run out, but *res* remains, then the final trustee will implead into the court the question: "What do I do now?"[23] The judge will decide and then *declare* a "resulting trust," which will be the legal form by which the judge takes the money from the trustee, relieves the trustee of fiduciary duty, and then disburses the *res* assets per that judicial decision. (The resulting trust form can be used in situations that don't directly impune real trusts, as well.)

Similarly, if—in any case, not just trust-related cases—the judge decides that Party A holds property that, under independent law or equity, really should be held by Party B, the judge may declare a "constructive trust," naming Party A as the trustee of the trust funds and Party B as the sole payee-in-full. It is merely a judicial form that partakes somewhat of the elements of trust.

---

23. Unless, that is, the trust itself explicitly directs the trustee about what to do in exactly those circumstances, in which case the trustee continues to do the will of the settlor under the normal rules we've already discussed.

C. POWERS AND DUTIES OF TRUSTEES

1. Powers

What acts and things may a trustee of right do in achieving her task of fulfilling the intent of the settlor for the benefit of the beneficiaries? The answer to this question has changed over time.

Under the traditional rule (which is now effectively dead), the trustee enjoyed only the authority to do those acts that had been specifically authorized by the settlor in the trust documents themselves or in the default list of powers found in state trust codes. (These lists of powers were akin to the lists of acceptable trust investments, considered *infra*.) So long as the trustee acted within the ambit of the authorized powers, then the acts were largely unreviewable; if the trustee violated those terms, even for an obviously good and settlor-intent-advancing purpose, the trustee was liable to sanction and recovery.

Under the modern rule, trustees have largely plenary powers (with increasingly few *per se* exceptions),[24] bounded by the very "high" (i.e., rigorously enforced and manifold) fiduciary duties considered below.

What has motivated this transition, and what explains the various features of the current structure?

2. Duties

As we have considered, if a trustee has no identifiable duties on which identifiable and identified and informed beneficiaries may sue, then

---

24. *See* UTC §815(a) (2000) represents the logical conclusion of the strategy of maximum empowerment of the trustee, giving trustees, as a default, plenary authority ("[E]xcept as limited by the terms of the trust," a "trustee, without authorization by the court, may exercise . . . all powers over the trust property which an unmarried competent owner has over individually owned property" and "any other powers appropriate to achieve the proper investment, management, and distribution of the trust property."). But the broader the authority, the higher the standards of fiduciary duty, as a practical matter. Enough of the old "list" mentality remains that the next section, §816, includes a safe-harbor list designed to give certainty to trustees and third parties for the actions listed: There is no question about the power of the trustee to undertake any of the actions that are specifically authorized there. (Per the official comment to that section, "the Committee drafting this Code . . . concluded that the demand of third parties to see language expressly authorizing specific transactions justified retention of a detailed list.")

the effort at settling a trust must necessarily have failed.[25] Instead, a gift will have been made, or the assets will never at law (or in equity) have passed from the would-have-been settlor.

It follows that when a settlor purports to grant a trustee absolute discretion in handling the trust and total absolution from damages arising from a breach of fiduciary duty,[26] something has gone wrong and the court must disregard some intentions of the settlor; either the grant of discretion and immunity must fail, or it must survive, and thereby doom the rest of the terms of the trust to crumble into the ash heap of history.[27] Simply as a matter of arithmetic, if nothing more, most courts take the former course.

So if, most of the time, the trust survives but the discretion and immunity must be cabined, this issue arises: what are the absolute, bare-bones mandatory-minima of fiduciary duty? Are they always the same minima? Whence do they arise? On what grounds?

KOLODNEY v. KOLODNEY

503 A.2d 625 (Conn. App. Ct. 1986).

Judges: Hull, Daly and Bieluch, JJ.

The plaintiff trustee, Abraham J. Kolodney, appeals from a judgment of the trial court ordering him to increase monthly payments to the defendant, Nancy Kolodney, beneficiary of the trust, from $ 1000 to $2500. The plaintiff claims, inter alia, that the court erred in finding that he had abused his discretion by failing to provide sufficient monthly payments for the comfortable maintenance, support and education of the defendant. We find no error.

---

25. This is true both legally and practically. As a legal matter, a trustee must inform identified and reasonably identifiable beneficiaries of their bounty. Good and honorable trustees will of course do this even if the beneficiaries have no idea of the existence of a trust. If there are no such beneficiaries, then the trust fails. If there are such beneficiaries but the trustee is bad and the beneficiaries have not been informed, then as a practical matter the trust fails too, as the bad would-be trustee will simply pocket the dosh.

26. Consider here our earlier discussion about the relative merits of direction and of discretion and of the practical fact that virtually all trusts end up with some admixture of the two. What might cause a settlor to grant some trustee absolute discretion and immunity absent some genuine misbehavior (i.e., undue influence, fraud, coercion, dishonesty, etc.) by the trustee? Can you construct a plausible hypothetical that genuinely lacks a base in real or constructive trustee misdeeds? Is it still a non-charitable trust?

27. And/or the dust bin of history.

The plaintiff was the brother of Ralph J. Kolodney, who was the father of the defendant and who created a testamentary trust[1] in her favor. The plaintiff was named as trustee and, pursuant to the trust, began to pay the defendant $1000 per month. The defendant applied to have the plaintiff removed as trustee but, instead of acting on the removal petition, the Probate Court ordered the plaintiff to pay the defendant a minimum of $2000 per month under the fourth clause of the will, retroactive to July 28, 1981, the date when the plaintiff accepted the trusteeship. The defendant had requested $30,000 per year, or $2500 per month.

The plaintiff appealed from this order to the trial court. That court, after a trial de novo . . . , increased to $2500 the minimum amount which the plaintiff was required to pay each month, retroactive to August 20, 1981, the date of his qualification as trustee.

From that judgment, the plaintiff has appealed to this court. . . . The plaintiff claims that the trial court erred (1) in failing to hold that the trust did not require him to make any payments to the defendant beneficiary, (2) in finding that the plaintiff delegated to his wife the duty to exercise independent judgment as to the financial needs of the defendant, (3) in holding that he abused his discretion, and (4) in ordering him, as trustee, to pay the defendant beneficiary $2500 monthly. . . .

The plaintiff's first claim of error is that the trust, by its terms, did not require him to make any payments to the defendant at all. This argument is based on the provision in the trust which provides the trustee with "the power to invest and reinvest [the trust *res*] and to

---

1. The provisions of that trust provide in part: "Fourth: All the rest, residue and remainder of my estate, of whatsoever the same may consist and wheresoever situated, I give, devise and bequeath to my said brother, Abraham J. Kolodney, to serve without bond, and if he is unable or unwilling to act, then to The New Britain National Bank, a national banking association located in said Town of New Britain, in trust, however, to pay over to my daughter, Nancy Kolodney, when she has reached or shall reach the age of fifty years. During the period while my Trustee, whichever one may act, shall hold any estate in trust, he or it shall have the power to invest and reinvest the same and to collect the income therefrom and expend so much of the net income and principal thereof for the comfortable maintenance, support and education of my said daughter as he or it shall, in his or its sole discretion, deem advisable, or in the event my said daughter shall not be living at the time of my death or shall not survive to receive all of the trust estate hereunder in accordance with the terms hereof, then I give, devise and bequeath all said rest, residue and remainder estate or all of said trust estate then remaining, whichever the case may be, to her children then living and the issue then living of any deceased child of hers, equally *per stirpes*."

collect the income therefrom and expend so much of the net income and principal thereof for the comfortable maintenance, support and education of my said daughter as he . . . shall, in his . . . sole discretion, deem advisable. . . ." The plaintiff equates the phrase "sole discretion" with "absolute discretion." This argument is unconvincing.

The plaintiff's claim hinges on his assertion that the language of this trust should be construed as was the language of the trust in Auchincloss v. City Bank Farmers Trust Co., 136 Conn. 266, 70 A.2d 105 (1949). In that case, however, the trust contained the express phrase "in their absolute discretion." That discretion was unbounded by any standard to be applied. Hence, the court held that the provision did not "impose upon [the trustees] a duty to use the income for the support and education of the child, leaving them merely a discretion as to time and methods of its disposition, nor is the provision one which conditions the application of the fund upon the needs of the child. . . ."

In the present case, however, the plaintiff's discretion was limited by a standard, that of "comfortable maintenance, support and education." "The well-settled rule in this state is that the exercise of discretion by the trustee of a . . . trust is subject to the court's control only to the extent that an abuse has occurred under the powers granted by the testamentary disposition. . . . To determine the discretionary powers provided, it is necessary to ascertain the dispositive intention as expressed by the language of the entire will 'in the light of the circumstances surrounding the testator when the instrument was executed, including the condition of his estate, his relations to his family and beneficiaries and their situation and condition.' [citation omitted]" . . . It is clear from the testator's use of the "comfortable maintenance, support and education" standard that the trustee's discretion was not intended to be absolute. . . . Had the testator so intended, he could have so provided in explicit terms. Any other reading of this trust would render the "comfortable maintenance, support and education" standard meaningless.

The plaintiff's claimed discretion not to make any payments to the defendant was modified by the standard expressed. The plaintiff trustee was obligated to maintain comfortably, to support and to educate the defendant beneficiary during the existence of the trust. That is the measure of his sole discretion. The defendant sought an allowance of $2500 per month to meet that standard, and the trial court found that amount to be necessary.

The plaintiff's next claim is that the court erred in concluding that the plaintiff had delegated to his wife the duty and judgment concerning the defendant's financial needs and thereby abused his discretion. This claim is without merit.

The transcript reveals that the plaintiff did direct his wife, Frances Kolodney, to visit the defendant at her apartment in New York's SoHo district. The plaintiff testified that his wife brought back a report on the defendant's living conditions which formed the basis for the amount of his payments to the defendant. From this testimony, the court could have concluded that the plaintiff delegated his duty to exercise independent judgment as to the defendant's needs. We will not retry the facts. . . .[4]

With regard to the plaintiff's remaining claims, his arguments are (1) that he was not obligated to make any payments to the defendant pursuant to the trust and, therefore, that he was not required to inquire into her financial needs which the court found he had failed to do, and (2) that in the absence of an abuse of his discretion, the court had no authority to control his discretion, or to substitute its own.

Both of these claims are based on faulty predicates. First, since we have concluded that the plaintiff was obligated to pay the defendant whatever sum was necessary for her comfortable maintenance, support and education, it follows that he had a duty to inquire as to what sums were necessary to maintain that standard of living. His failure to do so constituted an abuse of discretion. Second, since the trial court found, and we agree, that there was an abuse of discretion in this case, the trial court did have the authority to raise the monthly payments to the defendant to the level required by the provisions of the trust. The amount ordered was the sum requested as necessary by the defendant for her comfortable existence under the standard set forth by her father.

There is no error.

IN RE GUARDIANSHIP OF EISENBERG

719 P.2d 187 (Wash. Ct. App. 1986).

Judges: Scholfield, C.J. Williams and Webster, JJ., concur.

Lisa Yvette and the guardianship of Ian Karl Eisenberg appeal the trial court's determination that the liability to them of their guardian,

---

4. The trial court found that the defendant's apartment was a sixth floor walk-up which contained a makeshift shower installed by her, and had heating problems and a front door that was repeatedly being broken.

Arthur Joel Eisenberg (Joel), did not include amounts due on certain aircraft leases between the guardianships and companies controlled by Joel.

Joel Eisenberg and his then wife, June Eisenberg, operated several related businesses, including a nonprofit air travel club known as Air Club International, a travel agency known as International Travel, Inc., and American Aviation Services, Inc., which later merged into Aeroamerica, Inc., an air charter company. Joel petitioned the superior court to be appointed guardian of the estates of his two minor children, Yvette and Ian, in August 1973.

At the time the guardianships were initiated, Joel purchased five Boeing aircraft and sold one to each guardianship. Yvette's estate purchased N734T with funds acquired from gifts to her, along with a loan of $ 154,000 from Air Club and its Canadian affiliate, ACI, Ltd. Ian's estate purchased N736T with funds acquired from gifts to him, along with a loan from Joel of $ 153,000.

In September 1973, Joel sought and received court approval to lease Yvette's plane (N734T) to Air Club for a 5-year term. Joel did not disclose to the court his own involvement with Air Club. In March 1974, without court approval, Joel replaced this lease with a new lease agreement between Yvette and Aeroamerica. Air Club filed bankruptcy in the spring of 1975. Yvette's plane continued under lease to Aeroamerica until July 1979. Aeroamerica filed for bankruptcy in November 1979.

After the Aeroamerica lease of N734T expired, Joel leased the plane to a movie company as a prop for $ 8,900, which was deposited into the Aeroamerica account and never paid to the Yvette guardianship. Following this, Joel directed the dismantling and sale of N734T for parts. The reasonable scrap value of $49,350 was not deposited into the Yvette guardianship account.

As for Ian's plane, Joel sought and was granted the court's permission to lease it to Air Club for 5 years. Here again, there was no disclosure to the court of his control of Air Club. In 1975, following Air Club's bankruptcy, Joel petitioned the court for approval to lease N736T to Aeroamerica. While he was debtor in possession of Aeroamerica, Joel extended the lease of N736T to Aeroamerica for an additional 5 years.

In its order fixing final accounting, the trial court listed the following as the assets of the guardianships:

[Yvette's guardianship:]	
Asset	Amount
Cash on hand as of August 17, 1982	$ 29,555.92
Account receivable from Aeroamerica, Inc., for unpaid aircraft lease payments	1,562,125.00
Account receivable from Air Club International	21,000.00
Claim against A. Joel Eisenberg for funds received as rental of N734T as movie "prop"	8,900.00
Parts removed from N734T and converted by A. Joel Eisenberg	49,350.00
Claim against A. Joel Eisenberg for legal fees and expenses incurred in obtaining his final accounting	11,500.00

One Boeing 720-027 aircraft, Serial No. N734T	In process of scrapping
[Ian's guardianship:]	
Asset	Amount
Cash on hand as of August 17, 1982	$ 99,664.16
Account receivable from Air Club International for unpaid lease payments	226,500.00
Account receivable from Aeroamerica, Inc., for unpaid lease payments through 1979	306,000.00
Unpaid lease payments from Aeroamerica thereafter	328,905.00
Unpaid balance on loan from A. Joel Eisenberg	(15,375.97)
Claim against A. Joel Eisenberg for legal fees and expenses incurred in obtaining his final accounting	38,500.00
One Boeing 720-027 aircraft, Serial No. N736T	50,000.00[1]

1. The record does not provide a complete accounting of the guardianships. The net amounts listing the assets of the guardianships appear to have taken into account the loans which were used to purchase the aircraft.

In August 1982, Joel was removed as guardian of both estates and, ultimately, his ex-wife, June, was appointed as successor guardian. . . .

Breach of Fiduciary Duty

A guardianship has been described as "a trust relation of the most sacred character." . . . Therefore, analysis of a guardianship question may rely upon an appropriate trust concept.

Liability for losses to a trust is discussed under two sections of the Restatement (Second) of Trusts (1959):

§205. Liability in Case of Breach of Trust

If the trustee commits a breach of trust, he is chargeable with

(a) any loss or depreciation in value of the trust estate resulting from the breach of trust; or

(b) any profit made by him through the breach of trust; or

(c) any profit which would have accrued to the trust estate if there had been no breach of trust.

The trustee is liable for losses sustained by the trust which are the result of the trustee's breach.

Section 206 of the Restatement speaks to the breach of the duty of loyalty:

§206. Liability for Breach of Duty of Loyalty

The rule stated in §205 is applicable where the trustee in breach of trust sells trust property to himself individually, or sells his individual property to himself as trustee, or otherwise violates his duty of loyalty. Comments a and b to section 206 state in part:

The trustee is under a duty to the beneficiary to administer the trust solely in the interest of the beneficiary. . . .

The trustee violates his duty to the beneficiary if he sells trust property to himself individually or if he has a personal interest in the purchase of such a substantial nature that it might affect his judgment in making the sale.

Comment f to section 205 notes that:

[A] trustee is liable for a loss resulting from a breach of trust. A question may arise, therefore, as to the causal connection between the breach of trust and the loss. If the trustee commits a breach of trust and if a loss is incurred, the trustee may not be chargeable with the amount of the loss if it would have occurred in the absence of a breach of trust.

Comment f to section 205 continues its analysis by noting:

On the other hand, where the trustee purchases for the trust, property owned by him individually, and the property depreciates in value, it is immaterial that the trustee could properly have purchased similar property from a third person and that in such a case he would not have been liable for the loss. In order to deter self-dealing by the trustee, he is chargeable with any loss which results. . . .

Therefore, if a trustee is engaging in self-dealing, he will be liable for all losses to the guardianship arising from his self-dealing transactions. The extent of the liability of a trustee who violates the duty of loyalty is discussed in comment a to section 206:

If the trustee commits a breach of his duty of loyalty he is chargeable with any loss or depreciation in value of the trust property resulting from the breach of duty, or any profit made by him through the breach of duty, or any profit which would have accrued to the trust estate if there had been no breach of duty.

In In re Carlson, 162 Wash. 20, 297 P. 764 (1931), the appellant was guardian of the estate of a minor child. The guardian continued to invest guardianship assets in securities of the company of which he was the principal stockholder, despite the fact that the securities had declined in value and that the company ultimately failed. The trial court charged the guardian with the original inventory value of the estate. On appeal, the court found the guardian liable for the full amount of the securities, despite their depreciation, and noted:

[A]s a general rule, a person occupying a relation of trust or confidence to another is in equity bound to abstain from doing everything which can place him in a position inconsistent with the duty or trust such relation imposes upon him, or which has a tendency to interfere with the discharge of such duty. Upon this principle, no one placed in a situation of trust or confidence in reference to the subject of a sale can be the purchaser, on his own account, of the property sold.

Carlson, at 31-32. In Tucker v. Brown, 20 Wn.2d 740, 150 P.2d 604 (1944), the court found a trustee liable for the full amount of money he received from the sale of bonds belonging to the trust. The court noted that a trustee who finds himself in a conflict of interest situation has only one choice:

Where a trustee finds himself in the position where he has, either individually or as trustee for another, an interest which conflicts with that of the beneficiaries of the trust, he should resign from the trust so as not to attempt the impossible task of representing conflicting interests.

Tucker, at 769.

Joel arranged for the leasing of guardianship property to corporations in which he had substantial personal interest. He was in charge of the nonprofit organization, Air Club, and he and June were the sole shareholders in Aeroamerica. Joel did not disclose this information to the court when he sought approval for the leases, and certain changes in the leases never received court approval. At the demand of Aeroamerica creditors, Joel agreed to subordinate all Aeroamerica obligations due the two guardianship estates to the claims of all other creditors. It is obvious that Joel breached his fiduciary duty of loyalty to the guardianships. We hold that Joel is personally liable to the guardianships for their losses resulting from this breach of the duty of loyalty.

Measurement of Losses

In deciding the appropriate sanction to be applied to a trustee who has violated his duty of loyalty, the court must fashion the relief granted so that it will act as a deterrent to the errant trustee and other trustees in the future. The equitable relief granted in each case will vary according to the circumstances of both the beneficiaries and the trustee. . . .

The net effect of Joel's actions concerning the guardianships' airplanes was to appropriate them for his own use. The most proper measure of damages, therefore, may be found under section 205(c) of the Restatement (Second) of Trusts:

[A]ny profit which would have accrued to the trust estate if there had been no breach of trust.

Therefore, we hold that the guardianships are entitled to damages consisting of the fair rental value of the planes from the time of their purchase until the end of their usage by Joel's corporations, less any rental amounts already paid during that time frame. . . .

The trial court must take further evidence to determine the proper amount of damages, if any, relating to leases of the aircraft. Therefore, this case is remanded for further proceedings consistent with this opinion.

QUESTIONS AND ANALYSIS

In *Kolodney*, the court found that "the [trustee's] discretion was limited by a standard, that of 'comfortable maintenance, support and education.'" In other words, the trustee had discretion in making distributions from the trust, but the discretion was bounded by the obligation to ensure the beneficiary's comfortable support, that the beneficiary could get an education. It found on this basis a duty in the trustee to monitor the beneficiary so as to know whether the beneficiary was independently comfortably supported and had access to education, or whether trust funds need be provided. The trustee then had to provide funds to achieve the required standards.

The court contrasted the *Kolodney* language to the language of the trust in Auchincloss v. City Bank Farmers Trust Co., 136 Conn. 266, 70 A.2d 105 (1949). In that case, however, the trust contained the express phrase "in their absolute discretion." That discretion was unbounded by any standard to be applied. Hence, the court held that the provision did not "impose upon [the trustees] a duty to use the income for the support and education of the child, leaving them merely a discretion as to time and methods of its disposition, nor is the provision one which conditions the application of the fund upon the needs of the child. . . ."

Does it follow, then, that the trustee in *Auchincloss* should properly have been judged to have had *absolute* discretion to make—or never to make—distributions from the trust wholly at the trustee's discretion? To anybody? To the trustee himself? Would the last of these not actually create absolute ownership of the trust property in the purported trustee, such that no trust had been established?

A trustee must, remember, have *some* duties that a beneficiary can enforce at law against the trustee in order for a trust to be formed. Consider whether you can frame a minimum set of duties that might obtain to all trustees of valid trusts.

* * *

Do these minima of fiduciary duty arise from practical or principled considerations, or (inevitably, if the arc of the moral universe indeed bends toward justice) both?

Though fiduciary duties arise in many areas of the law, those of a trustee are particularly extensive and are generally enforced with relative vigor; duties are defined aggressively, and recognized infractions are taken seriously and met with heavy sanction. This vigorous enforcement arises for a couple of reasons (at least). First, some of the duties can be hard to monitor, the beneficiaries not necessarily being, *a priori*, aware of their status as beneficiaries or of the niceties of trust law and so potentially unlikely to themselves demand to oversee the trustee with the sort of knowledge and assertiveness that the settlor might have undertaken. Second, once the settlor has departed the stage, the trustee acts for the benefit of the beneficiaries, but at the continuing behest of someone who is gone,[28] which creates both relatively unique agency problems (usually the principal can monitor the agent himself, which narrows the distance between principal goals and agent incentives) and the general sense of obligation to the dead that the law generally embraces. Other explanations for the rigor of trustee fiduciary duties may occur to you. For an example of just how vigorously courts enforce duties, look upon the case of poor Gleeson, which follows.

IN RE WILL OF GLEESON
124 N.E.2d 624 (Ill. App. Ct. 1955).

Mary Gleeson, who died testate on February 14, 1952, owned . . . 160 acres of farm land in Christian county, Illinois. By her will admitted to probate March 29, 1952, she nominated Con Colbrook, petitioner-appellee (who will be referred to herein as petitioner), executor thereof. Petitioner was also appointed as trustee under the will and the residuary estate, including the aforesaid 160 acres of land, was devised to him in trust for the benefit of decedent's 3 children, . . . who are respondents herein.

On March 1, 1950, the testatrix leased the 160 acres for the year ending March 1, 1951 to petitioner and William Curtin, a partnership. On March 1, 1951, she again leased the premises to said partnership for the year ending March 1, 1952. Upon the expiration of this latter lease the partnership held over as tenants under the provisions thereof and farmed the land until March 1, 1953, at which time petitioner leased the land to another tenant. . . .

---

28. Usually, and especially in a study like ours, gone to a great beyond, whatever that might be. But even if the settlor yet lives, as with a trust established for the purpose of relieving the settlor of the day-to-day management of the trust assets, she is understood to have gone away, so that the trustee looks to his instructions rather than to the settlor's continuing oversight and input.

The petitioner's appointment as trustee was confirmed by the circuit court of Christian County on April 29, 1953. On July 22, 1953, he filed his first semiannual report. . . . To this report respondents filed certain objections. We are concerned here with only one of the said objections, which is as follows:

> 1. Report shows trustee was co-tenant of trust real estate but fails to account for share of profits received by trustee as co-tenant which by law should be re-paid by him to trust estate.

The record indicates no dispute as to the fact that petitioner as trustee leased a portion of the real estate of the trust to himself as a partner of William Curtin and . . . received a share of the profits realized by him and Curtin from their farming operation of said real estate. . . .

The courts of this state have consistently followed a general principle of equity that a trustee cannot deal in his individual capacity with the trust property. . . .

Petitioner recognizes the existence of this general rule, but argues that because of the existence of the peculiar circumstances under which the petitioner proceeded, the instant case must be taken to constitute one of the rare exceptions to such rule. The circumstances alluded to as peculiar are pointed out as being the facts that the death of Mrs. Gleeson occurred on February 14, 1952, only 15 days prior to the beginning of the 1952 farm year; that satisfactory farm tenants are not always available, especially on short notice; that the petitioner had in the preceding fall of 1951 sown part of the 160 acres in wheat to be harvested in 1952; that the holding over by the trustee and his partner was in the best interests of the trust; that the same was done in an open manner; that the petitioner was honest with the trust; and that it suffered no loss as a result of the transaction.

Petitioner's argument that the foregoing constitutes circumstances bringing this case within any exception to the general rule does not appear to be supported by the authorities. In Sherman v. White, 62 Ill. App. 271 and Bold v. Mid-City Trust & Savings Bank, 279 Ill.App. 365 cited by petitioner, the court followed the general rule announced in so many cases to the effect that a trustee may not deal with trust property in his individual capacity. While giving recognition to the rare exception that a trustee may, under certain circumstances, be entitled to make a personal gain out of the trust property, the court in both cases adhered to the general rule as above stated. . . . The question for decision on this appeal was whether the record reflects a sufficient reason for permitting the petitioner to deal with the trust property for his own individual benefit.

Petitioner contends that since only 15 days intervened between the death of Mrs. Gleeson and the beginning of the farm year, and that good tenant farmers might not be available at such a time, it was in the interests of the trust that the petitioner continue to hold over for the year of 1952. No showing is made that petitioner tried to obtain a satisfactory tenant to replace Colbrook and Curtin on March 1, 1952. The record discloses that [after] the death of testatrix, petitioner discussed continuance of the farming operation with two of the beneficiaries under the trust and voluntarily raised the cash rent from $6.00 to $10.00 per acre. This evidence tending to show that petitioner was interested in continuing a tenancy under which he was leasing trust property to himself would seem to refute any contention that an effort to lease the property to any one other than the partnership was made. The fact that the partners had sown wheat on the land in the fall of 1951 cannot be said to be a peculiar circumstance. It is not suggested that the trust would have suffered a loss if someone other than the petitioner had farmed the land in 1952 and harvested the wheat. It would appear that a satisfactory adjustment covering the matter of the wheat could have been made between the trust and the partnership without great difficulty.

The good faith and honesty of the petitioner or the fact that the trust sustained no loss on account of his dealings therewith are all matters which can avail petitioner nothing so far as a justification of the course he chose to take in dealing with trust property is concerned. . . .

We think the holding of the court in Johnson v. Sarver, supra, is applicable to the question to be decided in the instant case. Among the questions with which the court dealt in that case was the right of trustees to lease real estate of the trust to themselves. Holding that the trustees were without power to do so, the court had this to say:

> [A] trustee must maintain a high level of conduct and owes to those whose property he controls undivided loyalty. It is not compulsory or mandatory that any of the trustees accept the appointment made by their father. They have accepted and asked the court to instruct them as to their duties, and if they are dissatisfied with the amount of compensation or any other requirement which the court has imposed, there is a method by which they can be relieved of their duties. . . .
>
> The chancellor . . . properly decreed that appellants, as trustees, cannot lease the real estate involved in this trust to themselves or deal with themselves. . . .

We think the decision in the foregoing case suggests that the petitioner herein, upon the death of the testatrix, instead of conferring with her beneficiaries concerning continuance of his tenancy of the trust property, should have then decided whether he chose to continue as a tenant or to act as trustee. His election was to act as trustee and as such he could not deal with himself.

This court, therefore, reaches the conclusion that . . . petitioner should have been required to recast his first semiannual report and to account therein for all monies received by him personally as a profit by virtue of his being a cotenant of trust property during the 1952 crop year, and to pay the amount of any such profit to the trust.

QUESTIONS AND ANALYSIS

The result in *Gleeson* is one worth fleshing out and dwelling upon for a bit. Here we have a tenant who was so close to and trusted by the landlord-settlor that she named him trustee of her trust, intending him to look after her family beneficiaries. His trusteeship began when the settlor died, just two weeks before the planting season began. Faced with the deep unlikelihood of finding a qualified tenant to take his place in two weeks at the end of February in Illinois—not known for its mild winters in which moving house would have been plausible—he signed on for another season (clearly what the settlor landlord had intended) and nearly doubled, voluntarily, his own rent. There was no suspicion whatsoever that he had acted with any impropriety or malice; and given that his primary job was that of a farmer, it is unlikely that he acted with any expert knowledge that anything he did was in any way untoward.

Nevertheless, it was untoward, because it was self-dealing, in that he as trustee dealt with himself as tenant, and so was adjudged to have violated fiduciary duty without any "further inquiry" into his motives or the objective propriety of his decisions. (Hence the "no further inquiry rule" discussed below.) As a result, then, the tenant-trustee was obliged to disgorge to the trust all of his profits from his year's farming on the property—which, given the narrow margins of small-scale farming operations in the middle of the last century, may very well have been the ruin of him.

This case thus stands as a stark illustration of just how serious courts are about applying the very highest of fiduciary standards to trustees. It also demonstrates how the position of trustee can turn into a nightmarish trap for those selected to be trustees because they are stalwart family friends rather than trained lawyers: They can behave with the highest of motives and stick to the best objective standards and still find themselves bedeviled by the law. Finally, this is a warning to young lawyers-in-training of how much care they must take at every moment in their careers, because the world is full of awful people like the beneficiaries here, who sued within their rights at law, but in utter conflation of any notions of equity.

* * *

These fiduciary duties can be categorized, though not with complete nicety, a couple of different ways. Following a common method, the explication of duties that follows divides the realm into duties of loyalty, duties of prudence, and leftover duties that are arguably combinations of the two primary categories. Another (similarly messy, overlapping, and incomplete) distinction is that between general management duties, investment duties, and distribution duties.

The penalties for breach of fiduciary duty depend on the type of breach and the state of the *res*. Broadly, if the error is one made in good faith by the trustee *and* if the relevant error did not involve an improper disbursement from the *res* of the trust, then the trust pays to make good the error. If the failure of fiduciary duty is the result of bad faith, or involves non-safe-harbor self-dealing, or results in an improper payout from the trust, the trustee pays. Joint and several liability arises as between multiple trustees unless the innocent trustee(s) have fulfilled their duty to inform the court of irregular activities.

The penalties available to the courts, and the vigor of their enforcement when a breach is presented, explain a trait common amongst trustees (particularly professional trustees): conservatism, where the thing being conserved is the present value of the trust. While this functions in practice as an in-built and apparently unavoidable bias against present beneficiaries in favor of residuary takers,[29] —and, depending on the fee structure, might marginally increase the trustee's permissible

---

29. Do you see why I say *residuary* beneficiaries here instead of "future beneficiaries" more generally? Depending upon the structure of the trust and the disbursement provisions, some or all future beneficiaries *might* be at least nominally benefitted by this small-c conservatism, but the final takers more or less must always be. Do you see why the bias seems to be an unavoidable byproduct of the agency problems necessarily inherent to trusts? If you think this problem could be avoided, how might you achieve such a fix?

fee—it would arise even were a saint to serve as trustee, as it is driven fundamentally by the simple (and regrettable) human frailties of incomplete knowledge of either the past or the future.

An illustration here might be useful. Imagine that you are the trustee for a trust that requires you to pay out income annually to A, and then, upon A's death, pay out the remaining *res* to B. You act always in good faith and in the best interests of the beneficiaries given these instructions. One year one of the stock holdings in the *res*—which has always paid out significant dividends, which dividends you have treated as income—stops paying dividends and instead plows its earnings back into the corporation. The effect of this change is to cause a significant jump in the price of the stock, which you have always treated as principal (i.e., as part of the *res*). Imagine further, to maximize the value of the hypo, that the dividends paid by this company generally equaled about 25 percent of the income paid to A in any given year. In other words, A is going to notice, and be displeased, should you as trustee decide to treat this increase in value as *res* accretion rather than income.

What, as trustee, do you do? Well, you have two options (other than seeking conversion of the trust to unitrust form, which would be the best move).[30] Either you can count the increase in stock price as an accretion to principal, or you can treat it as the equivalent of a dividend, and take the amount of increase in the stock attributable to the nonpayment of the dividend out of the principal and pay it as income to A.

There is no way, as a matter of economics or finance, to make this decision. According to those disciplines, these two things—the paid dividend or the additional stock-value increase—are absolutely indistinguishable. So no help there. And assume that there's no settled law on the matter in your state.

So now what? You might think: Well, pay out to A, because A will notice the 25 percent hit if payment is stopped, while continued payment would be consistent with past years. So pay to A, and hope that B never notices or that he understands the logic of the decision when you explain it to him if he does notice.

But consider again the discussion about when trustees are held *individually* liable for breaches of duty, as opposed to when the *trust* makes good. Assuming you are acting in good faith—and there is nothing in this hypo to suggest otherwise—then if you follow the course of

---

30. Unitrusts will be discussed shortly.

action just considered, you will *presently* have paid out of the *res*. This means that if B later complains that you erred, and the court agrees, you are liable out of your own pocket to make up the difference, even though you were acting in good faith.

And so, I ask again, what would you do? Does your plan solve the potential liability problem? Other problems? What about next time? (The safest and wisest answer in these circumstances).

The safest and wisest answer in these circumstances is surely to plead the question into the court and get a judicially blessed instruction. This is an expensive and time-consuming process, though, and in the modern era, well-drafted trust documents will render such quandaries obsolete. Relatively recent developments, such as the unitrust have created ways (where adopted) for trustees to get out of such indeterminate messes.

Another penalty available to the courts—and one that may explicitly be sought by the beneficiaries, is trustee removal.

What follows is one of the standard means of dividing up and comprehending the duties of trustees. As mentioned above, other organizational methods are available.

a. Duty of Loyalty

The position of trustee is fraught with potential pitfalls in part because the trustee must demonstrate loyalty both to the settlor's intentions and to the beneficiaries of the settlor's generosity, and because—especially when the trustee enjoys some level of discretion in making disbursements to beneficiaries—there will almost always be some practical tension between the previously expressed desires of the settlor and the present wishes of the beneficiaries.

Consider, for example a trustee administering a spendthrift trust[31] which permits and requires disbursements to a traditionally prodigal and indolent (not to say louche) descendant of the settlor of trust. Disbursements are to be made to this descendant beneficiary upon the trustee's discretion, but the trust cabins that discretion: Disbursements may be made only "when [descendant] is, in the trustee's judgment, demonstrating real commitment to reasonable economy and productive career enhancement." Let's call the settlor Bert and the descendant Ernie.

---

31. These will be discussed in detail anon. For now, consider them to be trusts that limit what beneficiaries can do with future benefit streams.

As a theoretical matter, the trustee's duties can be stated fairly easily: The highest duty of the trustee is to do Bert's will, as expressed in Bert's trust instrument. Per that instrument, the trustee may (and in fact must) make disbursements to Ernie if Ernie is sticking to a budget, looking for value when making purchases, and buying only necessities rather than frivolities, while at the same time maintaining a job with a future or good standing in some sort of vocational training program. Should Ernie instead take up (amateur) snow boarding while investing heavily in Kentucky bourbon futures (in the sense that it will always be five p.m. in a couple of hours *somewhere*), then the trustee cannot make any disbursements to Ernie. Thus is loyalty demonstrated both to Bert's intentions and to Ernie's interests (at least as those "true" interests, for the purpose of trust disbursements, were established by Bert in the trust deed).

Actually performing these duties, though, may prove rather more difficult than stating them. After all, the trustee's best source of evidence that Ernie is living the straight-and-narrow life that Bert demanded will be . . . Ernie himself. Likewise, Ernie will be in the best position to obfuscate his failures and overemphasize his discipline and hard work if he's missing the mark—a thing that he will have every reason to do if he's not honestly achieving the goals that Bert set for him. In fact, Ernie is particularly likely to make it hard for the trustee to tell whether he's really meeting Bert's conditions if he's not meeting them. First, he will likely particularly need money if he's both spending wildly and not progressing in his career. Second, if he's the sort of person who would abjure Bert's improving strictures while still attempting to benefit from Bert's eleemosynary impulses, he's probably also the sort of person who would try to pull the wool over a trustee's eyes about it.

Too, there's a sort of "presentist" moral confusion that might arise as the trustee tries to evaluate the relative loyalties involved. After all, in most situations, Bert as settlor will have settled a trust rather than simply making disbursements to Ernie when he thinks best because Bert will have died. And so the trustee must do Bert's wishes without Bert actually being before him, guided only by the sterile instructions of a written deed. Ernie, in contrast, will still be fully before him in the flesh—perhaps literally and physically; perhaps only via written or telephone communications, but still as a living person. And, as we have noted, the further Ernie strays from Bert's expressed wishes, the more he will—in a certain sense, anyway—present a figure genuinely in need of the dosh which the trust might have provided him, had he actually lived up to Bert's expectations. This can lead to practical moral confusion, confusion likely to rise to the very extent that the trustee is less of an objective, removed—and experienced and careful—professional trustee, and more of an amateur, inexperienced, unwary family friend type of trustee. Thus does the law of trusts set unintended but (arguably) largely unavoidable traps for the unwary, generous, compassionate amateur trustee, because this potential, presentist moral confusion, however driven by either compassion or amateur status, provides no defense to the unwary trustee who, because of it, inverts the hierarchy of loyalty duties. These are, again: first to the settlor's intent as expressed in the trust instruments, then to beneficiaries, but only insofar as the acts of loyalty have been directed and cabined by those trust instruments.

i. No self-dealing

While there can in some instances arise some tension between loyalty to the settlor's intent and duty to the potential beneficiaries, that tension cannot extend to the realm of self-dealing. Regardless of any other considerations, a trustee *may not do any act or thing which would (or even could) redound to the trustee's benefit rather than to the benefit of beneficiaries as defined by the settlor's intent.* Any part of the trustee's management of the trust that could even putatively be understood to benefit the trustee will qualify as self-dealing and subject the trustee to the highest reasonable damages calculation available.

No further inquiry rule. So serious is the law of trusts about punishing any self-dealing by trustees that it imposes the "no further inquiry rule" in self-dealing cases. Under this rule, trustees found to have engaged in self-dealing of any kind are held liable for breach of fiduciary duty, without regard to whether they actually profited from the self-dealing, whether they dealt to themselves in bad faith (i.e., to make a profit at the expense of the trust) or *contra*. In other words, once self-dealing is discovered, then the court will make "no further inquiry" into the purposes or motivations behind the self-dealing; it will simply find liability. Upon the court's finding a breach of duty, trustees are liable to pay to the trust any (a) profits generated from the self-dealing; (b) any losses suffered by the trust as a result of the self-dealing, either make-good or expectational; and (c) any other reasonable accounting of loss to the trust.

Gleeson provides a powerful illustration of this rule in action. In that case, which you just read, Colbrook, a tenant farmer on the settlor's estate, was named trustee by the landlord-settlor. Being a farmer, he was naïve in the ways of trust law. Being a gentleman, he accepted the duty his landlord (and, presumably, friend) had placed upon him and did his best to do right by her. Being a sensible farmer, he recognized that—she having died just weeks before planting season was to begin again and before his lease was to expire—he had very little choice (from the trusts' perspective as well as his own; hiring out a farm to a working tenant is not an impulse-buy transaction) but to relet the land that he had worked under his landlord for the five previous years. In a gesture of nobility and a nod to fiduciary obligation, he nearly doubled his own rent on behalf of the trust for which he was acting as the (likely uncompensated) trustee.

All was for naught—and, from Colbrook's point of view, a great deal less than naught. The key to his catastrophe is contained within the last sentence of the last paragraph: *he* doubled *his own* rent on behalf of the trust. *He* (in his personal capacity) transacted with *him* (in his trustee capacity). This is self-dealing. This is forbidden. Once it has occurred, breach of his fiduciary duties as trustee has occurred. Once this breach is found, per the rule presently under consideration, there can be no more inquiry into things like motive or actual benefit or reasonableness—nothing. There is only penalty. In this case, the penalty was very steep indeed. Colbrook was obliged, having already paid the doubled rent, to disgorge all of his profit for the year. In case you have not enjoyed the opportunity to be a tenant farmer in the '50s in rural Illinois: He was almost certainly ruined by this decision, bereft of income and capital and credit facilities and hope. And yet, despite his obviously honorable behavior, the court ruled as it did.

The no self-dealing rule is a very serious thing indeed.

The trustee fee exception. However serious it may be, the no self-dealing rule has—it must have—a fairly obvious exception.

Trustees are compensated (out of trust funds) for their services, whether they are career trustees or cameo actors, unless they either explicitly agree to serve without pay or fail to draw their "salary" from the trust.[32] They must be compensated—only the very good (of independent means), the very dim, or the very devoted to a sole settlor of a manageable trust could possibly act otherwise, nothing in this life being free (including one's time), and the risks of a costly screw-up being relatively high.

---

32. All such voluntary trustees are, excluding a few instances of trust company *pro bono* service, on the amateur circuit, of course. If that realization makes you grumpy, stop a moment to consider what fraction of your caseload will be shouldered without fee or how many years you intend to work without salary.

These fees are technically a violation of the rule against self-dealing, as there's generally no one else around to cut the check to the trustee for her fees but the trustee herself. But it falls within a safe-harbor exception for the reasons considered above.

The settlor may (attempt to) establish a fee in the settlement documents himself; a potential trustee who accepts the position subject to express provision will be bound to it, unless perhaps some sort of procedural unconscionability argument were available thereafter. In the absence of such a provision (or other relevant contractual arrangement), the fee will be set by the court, often following a standard formula (e.g., 3 percent of the average balance of the *res*, *per annum*) but always designed to provide, of course, a "reasonable fee." (There is no uniformity amongst states in this regard, so the "reasonable fee" rule of thumb is a safe generalization.)

i. No Conflicts of Interest and the Baked in the Cake Exception

The duty of loyalty also forbids a trustee to serve if that trustee's personal situation is such that she cannot reasonably serve as trustee—with full fiduciary fidelity to the trust—without making decisions or undertaking transactions that might in any way be affected by personal, nontrusteeship motivated considerations. Alternatively, if our trustee-designate has agreed to serve, she may make no decision that would create a conflict of interest[33] between her personal situation (including her personal professional situation) and the interests of the trust.

These conflicts can come in many forms. Some of them are obvious and can be understood as a generalization of, or extension from, the no self-dealing rule. Assume for instance that our trustee manages a trust of significant size and broad investment. Our trustee works at GiantBank, which is a publicly traded company. Better yet, our trustee is a senior executive at GiantBank, competing for the position of CEO of the bank. Further, imagine that the trust assets are of such magnitude that investing them in GiantBank would materially matter to GiantBank's quarterly figures and to our trustee's all-important annual review.

Under these circumstances, our trustee has found herself in a nearly hopeless conflict of interest. She would benefit greatly (personally) from redirecting trust assets into GiantBank stock. Yet should

---

33. Or, in a common political trope, "create the appearance" of a conflict of interest.

she do so, she would be acting transparently in her personal interest, *whether or not that interest was also the best interest of the trust.* She would be conflicted. Therefore, she cannot, without ensuring her own breach, should suit arise, invest in GiantBank stock.

And yet, at least in high theory, our trustee's problems do not end there. What if it were the case that an investment in GiantBank, right now, was the wisest possible investment decision? This would be immensely hard to prove, of course, but so would the reverse—and very few beneficiary litigants, no matter how clever and how well counseled, would be able to argue that the GiantBank play had necessarily been the wrong play to make. But under the no further inquiry rule (which is the default rule in conflict-of-interest situations as well), they wouldn't have to. Rather, they would merely need to prove that some investment decisions—however wise—were implicated by trustee's personal interests, thus conflating, necessarily, in trustee's mind, personal interests with trust interest, thereby establishing a conflict of interest and thus a breach of fiduciary duty. To repeat: It does not matter if the conflicted move was objectively the best or even the only good move for the trustee to make, the fact of the conflict alone creates a breach of duty and damages.

All of this can create an astonishingly unstable situation. After all, very many trusts—especially large (and therefore particularly lucrative) trusts—require of their trustees a flexibility and capaciousness in nonconflicted investment breadth (as we will discuss further anon). Meanwhile, most people qualified both to take on such an investment responsibility and to have the professional knowledge necessary to avoid *Gleeson*-style disasters will be either lawyers or investment house bankers (often as trust house attorneys) and will have their own personal deployments in the markets such that conflicts might be thorny problems. Alternatively, they may be higher-ups in institutions with which the settlor had been deeply practically engaged, such that *any* decision will necessarily be conflicted.

Take again, for example, a situation in which settlor has dealt for decades with a specific banker, or bank, and therefore selects one of the principals at the bank to be his trustee. Imagine further (this is not a stretch; the reporters swarm with such cases) that, very naturally, the settlor has invested fairly substantially in the bank upon which he has placed so much reliance over so many years and has included his shares in the bank in his trust *res*. Now the trustee is in a pickle. Her responsibilities as trustee require her to invest, with prudence, the whole of the *res*. This of course includes making prudential decisions relating to further investment in, or divestment from, her employer bank. Any such decisions are objectively conflicted, especially because the no further inquiry rule forbids defenses that would, if permitted, demonstrate that the trustee had acted in a way opposed to her personal interest or without consideration to that interest.

Yet strict application of the no further inquiry rule in this narrow case doesn't seem quite sensible, does it? After all, we presume the settlor to be competent; this presumption includes the presumptions that the settlor was broadly aware of the content of his *res* and the situation of his trust-making.[34] And so we can presume that the settlor was OK with this specific, narrow conflict (that of trading the conflicted bank stock). We can go further and assert that the settlor built this specific conflict into the warp and woof of this trust, or, in the jargon of trust law, that the settlor "baked in the cake" of the trust this spice of conflict. And so the "baked in the case" exception.

Of course (and because there is no metaphor than cannot be ridden right down into the ground), it's better to include the ingredients of a cake expressly on the label, especially if the cake is to enter the stream of commerce. Or more coherently, an express assertion beats a background presumption every time. A well-drafted trust will thus explicitly acknowledge that a conflict has been baked into the cake and will expressly sanction and bless actions taken by the preferred trustee that would otherwise technically constitute conflicted dealing.

As a quick practical exercise, see if you can come up with a reasonable clause that would perform this function in a trust deed.

Next, consider these thoughts:

1. Did you find the result in *Gleeson* startlingly harsh?
2. Do you see a way to get to a better result, given what you've just read?
3. Why do you think these measures were not taken?
4. What—if anything—follows from these musings? Why?

iii. Loyalty to "All Masters"

Did your parents, when you were young, make sure that as between you and your siblings there were the same number of presents under the tree or on your respective birthdays or whensoever you may have celebrated by their giving to you stuff designed to fill the hearts and widen the eyes of the young? Did they strive to ensure that they were spending more or less the same amount on each of their progeny in each gift-giving cycle,

---

34. *See supra* Part II.B.

or perhaps according to some, perhaps vague, pre-established sense of the relative expense of the "needs" of life of children of certain ages and in certain relevant situations? If so—or if you make such calculations with members of your family—then you already understand the basic premise of loyalty to "all masters." (This duty is also called the duty of impartiality, a label that, however, is not as pedagogically illustrative as the other.)

We have already considered that a trustee's first fidelity must be to the settlor's instructions, to carry them out as far as the law permits and the *res* holds out. Within that ambit, we have seen, the trustee has the obligation of loyalty to the beneficiaries—not only to direct her efforts only on their behalf but also to avoid conflicted behavior that might raise even the specter of impropriety unless it has been approved in one of the narrow available ways.

Now we address the trustee's obligation to show *equal* loyalty and fidelity to *all* beneficiaries and classes of beneficiaries. This means, first, that the trustee may not play favorites—in fact, may employ no irrelevant (i.e., not settlor established) criteria of any kind in employing any discretion granted to the trustee by the settlement documents. Posit that A and B, children of the settlor, are the present beneficiaries of the trust. The settlement document instructs the trustee to disburse funds "to enable each of A and B to live a lifestyle comparable to that which they have heretofore enjoyed, provided that each of them maintains fulltime, legitimate gainful employment, regardless of relative remuneration; but should either fail of meaningful gainful employment, to enable such party to maintain only the basic necessities of life until such time as proper employment shall be resumed."[35] Loyalty to all masters requires that the trustee undertake to do the will of the trust without indulging in any extraneous considerations. It would violate the duty of loyalty both to the settlor and to A if the trustee held A to a higher definition of gainful employment, or provided A with smaller distributions, because the trustee had had an unrequited crush on A in high school or because A's politics are not to the trustee's liking or for any extraneous considerations of this kind.

Similarly, the trustee must demonstrate loyalty to all *classes* of beneficiaries. In the scenario we've already posited, A and B are the present beneficiaries (often—and as we shall see, not always terribly helpfully—called the "income beneficiaries"). Now let's posit further

---

35. As a drafting note: What entirely unnecessary bone of contention has been carelessly written into that wording?

that the trust is designed to provide A and B income support under the terms considered above for the lives of each of them and upon the decease of each of them, a grant of an equal percent of the principal of the *res* is to be disbursed to their descendants, if any; with equal shares also issuing to the descendants of C, a friend of settlor; and to the Commonwealth of Jefferson Youth Baseball Association.

Now the hypo includes separate *classes* of beneficiaries. Most important, the beneficiaries are distinguished as between present, or life-term, or "income" beneficiaries, and remainder or residue or "principal" beneficiaries. This addition of classes creates all sorts of potential problems for a trustee and all sorts of opportunities for good and thoughtful drafting, *vel non*, for a T&E lawyer.

The basic problem is this: Because the trustee must pay to each of the beneficiaries all of the amount, but only the amount, to which that beneficiary is entitled under the trust instruments, the trustee must make very sure not to overpay anyone, because that will necessarily leave too little to pay everyone else. We have already seen that this fact naturally (and unavoidably) biases trustees toward making smaller payments to present interest beneficiaries, thereby leaving more in the pot to pay later interest beneficiaries or to make good if the court were to decide that the present interest beneficiaries deserved more. Good drafting, though, will anticipate as many as are feasible of the issues that the trustee is likely to face in determining how much to pay whom, when, and therefore will minimize the trustee's difficulties and the possibility of expensive suits against the trust. (Remember, if the trustee impleads a question of trustee duty into the court, asking the court to decide in a nontrivial matter, then the court will do so, at no personal liability to the trustee. This means that the costs of the proceedings must be paid out of the *res* of the trust. Similarly, if the trustee makes a caution-informed judgment call and is then sued by the present beneficiaries, the trustee may defend the suit with trust assets. These drains on the *res* for the benefit of lawyers and the detriment of all beneficiaries cannot have been the settlor's will. In all cases, they are a shame, and a waste; when they arise as the result of demonstrably and culpably bad drafting, the loss will likely redound to the drafter in the form of settlement of a malpractice action.)

Good drafting requires thinking through with the client-settlor the issues that might arise in carrying out the settlor's wishes. Consider, for instance, this regularly arising issue: When settlor suggested that A and B should be maintained in the style of life to which they had become accustomed, what does that mean? While "style to which one has become accustomed" is a common term, perhaps even common enough to be considered a term of art of sorts, it is hardly very detailed. Similarly, what constitutes the provision of necessities? These issues should be fleshed out in the trust documents, as should details about what constitutes gainful employment and other terms or concepts that pop up in the trust. Meanwhile, should A's and B's other income and assets be considered when grants are made to keep them at the appropriate level of income? The Restatement of Trusts sets "no" as the default answer, but it is not at all obvious in a trust such as the one in our hypothetical that this would be the answer the settlor prefers. While considering this issue: Should just the assets and income of A and B be considered or also the assets and income of A's and B's potential spouses? What about any live-in partners?[36] Is the trust meant to keep the whole family of A and B in the relevant level of income or just the named parties? Should A or B be dropped from the accustomed level of support if they are determined to be incapable of work or if they go back to school to take another degree?

All of the foregoing questions are focused very much on the settlor's "central," personal wishes and instructions, and must be nuanced by those wishes themselves and the unique circumstances of the settlor's and the beneficiaries' lives. But there is another class of questions, of instructions, that the drafter must generally raise and guide the settlor through with care and clarity, as they are of the technical—but vastly important—sort that the settlor may not have considered at all.

This sort of issue arises most commonly with a problem that has been alluded to in the preceding pages: the "income and principal" problem. Traditionally, settlors have been wont to decree, and drafters to pen, terms that reserve the "income" of the trust, or some part of it, to one or more beneficiaries, called (see if you can spot this) income beneficiaries or—borrowing from real property law—present interest beneficiaries. The beneficiaries who are paid off when the trust is wrapped up are, then, the principal beneficiaries or remaindermen. Note that there can be more than one "tranche" of interest holders, so that the trust could grant "interest evenly divided between A and B for their lives, then to the children of A and B for life [in some

---

36. Does this latter question seem dated to you, in the era of same-sex marriage? Think again. If the assets of spouses are considered but the assets of live-in partners are not, then the trust has created a subtle but meaningful (depending on the size of the would-be spouse's assets) incentive not to marry. Does the ancestor-settlor mean to establish this incentive? These are the sorts of issues that thoughtful and successful drafters think through with their clients.

specified apportionment], then upon the death of the last of these, the principal divided between the Museum for the Preservation of Ugly Hats and the Society for the Advancement of Wayward Turtles."

The key problem that arises from such a designation is this: There really isn't any meaningful distinction between income and principal, and there is certainly no coherent rationale for investing in order to maintain a purely legal or accounting demarcation between income that is attributed to interest and income that is attributed to principal. As we have seen already, if a stock held by the trust switches from paying a dividend to increasing its principal value, then the value of the trust has not changed in any way. By normal accounting principles, though, the amount of value of the trust attributed to income has fallen, and the amount attributed to principal has risen. This creates a deep and serious dilemma for the trustee. As will become clear in the next section, the trustee's (modern) duty of prudence requires the trustee to invest well and carefully—with attention to diversity of assets and without a commitment to, or the protection of, a safe harbor list of approved types of investment. Given that the value or worth of Stock X has not changed at all because of the decision to switch from dividend to reinvestment, it is at best gratuitous busywork to require the trustee to switch out of Stock X and into some other stock or investment in order to keep the balance between income and principal balanced; at worst—if no assets are as good in the overall portfolio as Stock X—it constitutes a positive breach of prudence to sell Stock X to replace it with some inferior investment. On the other hand, the duty of loyalty, requiring equal loyalty between all parties and classes of parties, including between "income" beneficiaries and "principal" beneficiaries, requires that some equilibrium be maintained between the portion of the benefits flowing to the trust that accumulate as added principal and the portion that is paid out as present income.

Changes in stock dividend payments represent only the tip of a very big iceberg. Effectively the same problem arises if the trust holds any physical property, be it real property such as a house or personal property such as a painting. Assume that the trust owns a house, which house is rented. Rental income flows in every year, while the principal value of the house rises (or falls) along with the real estate market in the area. Minor but manageable allocation issues will arise: If the roof needs repaired, ought the costs of repair to come out of the rental income or from the principal value of the house? But now assume that it arises that the best use of the capital in the house is for the house to be sold at the end of the next lease period and for the proceeds to be invested in an asset that pays no income. Should it be done? Obviously, it will decrease what is usually denominated the "income" of the trust, while increasing the principal value; the impact of the change will be greater in proportion to the value of the house compared to the total value of the trust. Do loyalty and prudence point in opposite directions here? The results are reversed, but the situation the same, if the trust owns a painting by a great master. Assume that the settlor owned this painting for a long time but also was known to buy and sell paintings—often at significant profit—from his collection while he lived. Assume further that the trustee is well informed that the market for this particular master—or for fine art in general—is peaking. Prudence counsels him to sell and, if the general market is peaking, not to buy another great master painting. But if he sells, he has radically decreased the principal holdings of the *res* and realized a significant "income" in the year of sale. Should that income pass as windfall to the income beneficiaries? Should the trustee buy another painting, even if the market is bad? Must he buy some other principal-appreciation-only asset? What should be done about the increase in value of the painting from the time that it was bought until the time that it was sold? Is this realized income, or principal transitorily held as cash? Do these distinctions make any real sense to an investor?

The trustee will best be able to do his job coherently and successfully if he is able to invest the *res* in a manner most consistent with his duties of prudence—of seeking the highest overall return consistent with the risk level appropriate for the trust, given its settlor-established mission. He can do that only if he is able to discard considerations of the *form* of profit or appreciation (i.e., whether a given asset of the trust will throw off what has traditionally been considered income or would rather appreciate to the benefit of what is commonly called principal), and instead to invest with attention only to total net benefit.

This the trustee has in the vast majority of states been permitted to do by the adoption of the Uniform Principal and Income Act (the first of two UPIAs that will arise in this section), last amended in 2008 (though presently under further review by the Uniform Law Commission, the people who draft all of the varyingly successful uniform laws). The great genius of the present Principal and Income Act is the "unitrust." The unitrust form permits settlors to assign benefits under their trusts not in the broad forms of "income" and "principal" beneficiaries, but to specify exactly how much of the assets of the trust the settlor wishes to pass to any given beneficiary, however the settlor might care to make those distinctions. Thus, rather than settlor assigning income payments to A and B, and then to the children of A and B, and then to the charities, as described above, the settlor might, for instance, allocate "to A and B for their lives, and to their children upon their majorities for each of their lives, an equal share of 10 percent of the annualized average of the value of the assets of the trust during the year proceeding, with the principal remaining upon the death of the last of these" to pass to the charities.

While the central genius of the unitrust is (arguably, anyway) the fact that it frees trustees to make investment decisions without regard to the truly incidental and investment-irrelevant detail of the form of payments, another key benefit arises for the careful drafter: The unitrust encourages the drafter to urge the settlor to think about settlement details that might otherwise not have detained the settlor and then to help the settlor to draft a document that addresses these details as the settlor wishes. This gives additional autonomy to the settlor and additional guidance and surety to the trustee, which in turn can in many cases keep the trust out of the kind of confusions that send the trustee to court and draw down the *res* of the trust to no purpose of any benefit to settlor or beneficiaries.

Return, for instance, to the on-going hypothetical. The revision made above, granting to the one-time "income" beneficiaries equal shares of 10 percent of the whole value of the *res* every year is a reasonable—though clearer—transmogrification of the earlier distribution into unitrust terms (at least in most economic periods, as will be discussed further in just a moment). Discussing the matter in terms of percentages, however, may raise some considerations that might otherwise have been overlooked. For instance: During the years until A and B have adult children, the 10 percent draw will be split between only two beneficiaries, at 5 percent each. But if each or either of A or B prove particularly fecund, then A and B may find themselves— just as they reach their golden years and may be in greatest need of trust support—sharing their patrimony with three or five or more of their progeny and co-beneficiaries, their shares falling toward a mere one percent of the annual value of the trust. Then, later, the last holdouts amongst the grandchildren will, in their own dotage, enjoy ever-increasing shares of that 10 percent total. Is this what the settlor intends? It may be—or it may be that the settlor, having been brought to consider these issues more carefully, would prefer that the total amount granted to what were once "income" beneficiaries should swell and shrink along with the total size of the beneficiary pool. It matters little to the careful drafter what the settlor decides but enhances her skill in the field and her fidelity to her clients to consider and flesh out these details while preparing the trust documents.[37]

Inflation, and its consequences, is another problem of which the unitrust permits supple treatment. Though at the time of this writing official inflation has been quite tame for many years, it has not always been so. Since the Second World War there have been significant bouts of inflations from late 1946 to late 1948 after the World War II wage and price controls were lifted; in guns-and-butter circumstances in 1951 (Korea) and the late 1960s (Vietnam); and a massive (by American standards) and sustained period after Nixon closed the gold window that lasted through the 1970s and into the early 1980s.

When people talk about inflation, what they mean is that it requires more units of money to buy virtually everything, so that, if inflation is 10 percent in a given year, a bottle of Coke that cost $1.00 last year will cost $1.10 today, and a haircut that cost $25.00 last year will cost $27.50 today. This must be distinguished from appreciation (or depreciation), which is the change in the value of a certain asset or class of assets but not in all assets generally. Thus, for instance, if inflation in a year is zero percent, then the Coke will still cost a dollar and the haircut $25. But even in a year of no inflation, there can be appreciation of certain assets (or categories of assets)—increases in their value (and price) that is not reflected (or not reflected directly, anyway) in the broad economy.

So, for instance, consider the example of the painting mentioned above. The painting was a part of the *res* when the settlor died, he having bought it 10 years before his death. Now, 10 more years on, the trustee has it on good advice that the market for this sort of painting, or of paintings by this painter, is topping and thus that he would be well advised to sell the painting. Since the drafter of the trust was wise enough to have advised him to employ a unitrust, and he was wise enough to have agreed, the trust establishes how much of the value of the trust is to be paid out every year.

But now another question arises: What about inflation? Posit that at the end of 2019 the trust was worth $5 million. It is now the end of 2020, and the trust is worth $5.5 million. Posit further that the rate of

---

37. A half-way house to the unitrust, one designed in part to deal with trusts that have already been written in contemplation of the old income-generators/principal-generators method, is the policy of "equitable adjustment," which allows trustees to "denominate" certain revenues or increases in value as either "income" or "principal" as necessary to fulfill both the language of the trust and the settlor's intent while maximizing trust *res* value insofar as possible.

inflation during 2019 had averaged 5 percent. This means that for the *res* of the trust to have the same purchasing power at the end of 2020 as it had at the end of 2019, the nominal value of the trust must be $5.25 million ($5 million x 1.05). If there were only $5 million in the *res*, the real value of the trust would have fallen by about 4.75 percent.

Returning to our example: The trust document requires the trustee to pay out 10 percent of the assets of the trust to the beneficiaries each year. Ten percent of $5.5 million is $550,000. If this amount is paid out at the beginning of 2020, then the real value of the trust, on the day after disbursements, will be about 5 percent smaller than it was on the first day of 2019. Is this what the settlor intended? Now let's posit that in 2020 there is a spike in inflation such that the average inflation over the year is 12 percent. The total return on the investment for the year is a little more than 20 percent so that the total value of the trust is now $6 million. The payment to the beneficiaries this year, then, will be $600,000, but because of the spike in inflation, the $600,000 will be worth appreciably *less* than the $550,000 that had been paid out the year before, even though the trust had earned an eight percent real return (20 percent nominal return less 12 percent inflation) instead of the 5 percent real return (10 percent nominal return less 5 percent inflation) it had earned the previous year. Is this what the settlor intended? Meanwhile, if a high inflation keeps up for many years, then the value—the purchasing power—of the 10 percent annual payment to the beneficiaries will continue to fall, steadily and appreciably, while the value of the *res* (and the purchasing power that will pass eventually to the charities) will rise accordingly. Conversely, if there are years of very low inflation, then the real value of the payouts will increase year by year (at least in the short term), while the real value of the *res* will fall year by year, so that eventually the real value of the payouts will also begin to fall (because they will be 10 percent of a smaller real value), and the real value of the *res* may well effectively exhaust long before the charities see any of it at all.

Is any of this what the settlor intends? Probably not. It is the rare settlor who sets out to fashion a trust to take care of his family or friends or charities into the distant future but who then is willing to leave his plans to chance and to the vagaries of central banks. Rather, most settlors very likely wish to design their trusts to be as inflation (and recession, for that matter) proof as possible. Thus, the wise practitioner will guide her client toward unitrust arrangements that not only eliminate the old concern about income versus principal labels, but will set a disbursement level that is not a fixed, constant percentage (e.g., the previous 10 percent example) but instead varies to take account of inflation rates; the level of actual real return achieved in any given year; the settlor's interest *vel non* in "smoothing" the possibly spikey results of a pure formula over several years, to create a more predictable support level for beneficiaries, and other concerns.

These steps will help to ensure that the trust is technically easy to manage, which will minimize trust expenses and maximize benefits to beneficiaries, while allowing for the settlor's true goals to be most fully understood, captured, and executed.

b. Duty of Prudence

The second fundamental category of trustee fiduciary duty is the duty of prudence. The most important of the prudence duties is the duty of prudent investment, discussed first below. An ancillary prudence duty is that of knowing how to contact the beneficiaries and how they're getting on (if relevant) and where the *res* assets are and ensuring their safety and the protection of their value.

i. Prudent Investment

A trustee must invest prudently. This means that the trustee must invest in ways that are recognized by the law to be reasonably safe and reasonably likely to bring in a return that will maintain and enhance the value of the *res*. Under current law, that means following the prudent investor rule as established in the Uniform Prudent Investor Act (the second UPIA of this section. It's not an accident that these are both UPIAs, as they deal in interrelated ways with the same subject matter). This second UPIA will be discussed shortly. First, though, a short digression into the history of the standards of prudent investment, which will help to illustrate the current rules and the specific fixations of those rules.

Cast your mind back to the beginning of the eighteenth century. Columbus had long-since sailed, the Spanish Empire had risen and declined, the Age of Pirates had passed, and the British were well on their way to building their First Empire. Building an empire—while not so subtly nudging another empire off stage and holding yet another at bay—is expensive and bloody work, and so England found itself in a fairly continuous string of wars throughout this era with Spain, France, and Holland.

After one of these wars, the War of the Spanish Succession, the British employed what today seems a novel way of paying off its war debts: It sold them to a private company, the South Sea Company, in exchange for granting that company a permanent annuity and the exclusive right to trade with Spain's colonies in the Americas (so, much of Central and South America, excluding Brazil, as well as parts of what is now the southern United States) and in the West Indies. British investors thought that the company had made a pretty good deal and so bought shares in the company, which gave the company capital to buy ships in order to conduct the trade and to pay down the war debt it had assumed.

This was one of the first stock (or, in British English, share) exchanges on a national scale in world history, and it led—as hindsight has taught us all too well to expect—to a speculative bubble. In this bubble, as in all bubbles, investors started to think that "this time was different" than all times prior in history and that something—the opening of the colonial trade, the financial innovation of the joint-stock company, the government's clever method of privatizing the war debts, something—meant that the old rules of prudence and the old expectation of slow and steady returns had fallen away and that fantastic gains (the invariable "striking it rich") lay just around the corner.[38] So, in an astonishingly short time, vast amounts of capital had been invested in these South Sea Company shares, and the price of those shares skyrocketed concomitantly. Some folks who bought early and sold relatively early did in fact make fortunes, as is true in all speculative bubbles. But those who bought late and held long were—or their finances were, anyway—massacred. Practical barriers to the Company's being able to meet the bubbly expectations were legion. First, under the treaty with Spain that had ended the war, *all* English merchants were only allowed to send one trade ship to Spanish America each year, so profit potential was limited. Second, the directors of the company were not traders by vocation and did a fairly bad job of it. Third, by the time the bubble peaked, taking the price of the stock from £100 to £1,050 per share in a few months, the putative wealth involved in the company—based as it was, initially, on a significant portion of the national debt and then exploded to more than 10 times its initial value—involved a hefty fraction of the total wealth of the Kingdom, such that *no* conceivable venture in that age could possibly have justified it.

---

38. A little friendly advice that adds nothing to the cost of this textbook: "this time" is *never* different. If you're still in a market that has gotten so oversold that the touters have been reduced to assuring investors that "this time it's different," then for the love of all good things, sell quickly. The results won't be pretty for those who don't.

But that's not all. Before the South Sea Bubble had popped, the fabulous paper wealth being accrued had drawn all sorts of other opportunistic joint-stock companies into existence and sent their stocks soaring—including a company founded for a special purpose that was to officially remain secret. Didn't matter; the frenzy was on, and speculators leapt in, bidding up the prices of these increasingly absurd ventures. The government stepped in, requiring that joint-stock companies get a royal charter before setting up business,[39] but the legislation merely fixed the government's imprimatur on the financial shenanigans and actually fed, rather than calmed, the bubble.

Eventually, of course, it all burst, and when it did, preposterous amounts of paper wealth disappeared. But that, of course, wasn't all either; if play money had just been piled up by some people, and then lost by those people, very little would really have changed. The problem—as noted above—is that there must be some final holders, sometimes these days called the "dumb money," that went in late and lost their shirts. These folks tended to be the less well connected and the less financially savvy. Included in the group that lost everything were lots of funds that we would today organize as trusts, some of which were organized that way at the time. So lots of people who were in effect being looked after as beneficiaries of trust funds found themselves bereft.

The results of this debacle were legion. The South Sea spectacular did not unfold in isolation; it was accompanied by bubbles in Holland (the Tulip Mania) and in France (the Mississippi Company crash), which hobbled French finance for the rest of the century and led—indirectly but distinctly—to the bankruptcy of the monarchy and thus to the French Revolution. (There were other contributing causes, fore and aft, of course.) They all popped more or less together. English parties who had contributed to the escalation of the bubble by insider dealing or by falsely fanning the flames of financial foolery found themselves drained of their ill-gotten gains in order to try to make right some of the losers. Parliament established some perpetual debt obligations that it has only gotten around to begin repaying in 2015. And, most importantly for our purposes, parliament drew up laws that forbad trustees and other fiduciary investors from participating in "speculation" in shares and limited them to investing in only a set list of supposedly safe assets. Ironically, as those of you who remember the 2008 market crash will appreciate, one of the investments that these

---

39. *See South Sea Bubble Act* 1720.

lists judged to be safe was real estate. In fact, in (particularly) British usage, the phrase "safe as houses" was so recognized an analogy that it could have been played during the Analogy Game at the end of *A Christmas Carol*.

The colonies and later the states of the American Republic copied these "investment list" statutes, which remained in place well into the twentieth century. The lists pretty much permitted investment in mortgages and government bonds and in some cases perhaps in utility stocks and in Savings and Loan organizations. Shareholding was forbidden.

The flaws of this safe-harbor list method became increasingly clear as a few bouts of inflation wiped out trusts invested in fixed-rate, low-interest government bonds and as understanding of markets and of investment theory improved. A first round of attempts to revise the system to permit broader investment occurred after the Second World War, as states passed what were called Prudent Man statutes. These statutes attempted to allow trustees to invest, given the trust's unique situation, in whatever manner a "prudent man" in the same situation might invest. In other words, it attempted to shift the measure of duty (and of breach) from a safe-harbor list (i.e., follow the list and no breach can obtain) to a generalized rule that permits broad discretion to the trustee upfront but that will be subject to later review to determine if prudence had been used (but not, per the hindsight discussion *infra*, that perfection be achieved).

These Prudent Man standards were a noble attempt, but they ultimately failed because judges were so used to applying safe-harbor list statutes that they eventually, through misunderstanding and then later misapplication of precedent, ended up reviving by fiat the list statutes that had been replaced, because later judges read earlier cases not as a review of the specific facts at hand in that case, but as a blessing or rejecting of the entire class of investments under review there.

So the legislators had to try again. This second round of revisionary statutes took place in the 1990s, when the legislators—and the Uniform Laws Commission—had recognized that ladies, too, could serve as trustees, and so were called some state-specific iteration of the Uniform Prudent Investor Act.[40] The UPIA finally achieved what the Prudent Man Acts had failed to manage: it shifted the rules for investment

---

40. Unif. Prudent Investor Act (Unif. L. Comm'n 1995). To wit:

SECTION 2. (a) A trustee shall invest and manage trust assets as a prudent investor would, by considering the purposes, terms, distribution requirements,

from a list to a standard. In the shadow of the UPIA, enacted virtually everywhere in some form, a trustee's key duty of prudent investment is to achieve a sufficient level of portfolio safety *not* by finding magically safe and remunerative assets to invest in. (Magical, because if some such investments existed, everyone would invest in them, which would increase the price of those investments for any given amount of yield, which would decrease the return per dollar, which would eliminate the attractiveness of the investment. Hence, magical—because impossible.) Instead, the trustee should fulfill the duty by *diversifying* the trust's assets to minimize the possibility that a shock in any given market could crush the value of the portfolio.

There is nothing that can completely eliminate risk in investment, because, among other things: (1) investments must always happen on

---

and other circumstances of the trust. In satisfying this standard, the trustee shall exercise reasonable care, skill, and caution.

(b) A trustee's investment and management decisions respecting individual assets must be evaluated not in isolation but in the context of the trust portfolio as a whole and as a part of an overall investment strategy having risk and return objectives reasonably suited to the trust.

(c) Among circumstances that a trustee shall consider in investing and managing trust assets are such of the following as are relevant to the trust or its beneficiaries:

(1) general economic conditions;

(2) the possible effect of inflation or deflation;

(3) the expected tax consequences of investment decisions or strategies;

(4) the role that each investment or course of action plays within the overall trust portfolio, which may include financial assets, interests in closely held enterprises, tangible and intangible personal property, and real property;

(5) the expected total return from income and the appreciation of capital;

(6) other resources of the beneficiaries;

(7) needs for liquidity, regularity of income, and preservation or appreciation of capital; and

(8) an asset's special relationship or special value, if any, to the purposes of the trust or to one or more of the beneficiaries.

(d) A trustee shall make a reasonable effort to verify facts relevant to the investment and management of trust assets.

(e) A trustee may invest in any kind of property or type of investment consistent with the standards of this [Act].

(f) A trustee who has special skills or expertise, or is named trustee in reliance upon the trustee's representation that the trustee has special skills or expertise, has a duty to use those special skills or expertise.

SECTION 3. A trustee shall diversify the investments of the trust unless the trustee reasonably determines that, because of special circumstances, the purposes of the trust are better served without diversifying.

earth, and some events, such as world wars or ice ages or solar electromagnetic pulses or giant meteor strikes have worldwide effects; and (2) in any world in which the prudence and discretion of a human trustee matters, all investments are going to involve layers and layers of human involvement,[41] and people are both fallible and unpredictable. But *some* investment risks can be minimized by holding properly diversified assets. (Of course, this risk minimization comes at the expense of reducing the possibility of gigantic spikes in *res* value, as if the trust had held exclusively Apple stock when the first iPod was introduced. But that sort of gambling, if not illegal because based on some kind of inside knowledge, is the very definition of imprudence.)

There are four levels of diversity that can be achieved.

- Firm diversification: The first level of diversification is achieved by owning the assets of more than one company in a class. So, for instance, it would be, in normal circumstances, imprudent to own only Ford stock, when diversification into other auto-company stocks is possible and easy, or to own only Citibank when diversification into other banking properties is possible. The reasoning here is that shocks can affect a single company that have no effect on the industry as a whole. One company's management can be particularly bad or crooked or unlucky. Firm diversification mitigates this problem.

- Industry diversification: Risk to the portfolio can also be reduced by holding assets in different industries. A portfolio that has various auto assets should have, for instance, various bank assets as well. The reasoning here is that one industry can tank because of increased regulation or changing consumer tastes or more expensive inputs, but that tanking will have a smaller or no effect on the economy as a whole. One thing to consider in achieving diversity of industry is the concept of complementary goods. In creating diversity, pick industries for which success is not deeply interrelated. Autos and banks are more diversified holdings than autos and tires, for instance.

- Geographical diversification: A third method of risk management is to own shares in companies based in different areas and countries. Different countries "get hot" or fall into recession at different times, depending on the quality of their governments, the interests and dedication to work of their populations and other factors.

---

41. It does not answer this objection to point out that much trading these days is done by computers. The computers still have to be programmed by people to undertake some sort of human reasoned logic.

Owning both American and Japanese auto shares, for instance, will increase diversification as well.

- Form of Asset diversification: A final lever, one aimed more at "pegging" the level of risk than at mitigating risk overall, comes in the form of the type of assets that the trust holds. Holding government bonds or other securities traditionally decreases the range of potential return but also decreases the risk to the portfolio. Likewise (and relatedly), holding more liquid assets, like bonds or stocks, traditionally decreases risk and potential gain, while holding less-liquid assets (like real estate, or close ownership of a business) tends to increase both potential reward and portfolio risk. In determining the risk/potential "ratio," as it were, a trustee is obliged to consider the needs of the trust as established in the trust instruments by the settlor. Does fidelity to the settlor's intent require a guaranteed, steady stream of income? Is it likely that big payouts may have to be made out in a relatively short time frame, with little notice? Are there assets enough and time enough to permit some investment in riskier or more illiquid assets? These are the sorts of questions that a prudent trustee will answer in picking stocks.

Note a necessary corollary to the UPIA's theory of prudent investing. Prudence must be judged from the vantage point of *the portfolio as a whole*. It doesn't matter whether one particular asset, if viewed alone, is relatively risky. In fact, in portfolio theory it doesn't really make a whole lot of sense to talk about the riskiness of a single asset. Rather, the question is whether the whole basket of assets owned by the trust presents a total weighted average that is protected from as many of the vagaries of luck and preventable exposure as is *reasonably*, without the benefits of hindsight, possible.

There is one big exception to this system of prudent *res* management. It is, in effect, another "baked in the cake" exception. Consider two scenarios.

Scenario One. Settlor establishes a trust, makes herself trustee of the trust until she dies, then passes management of the trust to Trust Company. At the time that Trust Company takes over management, the *res* of the trust is invested in five assets:

(1) Ownership of a family house and household goods and personal effects worth about $1 million;
(2) Stock in Apple worth $3 million;
(3) Her (deceased) mother's condo in Florida, worth $500,000;
(4) A half-share in her brother's appliance store in the town they both lived in, worth $2.5 million; and
(5) Stock in a Montana mining interest worth $1 million.

In her trust, settlor granted as gifts outright some of her personal property, while specifying that the trust would own the house and the remainder of the household goods as a residence open to the whole of the family for the remainder of the lives of her children and grandchildren, unless a vote by two-thirds of the adult members of that group were in favor of selling it. With regard to the rest of the trust *res* the settlor included instructions about how various benefits were to be paid to various beneficiaries, but no instructions were given about how to hold any portion of property.

Were the trustee to consider *only* the interests of portfolio maximization, then he would obviously sell the family house, as ownership of the house is the investment of a significant portion of the family's wealth in one single asset, while much of the remainder of the wealth (the $2.5 million in the appliance store) is also invested in the same locale. But the settlor here obviously has a distinct, asset regarding interest, and has established a way in which that asset can be divested of—but one that leaves no discretion in the hands of the trustee at all. In this instance, the express and thoughtful wishes of the settlor outweigh the obligations of asset diversification; the trustee not only needn't sell the house on his own initiative but cannot.

Now, were you the drafter of this trust, you would have wished in your masterful competency to raise with the settlor the question of what should happen if the value of the house started to slide precipitously, perhaps because the neighborhood or the area started to go south or for some other reason. It might be that a settlor who had fully thought through the possibility of asset decline might have preferred to include an "objective trigger," one that, say, allowed the trustee to sell the house upon the vote of only a bare majority of qualifying descendants if asset values were on a declining trend or some other fail safe. On the other hand, the settlor's purpose might have been so family—rather than asset—oriented, that she should have rejected this option. Were she to have considered and rejected it, it might be worthwhile for the drafter to communicate that consideration process in writing to the trustee, or along with the trust documents at any rate, so that the trustee can rest especially assured—and demonstrate to any later court—the fixity of the settlor's intentions.

So the trustee has a significant, fixed, immutable asset to take into account when diversifying the portfolio. But, with that fixed instruction in mind, the trustee still is obliged to diversify as much as possible. It will not do, for instance, for the trustee to leave the investments in Apple and the mining interest as they are; this represents only a bare minimum of diversification. There is interindustry diversification, but only in two assets; more diversification is necessary.[42] There is no inter-firm diversification. Settlor's other assets are also far under-diversified. She has too many assets in her home town, too much in real estate, and too much in too illiquid a form.

The trustee should act as swiftly as is reasonable, given market conditions, to correct these deficiencies. Since the asset he cannot sell is real estate in the settlor's home town, he should sell the other real-estate asset (the settlor's mother's condo) and the other home-town asset (the half-interest in her brother's store). Yes, these are family related assets, but the settlor has expressed no particular regard for them, and so they are assets that the trustee must sell to achieve prudent diversification. With the proceeds of all of these sales, the trustee should purchase a broad set of assets diversified on the axes indicated above.

Note that if the trustee fails of his duty, it will avail him nothing to argue to the court that he merely held onto the assets that had constituted the *res* when he took over. Trustees—whether sophisticated or not—are obliged to act with investment prudence, regardless of whether the settlor showed such sophistication or prudence.[43]

Scenario Two. Settlor establishes a trust, makes himself trustee of the trust until he dies, then passes management of the trust to Trust Company. At the time that Trust Company takes over management, the *res* of the trust is invested in five assets:

(1) Ownership of a family house and household goods and personal effects worth about $1 million;
(2) Ownership of his hardware store downtown, worth $3 million;
(3) His father's hunting lodge upstate, worth $500,000;
(4) A half-share in his appliance store in the town he and his sister lived in, worth $2.5 million; and
(5) Stock in a Montana mining interest worth $1 million.

---

42. The diversification obligation may seem daunting, but much of it can be achieved by buying shares in index funds that are themselves already diversified in various ways.

43. It is well established at modern law (though not universally adopted, *see*, *e.g.*, Ill. Comp. Stat. 5/16.3) that a trustee who is not sophisticated in investment matters may hire a sophisticated investor to undertake these sorts of prudent investment efforts. If the trustee does "hire out" the job, then the trustee is still responsible to make a prudent decision in picking the investment advisor and in monitoring the investments (as, perhaps, by having an independent auditor review them once in a while), but liability for actually investing prudently descends to the investment professional.

Obviously, the conditions here are largely the same as before. Let's make them more similar, in that the settlor here gave away many of his household and personal goods outright in the trust documents. Here's the difference: Instead of leaving his house to the descendants, as his sister did, he left his hardware store "to his children and his grandchildren, to run as long as any of them live, and then the business to be sold to any great-grandchildren willing to buy it at market value and the assets distributed to the family; or if none, to be sold publicly and the assets to be granted by charitable gift to the Home for Aged Entrepreneurs. Either that hardware store stays in the family, or the family doesn't get its value."

Much of the analysis here will be the same as it was in the first scenario. This *res* has *far* too many assets located in the home town; the house and the interest in the appliance store, having gone unmentioned, must be sold.[44] The mining interests must be sold (at least in significant part) and replaced with diversified assets as well.

What about the store? The settlor was about the store as clear as his sister had been about her home. Should the trustee behave any differently? Some states' courts say no, reasoning that the settlor's autonomy regarding the store is, during his life, the same as regarding his house, and he is privileged, should he wish, to do with it as he will, or set any conditions he might. Other states' courts have reached the contrary conclusion and determined that when a settlor leaves non-sale conditions on noncommercial property, the trustee must respect them, but where the assets are commercial, the trustee must treat them as though the prudent investor rules were mandatory rather than default. In all circumstances, the trustee must make very sure that the instructions not to sell a commercial asset are *mandatory* rather than *permissive* (i.e., the trustee "must not sell," or "must hold" as opposed to "the trustee may maintain"), as the latter, leaving discretion in the trustee, will do nothing more than offer the trustee a temporary safe

---

44. This may seem harsh, or at least odd, regarding the house, but because the settlor has given no instructions about the house, the trustee cannot exempt it from the default diversification rules, which require that such a fixed asset in the same locale as other fixed assets that the settlor insists on retaining be sold and reinvested. There is no reason at all that the trustee couldn't undertake to sell the house privately to any set of descendants who might be interested in buying it, but in the interest of loyalty to all descendants, the trustee would have to have an independent valuation of the property and sell it, even in this private sale, at full market price.

harbor derived from the conditions under which the trustee may hold onto those assets despite portfolio imbalance, and for what purpose.[45]

ii. *Prudent Distribution to Beneficiaries (Prudent Monitoring and Care)*

The duty of prudent monitoring and care applies both to the beneficiaries and to the *res*. The duty of monitoring beneficiaries has already been discussed in some measure. It includes the duty to make reasonable efforts to keep track of the beneficiaries, as "lost" beneficiaries can hardly be paid their benefits. The reasonability stipulation is one of common sense; the trustee may of course expend the trust's funds to keep track of the beneficiaries, and so the trustee neither must nor may bankrupt the *res* tracking down beneficiaries who either refuse to make reasonable efforts to be findable or who cannot with proper attention to cost be found. This is one of those judgment calls that every trustee must necessarily make. It will not do for a trustee to place all the burden of contact on the beneficiaries, especially if the beneficiaries are young or incapacitated in any way or if finding them after a lapse would prove relatively painless and inexpensive. On the other hand, the trustee would ill serve the other beneficiaries (if there are others) if the burden of the trust assets were to be burnt up in locating some long-lost or distant grantees, unless such purpose were explicitly designated by the settlor as one of the primary purposes of the trust. In general, common sense and diligence will serve the trustee to avoid breach of this duty.

The second beneficiary-regarding duty of monitoring and care has been raised explicitly before: It is the duty to know, broadly, the financial and personal situation of any beneficiary if the trustee has discretion as to when and how much to disburse to that grantee, so that the trustee can informedly fulfill that duty. Thus, if a trustee has been granted discretion to pay benefits "in order to maintain [beneficiary] in [a certain level of comfort]," then the trustee must make reasonable efforts to discover how the beneficiary lives, so as to fulfill the discretion within the established constraints.

---

45. An example of this might be "The trustee may, without regard to the Prudent Investor Act, maintain shares of the First Central Bank, in which settlor served as a director, so as to permit managed sale that does not reduce the FCB stock price." This is discretion, but *bounded* discretion, and so creates as many responsibilities as it mitigates.

The duty to monitor also applies to the assets of the *res*. These include the duty to "collect and protect" trust assets.[46] The trustee must know the condition of the assets at the time the trust comes into force,[47] must take control of those assets, must insure them against loss, must maintain their value (as by ensuring proper climate control for paintings or cigars or wine, keeping physical property wind- and water-tight and free of pest or squatters, and so forth), and must generally behave as a careful and conserving owner would behave toward those assets.

c. Hybrid Ancillary Duties

These final duties are called "hybrid" because they partake somewhat of a duty of loyalty and somewhat of a duty of prudence; they are called "ancillary" because they could each be derived entirely from the prudence and loyalty rules that you have already learned. For convenience, some of these hybrid ancillary duties are spelled out below, but note the vital point: These are merely commonly arising corollaries of rules that you have already learned. This does not constitute a complete list of "left-over" fiduciary rules. The law is best learned as a web, not as a set of lists.

i. Duty to earmark trust property

Trust property must be earmarked as such to make sure that it is not commingled with nontrust property. The duty to earmark also underscores the duty to search out and locate all trust property at the beginning of the trusteeship and to keep track of it for the length of that trusteeship. UTC §810 provides as follows:

(a) A trustee shall keep adequate records of the administration of the trust.

(b) A trustee shall keep trust property separate from the trustee's own property.

(c) Except as otherwise provided in subsection (d), a trustee shall cause the trust property to be designated so that the interest of the trust, to the extent feasible, appears in records maintained by a party other than a trustee or beneficiary.

---

46. *See e.g.*, UTC §809 (2000) says: "A trustee shall take reasonable steps to take control of and protect the trust property.")

47. Restatement (Third) of Trusts §76, cmt. d (2007) says: "The trustee's duty to administer the trust includes a duty, at the outset of administration, to take reasonable steps to ascertain the assets of the trust estate and to take and keep control of those assets."

(d) If the trustee maintains records clearly indicating the respective interests, a trustee may invest as a whole the property of two or more separate trusts.

ii. Duty Not to Commingle

The question of commingling is a matter of pockets. Imagine a trustee. He keeps his wallet—his own money, as well as the means by which he accesses his assets—in his back right pocket (or, if you're of a slightly nostalgic bent today, in the right inner breast pocket of his suit jacket). This means he has three other pockets (assuming standard business-suit pants) in which to corral the assets of settlor, passed to him as trustee for his maintenance and protection. It matters little which pocket he picks; rather, the key is that he under no circumstances put any of this trust money in his back right pocket—the "personal assets" pocket. Should he do so—even occasionally, even a little bit—he opens himself to a world of hurt.

The Restatement (Third) of Trusts §84 says: "The trustee has a duty to see that trust property is designated or identifiable as property of the trust, and also a duty to keep the trust property separate from the trustee's own property and, so far as practical, separate from other property not subject to the trust."

iii. Duty to Inform Beneficiaries

This duty is straightforward. Trustees must inform beneficiaries of their interests in a trust, even if those interests are contingent or con-testable. The trustee needs to make significant efforts to get and stay in touch with present and contingent beneficiaries, balancing the duty to keep track of beneficiaries against the obligation to use the trust funds wisely and to maximize the purposes of the settlor. (When in doubt here, as when in real doubt in any situation, the trustee is best served by pleading hard questions to the court.)

One somewhat "interesting" issue arises on this front. Trusts, unlike wills, are not public documents; settlors may stipulate regarding secrecy, and the trustee is—absent express instruction—obliged to attempt to do the settlor's putative desire regarding discretion. On the other hand, beneficiaries *must* know (in order for them to be beneficiaries and for the trust to be a trust) enough to be able to identify what sort of emoluments ought to be flowing to them from the trust and under what terms, so that they might have knowledge sufficient to bring action against a trustee in miscompliance. It does *not* follow, however, that the trustee must reveal the whole of the trust's provisions to each beneficiary.

Of course, nothing in the law can be entirely straightforward. There is a hitch here, too: the quiet (or silent) trust. Some states, following the traditional rule, do not permit such quiet trusts at all, and the UTC frowns on them.[48] Where they are permitted, the rules are not entirely uniform. Broadly, however, quiet trust rules permit settlors to establish trusts that forbid the trustee to reveal the provisions of the trust to the beneficiaries.

The usual argument in favor of such trusts is that an ancestor settlor may not care to have descendant beneficiaries know the extent of the settlor's assets. This is particularly true when the beneficiaries (or some of them) are thought to be dissolute in one of the various ways that might spur the settlor to set up a trust in the first place. Yet the problem with quiet trusts should be plain: If the beneficiaries are not informed at least of the provisions of the trust that apply to them, then they cannot possibly patrol the trustee's fiduciary duties. A few of the states that permit quiet trusts just ignore this problem, while others require the appointment of some third-party, playing a role that is often these days called a "trust protector," who is apprised of the whole content of the trust and who stands *in loco legatarius*, as it were.

3. Resulting Liability for Breach

It would be hard to stress any more than has already been done just how high are the fiduciary duties of trustees, how seriously they are taken by the courts, and how significant are the penalties for misbehavior. As a rule of thumb when trying to determine what penalty will flow from a breach: Unless the breach is technical, unintentional, and disinterested, the courts will use the damages calculation that will result in the highest possible plausible recovery from the wayward trustee for the trust *res* and the ultimate benefit of the beneficiaries.[49]

---

48. UTC §813 includes a duty to inform beneficiaries and report developments to them that would obviate the quiet trust under the code. It then covers its bases, though, by including only as optional elections, at UTC §105(b)(8)-(9), provisions that make the §813 obligations unwaivable by settlors. This latter is a recognition that some states are quite enamored of their quiet trust provisions and unwilling to forego them.

49. "Plausible" here because the damages must bear *some* coherent relationship to the breaching behavior itself. However motivated to punish a bad actor trustee, the court is not simply going to fine the trustee *ex nihilo*. Of course, a trustee whose breach reaches to levels of theft may also face criminal liability.

a. "Technical, Unintentional, and Disinterested" Breach

Examples of "technical, unintentional, and disinterested" breach have appeared above, and give rise to the small-c conservative instincts of trustees. Recall the situation in which a trustee must decide whether to pay the present beneficiaries more now or keep more in the trust for the benefit of future beneficiaries. The trustee will have a natural, self-protecting instinct, when in doubt, to pay less to the present beneficiaries, for reasons already considered. In sum, these are that if the money is still in the trust, and the error is one of this "minor" kind, the trustee's "damages" for breach will come out of the trust, rather than out of the trustee's pockets, even though the determination of the court will technically be to find a breach of the trustee's fiduciary duty.

Here's an example. Trustee Tom manages a trust on behalf of present beneficiary Alex and future beneficiary Brenda. The trust instrument instructs Tom to ensure that Alex lives "in the style in which he was reared," which was a situation of upper middle class comfort but not great wealth, with the *res* of the estate passing at Alex's death to Brenda.

The trust became effective in 1980. Between 1980 and 2000 the standard of living of the average person in the upper middle class had risen significantly. Tom had recognized this "status appreciation" and increased Alex's disbursements by what he considered an appropriate amount. In 2000, though, Alex had come to Tom to ask for a further increase, suggesting that scions of the upper middle class could now afford nice retirement homes in Florida as well as their family homes in snow country, while he had thus far satisfied himself with a rural hunting cabin as his vacation home. Tom looked diligently into the question, but in the end decided -- perhaps nudged by the small-c effect—that his fiduciary duty did not permit him to disburse enough money to permit a down-payment and regular mortgage payments on a southern snow-bird perch of the sort that Alex desired, especially since Alex had proven unwilling to sell his upstate hunting property to provide some of the assets for the vacation home.

Despite his refusal, Tom recognized amiably that he might be wrong in his decision and invited Alex to address the question to a court, a thing that Alex would achieve by suing Tom in his capacity as trustee, claiming that Tom had breached his fiduciary duty in underpaying Alex now, in implicit favoritism of Brenda later. Tom would then defend his decision.

If Tom is found not to have breached his duty, then Alex does not get the extra disbursement, and Tom proceeds per his previous determination. If Tom is found to have breached his duty, then Alex *does* get the extra disbursement *out of the res of the trust* while Tom faces no penalty that reduces his assets as an individual, and all go their merry way.

Now keep the hypo, but reverse Tom's behavior. That is to say, imagine that when Alex came to Tom to request the extra funding, Tom researched the issue, considered the request, and with all careful solemnity granted it. Then Alex bought the house, and maybe took a Caribbean vacation and enjoyed some other incidents of comfortable living as well.

All proceeds nicely until Alex slips off his vacation-house diving board during an Active Ageds party and passes away. Tom, no more "present" beneficiary being present, makes to pay out Brenda. Shortly after he makes his final disbursement from the trust, however, and is preparing his accounts for a final review, and blessing, by the courts (which review and blessing will absolve Tom from any future liability for his service as trustee), Brenda appears in his offices, complaining that her check had been too light, and declaring her intention to sue Tom in his capacity as trustee, claiming—just as Alex did in the previous iteration—that Tom had violated his fiduciary duty by overpaying Alex during his life, leaving too little for Brenda and therefore violating his duty of loyalty to Brenda.

Note what happens now. Everything in these two versions of this hypothetical is the same, except that in a "leaner" situation, Tom had decided to favor the present beneficiary. Yet the outcome is not at all the same for Tom. In this second iteration, if the decision in the court goes against Tom, he cannot simply reach into the *res* of the trust to satisfy the judgment and correct his technical, good-faith error. The *res* has all been disbursed. Tom has no choice but to satisfy the judgment *out of his own pockets*, taking a loss because of his entirely diligent and good faith efforts on behalf of the trust. The impetus behind the almost implacable tendency to favor later disbursements over earlier ones should now be very clear indeed.

b. Gross, Willful, or Interested Breaches

It should also be clear that if even some perfectly "innocent" breaches result in damages flowing from the trustee's personal funds to the trust account, then willful and interested breaches are going to be treated with aggressive severity.

Recall the *Gleeson* case. There the court determined that Colbrook, the trustee/tenant-farmer had acted in his own self-interest, even though everything in the record absolutely testified to his good faith and that every action was design to do his duty to the settlor/landlord/decedent/friend and to the beneficiaries of the trust. Because his actions were self-interested, though, no inquiry into his motives or the objective effects of his actions were permitted. (This "no further inquiry" rule is itself one of the measures of the severity of damages applied in trustee fiduciary duty cases.) Instead, Colbrook was obliged to relinquish all of the profits he had made because of his "self-dealing," (i.e., the dealings between "himself as trustee" and "himself as tenant of the trust.") As was considered above, that may have been the end of poor Colbrook, who had done nothing more than to try his best to do right by his former landlord and friend in every way he could think of. The courts do not care.

In fact, the general rule in the case of conflicted (i.e., interested) behavior is that the trustee must disgorge to the trust or to the beneficiaries from his own assets any appreciation of the self-dealt assets that has occurred from the time of the breach (i.e., the time of self-dealing) until the time of trial of the question of breach. The *Gleeson* case provides an example of that —the profits from the year's planting providing the measure of the appreciation in value of the self-dealt asset (i.e., the lease of the farmland for the relevant year).

This measure assumes that there has been an appreciation in assets. If there has been a *depreciation* in the asset, then the trustee must pay the trust the full market value of the self-dealt goods at the time of the self-dealing (unless the self-dealing, as in the *Gleeson* case, resulted in there having already been a full market payment for the asset). In other words, if a trustee undertakes an interested transaction with the trust and gets caught, the trustee is—without any further inquiry—on the hook to pay the trust any appreciation of the asset that may occur after the self-dealing but must personally absorb any losses that accrue after the self-dealing, while making the trust whole from the moment of self-dealing. The idea here is to make sure that under no circumstances can any trustee caught in any self-dealing (that has not been properly sanctioned, as by having been "baked in the cake," as discussed above) ever profit from that self-dealing; instead, he will almost always lose from the transaction, while insulating the trust from any possible losses. If the trustee will always lose from self-dealing, he will never try (unless he doesn't think he's going to get caught, or, like Colbrook, just doesn't know the rules).

The standard of recovery is slightly different for negligent or willful trustee breach that is nevertheless not self-interested. In these latter circumstances, the standard measure of damages that the trustee must return from her own assets to the trust is the true value of the assets at the time of the negligent or willful action plus interest on the damages amount from the time of the breach until the time of damages payment.

This explanation needs an example. Return to Tom, Alex, and Brenda, but this time assume that Tom has retired from the practice of trust administration, has properly submitted his accounts for review and approval by the courts, and has passed along the trust account to his partner's son, Jack. Jack, sadly, just isn't the man that Tom had been, at least in the office. While Jack did not steal from the trust or undertake interested deals, he did make some bad investments and some sloppy deals. For instance, he sold a property held by the trust for $100,000, when its real value was somewhere between $125,000-$140,000, while he traded the trust's natural-gas stocks away right before a rise in world energy prices saw them increase steeply in value.[50]

Alex, to whom Jack disbursed an agreeable amount every month, never noticed these failures of prudence, but Brenda, upon receiving a final payment smaller than she had expected, did inquire and did discover the events. She sued.

What result would you expect under the rule described above? Consider the property first. If Jack had sold the property exactly two years ago (again, for ease of the hypo), then he would owe the trust, out of his own pockets, the difference between the price he got for the property ($100,000) and its "real price" plus interest for the intervening two years. If the range of the real value is between $125,000 and $140,000, the court is likely to err on the high side, under the theory that when a trustee fails of his fiduciary duty (here, the duty of prudent investment of the assets, which includes judicious and market-price purchase and sale), he should bear any risk or doubt appending to that imprudent behavior. Meanwhile, in some states the courts use a "statutory" interest rate in a context like this, set by the legislature, while in other states the court could take evidence on the question of

---

50. For the sake of this hypothetical, just assume that the "real value" of the property was easily and incontrovertibly demonstrable. Often assertions of the "real value" of a good at any given time will be highly contentious and will require expert testimony. Often experts are available to testify on both sides of the question, and in the end the trier of fact must squint and make a judgment call. All of this can be very expensive and often to very little purpose.

an appropriate interest rate and set that as part of the unique damages in the case.

So far so good. Some critics argue that this metric over-compensates trusts at the expense of trustees, but the riposte to such criticisms is that they miss the point: The *goal* in a case of breach of fiduciary duty is to cause the trustee to suffer a loss because of his breach, and if there's any doubt about how big the loss to the trust has been because of that breach, the risk should fall on the trustee, who should pay in damages the highest reasonable amount to make the trust whole.

Now, though, let's consider the natural gas stock. Say that Jack sold the 10,000 shares of natural-gas stock (of different companies, thus achieving a diversification goal) at $60. Shortly thereafter, the stock rose precipitously to $90, and stayed in the $90 range through the wrapping up of the trust and the suit by Brenda.

Under the formula employed for disinterested breach, Jack would owe the trust $30,000 (the difference between the prudent sale price and the actual sale price) plus interest from the date of sale. And, again, this formula suits the logic of damage calculations against trustees—if the claim of breach on this count is justified. But is it?

This being a hypo, the existentially true answer is that it is justified if the HypoMaster makes it justified. But what could make a determination of breach justified on these facts? The problem here is this: If a trustee is required to serve as an insurer against his business decisions later proving suboptimal, then no sane person would ever be willing to serve as a trustee.

The issue is one of hindsight bias. It is not fair—it is straight-up absurd—to hold a trustee liable for imprudence for selling assets at time A merely because the price of those assets was higher at time B. Asset prices fluctuate, especially prices of assets sold in highly traded markets like stock exchanges. At any given time, you can find various traders and market advisors who think that the price of any given stock will be higher in the coming days and weeks, while others think it will be lower. In fact, this more or less *must* be so: If *everyone* thought that a stock was overvalued at, say, $100/share, then no one would pay that $100 for a share, which means that the price would fall, instantly, to a price at which people were willing to buy it—which is the price at which an equal number of people think it likely to go higher in the coming days and weeks as think it will go lower. This is, in a very simplified form, the market-clearing price.

This means that if the market price of the natural-gas stocks that Jack sold, on the day he sold them, was $60, then on that day an equal number of people[51] thought that natural gas stocks would go higher as thought they would go lower, and that the *real price* of those stocks on the day he sold them was *really* $60, regardless of what may have happened *after* he sold them. For a court to look back at that transaction "with the benefits of hindsight" (as the saying goes) and declare that Jack had been imprudent to sell when he did is absurd.[52] Jack should owe no liability if he sold at an open market price, because he had committed no breach—at least not on these facts.

It is possible to construct a hypo in which Jack really should be held liable on these facts—except that the fact that the market price later rose to $90 is always irrelevant. Jack may properly be held liable if he sold at $60, in, say, a private transaction to a buyer, on a day on which he could have gotten more for the stocks in a public market transaction. Then he really did fail to be prudent, in that he didn't check the public sale price. Likewise, he could have been considered imprudent if he had sold at the public sale price when some potential purchaser had for some reason offered him *more* than the price on the public markets, and he turned down that offer. But he shouldn't be held liable for selling on the public market without searching the world for any nutty buyer who might for some private reason be willing to pay him more than the public market price. He might also have been held liable if, say, he had sold all of the stock in a single transaction, if it could be demonstrated that prudent procedure had been recognized as selling slowing into the market to avoid flash-crash conditions. None of these bases of liability, though, have anything to do with the incidental fact that the price of the stock later rose to a level higher than he sold at. Trustees are obliged to be prudent, not superhuman.

---

51. Actually, it's the number of total shares bid for, as one very deep pocketed bidder who felt strongly in one direction could "weigh out" a lot of smaller bidders who think the opposite. But that's an incidental detail for our purposes right now.

52. Explained in this way, I hope that hindsight bias does seem absurd. And it has been deployed in truly ludicrous ways, as in a case from the 1930s in which a judge held a defendant liable (in a slightly different context) for failing to anticipate the stock market crash of 1929 and the Great Depression. You know that the judge was engaging in the purest and ugliest hindsight bias from the simple fact that he was still, in the 1930s, a judge. If he had really seen the stock-market crash coming, he could have shorted everybody and made an absolute killing, just as President Kennedy's father is said to have done, advancing that family's already impressive fortunes tremendously. On the other hand, though, hindsight bias infects everyone to some degree and some people to preposterous degrees. In a somewhat different context some of those people are known as Monday morning quarterbacks. Or in-laws.

Finally on this topic, a reprise of an earlier consideration: co-trustee liability. The majority rule is that, as a default, all trustees are jointly and severally liable to beneficiaries for any breach that occurs on their watch. This is because each trustee is charged not only with behaving with prudence and loyalty herself, but with ensuring prudence and loyalty in her colleagues by prudent monitoring of those colleagues. If one trustee has been particularly infidelitous, as by self-dealing or acting willfully, while the other trustee(s) merely failed of their monitoring duty, then the relatively innocent trustee(s) may seek to recover from the real wrongdoer by indemnity.[53] But in the first instance, the wronged beneficiaries may sue all the trustees, recover from all or any of them, and let them sort it out.

D. MODIFICATION AND TERMINATION OF TRUSTS

The settlor's intent being paramount, trusts are not easily modified or terminated in contravention of the substance of that intent. Nevertheless, many instances do arise in which modification or termination is permissible, wise or necessary.

If the settlor lives and the trust is revocable, the settlor's determination—not the intent as expressed in the trust documents—is the touchstone. After all, a settlor could simply revoke the instrument entirely, so amendment can cause no difficulty.

If the settlor lives and the trust is irrevocable, what occurs if modification is desired? Why? (If the answers to these questions are not perfectly clear now, they should be after the next section.)

Meanwhile, a trust can be modified or terminated in some circumstances by the trustee or beneficiaries without the settlor's consent, as when the settlor has passed away. Of course, the settlor's intent remains the touchstone for whether the change sought is permissible.

---

53. UTC §703 says that "a trustee who does not join in an action of another trustee is not liable for the action," but the dissenting trustee must "exercise reasonable care to prevent a co-trustee from committing a serious breach of trust" and must "compel a co-trustee to redress a serious breach of trust." *See also* Restatement (Third) of Trusts §81(2) (2007), to similar effect; UTC §705(a)(1), which permits resignation with *notice* to the beneficiaries, settlor (if living), and all co-trustees. However, under §705(c), the "liability of a resigning trustee . . . is not discharged or affected by the trustee's resignation."

Courts will go far to give effect to the settlor's intent, which explains why such intent (as inferred from the terms of the trust) cabins the ability to change or terminate the trust by someone other than the settlor.[54]

Under the Restatement (Third) of Trusts and the UTC, modification (or deviation) is available for any provisions, whether administrative or dispositive, as long as the deviation will "further the purposes of the trust" in view of changed circumstances.[55] These might reasonably be referred to as the "revised *Claflin* doctrine."[56]

These provisions state a different deviation rule from that of the Restatement (Second) of Trusts, which forbade any modification (or deviation) the purpose of which would simply be bettering the beneficiaries' position. This might be called the "traditional *Claflin* doctrine." The more modern authors, including the UTC drafters, thought—with the benefit of experience—that the original doctrine, named after the case in which it was first formulated, had proven too narrow and hence improvable. Here's why. Imagine that the trust instrument declared that disbursements were to be made annually. Some years after the settlor's death and the trust's activation, changes in tax law rendered it the case that the trust would save significantly on taxes were it to make disbursements quarterly instead of annually. It would absolutely be to the benefit of the beneficiaries to make this change, because more post-tax dosh would remain in the *res* or would be available for present payouts. But the changed payouts would constitute a deviation from the trust. Under the old rule, at least some courts thought it their duty to deny this modification in accord with the Second Restatement provision. The modern rule clears up this difficulty.

Another fairly straightforward form of nonsettlor generated modification is the process of "decanting." Decanting involves breaking up a trust into baby trusts, an administrative matter that a wise settlor counseled by a careful attorney would include as an explicit power in the trust document, but which a trustee may undertake—upon court blessing—whenever such decanting would provide benefits to the trust

---

54. *See* Restatement (Third) of Trusts §66 (2003) and Uniform Trust Code §412 (2000).

55. *See id.*

56. The label derives from the case Claflin v. Claflin, 20 N.E. 454 (Mass. 1889) in which the original doctrine was propounded.

(usually by making administration of the trust by the trustee(s) simpler and cheaper) without undermining any material purpose of the trust.

Here's a specific iteration of a typical situation in which modifications can occur to the betterment of some beneficiaries and the non-detriment of any beneficiaries. See if you can formulate the typical situation from the specific instance.

IN RE CARNIOL

861 N.Y.S.2d 587 (N.Y. Sur. Ct. 2008).

Opinion

John B. Riordan, J.

This is a first and final accounting of Rhonda Carniol, the executor of the estate of David Carniol. The prayer for relief includes a request to allow the executor to modify the terms of the article fourth trust created under the will.

The decedent, David Carniol, died on March 2, 2005. The decedent's will dated August 26, 1998 was admitted to probate and letters testamentary issued to Rhonda Carniol on May 23, 2005. Article fourth of the will provides as follows:

> I give the proprietary lease or leases to, and the stock evidencing ownership of, any cooperative apartment or apartments which I own at the time of my death, together with any applicable insurance policies, including prepaid premiums, to my wife, diane carniol, or, if she does not survive, to my trustee, in trust, who shall retain the apartment for use by my granddaughter, aimee robin carniol, if and for as long as she wishes to reside there. Payments for expenses regarding the use or preservation of the property, including maintenance, real estate taxes, insurance premiums, repairs, and interest and principal on any mortgage on any apartment or on the underlying property, and for capital improvements shall be made by my granddaughter. Neither my granddaughter nor my trustee shall be liable for loss, destruction, usage or waste of any apartment held hereunder, or for any decline in its value or its failure to appreciate in value.
>
> My trustee may, with the consent of my granddaughter, sell any apartment held hereunder at any time for such price and on such terms and conditions as my trustee shall determine and invest as much or all of the proceeds as my trustee shall determine in another residence, on the same terms that apply to the original residence.

Any proceeds of sale in excess of the amount used to purchase another residence shall be added to the trust under article fifth.

Upon the death of aimee robin carniol, my trustee shall sell any apartment held hereunder for such price and on such terms and conditions as my trustee shall determine and distribute the proceeds of sale to the trust under article fifth.

[Article 5 of the will created a trust with a *res* of $150,000. Aimee Carniol and Steven Carniol, the testator's grandson, were the beneficiaries of the Article 5 trust, which was to be divided evenly between them.]

Decedent's wife Diane predeceased the decedent. Both Aimee Robin Carniol and Steven Carniol survived him. . . .

The petitioner avers that inquiry was made to the Hillpark Co-op Association regarding the proposed transfer of the apartment to the trust. According to the petitioner, the co-op association advised that it would not approve a transfer to a trust and, in addition, that any person residing in the apartment needed co-op board approval, which could be granted only after all required forms are completed and the proposed resident appears before the board. To determine whether this was accurate, petitioner's counsel wrote to the attorneys for the co-op association on two separate occasions and was advised in writing both times that the board would not approve a transfer to a trust.

Petitioner further states that Paul Carniol, the trustee of the article fourth trust, obtained the required forms and sent them to Norman Carniol, Aimee's father, with a request that he assist Aimee in completing the forms. The trustee claims that he never received a response despite following up numerous times with Aimee's father, Norman. Petitioner believes that based upon Aimee's financial situation and "certain other aspects of her history," it is unlikely that the co-op board will approve her tenancy even assuming she could overcome the board's policy prohibiting transfers to a trust. Accordingly, petitioner asked Aimee if she would consent to a sale of the apartment; however, Aimee never gave a definitive response to petitioner's request.

Under these circumstances, petitioner now asks the court's permission to modify the terms of the article fourth trust to permit her either to (1) sell the cooperative apartment and to pay the proceeds, net of the existing debt on the property and expenses of sale, to the article fourth trust, or (2) transfer, with or without co-op board approval, the decedent's right, title and interest in the cooperative apartment to the article fourth trust with a direction that the trust immediately sell such apartment. Once the property is sold, either by the executor or by the trustee, petitioner asks that the trustee of the article fourth trust, at his discretion, be permitted to purchase a replacement apartment or home for Aimee and that any excess funds be used to defray the cost of housing, including rent on an apartment or home, utilities, real estate taxes and other appurtenant charges for Aimee for her lifetime, or until the trust proceeds are exhausted. The petitioner also seeks a direction from the court ordering Aimee to pay the costs of carrying the apartment until this proceeding is completed, and, if Aimee fails to meet such obligation, authorizing her to sell the cooperative apartment and apply the proceeds in the manner described above. . . .

It is a basic rule of reformation, that a testator's intent must be gleaned from a reading of the entire instrument. . . . It appears from the will, in its entirety, that the testator intended for Aimee to have a place "to reside" for as long as she wishes. The testator, however, placed the burden of expenses "regarding the use or preservation of the property" upon Aimee. The testator also restricted the trustee's ability to sell the property absent Aimee's consent. Absent from the will, however, is a provision considering the possibility that Aimee would fail to pay for the expenses and would also fail to consent to a sale.

Based upon the co-op board's restriction on transfer policy as evidenced in the letters from the co-op board's attorney submitted to the court, the executor is unable to transfer ownership to the article fourth trust. Aimee has failed to meet the obligation imposed on her by the terms of the will to pay the expenses of the apartment. Moreover, a sale cannot be effectuated because Aimee has not consented. For these reasons, the executor has asked the court to reform the will. The terms of the will, however, are clear as is the testator's intention to provide a place for Aimee to reside. Nevertheless, "[t]he doctrine of equitable deviation has been applied to allow trustees to depart from the terms of a trust instrument where there has been an unforeseen change in circumstances that threatens to defeat or substantially impair the purpose for which the trust was created" (Matter of Aberlin, 264 AD2d 775, 695 NYS2d 383 [2d Dept 1999] [citation omitted]).

It appears that the testator did not foresee the possibility that Aimee would be unable to pay for the upkeep of the co-op apartment and withhold her consent to a sale, or that the board would not approve a transfer of the shares to a trust. Also, estate assets are being depleted to maintain the apartment, even though the testator's intention of providing this residence for Aimee cannot be realized. Thus, the circumstances of the instant case justify an equitable deviation from the literal terms of the will and the court authorizes the executor to sell the cooperative apartment and pay the proceeds, net of the existing debt on the property and expenses of sale, to the article fourth trust. . . .

Concerning the request for authorization to purchase a replacement residence for Aimee, the court finds that an evidentiary hearing is necessary in order for a finding to be made as to Aimee's ability and intention to pay the expenses of upkeep. If Aimee is unable to pay these expenses, the same problem will arise in connection with a replacement residence. If the court finds that Aimee is unable to pay the expenses of upkeep on a replacement residence, the article fourth trust will be collapsed and the funds held therein will be paid over to the article fifth trust. Since one half of the income from the article fifth trust is payable to Aimee, Aimee will receive some immediate benefit in accordance with the testator's intention.

* * *

Now consider a short excerpt from a fairly standard tax case.

GRASSIAN v. GRASSIAN

835 N.E.2d 607 (Mass. 2005).

Opinion

Stuart E. Grassian, trustee of the Nancy Friedman Revocable Family Trust of 1995 (trust), commenced this action in the county court, seeking reformation of the trust. A single justice of this court reserved and reported the case to the full court.

The facts are not in dispute. The settlor, Nancy Friedman, executed the trust as part of her estate plan in 1995. Her intent in doing so was, according to the drafting attorney's affidavit, "to avoid paying taxes unnecessarily and to minimize and if possible eliminate the federal and state estate taxes payable upon either of [her or her husband's] deaths to the extent permissible by law." The trust provides that if the settlor died before January 1, 1997, survived by her spouse, a portion of the trust assets was to be allocated to a subtrust (Trust A) intended to qualify as a qualified terminable interest property (QTIP) trust under 26 U.S.C. §2056(b)(7) (2000). The balance of the assets was then to be allocated to a subtrust intended to qualify as a marital deduction trust (Trust Q). All assets allocated to Trust A and Trust Q were intended to pass free of both Federal and Massachusetts estate taxes. The trust further provides that if the settlor died on or after January 1, 1997, Trust A would not be funded; in that situation, a portion of the assets would be allocated to Trust Q and the balance of the assets to a subtrust intended to qualify as a Federal credit shelter or bypass trust (Trust B). Trust B was intended to hold assets equal to the settlor's unused Federal exemption.

The trust was structured in this way because, at the time of execution, a relevant change in Massachusetts law was expected to take effect on January 1, 1997. Effective that date, Massachusetts imposed a so-called "sponge tax" on estates of decedents valued over the Federal exemption in the year of death. Under the sponge tax system, if any Federal estate tax was due, the Federal government directed a percentage of the Federal estate tax dollars to Massachusetts. If no Federal estate tax was due, then no Massachusetts estate tax was due. Trust A was meant to address the possibility that the settlor might die before the sponge tax system took effect. Trust Q, and not Trust A, was to be funded if the settlor died after the sponge tax system was in place.

The settlor died on February 27, 2004, survived by her husband and three children, all of whom are beneficiaries of the trust. Unknown to the settlor, effective January 1, 2003, the sponge tax system was eliminated in Massachusetts. G. L. c. 65C, §2A, as appearing in St. 2002, c. 364, §§10, 23, 24, and St. 2002, c. 186, §§28, 34 (the 2002 amendments). As a result of the 2002 amendments, the settlor's estate owes approximately $ 64,400 in Massachusetts estate taxes. The trustee requests that the trust be reformed essentially to provide that Trust A be funded not only if the settlor had died before January 1, 1997, but also if she died after December 31, 2002 (as she in fact did). We agree that the trust should be reformed as requested.

We may reform a trust instrument to conform to the settlor's intent. . . . We have reformed trusts in light of a change in the law that frustrates a settlor's intent to minimize his or her tax liability. . . . We require clear and decisive proof that the instrument fails to embody the settlor's intent. . . . Here, the settlor's intent to minimize or eliminate estate taxes is clear from the trust instrument as well as from the drafting attorney's affidavit. The structure of Trusts A, B, and Q—in particular, the changes in whether and how these subtrusts were to be funded depending on whether she died before or after January 1, 1997—shows her intent to minimize taxes even in light of anticipated changes in the tax laws. The 2002 amendments frustrate this intent.

We remand the case to the county court for entry of a judgment reforming the trust as proposed in the complaint.

So ordered.

E. CREDITORS

Now the focus must shift to that third set of trials upon the patience and goodness (and competence and luck) of the trustee: creditors. There are potentially three sets of creditors whose interests could be raised: creditors of the settlor, creditors of the beneficiaries, and creditors of the trustee.

The last should be dealt with first because it can be dealt with so swiftly. The creditors of the trustee in her individual capacity may take nothing from the trust. Period. The trustee must—*per* the very root and core and brains of the operation—keep trust assets separate from personal assets; likewise, the trustee's ownership of the trust *res* remains wholly separate from (and favored against) her ownership of her own property. Should the trustee use trust funds for personal purposes, then the beneficiaries will have a chose in action against the trustee, the damages arising from which will be very great. This will make the trust beneficiaries judgment creditors against the trustee; they can seek compensation out of the trustee's personal assets. But the reverse is never true; no personal creditor of the trustee, from whatever corner, can seek access to trust assets.

Regarding questions of creditors of settlors and beneficiaries, the fundamental rule is nearly as simple: *Creditors may step into the shoes of their debtors.* This means that a creditor can force a settlor or beneficiary to do—or, generally, can do directly—anything that the settlor or beneficiary can do with the *res*, but no more. This concept will rather quickly make a great deal of sense, but it first may require a bit of unpacking.

1. Creditors of Settlor

Again, remember the central rule: Creditors may step into the shoes of their debtors. Regarding settlors, then, the great question is whether the trust from which the creditors wish to collect is revocable or irrevocable.

a. Revocable Trusts and Provisions

If the trust (or some portion thereof) is revocable, then the settlor must be alive.[57] If a live settlor has settled a fully revocable trust, then

---

57. I won't insult you by asking you whether you can see why that's true.

he can revoke it entirely, making the assets his untrammeled property again. The "stepping into the shoes" doctrine means that if he can do it, his creditors can do it. And so, creditors have complete access to the assets in a wholly revocable trust. (When you remember that the IRS and those who win judgments against a person are also their creditors, you see why a wholly revocable trust serves so little purpose, and why many states presume as a default that a trust not otherwise designated by the settlor is an irrevocable trust.)

Once a settlor dies, even a fully revocable trust becomes irrevocable. And yet, while the settlor lived, the assets were fully available to the settlor by any act of revocation, just as though the assets had remained in the settlor's estate until the moment of death. Under these circumstances, the Restatement (Third) of Trusts §25, cmt. e (2003) and the UTC[58] treat trust property that was revocable until the settlor's death as if it had been owned by the settlor at that time. The UTC further specifies that a revocable trust is subject to the settlor's creditors after the death of the settlor to the extent that the settlor's probate estate is inadequate to satisfy the creditors' claims, suggesting that the nontrust probate assets are to be exhausted first.

b. Irrevocable Trusts and Provisions

With regard to irrevocable trusts (or provisions), the questions change substantially. A settlor of course cannot by definition revoke or (materially) alter an irrevocable trust so standing in the shoes of the settlor will not do any good. Rather, the settlor's creditors can only reach the settlor's former assets (now transferred to become the trust's *res*) if the settlor is also *a beneficiary* of the irrevocable trust—and so the analysis of the creditor's chances in such circumstances rightly falls into the next section, which considers creditor's access to beneficiary distributions.

One extremely important caveat arises to this easy rule: A trust may not be used to defraud creditors. Should a settlor who has already contracted a debt form an irrevocable trust or should that trust be formed in contemplation of defrauding a creditor, then the trust will be treated as *null* with regard to that creditor so as to defeat the attempted fraud or fraud adjacent action.

---

58. *See* UTC §505(a)(3) (2000). *Contra* the traditional rule as expressed in the Second Restatement.

2. Creditors of Beneficiaries (Protective Trusts and the Hamilton/Spendthrift Shuffle)

Now comes the lively action. Most trusts within the purview of this course arise because settlors seek to guide the actions of their beneficiaries, or at least the use of their property, from beyond the grave. And those settlors, of course, have little interest in settling a trust merely for the money to pass from the hands of their less careful beneficiaries into the maw of the beneficiaries' creditors either already established or yet to arise. This leads to a common set of "moves" by settlors, so common that while, due to the potential variability of any given trust or set of trusts, the mind runneth not to the potential variety of possible trusts, some few trust forms or clauses have earned shorthand names and bear a bit of consideration. And almost all of these, except for (and, as we have seen, even including) the revocable vs. irrevocable categorization, "meet the road" with regard to issues of creditors.

In the context of beneficiaries, the next deep distinction available between trusts and provisions is that of mandatory and discretionary. The basic distinction is fairly obvious. Mandatory provisions provide the trustee no discretion, no decision-making authority or responsibility. So, for instance, "pay to the following ten named beneficiaries $1,000/ month for the remainder of each of their natural lives" is a wholly mandatory provision, with no discretion involved. By comparison, a provision that charges the trustee to "pay out to each of my descendants as much as may be required to permit them to live at twice the poverty line, should those descendants prove themselves morally upright," is most obviously a discretionary provision and allows—requires—lots of decision making (and research) by the trustee.

The relevance of the mandatory vs. discretionary distinction to the question of collection by beneficiaries' creditors should be obvious by now—if you recall the first rule of creditors' rights: The creditor may step into the shoes of the [creditor's debtor]. If a trust provision is mandatory, then the trustee has no opportunity to deny the distribution, for any reason; she is merely a cipher. In such instances, when the payment is due, the beneficiary may sue to demand it if the trustee is foolish enough not to pay. So too, therefore, may the beneficiary's creditors. In fact, the beneficiaries' creditors can go to court to obtain a *Hamilton* Order,[59] which not only establishes that the debt is due to

---

59. These orders are named after the case in which they were "invented."

the creditor but requires the trustee to make the distribution from the trust *directly to the creditor* until the debt has been discharged.

Settlors find this situation, and *Hamilton* Orders generally, rather frustrating. Very often one of their primary reasons for establishing a trust is to keep those of their descendants who have demonstrated proclivities for financial imbecility from blowing through their inheritance both quickly and stupidly. Consider, for example, a settlor—we'll call her Murphy—who has made her fortune and her fame as a newspaper reporter, author, television commentator, and in other related pursuits that, before the internet, could result in the accretion of a significant fortune. Murphy has accreted that fortune. She also, rather late in the maternal cycle, delivered herself of two non-marital children.

Let us assume further that Murphy retired (or at least semi-retired) at just about the same time as the inimitable David Brinkley,[60] and by a wise recognition of the opportunities and limitations of the internet—both on the news, in publishing industries, and in general—turned her small fortune into a large one. As portents of mortality began to infiltrate Murphy's successes more than a tenth-part through the twenty-first century, her thoughts drifted towards the here-after, and to the still-remaining. She recognized that her eldest child was undoubtedly headed toward remarkable success and financial acumen. Her younger child, though, little Eliza, demonstrated different strengths: She was a painter, a dreamer, and—as with many similar artistic types—financially inept. (The previous, more Victorian term for this type of person was "spendthrift." This term will become important in a moment.)

And so Murphy, upon consultation with counsel, decided to establish a trust, one that dispensed mandatory grants to her eldest both annually and upon certain triggers (graduation from graduate school, permanent employment, marriage, or procreation without marriage, etc.), but which left disbursements to her younger child in the discretion of the trustee. After all, if the trustee had discretion as to whether the younger daughter got a disbursement, then a *Hamilton* Order would be of no use.

And yet, as Murphy's counsel quickly pointed out to her, trustee discretion provided only a partial solution. After all, if the younger daughter were ever to benefit from Murphy's largesse, the trust would eventually have to make some sort of disbursement to her. And *Hamilton* Orders reach beyond mandatory disbursements; they can, in the absence of further protections, require that any disbursements

60. Middle '90s.

made from the trust in favor of Eliza be paid to any of Eliza's creditors until such creditors had been paid off, whenever such disbursements might be made. In other words, the trustee would—upon the creditor being granted a *Hamilton* Order—be entitled to full recompense before another nickel could be passed along to Eliza. If Eliza bought, say, an art gallery on credit, then Eliza could never receive another distribution, even were she starving, until the art gallery had been paid off.

Murphy's counsel explained to her the further line of defense against Eliza's rapacity: the spendthrift clause.[61] A trust that includes a spendthrift clause effectively pre-defeats a *Hamilton* Order. It forbids trust assets to be encumbered by beneficiaries to which the clause applies.[62] As a result, in trusts that include spendthrift clauses, a beneficiary's creditors can never collect directly from the trustee, but must wait until a distribution—whether mandatory or discretionary—has been distributed to the beneficiary, and may then collect from the beneficiary individually.

Murphy accepted this solution, and the trust was thus written. What do you think? How effective is the spendthrift protection? In what circumstances?

There is nothing that can stop a creditor from collecting debts from a beneficiary-debtor once the money has passed into the hands of that beneficiary-debtor. But having to wait until the money flows to the beneficiary, and then having to keep track of the beneficiary in order to enforce collection, can add some—sometimes significant—costs to the process of debt collection.

3. The Self-Settled Asset Protection Trust

Self-settled asset protection trusts (SSAPTs) are irrevocable spendthrift trusts for which the settlor is the primary (or only) beneficiary. Because they are irrevocable, creditors can't get at the assets through the settlor *qua* settlor. And because they are spendthrift, creditors can't get at them from the settlor-as-trustee directly by stepping into the shoes of the settlor wearing his beneficiary hat. Rather, the creditor must wait until the settlor as trustee pays the settlor as beneficiary before the creditor can collect from the settlor as beneficiary.

---

61. This should really be called the anti-spendthrift clause, for reasons that will become immediately apparent. Yes, the terminology is incoherent to the modern eye at a variety of levels here, but it's built into the system by now.

62. *See* UTC §§502-503. The UTC recognizes spendthrift trusts (§502), and an exception to them for spouses and children (§503), but not for tort creditors.

As the following case makes clear, nothing in this set up avoids the settlor's obligation not to commit fraud, so any debt of the settlor that had been incurred before the settlorestablished the trust would still be reachable "through" the settlor, because to that extent the trust would be a fraudulent instrument and would be ignored. Now consider the following case for an object lesson in how the law treats people who try to rook their creditors so obviously. Think also about whether (and, if so, when) SSAPTs might do legitimate work. A number of states have adopted SSAPT statutes, but they have played very little role in trust litigation so far.

WALDRON v. HUBER (IN RE HUBER)

493 B.R. 798 (Bankr. W.D. Wash.2013).

Opinion

This matter came before the Court on April 15, 2013, on the Motions for Summary Judgment as to Claims Relating to Transfers by Debtor & Invalidity of Trust and as to Claim of Denial of Discharge, filed by Mark D. Waldron, Trustee for the estate of Donald G. Huber (Trustee) against Donald G. Huber (Debtor). At the conclusion of the hearing, the Court took the matter under advisement. Based on the arguments and pleadings presented, the order of the Court is as follows:

The Debtor has been involved in real estate development and management in the Puget Sound area for over 40 years. He graduated from Pacific Lutheran University in Tacoma with a degree in Business Administration and Sociology. In 1968, he founded United Western Development, Inc. (UWD) with its principal place of business located in Tacoma, Washington. The purpose was to use it as a vehicle to engage in real estate development. The Debtor still serves as its President, although he is partially retired. The operation of UWD and the Debtor's other businesses is now primarily performed by his eldest son, Kevin D. Huber, who has served as UWD's Senior Vice President —Business Development since 2001. . . .

Many, if not all, of the projects of the Debtor were undertaken by him through the use of an entity separate and apart from UWD, such as through a corporation or limited liability company, with the Debtor owning all, or a portion, of the project. The Debtor, however, was required on many projects to sign as guarantor in favor of third party lenders, many of them local banks. These appear to be the largest creditors of his bankruptcy. . . .

In 2007, UWD hired an individual who was experienced in investment banking and real estate securitization with a plan to secure additional financing. Subsequently, UWD entered into an engagement letter with Houlihan Lokey, a private finance group, to assist it in raising approximately $55 million in capital. . . . The funds were to be used to pay off existing debt, provide additional working capital for present and future needs, and to fund the transaction fees. The cost of the "due diligence" requirements was substantial, but in late September or early October 2008, the Debtor embarked on a fund raising trip to New York City. The Debtor/UWD, however, proved to be unsuccessful in its attempt to secure additional financing, receiving only one verbal offer and no written offers. On October 10, 2008, UWD terminated the agreement with Houlihan Lokey, partly due to the market turmoil that was by then affecting the real estate market nationwide, further dimming their chances of securing additional funding.

In 2007, the Debtor had and was in partnership on many of his projects with Robert Terhune, who was also a guarantor of many of the same projects. In a series of emails . . . between the Debtor and Mr. Terhune, it became apparent that several of their joint projects were beginning to unwind due to a lack of capital. . . . The Debtor placed ever increasing pressure on Mr. Terhune from the spring of 2008, through the end of the year to become current on monies he believed he was owed. When Mr. Terhune also threatened to set up his own spendthrift trust, the Debtor through his counsel made it clear to Mr. Terhune that the setting up of such a trust would be fraudulent as to him, as he considered himself a creditor.

The Examiner indicated in his report filed with the Court that the Debtor was or had to be aware of the "gathering storm clouds." In addition to the threat of a collapsing housing market, a review of court files after the establishment of the Trust reflects that several loans in existence in August 2008 were fragile at best. . . .

It is well documented that in 2007 and 2008 nationally, as well as locally, the real estate market began to deteriorate due to the collapse of the subprime mortgage market and the implementation of more restrictive lending standards. On August 19, 2008, Kevin Huber, on behalf of his father, emailed attorney Harold Snow, an estate planning attorney, because "[m]y father has some assets that he would like to protect and shield." The Debtor subsequently retained Mr. Snow to set up an asset protection trust, called the Donald Huber Family Trust (Trust), which was established on September 23, 2008. Correspondence after drafting the Trust document acknowledges that one of the Debtor's principal goals for creating the Trust was to "protect a portion of [the Debtor's] assets from [his] creditors." In a number of emails between the Debtor and Mr. Snow, the Debtor expressed urgency in setting up the Trust.

With the assistance of Mr. Snow, the Debtor transferred $10,000 in cash and his ownership or membership interest in over 25 entities into DGH, LLC, an Alaska limited liability company, set up on September 4, 2008, to receive those interests. DGH, LLC, after it was established, was owned 99% by the Trust and 1% by Kevin Huber, its manager. UWD's shares were transferred directly into the Trust and not through DGH, LLC. Assets such as the Debtor's residence at 8310 Warren Street in Tacoma were conveyed to an Alaska corporation (8310, LLC) and then into DGH, LLC. The 8310, LLC then leased the residence to the Debtor, and the Trust made the mortgage payments. The corporate assets were transferred in a similar fashion via quit claim deed to an Alaska corporation, then the new entity's interest into DGH, LLC. The Debtor acknowledges that he received no consideration for the transfers.

In summary, the assets owned or partially owned by the Debtor, either directly or indirectly, prior to the Trust implementation consisted of approximately 13 development projects, his residence and the residence of his disabled daughter, interests in several shopping centers, a few corporations, and $3 million dollars in uncollectable receivables. As of July 2010, and after the Trust was created and further after several entities/projects were either foreclosed or sold, the Debtor personally owned only a 5% interest in the James Center Professional Plaza, worthless notes and accounts receivable, and a 50% interest in Burnett Highlands, LLC. Meanwhile the Trust appeared to own the Debtor's holding and real estate operating companies, such as UWD Group, LLC, UWD Management, LLC, and DGH, LLC, as well as the residence occupied by his disabled daughter, an 85% interest in both the Kimball Center, LLC and Pioneer Plaza, LLC, PSEA, LLC, and Sure Seal, LLC. The Debtor was the trustor of the Trust, while Kevin Huber, Amber Haines, and Alaska USA Trust Company (AUSA) were trustees. There was only one asset of the Trust held in Alaska, which is a certificate of deposit for $10,000 transferred there by the Debtor. All other assets are located in Washington State.

The ultimate beneficiaries of the Trust, beside the Debtor, consist of his sons Kevin and Dillon, daughters Darby and Neysa, and stepchildren Amber, Seth, Cedar and Star. The Debtor also has grandchildren that the Trust assists in paying for their educational expenses. The Trust established by the Debtor generated $345,248 in discretionary beneficiary income in 2010, and $360,000 in 2009.

In August 2011, the Debtor filed an amended Schedule I reflecting then current income of $17,444 per month. Of this amount, $1,300 was in the form of the Debtor's social security benefit. He also received social security income for each of his two minor children. The Debtor received trust income of $14,500 per month. . . .

The total amount paid out from the Trust assets between October 1, 2010, and July 30, 2012, [almost entirely for personal and educational expenses for the Debtor and other beneficiaries,] was $571,332.81. From the date of the filing of the chapter 11 petition on February 10, 2011, through July 30, 2012, the amount of the distributions was $406,837.27. . . .

The Debtor filed for chapter 11 bankruptcy protection on February 10, 2011. . . . The case was converted to chapter 7, title 11 on October 21, 2011. The Plaintiff in this action is the duly appointed chapter 7 trustee. . . .

A. Validity of the Trust

The Trustee initially contends that the Trust should be invalidated under Washington State law. The Trust was created in the State of Alaska and designates the law of Alaska to govern the Trust. Alaska recognizes self-settled asset protection trusts, see AS 34.40.110, but Washington does not, see RCW 19.36.020. As such, the parties agree there is a conflict in the laws of the two states, and the Court must look to choice of law rules for guidance.

1. Choice of Law

"In federal question cases with exclusive jurisdiction in federal court, such as bankruptcy, the court should apply federal, not forum state, choice of law rules." . . . In applying federal choice of law rules, courts in the Ninth Circuit follow the approach of the Restatement (Second) of Conflict of Laws (1971) (Restatement). [When the settlor of an inter vivos trust chooses a state's law to govern the trust, the trust is valid if (1) the chosen state has a substantial relation to the trust, (2) the trust is valid under the chosen state's law, and (3) application of the chosen state's law does not violate "a strong public policy of the state with which, as to the matter at issue, the trust has its most significant relationship. . . ." Restatement (Second) of Conflict of Laws §270 (1971).]

[T]he local law of the designated state . . . will not be applied if this would violate a strong public policy of the state with which as to the matter in issue the trust has its most significant relationship. Thus, where the settlor creates a revocable trust in a state other than that of his domicil, in order to avoid the application of the local law of his domicil . . . , it may be held that the local law of his domicil is applicable, even though he has designated as controlling the local law of the state in which the trust is created and administered.

Under the Restatement, the Debtor's choice of Alaska law designated in the Trust should be upheld if Alaska has a substantial relation to the Trust . . . . Comment b provides that "a state has a substantial relation to a trust if at the time the trust is created: (1) the trustee or settlor is domiciled in the state; (2) the assets are located in the state; and (3) the beneficiaries are domiciled in the state. These contacts with the state are not exclusive." . . . In the instant case, it is undisputed that at the time the Trust was created, the settlor was not domiciled in Alaska, the assets were not located in Alaska, and the beneficiaries were not domiciled in Alaska. The only relation to Alaska was that it was the location in which the Trust was to be administered and the location of one of the trustees, AUSA.

Conversely, it is undisputed that at the time the Trust was created, the Debtor resided in Washington; all of the property placed into the Trust, except a $10,000 certificate of deposit, was transferred to the Trust from Washington; the creditors of the Debtor were located in Washington; the Trust beneficiaries were Washington residents; and the attorney who prepared the Trust documents and transferred the assets into the Trust was located in Washington. Accordingly, while Alaska had only a minimal relation to the Trust, using the test set forth in Comment b, Washington had a substantial relation to the Trust when the Trust was created.

Additionally, Washington State has a strong public policy against self-settled asset protection trusts. Specifically, pursuant to RCW 19.36.020, transfers made to self-settled trusts are void as against existing or future creditors. . . . This statute has been in existence for well over a century, as it was first enacted in 1854. This policy is consistent with those in other states. For instance, in Marine Midland Bank v. Portnoy (In re Portnoy), 201 B.R. 685, 701 (Bankr. S.D.N.Y. 1996), the bankruptcy court considered the public policy of New York against self-settled trusts when determining a choice of law issue: "Portnoy may not unilaterally remove the characterization of property as his simply by incorporating a favorable choice of law provision into a self-settled trust of which he is the primary beneficiary. Equity would not countenance such a practice." As with New York, Washington has a policy that a debtor should not be able to escape the claims of his creditors by utilizing a spendthrift trust. Thus, in accordance with §270 of the Restatement, this Court will disregard the settlor's choice of Alaska law, which is obviously more favorable to him, and will apply Washington law in determining the Trustee's claim regarding validity of the Trust.

2. RCW 19.36.020

Interests in property are determined by state law. . . . RCW 19.36.020 provides in relevant part as follows:

> That all deeds of gift, all conveyances, and all transfers or assignments, verbal or written, of goods, chattels or things in action, made in trust for the use of the person making the same, shall be void as against the existing or subsequent creditors of such person.

The Trust is admittedly a self-settled trust. In accordance with RCW 19.36.020, the Debtor's transfers of assets into the Trust were void as transfers made into a self-settled trust. See Rigby v. Mastro (In re Mastro), 465 B.R. 576, 611 (Bankr. W.D. Wash. 2011) (where a bankruptcy judge applying Washington State law held that the debtors' transfers of assets into a self-settled trust were void). The Debtor has provided no legal authority to the contrary. Accordingly, the Debtor's transfers of assets into the Trust are void, and the Trustee is entitled to summary judgment as a matter of law to the extent the Trustee seeks to have the transfers invalidated. . . .

C. 11 U.S.C. §548(e)(1)

The Trustee also seeks summary judgment under 11 U.S.C. §548(e)(1), arguing that the Debtor's transfers of assets into the Trust should be avoided. That this Court has determined already that such transfers are void under RCW 19.36.020 does not preclude a determination that the transfers also are fraudulent under §548(e)(1). . . .

11 U.S.C. §548(e)(1) provides as follows:

> In addition to any transfer that the trustee may otherwise avoid, the trustee may avoid any transfer of an interest of the debtor in property that was made on or within 10 years before the date of the filing of the petition, if —
>
> > (A) such transfer was made to a self-settled trust or similar device;

(B) such transfer was by the debtor;

(C) the debtor is a beneficiary of such trust or similar device; and

(D) the debtor made such transfer with actual intent to hinder, delay, or defraud any entity to which the debtor was or became, on or after the date that such transfer was made, indebted.

The parties agree that each of the elements of §548(e)(1) has been established except for the last element: whether the Debtor made the transfers to the Trust "with actual intent to hinder, delay, or defraud any entity to which the debtor was or became, on or after the date that such transfer was made, indebted." The Trustee contends that the overwhelming evidence establishes the Debtor's intent to hinder, delay and defraud his creditors, while the Debtor argues there is an issue of material fact as to his intent.

The Trustee has the burden of proving the elements of a fraudulent conveyance by a preponderance of the evidence. . . . Fraudulent intent may be established on the basis of circumstantial evidence. . . . In assessing the evidence, courts consider "badges of fraud," which are "circumstances so commonly associated with fraudulent transfers that their presence gives rise to an inference of intent.". . .

The Ninth Circuit has articulated that

[a]mong the more common circumstantial indicia of fraudulent intent at the time of the transfer are: (1) actual or threatened litigation against the debtor; (2) a purported transfer of all or substantially all of the debtor's property; (3) insolvency or other unmanageable indebtedness on the part of the debtor; (4) a special relationship between the debtor and the transferee; and, after the transfer, (5) retention by the debtor of the property involved in the putative transfer. . . .

"The presence of a single badge of fraud may spur mere suspicion; the confluence of several can constitute conclusive evidence of actual intent to defraud, absent 'significantly clear' evidence of a legitimate supervening purpose." . . . Once the trustee establishes indicia of fraud, the burden shifts to the transferee to prove some "legitimate supervening purpose" for the transfer. . . .

In support of his motion for summary judgment, the Trustee submitted over one hundred exhibits containing declarations, emails, documents, and pleadings to establish the Debtor's intent to hinder, delay, or defraud his creditors. Conversely, the only evidence submitted by the Debtor on summary judgment is the Debtor's deposition testimony taken on September 20, 2011, by counsel for the Examiner. . . . Notably, while the deposition references numerous exhibits, the Debtor did not file these exhibits with the Court. Accordingly, the deposition it is of minimal value to the Court, particularly as it fails to designate specific portions rebutting the very specific allegations of the Trustee. . . .

Considering each of the badges of fraud, the evidence submitted by the Trustee first establishes that at the time the Debtor transferred his assets into the Trust, there was threatened litigation against the Debtor. Specifically, it appears that foreclosure of several properties for which the Debtor had guaranteed the bank loans was becoming increasingly certain. . . . The maturity dates on these loans had been extended at least one time; the local and national real estate markets were collapsing; Robert Terhune had not, and apparently could not, repay the Debtor an approximately one-million dollar debt, on which the Debtor depended to service the loans; and by March 2008, the Debtor was not making timely payments on his project debts, which he had guaranteed. Ultimately, litigation ensued, beginning in spring 2009. While the Debtor's responsive pleading states that nothing indicates the Debtor anticipated that the loans would not be further extended, the Debtor submitted no declaration or evidence in support of this proposition.

The Trustee also has established that the Debtor transferred all or substantially all of his property into the Trust. It is undisputed that the Debtor transferred $10,000 in cash and his ownership or membership interest in over 20 entities into DGH, LLC, which was owned 99% by the Trust and 1% by Kevin Huber. These entities included the Debtor's residence at 8310 Warren Street; his daughter's residence; interests in several shopping centers; 13 development projects; and a few corporations. The Debtor also transferred UWD's shares directly into the Trust. The Trustee presented evidence that after the Trust was created and several entities were either foreclosed or sold, the Debtor personally owned only a 5% interest in the James Center Professional Plaza, worthless notes and accounts receivable, and a 50% interest in Burnett Highlands, LLC. The Trust, on the other hand, appeared to own most of the Debtor's income-producing assets. According to the Examiner, 71.1% of the Debtor's assets were transferred to the Trust, while 28.9% remained outside the Trust. This has not been rebutted by the Debtor.

The Trustee further has established significant indebtedness on the part of the Debtor when he transferred his assets into the Trust. The Trustee's evidence indicates that in 2007, the Debtor began to experience substantial financial problems. To raise money, he had to sell a portion of his interest in the James Center Professional Plaza, which generated a $177,000 tax in 2007. The evidence, including emails from the Debtor, establishes that the Debtor was unable to pay this tax debt when due, and it remains unpaid to date. Additionally, during the period that the Trust was formed and assets transferred, the Debtor had increased his pressure on Robert Terhune, without success, in order to obtain capital to service his debts. As set forth in the Debtor's emails, the debt load was "strangling" the Debtor and "bills [went] unpaid." Furthermore, during this period, the Debtor had expended approximately $70,000 - $100,000 per month for one year in his efforts to obtain funding through Houlihan Lokey, which also proved unsuccessful.

As to the fourth badge of fraud, the Debtor does not dispute that there is a special relationship, as he is both the trustor and beneficiary of the trust.

The Trustee also has established that the Debtor effectively retained the property transferred into the Trust. While the Debtor indicated in his deposition that he did not retain the right to direct how or if distributions were made from the Trust, it appears that substantially all of the Debtor's requests for distributions were granted. Only one reference was set forth in the deposition of any refusal. Furthermore, the only party to review the requests was his son Kevin Huber, with whom he was in business at the time. The record indicates that AUSA did absolutely nothing to become involved with the preservation or protection of the Trust assets, but merely acted as a straw man. Additionally, the Debtor continued to reside in a Trust asset and to receive some $14,500 per month in trust income, which went toward his personal expenses, loan payments, cash, education expenses for his family, and payments to his former spouse, all at the expense of his creditors. Based on the evidence before the Court, the only reasonable conclusion is that the Debtor continued to use and enjoy the Trust assets just as he did before the transfers.

The Trustee has established that the five badges of fraud exist in this case; the Debtor has not raised a genuine dispute as to these badges. In addition, the Trustee's evidence indicates that in the face of the declining real estate market, the Debtor's inability to secure funding, and mounting debt, the Debtor was afraid that he would lose everything he had worked so hard to achieve. While the Debtor alleges that he consulted Mr. Snow and created the Trust merely for estate planning purposes, the timing of the Trust's creation, the facts surrounding its creation, and timing of the asset transfers support a finding of a motive other than estate planning, that of asset protection at the expense of his creditors. Furthermore, the Debtor has not presented any evidence refuting the Trustee's overwhelming evidence that when the Trust was created, the Debtor was desperate to protect his assets and knowledgeable of the purpose of a spendthrift trust.

The Debtor argues that his reliance on legal counsel in creating the Trust negates fraudulent intent. Even if the Debtor had presented evidence that he relied on the advice of counsel in creating the Trust and transferring his assets, such reliance must have been in good faith. . . . A finding that the debtor knew that the purpose of the transfers was to hinder or delay creditors "precludes the defense of good faith reliance on the advice of an attorney even if the client is otherwise innocent of any improper purpose." . . . In the instant case, the Debtor's deposition testimony establishes that he was well aware of the effect of a spendthrift trust, as he testified that through counsel he forbid Mr. Terhune from putting his assets into a spendthrift trust until the parties reached an agreement as to the debt Mr. Terhune owed him. The Debtor clarified his reasoning: "Mr. Terhune didn't have anything other than the properties that we owned together and his house. So if he transferred them, I'd have nothing to secure me." Additionally, at the hearing, the Debtor failed to present any plausible reason to create a self-settled asset protection trust other than to shield assets from creditors.

Accordingly, the evidence presented by the Trustee supports an inference of actual fraudulent intent by the Debtor to hinder, delay, or defraud his current or future creditors, in violation of §548(e)(1)(D). The Trustee is entitled to summary judgment on this claim as a matter of law.

D. 11 U.S.C. §544(b)(1) and RCW 19.40.041(a)

Section 544(b)(1) gives the Trustee the authority to bring an action to avoid fraudulent transfers under state law. Under the Uniform Fraudulent Transfer Act (UFTA), a transfer is fraudulent if the debtor acts with actual intent to hinder, delay, or defraud a creditor, or transfers "[w]ithout receiving a reasonably equivalent value in exchange for the transfer or obligation." RCW 19.40.041(a)(1) - (2). The party alleging the fraudulent transfer must demonstrate actual intent to defraud by "clear and satisfactory proof." . . . Circumstantial evidence of intent may be considered. . . . In determining whether actual intent exists, a court may consider eleven factors, or badges of fraud, set forth in RCW 19.40.041(b):

(1) The transfer or obligation was to an insider;
(2) The debtor retained possession or control of the property transferred after the transfer;
(3) The transfer or obligation was disclosed or concealed;
(4) Before the transfer was made or obligation was incurred, the debtor had been sued or threatened with suit;
(5) The transfer was of substantially all the debtor's assets;
(6) The debtor absconded;
(7) The debtor removed or concealed assets;
(8) The value of the consideration received by the debtor was reasonably equivalent to the value of the asset transferred or the amount of the obligation incurred;
(9) The debtor was insolvent or became insolvent shortly after the transfer was made or the obligation was incurred;
(10) The transfer occurred shortly before or shortly after a substantial debt was incurred; and
(11) The debtor transferred the essential assets of the business to a lienor who transferred the assets to an insider of the debtor.

These factors are "non-exclusive and precatory, indicating that other evidence impacting on intent should also be considered.". . .

Several of these badges of fraud overlap those considered in the Ninth Circuit in analyzing 11 U.S.C. §548. The Court already has determined that the Trustee established the Debtor was threatened with litigation when the transfers occurred; the transfers were of substantially all the Debtor's assets; and the Debtor retained control of the transferred property. The evidence also establishes that as a self-settled trust, the transfer from the Debtor to the Trust was to an insider. For the same reason, the Debtor concedes he did not receive consideration for transferring his assets to the Trust. Additionally, the evidence establishes that by transferring the property into the Trust, the Debtor was attempting to remove the assets from the creditors' reach.

In addition to these factors, as set forth in the Court's §548(e) analysis, the Trustee's evidence further shows that in the face of the declining real estate market, the Debtor's inability to secure funding, and mounting debt, the Debtor was concerned that he would lose all of his assets to his creditors. A review of the evidentiary record before the Court is overwhelming that the Debtor was desperate to protect and shield his assets. There is almost no evidence to the contrary.

The Debtor, however, contends that his denial that he had fraudulent intent is sufficient to raise an issue of material fact. In *Sedwick* [*v. Gwinn*, 873 P.2d 528 (Wash. App. Ct. 1994)], the court concluded that "where the debtor denies that his or her intent was to defraud, the issue cannot be conclusively determined by the trier of fact until it has heard the testimony and assessed the witnesses' credibility," making summary judgment inappropriate. . . . *Sedwick*, however, is inapposite because the debtor there submitted not only his own affidavit, but the affidavit testimony of other witnesses that was consistent with the debtor's affidavit. In these affidavits, each witness stated that there was no intent to defraud the plaintiff.

In the instant case, the Debtor failed to submit his own declaration regarding his intent, let alone the declarations of other witnesses, such as Mr. Snow and Kevin Huber, who would be the witnesses most likely to testify as to the Debtor's intent in creating the Trust and transferring his assets. Moreover, while the Debtor's deposition testimony states that he created the Trust for estate planning purposes, it does not directly address or deny the evidence submitted by the Trustee establishing that the Debtor wanted to protect his assets in light of his increasingly bleak financial situation. The Court finds that the Debtor's desire to provide for his children and grandchildren through estate planning by protecting his assets that they would otherwise stand to inherit, is not mutually exclusive of the desire to shield his assets from creditors. Accordingly, estate planning alone does not create an issue of fact as to intent. . . . Furthermore, as previously indicated, the Debtor's deposition testimony regarding Mr. Terhune's goal to transfer his assets into his own pendthrift trust establishes that he knew the purpose of a spendthrift trust.

Accordingly, viewing the evidence in the light most favorable to the Debtor, the Trustee has established that there is no genuine dispute as to any material fact, and the Trustee is entitled to summary judgment as a matter of law on its UFTA claim based on actual fraudulent intent.

* * *

And that's about it. I hope you've enjoyed this presentation of wills and trusts about as much as one really can enjoy a law-school class. Many of you will be going on now to test your learning by taking on the practicum; others will be facing a final; perhaps others will follow a different course. Almost all of you will be taking the bar exam before too long, and many of you will see one or more wills or trusts questions; they are often tested there. Whatever lies ahead for you, I thank you for your time this semester and wish you the very best!

TABLE OF CASES

Primary cases are indicated by italics.

TABLE OF STATUTES AND RESTATEMENTS

INDEX